	DATE DUE	
APR 13 2004		
JUN 10 2006		

623.862 Blandford, Percy W
B
Modern sailmaking / by Percy W. Blandford. -- 1st ed. -- Blue Ridge Summit, Pa. : Tab Books, c1979.
320 p. : ill.

ISBN 0-8306-8937-0 : $12.95. [ISBN 0-8306-7937-5 : pbk. :]

N
11/79

1.Sails.

MODERN SAILMAKING

Other TAB books by the author:

No. 788 *Handbook of Practical Boat Repairs*
No. 860 *The Woodworker's Bible*
No. 894 *Do-It-Yourselfer's Guide to Furniture Repair & Refinishing*
No. 910 *How to Make Your Own Built-In Furniture*
No. 1004 *The Upholsterer's Bible*
No. 1008 *Woodworking with Scraps*
No. 1044 *The Woodturner's Bible*
No. 1114 *How to Make Early American & Colonial Furniture*

No. 937
$12.95

MODERN SAILMAKING

BY PERCY W. BLANDFORD

TAB BOOKS
BLUE RIDGE SUMMIT, PA. 17214

FIRST EDITION

FIRST PRINTING—JANUARY 1979

Printed in the United States of America

Library of Congress Cataloging in Publication Data

Blandford, Percy W.
Modern sailmaking.

Includes index.
1. Sails. I. Title.
VM532.B53 623.86'2 78-15404
ISBN 0-8306-8937-0
ISBN 0-8306-7937-5 pbk.

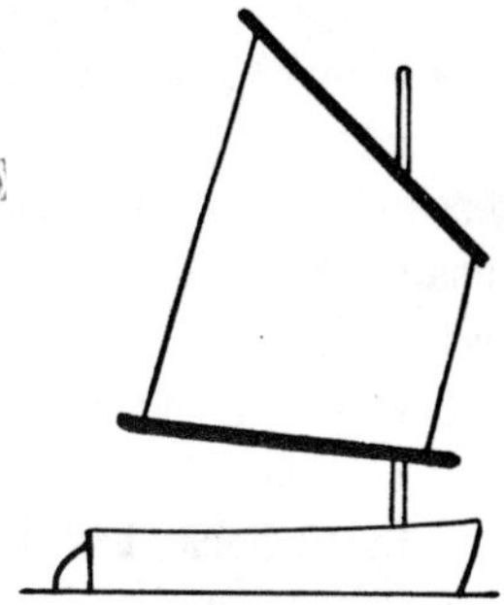

Preface

There has always been something of a mystery associated with the art or craft of sailmaking. In the days before the coming of steam, not much was known about theory, and aerodynamics was a science yet to come, but certain sailmakers had a feel for a sail and could cut and sew a more effective sail than their competitors. This carried over into pleasure boating. Certain sailmakers gained a reputation for making sails that were just a little bit faster than others, or they would keep their shape longer. A sail with the label of one of these makers was prized and their claims to superiority were usually substantiated by results.

Those were the days when cotton and other natural fibers were used for sailmaking. These have been replaced by cloths made from synthetic fibers. The coming of these man-made fibers has revolutionized sails. Natural fibers will rot. They would also stretch and shrink. Synthetic fibers do not rot. Those used for most sails do not expand or contract, while those that will expand have a calculated elasticity.

Apart from the freedom from worry due to the effect of water, it is the relative stability of these modern fabrics that has caused the sailmaking revolution. Much of the mystique associated with earlier sailmaking was due to the effect of experience in allowing for stretch in new natural fiber sail cloth so when a new sail had stretched it would be the desired shape and size without creases or distortion.

With modern materials, the size it is made is its final size, so no stretch allowances have to be made. The main reason why an experienced sailmaker and a beginner got different results, therefore, has been removed.

Of course, a man who has spent a lifetime making sails should be able to make a better sail in modern materials and if the best sail is needed for a first-class racing yacht he should be given the job. For lesser craft, and particularly smaller boats, there is no reason why an amateur sailmaker should not be able to make an acceptable sail that will perform well. There is a tremendous satisfaction to be gotten out of building your own boat. It is even more satisfying to make its sails as well.

In this book I have broken down the work into many steps, so a sail can be tackled progressively. The techniques that give the sail its shape are described, and there is no reason why an amateur with a sewing machine and just a few tools should not be able to make a success of his or her first sail, and then move on to more ambitious sails. Most sailmakers soon find a need to make other things besides sails and I have included some examples, but it will be seen that sailmaking constructions and techniques can be applied to many fabric-covered items needed on or about a yacht. Even the man whose interest is in power rather than sailing cruisers has canvaswork on his ship.

In gathering material for this book I was surprised to find how little has been published before and nearly all that has been published dates from the days of natural fiber sails. Consequently, I hope this new book concerned with modern materials will help a great many readers to understand more about sailmaking and will serve as a guide to them when they start to make their own sails. I hope they find this a very absorbing and worthwhile activity.

Percy W. Blandford

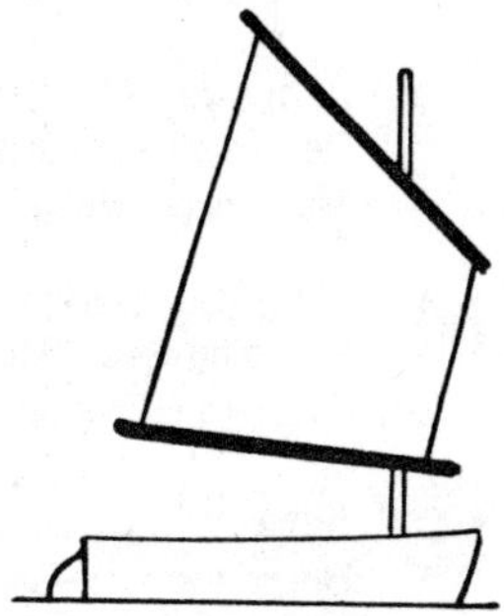

Contents

Sailing Rigs

Single-sail rigs probably evolved by trial and error from earliest man, who ventured afloat in a dug-out boat or on a raft. When the wind suited, he raised a skin or a coarsely woven cloth on a mast so his craft blew downwind before it. He must have soon discovered that he could steer a little each side of directly downwind by trailing a paddle astern, and that he could have a measure of control by holding the lower corners of the sail while the top was spread by another spar.

SAIL SHAPES

This simple square sail (Fig. 1-1) has been the basic form for all sizes of craft from small boats to large ships for a very long time on most of the waters of the world. If you only expect to sail in the direction the wind is blowing, a rectangular sail is as good as anything. The finer points of sail design do not come into it. Almost any shape of sail of adequate area will drive the boat before the wind. Square sails are still used on ocean-going craft. There are still sailing ships equipped almost completely with a multiplicity of square sails, while a yacht of more modest size may carry one or more square sails in addition to its normal fore-and-aft rig. The square sail, on its own yard, then comes into its own for "trade wind" sailing in those parts of the oceans where a following wind can be expected.

square

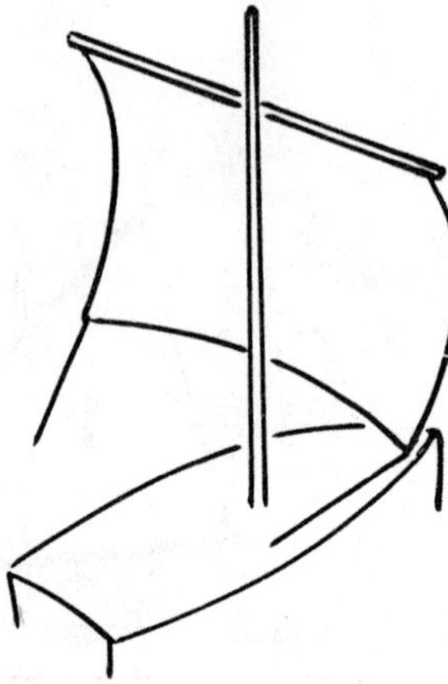

Fig. 1-1. Single-sail rigs developed from the square sail, which was turned fore-and-aft and given different shapes.

Early sailors must have discovered that if a square sail is pulled around more nearly in line with the boat, it is possible to sail across the wind, or even at an angle towards it if the boat hull is of a suitable design to grip the water and prevent leeway. A square-rigged ship would not normally make any worthwhile progress to windward, so sailing ship routes were planned to take advantage of prevailing winds in areas where they could be expected to be favorable. Such a ship might waste a considerable amount of time waiting for the wind. Those ships that remain are mostly used for training. They have a motor to get them out of that sort of situation.

In a smaller craft with a single sail, the square sail began to take on other forms as it was used for *reaching* (sailing across the wind) or for sailing *close-hauled* (at an angle towards the wind). The forward corner was held down, often to the stem head and the aft corner was given a rope sheet for control. The shape was then modified to suit the changed circumstances and the result was the *dipping lug* (Fig. 1-2). This sail was a favorite on the open boat working rig for a very long time from the Middle Ages almost to the present day. The sail was kept on the leeward side of the mast, so when the vessel went about on to the other tack, during the period when the boat was head to wind and the sail was empty, the tack was released and the yard dipped to the other side of the mast, so the tack could be refixed before the sail filled again.

Leaving the foot of the sail loose led to complications when the boat was sailing off the wind, as it would pull into too much of a bag.

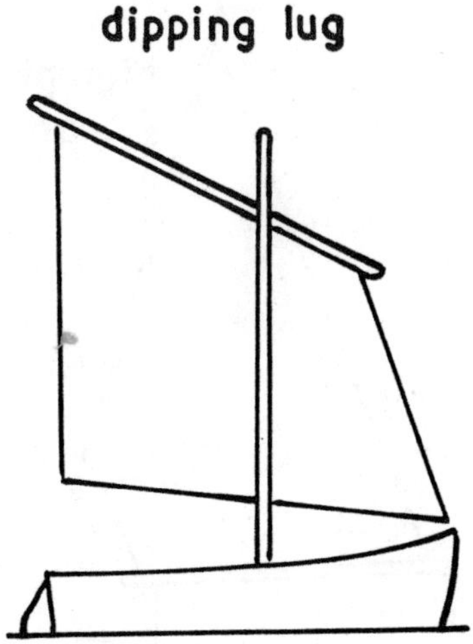

Fig. 1-2. The dipping lug.

The answer was the addition of another spar (see glossary for any unfamiliar terms), and with the addition of this boom the tack ceased to be taken to the stem head. Instead, a tack line held the forward end of the boom to the mast and pulled it down. This was the *balanced lug sail* (Figs 1-3 and 1-9).

Early balanced lug sails were not far from square, but it was soon found that a better performance to windward came from cutting

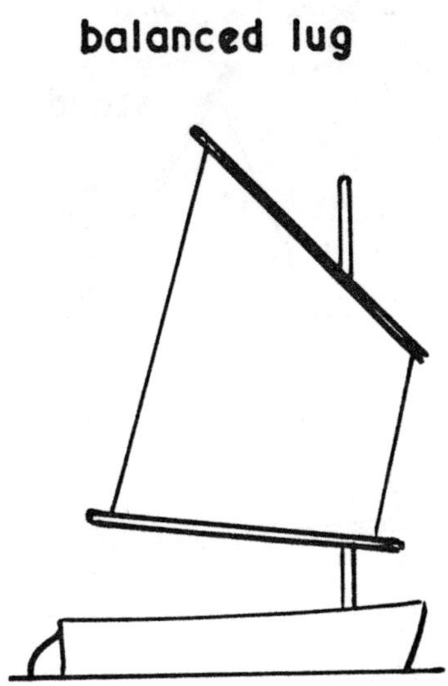

Fig. 1-3. The balanced lug.

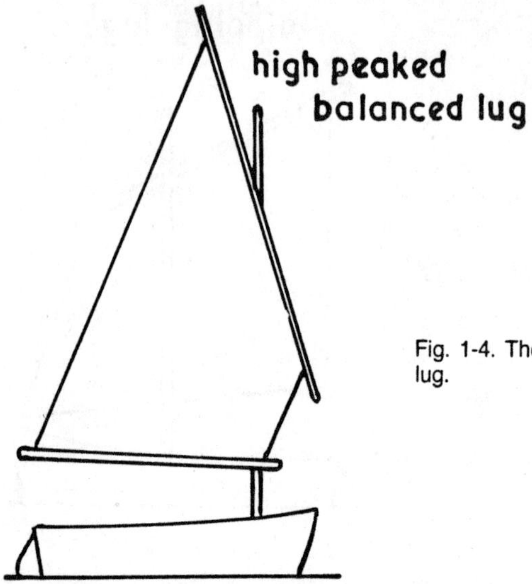

Fig. 1-4. The high-peaked balance lug.

the sail so the yard was at a steeper angle. Such a high-peaked sail (Fig. 1-4) would sail on either tack with no appreciable difference in performance when the boom was kept the same side of the mast.

The short forward edge of the sail did little to help the boat forward and one step to counteract this was to attach the boom to the mast with a *gooseneck* (a universal joint), cutting out play between the boom and mast and allowing the sail to set better. This was the *standing lug* (Fig. 1-5). Both balanced and standing lug sails still have

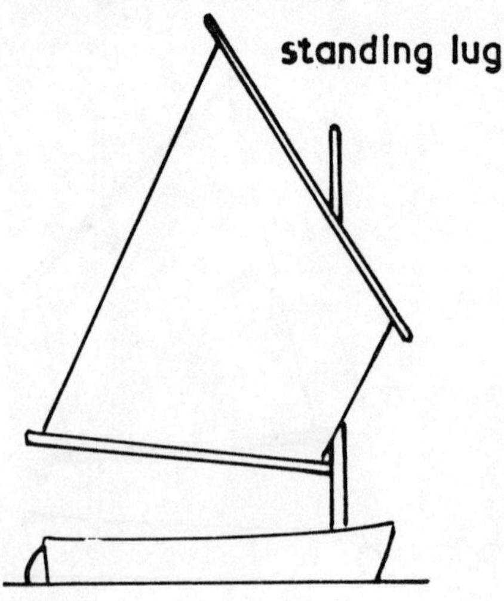

Fig. 1-5. The standing lug.

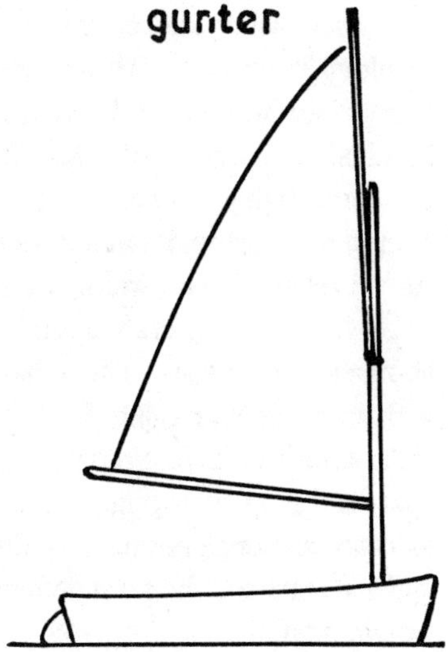

Fig. 1-6. The gunter.

their uses where simplicity and ease of stowing spars are important—especially in craft where sails are only needed occasionally. Normally the mast and both spars are shorter than the boat.

The next step in the evolution of the single-sail rig was to bring the yard entirely aft of the mast and peak the sail even higher, so the yard (now more correctly called a *gaff*) almost continued straight up the mast. This was the *gunter lug sail* (Fig. 1-6).

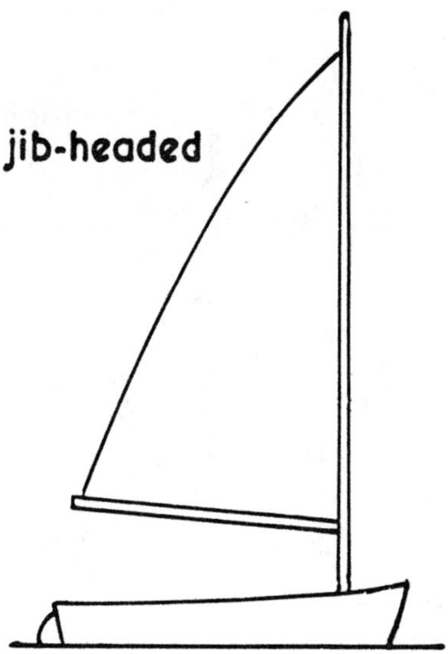

Fig. 1-7. The jib-headed sail.

The obvious step after this was to make gaff and mast one. The resulting jib-headed sail has been called leg-of-mutton, Marconi, and Bermudan (Bermudian, Bermuda). There have been earlier triangular sails, but tall jib-headed sails (Fig. 1-7) are what are envisaged by the name today. It was the aerodynamic knowledge gained from aircraft development that showed the value of a high aspect ratio sail (tall in relation to its width) for getting to windward.

Most modern craft intended for the best performance have jib-headed main sails. These have the complication of a tall mast, with its attendant rigging. For smaller craft, a gunter main sail of the same area will have almost as good a performance, with shorter spars and simpler rigging. There are limits to the size of a gunter sail as there are engineering problems of dealing with the overlapping gaff and mast and the arrangement in large sizes produces too much weight aloft.

In some parts of the world, single-sail rigs have developed in other ways. Chinese junk sails are basically square, but they have a number of light spars across them (Fig. 1-8A). In recent years some modern yachts have made creditable voyages with junk rigs and the Chinese have not been influenced away from them by Western rigs, so a modern sailmaker may be called on to make these sails. There are several modifications and compromises in Western craft, but the junk principle remains (Fig. 1-8B).

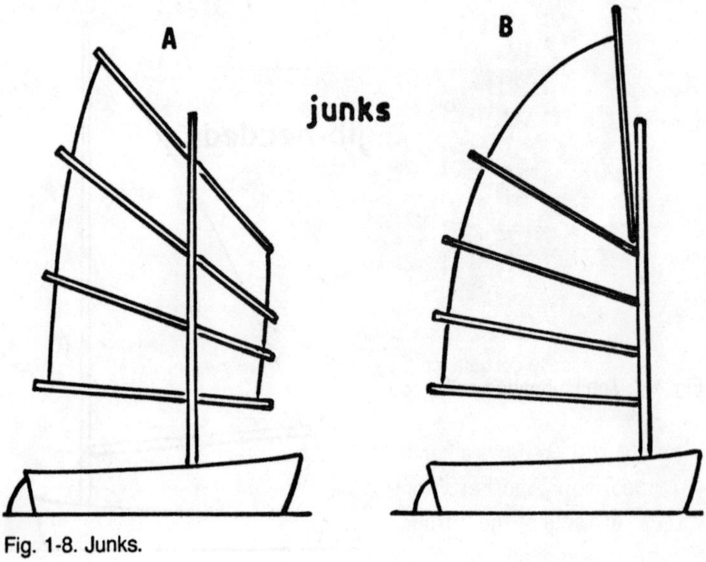

Fig. 1-8. Junks.

Fig. 1-9. A vertically-cut balanced lug sail, with grooved spars and three rows of reef points on a scow-shaped modified board boat.

Figure 1-9 shows a vertically cut, balanced lugsail, for purposes of comparison. Another variation of the square sail is the *sprit sail*. Instead of a spar at the top and usually another at the bottom, there is one going diagonally across the sail (Fig. 1-10A). This is the sprit.

Sprit sails are used on the popular little Optimist, but the biggest example is the British Thames sailing barge, many of which are still used as yachts. On a barge the sail is never brought down, but is gathered to sprit and mast with brailing ropes. In the days of commercial sail this was the largest rigged craft that could be handled by a man and a boy.

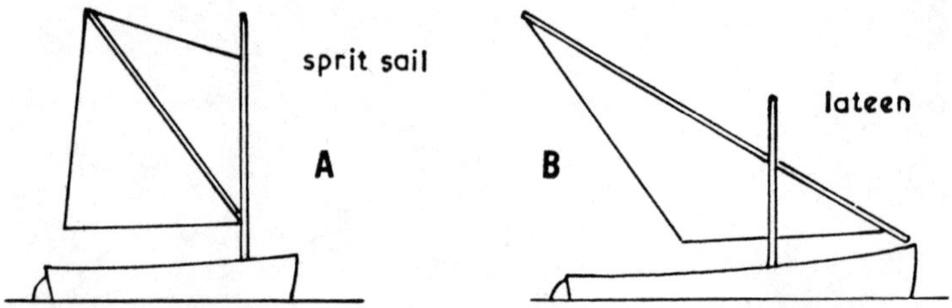

Fig. 1-10. Rigs developed from single sails to those with two or more sails on a single mast.

The normal sail tends to push the bow of the boat down when it is driving. In places where common courses make use of a beam wind it is possible to have a lifting sail. Two places very far apart arrived at very similar answers—the ancient Egyptians on the Nile and some of the natives of Pacific Islands. In both places the sails were lateen (Fig. 10B), having a very long spar supporting the top of a triangular sail on a short mast. In some cases, as when outriggers were used and these always had to be to windward, the sails were symmetrical and the mast central on a double-ended hull. For the return journey the rudder was taken to the other end and the sail dipped the other way. A lateen sail is not a good performer where following or head winds may have to be used.

MORE THAN ONE SAIL

The greatest use is made of a given sail area by having it all in a single, properly designed sail. Although this gives the maximum propulsion, there are practical problems of rigging larger craft and there are occasions when it is easier to maneuver a boat under sail, particularly when changing course sharply, if the rig is arranged in two or more sails.

There have been craft rigged with two or more masts, each carrying one of the types of sail already described. Such rigs are still sometimes seen, but the more usual arrangement is to have a single mast with a main sail aft of it and one or more triangular sails forward of it. The main sail may be a variation of the lug, with a gaff having jaws around the mast and ropes to hoist and control its angle (Fig. 1-11). At one time another sail might be hoisted above it, but this complication has been abandoned. Although the majority of yachts have jib-headed main sails there are gaff rig enthusiasts who claim advantages for these sails.

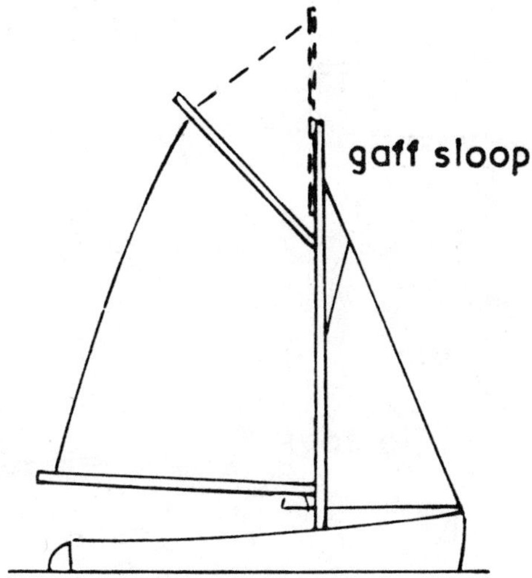

Fig. 1-11. The gaff sloop.

Whatever the type of main sail the rig is described as a sloop if there is a single head sail (Fig. 1-12A). If there are more sails forward of the mast, it is a cutter (Fig. 12B). The names of head or fore sails have gone through a change. The single head sail of a sloop is often called a jib, although traditionally this is the name of one sail of a cutter (Fig. 1-12C).

Another sail right aft may help in steering, even if quite small. The Thames sailing barge has quite a tiny mizzen sail sheeted to the rudder for this purpose. On a more conventional yacht the rig is called a yawl if the mizzen mast is stepped aft of the rudder head (Fig. 1-13A). A mizzen sail, used alone, can give a weather vane effect and keep a boat head to wind when heaving to or being used for fishing.

Some trading craft have been given a larger mizzen sail on a mast stepped forward of the rudder head, but the sail area is less than that of the main sail. This rig is a *ketch* (Fig. 1-13B). It has

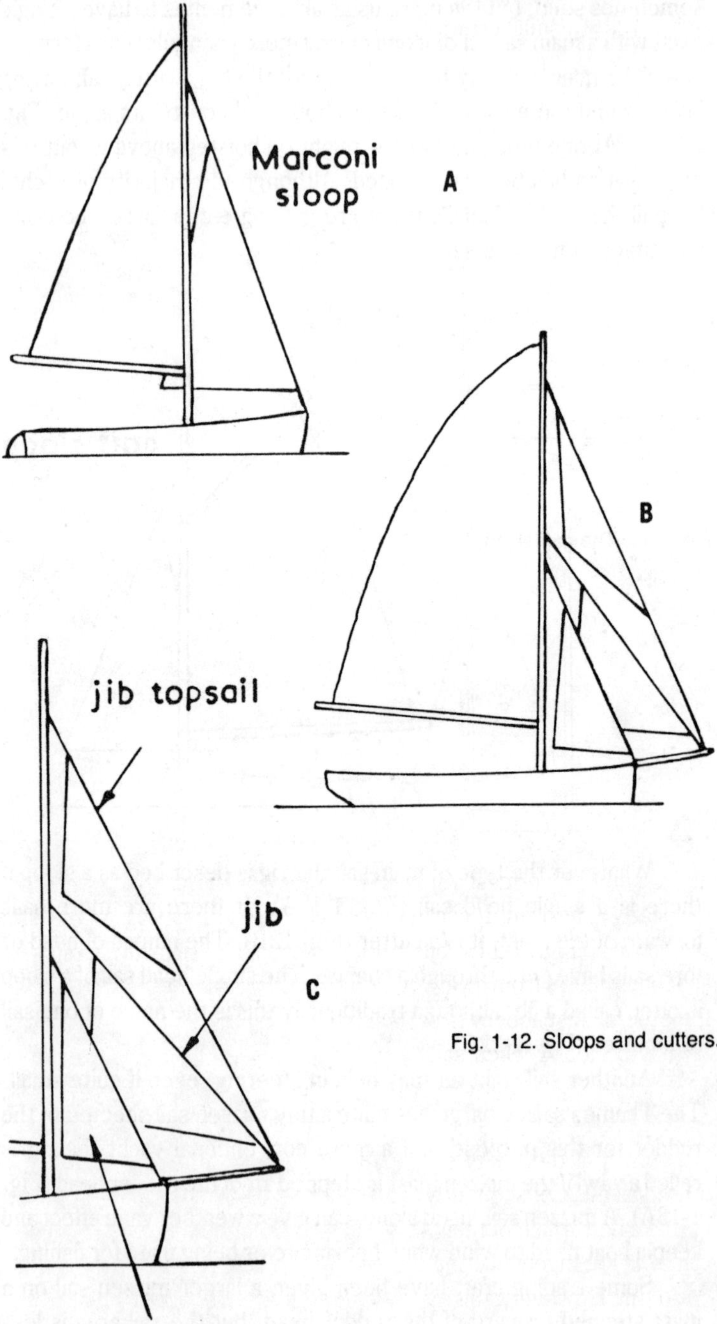

Fig. 1-12. Sloops and cutters.

advantages in breaking the total sail area down into sizes that can be managed by a small crew, but the ketch rig has never been popular for yachts.

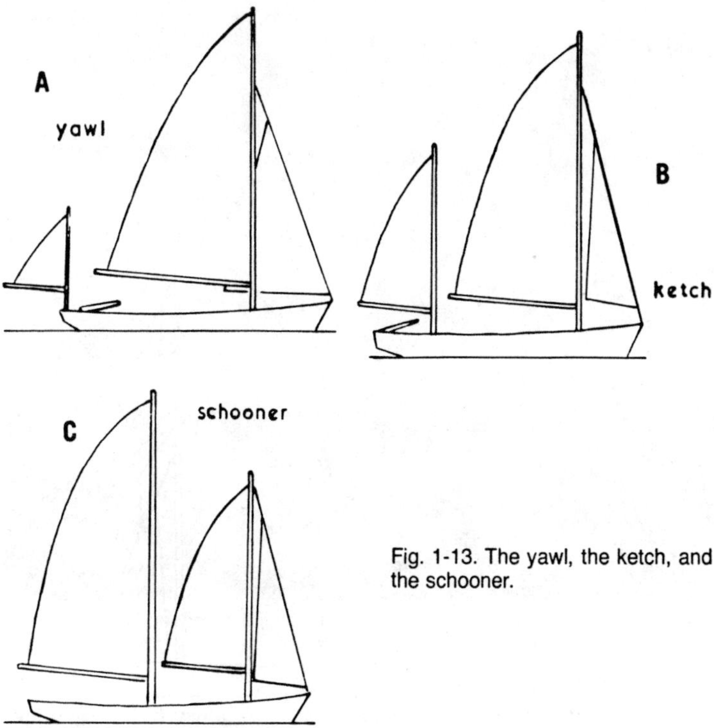

Fig. 1-13. The yawl, the ketch, and the schooner.

Another two-mast rig is the schooner (Fig. 1-13C), which is peculiarly American. It can still be a schooner if there are more than two masts (Fig. 1-14), but two are usual for pleasure craft. A schooner differs from a yawl or ketch in having the aft sail larger than the others. A schooner is particularly efficient in a beam wind, such as may be found when sailing up or down the U.S. coastlines.

SAIL POWER

Much of the joy of sailing lies in learning more and becoming more skillful. Consequently, sailing enthusiasts are always striving to make better use of their sails and, obviously, the theory of sailing can be quite involved. Any attempt to simplify it is liable to lead to criticism. However, this is not a book on how to sail—there are plenty of publications on that subject. The following notes are in-

Fig. 1-14. The 'Malcolm Miller', a British sail-training schooner. Note the complexities of rigging and the yards for square sails.

tended to give a very basic outline of sailing theory to help anyone wanting to make sails, regardless of whether he is a very experienced sailor.

This is most easily understood if the boat is regarded as having only a single sail. For maneuvers, second or other sails are set at the same angle as that shown for a single sail. Sailing before the wind is not the easiest way to sail. *Reaching* across the wind (Fig. 1-15A) is easiest and the sailor may describe this as a *soldier's wind*, with the implication that even a soldier could sail that way. If the wind direction is indicated by a line through the mast and the angle between this and the direction the boat is to go is bisected, that is the theoretical angle of the sail (Fig. 1-15B). Because the sail is made of flexible cloth, and this is the average angle, the foot of the sail has to be hauled in further than this.

If the rudder is used to turn the boat more towards the wind (close-hauled), the same theory holds—the mean sail angle is the result of bisecting the wind and direction lines (Fig. 1-15C). A point is reached when turning towards the wind, when the sail starts flapping and ceases to drive the boat forward. This is in the region of 45 degrees, so the boat cannot progress nearer to the wind than that

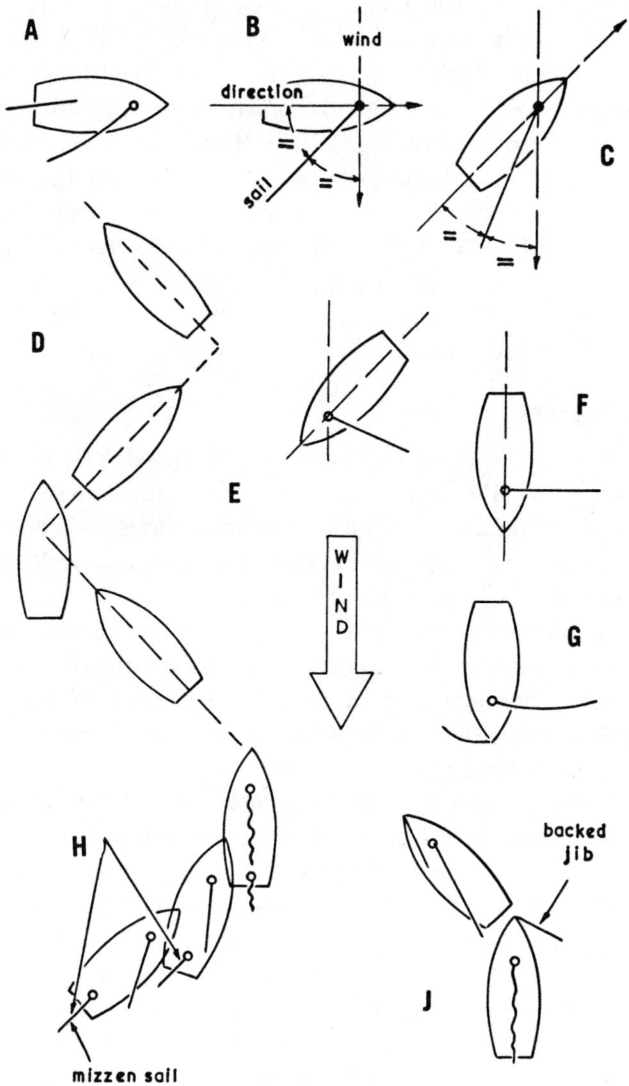

Fig. 1-15. Sails are set in relation to the wind and the intended course so most craft will go in any direction except within about 45 degrees of directly towards the wind.

and has to follow a zig-zag course, making a series of *boards* and *tacks* (Fig. 1-15D).

If the rudder is used to turn the boat away from the wind, bisecting the angle shows the sail going further out (Fig. 1-15E), until the wind and direction lines are the same and the sail is out at a right-angle so that boat is "running" (Fig. 1-15F).

With two or more sails, they will normally be set at approximately the same angle for reaching and sailing close-hauled. When running, one sail may screen the other, unless they are goose-winged to opposite sides (Fig. 1-15G). Having the sail area broken down into several sails allows the wind to be used to aid the rudder. Hauling in an aft sail will help the rudder make the boat *go about* when tacking (Fig. 1-15H). This is probably one of the main reasons for the tiny mizzen sail on a yawl or a Thames barge. If a boat gets *in irons* (head to wind and unable to turn), backing a head sail (Fig. 1-15J) may get the bow around.

SAIL BALANCE

If all that is expected of a sail is that it will drive the boat downwind, it can be mounted on a mast so its area is well forward and this result will be achieved. But if the steersman tries to alter course with the rudder, he may find that although he alters the angle of the boat, the direction sailed will still be downwind. He will be unable to turn the boat into the wind. Except for lowering the sail, which is not always possible when it is full of air, the only way to stop a sailing boat is to turn it bow into wind, so the sail is in line with the mast and flapping ineffectually like a flag. A boat that cannot be turned into the wind could be dangerous.

For a sailing boat to answer its helm the sail plan has to be balanced in relation to the boat, particularly its underwater profile. If a correct balance is achieved, the rudder can be used to turn the boat when sailing in any direction, including towards the wind. In fact it is usual to relate the sail plan to the boat in such a way that if the rudder is released and the boat is left to its own devices, it will turn into the wind and stop. This weather helm is only slight, but it is a safety arrangement that automatically stops the boat in emergency. Having to keep the rudder excessively in one direction to maintain a straight course indicates a sail plan out of balance with the hull.

The meaning of rudder angle is best seen in a dinghy steered by a tiller, as the angle of the tiller can be observed. The helmsman normally sits on the side nearest the wind (weather side). Opposite is the lee side. In a theoretically correctly balanced sail/boat combination the course will be held with the rudder and tiller central. There are too many variables for this to always be practicable. If the helmsman has to pull the tiller slightly towards him, that is *weather helm* (he is pulling the tiller to the weather side), as shown in Fig. 1-16A. If he lets go of the tiller, the rudder is pulled central by the flow of water past it and the sails turn the bow into wind, they flap and the boat stops, which is the safe position.

If the helmsman has to hold the tiller to leeward, there is *lee helm* (Fig. 1-16B). This could be dangerous. If the helmsman fell overboard, the centering rudder would cause the sails to turn the boat downwind and it would continue to sail away unattended.

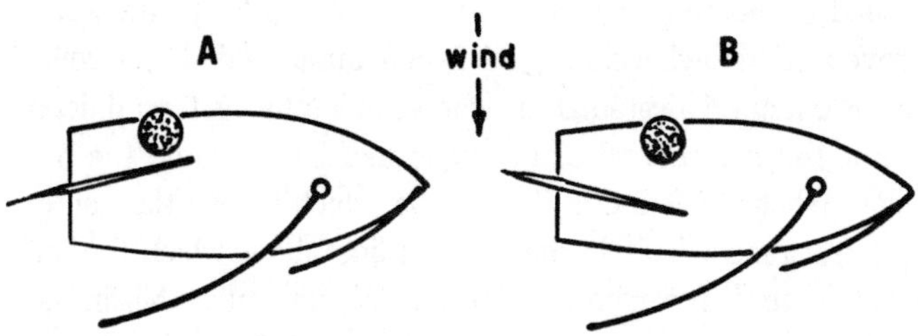

Fig. 1-16. A sailing boat makes some leeway as well as head way. Its performance is dependent on the correct relation between the center of lateral resistance of the hull and the center of effort of the sail plan.

If steering is by wheel the need to keep a pressure one way or the other to maintain a course will indicate weather or lee helm.

A boat needs keel surface to prevent leeway when under sail in any direction except sailing directly downwind. If there is insufficient keel surface the boat may sail forward while also going sideways, so the course made good will be nowhere near the direction the boat is apparently heading. Such a boat might be useless to windward as any course made good on a tack would be cancelled out by leeway (Fig. 1-17).

The keel surface is the total of all the boat that is under water when viewed in profile, not just the keel, whether fixed or drop, or any leeboards or other device. The area of the rudder is included, as well as all the underwater parts of the hull (Fig. 1-18). Obviously, the underwater profile may vary if the boat heels. Most boats are

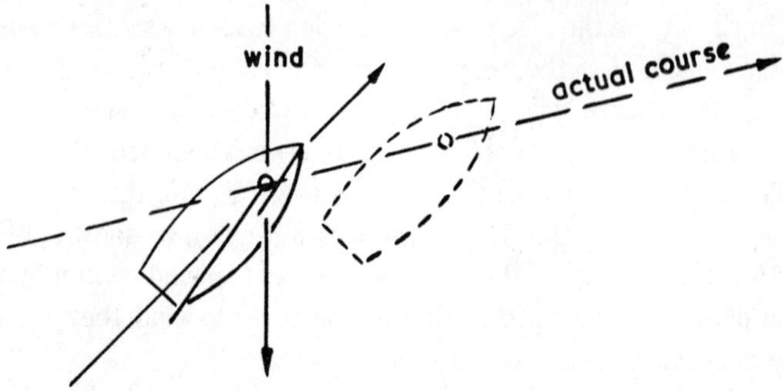

Fig. 1-17. A boat needs keel surface to prevent sailing downwind.

designed to be sailed near upright, as the effective keel surface is often reduced considerably at much angle of heel. Exceptions might be found on some chine boats, where the grip on the water is improved when the lee chine gets deeply immersed. There could be a similar effect on a catamaran, when the lee hull is forced deeper.

For sail balance calculation it is usual to assume the hull is upright. What is needed is the line on which comes the center of lateral resistance. This is the vertical line about which the hull is assumed to turn. It can be found by calculation, but as this line is the balancing point of the underwater profile it is much simpler, and often more accurate, to find its position practically.

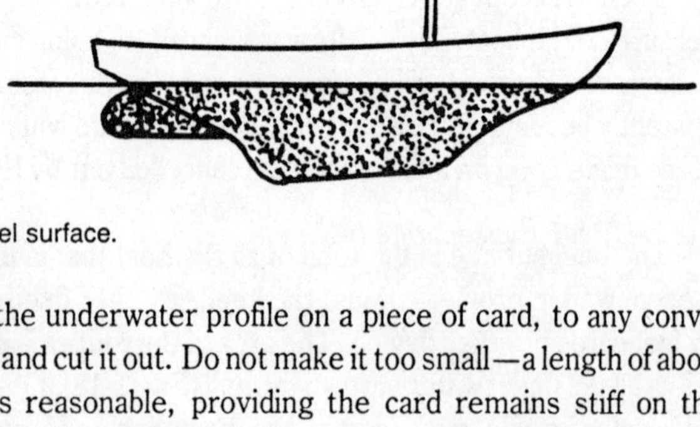

Fig. 1-18. Keel surface.

Draw the underwater profile on a piece of card, to any convenient scale, and cut it out. Do not make it too small—a length of about 12 inches is reasonable, providing the card remains stiff on this length. Balance the card on a knife edge, with the waterline at right-angles to the edge. When a balance is achieved, mark the line of the knife edge. That is the line of the center of lateral resistance (Fig. 1-19A).

On the sail plan it is necessary to find the vertical line on which the center of effort comes. This is the point at which all the effort of the sail might be considered to be concentrated to get the same effect as that obtanied by the wind spread over the whole sail surface. So the center of effort is actually the geometric center of the sail plan and can be found by a little simple geometry.

The center of a triangle is found by joining two corners to the centers of the opposite sides. The center is where they cross (Fig. 1-19B). Do it the third way if you wish to prove it. The area of a triangle is found by multiplying the length of one side by half the height of the opposite corner, measured perpendicular to the side (Fig. 1-19C).

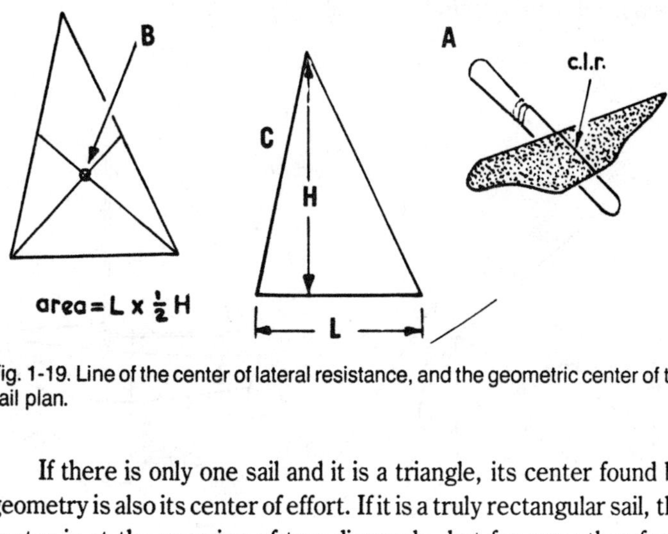

Fig. 1-19. Line of the center of lateral resistance, and the geometric center of the sail plan.

If there is only one sail and it is a triangle, its center found by geometry is also its center of effort. If it is a truly rectangular sail, the center is at the crossing of two diagonals, but for any other four-sided shape it is necessary to divide it into triangles, find their centers and areas, then combine them.

Deal with the separate triangles, as just described, then draw a line between the two centers (Fig. 1-20A). The combined center of effort is on this line at a position proportionate to the areas of the triangles. This could be found by calculation, but it is easier to erect lines at right-angles to each end and measure distances proportionate to the opposing areas along them. A line joining these points will give the position of the combined center of effort (Fig. 1-20B). Choose any convenient scale for the distances at the ends, but too small a scale results in the lines crossing rather acutely so the exact crossing point is not as easy to define as it is when the crossing angle is rather wider.

This can be carried on, taking in more triangles. For instance, in a gaff sloop rig the center of effort of the main sail can be found on a line joining its two triangles, then the center of the jib is found and joined to it (Fig. 1-20C). Distances are marked along lines at the ends of this, in proportion to the total main sail and jib areas. A line joining them crosses the other line at the combined center of effort. In designing a rig in relation to a hull it is usual to work on all plain sail—the normal working sails—and ignore special sails that may be used for light airs or strong winds. Such sails as storm jibs should be of size that brings the center of effort to about the same position when used with a reefed main sail.

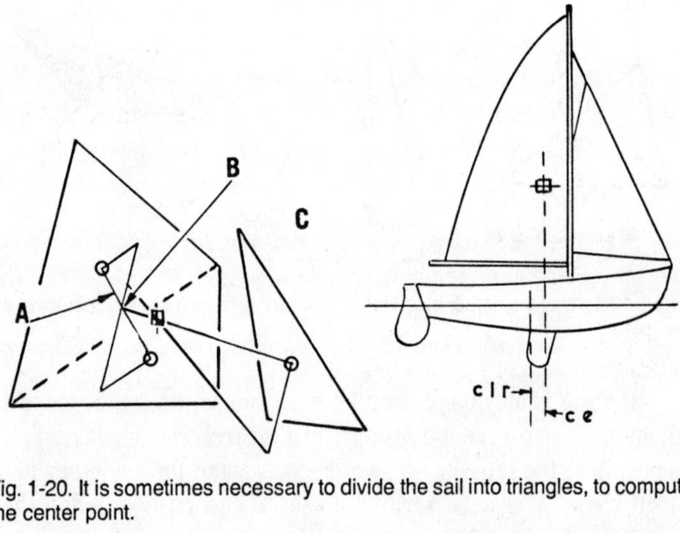

Fig. 1-20. It is sometimes necessary to divide the sail into triangles, to compute the center point.

It is the vertical line on which the center of effort comes that has to be related to the center of lateral resistance line. It might be thought that the two should coincide, but this is geometry and not sailing practice. The work can only be used as a guide. Sails are never sheeted tightly fore and aft. They sag off according to how they are set in relation to the direction relevant to the wind that is being sailed, and the center of effort tends to move aft as speed increases. When a hull moves through the water its center of lateral resistance moves forward slightly.

Theory at this stage has to be matched with experience. In theory the center of effort should come slightly aft of the center of lateral resistance to give the recommended slight amount of weather helm. If this was done according to the geometric positions the amount of weather helm in most cases would prove in practice to be excessive. It is more usual to let the center of effort come slightly forward of the center of lateral resistance (Fig. 1-20D) as found on paper. When the vessel is underway, this will give the desired amount of weather helm.

As with many things connected with yacht design, there are so many variables that cannot be calculated, that what calculations there are and what drawings are done are important as guides, but experience (not necessarily your own) has to follow. There is a lot of truth in the sayings that "yacht design is more art than science" and "what looks right is right." Fortunately, there are several practical things that can be done for final corrections. Moving the crew or ballast will alter the underwater profile and it is possible to alter the set of sails or the angle of mast. If reasonable care is taken in designing, it is rare for drastic alterations to be needed in practice.

SAIL PERFORMANCE

Sails have been used for thousands of years, yet during most of that time there has been little understanding of how they did their work. Sailing with the wind aft may have seemed obvious, but how they got a boat to windward was not appreciated. Experience showed what had to be done in setting the sails and showed what sails performed to windward best, but the reason behind it was still a mystery. It was not until the development of aircraft in comparatively recent years that scientific thought was brought to bear on sail design.

A sail going to windward has to perform a similar task to the wing of an aircraft. The wing has to provide *lift* to get the aircraft off the ground and keep it in the air as it is pulled forward. The boat sail has to provide *lift* to get the craft to windward.

The aerofoil section of a wind is such that air is deflected away from its upper surface, while that on its underside follows a smoother curve (Fig. 1-21A). The effect on the upper surface is to create a partial vacuum and it is the suction of this, more than the air pressure below, that provides lift. In early slow aircraft there was more curve to the wing than in modern fast machines, and some even had wings of single fabric thickness, like sails.

There have been wing sails, like aircraft wings on edge, but they were only suitable for sailing close-hauled one way. No one has yet devised a wind sail that proved satisfactory by altering its section according to direction. With rigid wing sails there is also the problem of what to do with them when not sailing, or even how to stop the boat.

Sails can be cut so their section to windward approximates an aircraft wing (Fig. 1-21B). A streamlined mast, with the sail in a groove gives a much better section than the older lacing to a round mast (Fig. 1-21C). The thin leading edge of a fore sail is not necessarily better than having some thickness there, due to roller reefing, or twin head sail track (Fig. 1-21D). If a streamlined mast can be rotated to match the angle of the sail, a better section can be achieved (Fig. 1-21E). Whether there is much practical gain depends on the craft, and, in many yachts, turning the mast is not feasible.

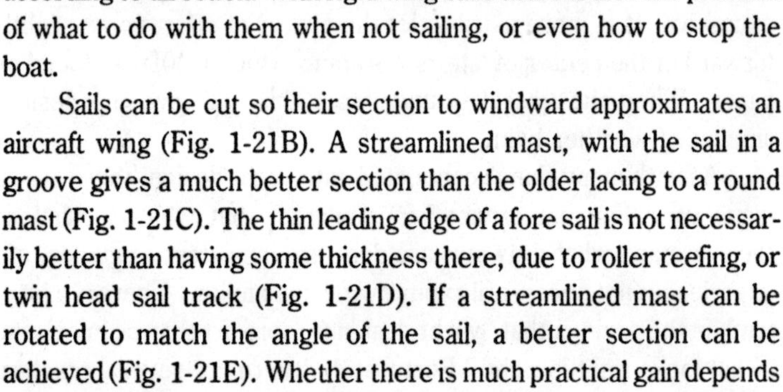

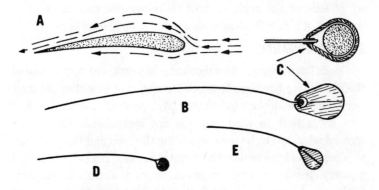

Fig. 1-21. The performance of a sail going to windward is similar to that of an aircraft wing in flight.

As a potentially fast boat increases its speed to windward due to its design or high winds, there is an advantage in flattening the curve of the sail. The boom at the foot of most modern main sails is there to get the flat angle to windward, as well as for other reasons. A boomless sail sags to a curve more than is desirable for the most efficient sailing. For downwind sailing there is some advantage in more curve to the sail.

This means that most sails are compromises, although there are devices to adjust sails and a racing yacht may have flatter sails for use in strong winds. Fortunately, an average sail is likely to give a satisfying performance on most angles of sailing for cruising and pleasure sailing. It is the racing sailor who appreciates the finer points of expert cuts and special features that only the experienced, professional sailmaker will be able to include successfully. The person who makes his or her own sails may not be aiming to join the go-fast set with the first suit of sails, but there is no reason why practice should not bring about the skill to make racing sails.

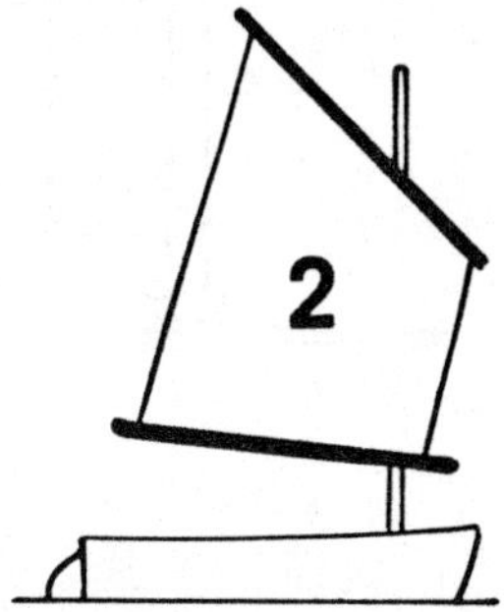

Rigging Details

Sails have to be hoisted and held at the correct attitude to the wind by a system of spars and ropes. There have been many experiments. Rigging design has not yet reached finality, nor is it ever likely to, but there are certain generally accepted arrangements that are found in most sailing craft. The method of hoisting and supporting sails affects the design of sails in general and detail planning, so anyone making sails should be aware of how they will be rigged. The purpose of this chapter is to provide background information of use to a sailmaker, rather than giving detailed instructions on the construction of spars and rigging.

The simplest mast arrangement is a spar resting on the keel and held at deck level (Fig. 2-1A). This means that most of its length depends on its own stiffness for support. If the wind puts exceptional loads on the sails which are transferred to the mast, the strain on the two support points could be so great as to cause failure. This means that such a cantilever mast is usually limited to fairly small boats.

However, with improvements in design of metal and wood spars there are unstayed masts carrying much larger sail areas today than would have been expected not so very long ago. For most rigs the mast has been expected to remain rigid and sails were designed to suit this requirement, but some modern single-sail rigs incorporate bendy masts, deliberately designed to alter shape and so affect the curve and shape of the sail (Fig. 2-1B).

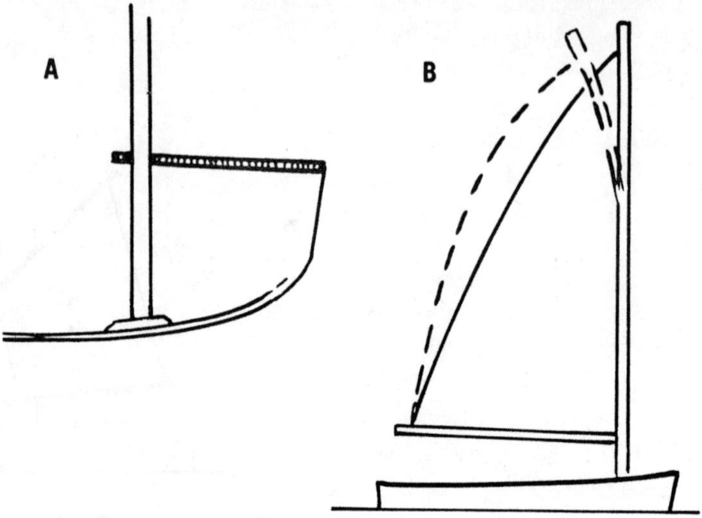

Fig. 2-1. Simple mast arrangement.

STANDING RIGGING

The obvious way to support a mast is to provide a stay to the bow, another to the stern and one each side (Fig. 2-2A). This is possible with a jib-headed main sail, but most other main sails would foul the backstay. Even with some jib-headed sails it is necessary to take the backstay to a projecting spar called a *bumpkin* (bunkin, boomkin), as shown in Fig. 2-2B, so it will clear the sail and its boom.

For rigs where a permanent backstay was impractical, the traditional aft support was a pair of running backstays. These went to points on the gunwale well aft and had arrangements that allowed them to be quickly set up or released, because only the one on the side opposite to the sail position could be used (Fig. 2-2C). A danger with this arrangement came if there was an unintentional gybe and the boom swung over before one backstay was released and the other set up. Without one or both backstays the mast could collapse forward and if the boom hit a taut backstay it could cause a capsize.

In addition, or in place of running backstays, the side stays (*shrouds*) may be brought aft of the mast (Fig. 2-2D), to provide some aft, as well as side, support. In a dinghy or small yacht, one or more shrouds arranged in this way may give sufficient support.

A stay is much more effective at a wide angle than at a steep angle (Fig. 2-2E). This is one reason for the use of a *bowsprit*, as well as a bumpkin (Fig. 2-2F). The bowsprit was also there to give a wider spread of sails forward of the mast, but modern scientific approach does not favor that so much. The problem of getting a wider angle is greater in the width of the boat. A shroud from a tall mast may be too near vertical to be very effective in stiffening the top of the mast (Fig. 2-2G). That is why *spreaders* are used (Fig. 2-2H). The compressive strain on the ends of the spreader and the wider pull of the upper part of the shrouds have more effect in preventing the top of the mast from bending.

Spreaders are not necessarily straight across, but may be angled aft to suit shrouds meeting the gunwales aft of the mast. When the yacht is on a broad reach or is running, the main sail may touch the spreaders. Even if the ends of the spreaders are suitably padded, there may be a risk of chafe and this has to be anticipated by the sailmaker. This method of staying has been used for parts of the mast (Fig. 2-2J), but with modern mast materials and design that sort of thing is less often seen.

Apart from the improvement in materials and design, one other reason for the simplification of rigs is the realization that spars and their supports do not contribute to the drive of the sails and are useless windage, so are better kept to minimum size and complexity.

On most craft, particularly in larger size yachts, the mast goes through to the bottom, where the structure is better able to take the downward thrust, and there is some support at deck level. This supplements the support provided by rigging. It fixes the mast position and angle. In an ideal situation this may be found to be exactly right, but yacht design is not always so precise. This is not incompetence on the part of the designer, but there are so many factors that cannot be exactly stated or anticipated,and no amount of experience can produce exactly the right answer every time. In a racing yacht there is an advantage in being able to move a mast or alter its angle slightly to get it arranged so the sails are most effective.

The mast step may be adjustable or there can be several positions over the keel. The hole through the deck may be much bigger than the mast. Rigging can be adjusted to get the mast as desired, within fairly broad limits. Wedges can be driven between the mast hole and the mast, if support there is required (Fig. 2-2K).

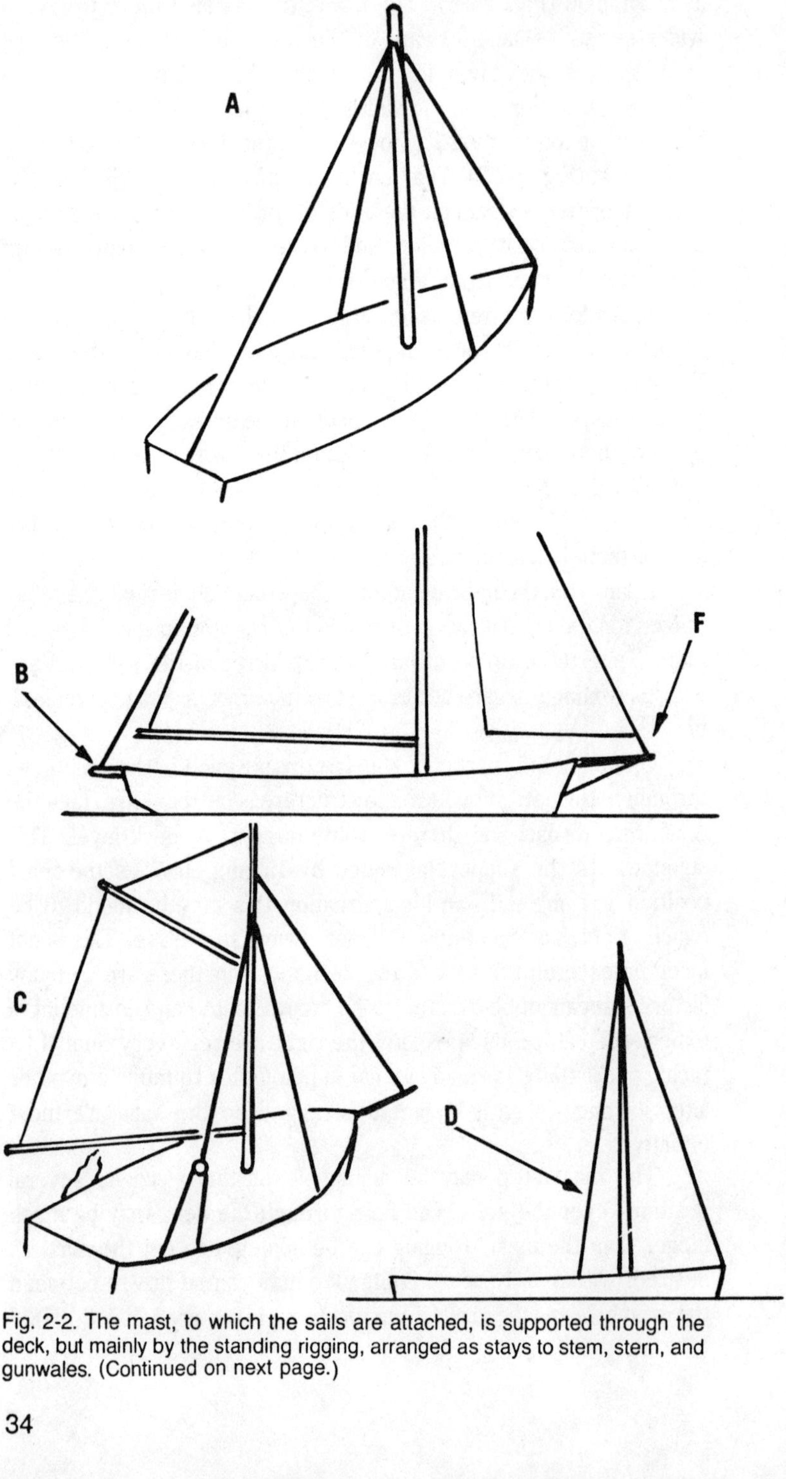

Fig. 2-2. The mast, to which the sails are attached, is supported through the deck, but mainly by the standing rigging, arranged as stays to stem, stern, and gunwales. (Continued on next page.)

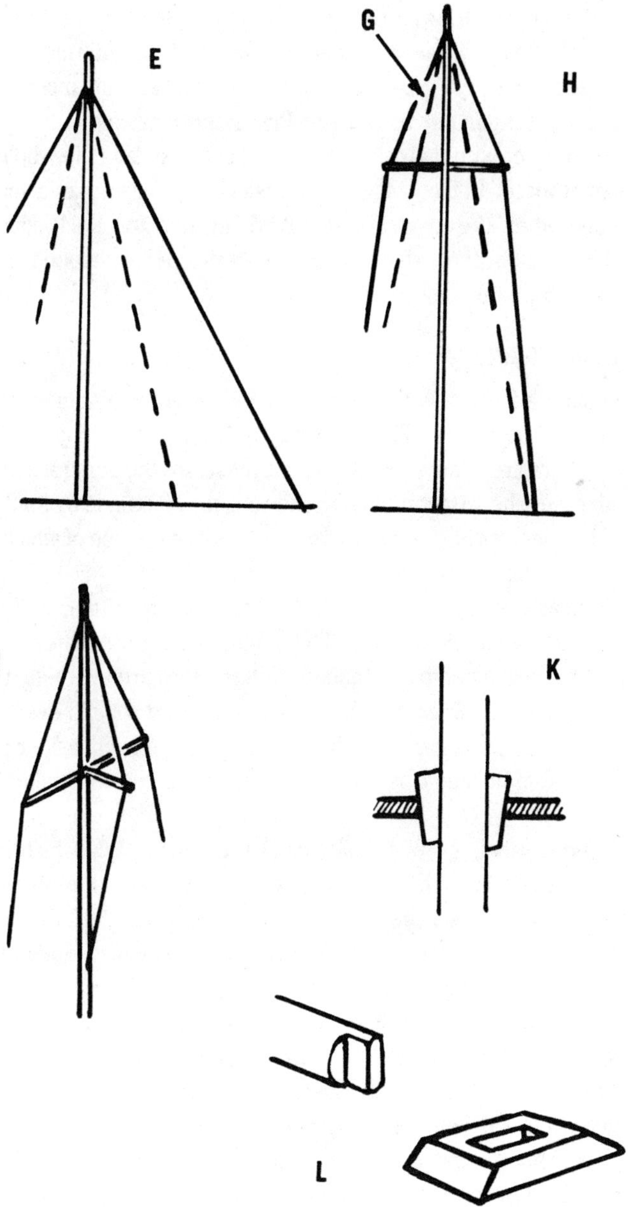
E
G
H
J
K
L

In a smaller boat, such as a racing dinghy class, the mast may depend entirely on its stays for support. It can be mounted over the keel of an open boat or on the deck. In its simplest form a tenon on the mast fits a mortise on its step (Fig. 2-2L), but this can be elaborated into slides with adjustments fore and aft, and incorporating a jack arrangement to raise or lower the mast foot.

Of course, with this arrangement, if any stay fails the whole rig goes overboard. In fact this may be less of a disaster than a similar breakage when the mast is supported through the deck and the remaining support is unable to take the strain so that a wooden mast breaks or a metal mast bends.

RUNNING RIGGING

Sails are hoisted by *halliards*, or *halyards* from haul yards of square sails up masts. They are controlled by other ropes called *sheets*. There are a few exceptions, but these are the general names. In both cases the attachments to the sails may be made by knotting or by shackles, spring fasteners, or other devices, some of which are described later.

In nearly every case a sail has to be hauled up taut, so there must be no give in the halliard. The traditional natural materials for these ropes were hemp and manila. Today there are synthetic rope materials, such as Dacron, which are used. Wire rope is even less likely to stretch, so a wire rope halliard may be used with a fiber rope tail for ease in hoisting; but when the sail is up, the wire takes the load.

A line associated with halliards is the *topping lift*, which goes from near the end of the boom through a block near the top of the mast. It is used to take the weight of the boom when the sail is off or not fully hoisted. It stays in position, but should be slackened off so as not to press against the sail when the boat is sailing.

Sheets for many sails are required to be without stretch, so Dacron and other non-stretch synthetic fibers are used for these ropes. In places where some elasticity in the sheet is required the synthetic rope chosen is usually nylon.

With the coming of synthetic fibers for ropemaking, almost completely superseding natural fibers, ropes have gone through a change in design. Most rope has been three-stranded. Although there had been braided rope in natural fibers, it was less common.

Many ropes in synthetic fibers are braided, giving a more comfortable feel and less tendency to kink or twist. Three-stranded ropes, in synthetic as well as natural fibers, are still used, but braided fiber ropes are now found in many applications afloat.

Traditionally, three-strand rope was used for bolt ropes on sails and the method of stitching allowed for this construction. This may still be needed, but differences in rope design and sail materials have brought the introduction of other ways of finishing the edges of sails.

At one time nearly all wire rope was seven-strand. This was made by twisting six strands around a core strand, which might be wire or could be fiber. Standing rigging might be made of iron wire, and running rigging was steel—in both cases the metal was protected from rust by galvanizing (coating with zinc). Ends were spliced.

Although seven-strand is still found, there are nineteen-strand ropes and the usual metal is salt-water resistant stainless steel, with similar ropes used for standing and running rigging, usually with one of several types of terminal fitting instead of a splice.

Halliard arrangements are usually straightforward, although winches, levers, and other means of applying purchase may be used to increase pull. The sailmaker has to ensure that the part of the sail

Fig. 2-3. An old gaff-rigged yacht with vertically-cut sails and the main sail hooped to the mast. The head sail has a boom and pivots on the forestay.

subjected to this strain is able to take it. This is usually the leading edge of the sail. In the case of a head sail a wire rope may relieve the fabric of strain. For the greatest efficiency, it is important that this edge of a head sail is as tight as possible. If it sags into a curve the boat may not sail as well to windward.

At one time the main sail was attached at intervals to the mast by hoops (Fig. 2-3 and 2-4A), ropes, and parrels (Fig. 2-4B) or merely by roping around with a line through eyelets after hoisting (Fig. 2-4C). None of these ways gave a very satisfactory set to the sail, particularly when going to windward. A step forward was the use of a track on the mast and fairly close runners (Fig. 2-4D). Sails to be hoisted in these ways may still be needed for traditional craft, but for most newer craft the edge of the sail slides in a groove in the mast (Fig. 2-4E), giving a much better set to the sail and a far better approximation to an aerofoil section when going to windward.

Coupled with this, the halliard may pass down through the mast and reduce windage. Other masts have been designed to allow the sail to be rolled inside the groove. Mast sections can be made in many ways, but the main consideration of a sailmaker is the production of a sail edge that will work in a groove and have sufficient strength to take the strain of hoisting tightly without allowing the fabric to distort.

Sheet arrangements can be quite complex, but they need not concern a sailmaker very much, except that strength will be required at points of strain. The foot of a main sail may only be attached at its ends to a boom. It may be laced in a basic rig (Fig. 2-5A), there may be a track or a very similar section to a grooved mast may be used. Normally the boom is sufficiently rigid to take care of the strains due to sheet attachment points, but the sailmaker may need to be aware of the different loads imposed by end or center sheeting (Fig. 2-5B).

In some simple craft the single sail has a pocket to slip over an unstayed mast (Fig. 2-5C and 2-6). While this makes for simplicity and the sail and mast can have a good section when sailing to windward (Fig. 2-7), there is the objection that such a sail cannot be lowered in an emergency. The sailmaker needs to produce an even loose-fitting pocket with reinforcing to prevent the mast from pushing through.

REEFING

The need to reduce sail when the area exposed is too much for the strength of the wind has been approached in several ways. A

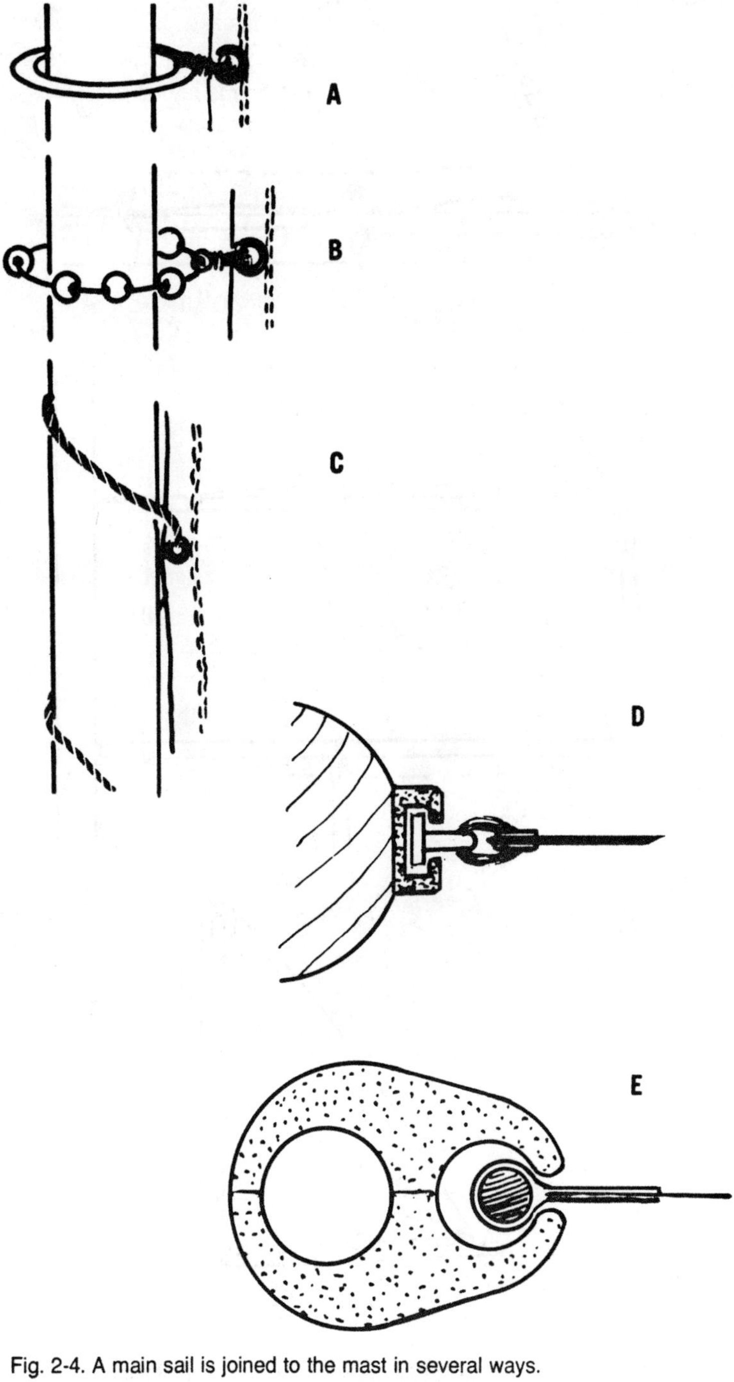

Fig. 2-4. A main sail is joined to the mast in several ways.

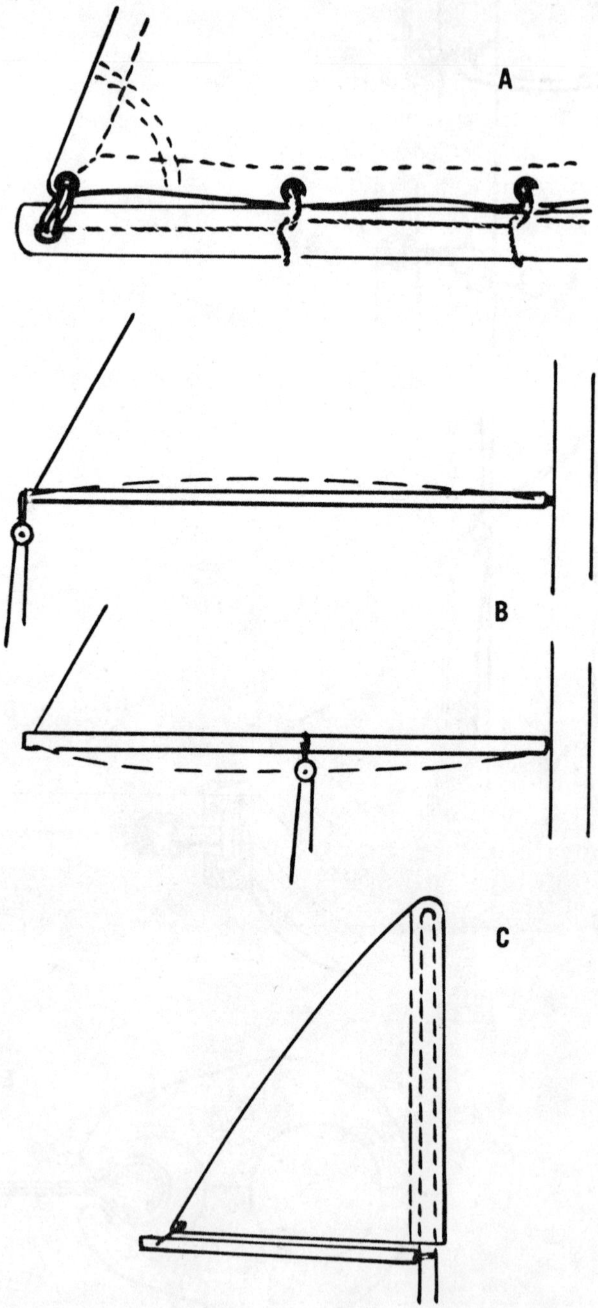

Fig. 2-5. The loads on a sail's foot depend on the method of sheeting.

large sail can be lowered and replaced with a smaller one. This is often done with fore sails. In a multi-sail rig some of the sails can be lowered and the boat continues to sail with the remaining sails. The area of a sail exposed can be reduced by gathering up some of the canvas. This is called *reefing*.

Whatever method of reducing canvas is employed, the remaining rig should still retain a similar balance in relation to the hull,

Fig. 2-6. A sleeved sail pocketed on an unstayed bendy mast, made with colored cloths alternating with white.

otherwise there may be excessive lee or weather helm. Some two-masted rigs are arranged so mizzen and fore sails without the main sail will still be balanced, or if the main sail alone is used there will still be balance. In a rig where sails can be changed the line on which the center of effort of the smaller sail comes should be about the same as that of a larger sail. If reefing a sail moves its center of effort laterally, this may have to be compensated by changing another sail. This may mean having a smaller fore sail when the main sail is reduced, to maintain a proper trim.

Details of the constructional work on a sail connected with reefing is given in the practical instructions later, but the methods are outlined here. The traditional method of reefing seems to have been used for as long as sails have been used, and it is still found. It may be called jiffy reefing. It is an effective method and is without the mechanical arrangements of other systems, that can go wrong.

The sail has one or more rows of reef points (Fig. 2-7). Usually, the reef pendants (pennants) are sewn to reinforced patches on the sail, and are always there. Sometimes there may only be grommets in the sail and the ropes have to be threaded through for reefing. At the ends of the rows of reef points there are more substantial cringles, with lines already attached or needing them to be attached.

To reef a sail, the boat is turned so air is spilled from the sail, then the halliard is eased so the sail partly lowers. The weight of the boom is taken by the topping lift. The cringle at the forward end is hauled down and fastened to the boom (Fig. 2-7A). That at the outboard (*clew*) end of the row is hauled down and outwards so as to stretch the sail along the line of reef points (Fig. 2-7B). This brings the line of points just above the boom with baggy canvas below it. This is gathered up by tying the reef points together, normally above the boom (Fig. 2-7C), but around the boom if the sail slides in a groove in it. The ends are joined with reef knots, and it is this application that gives the knot its name.

The use of reef points is also found on square and fore sails and may be used on a boomless main sail. In all of these cases there is no spar to provide tension and the reefed edge may be bad aerodynamically, but when there is too much wind and the aim is to reduce some of the drive, a little inefficiency to windward may have to be accepted.

The alternative to the use of reef points is to roll some of the sail away. There is a system of rolling within the mast, but rolling around

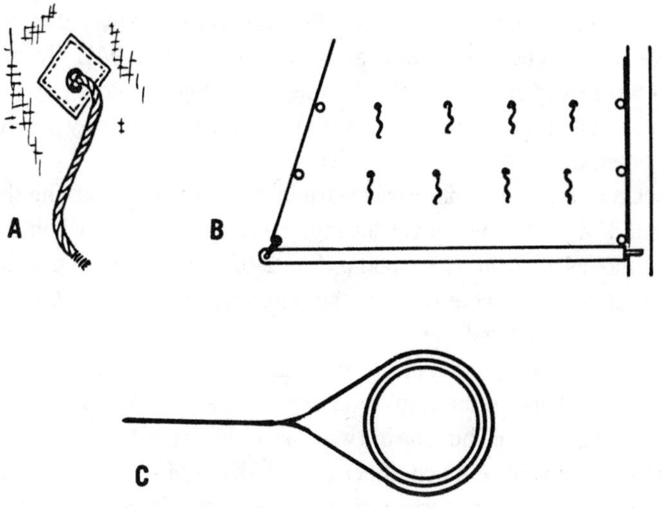

Fig. 2-7. Sail and mast can have a good section when sailing to windward.

the boom is more usual. There are a few requirements if this is to be possible. The boom needs to be parallel, or nearly so. It need not be round, but if it is that is helpful. Sheeting should be at the end only. A *boom vang* (kicking strap) cannot be used in the ordinary manner, but there are ways of incorporating one with a rolled sail, and there are rigs where a sheet attachment away from the end of the boom uses a claw and rollers outside the rolled canvas.

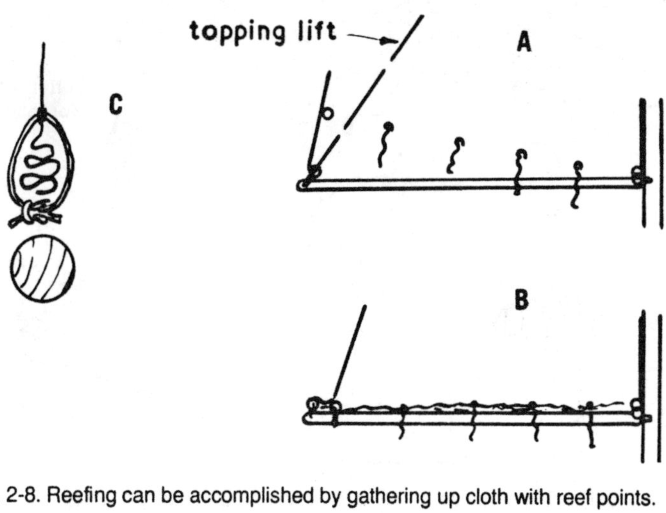

Fig. 2-8. Reefing can be accomplished by gathering up cloth with reef points.

In a dinghy of modest sail area the end of the boom may fit over a spike on the gooseneck with a square part (Fig. 2-9A). Normal pressures keep it there without fixing. If reefing is necessary the boom is pulled aft a few inches and the surplus fabric rolled by turning the boom by hand.

On a larger craft differences are in the methods of turning the boom. There may be a lever arrangement, in which a pawl on the lever moves a pinion on the boom (Fig. 2-9B). A further step is the use of a geared handle to wind the boom around (Fig. 2-9C) in a similar way to a windlass.

Sails are not just flat pieces of cloth so reefing may be found to distort the shape of the remaining exposed canvas. Much depends on the particular sail, but one or two rolls or the use of the first row of points may not have much effect on the shape of an average sail.

Roller reefing or furling has been used on fore sails for some time and several schemes and sets of equipment have been available. There may be a long wood or plastic roller included along the luff of the fore sail or the sail may merely wind up on a wire rope. At the bottom there is a drum with a line around it. When the sail is fully set, the line is rolled on the drum. Pulling on the line rolls the sail (Fig. 2-9D). Pulling the fore sail sheets unfurls it. This is the principle. Differences between makes and systems are mainly in refinements and quality.

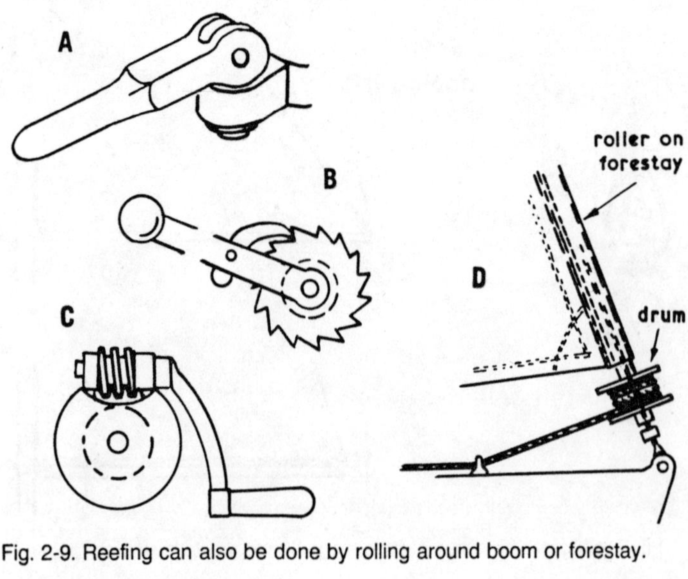

Fig. 2-9. Reefing can also be done by rolling around boom or forestay.

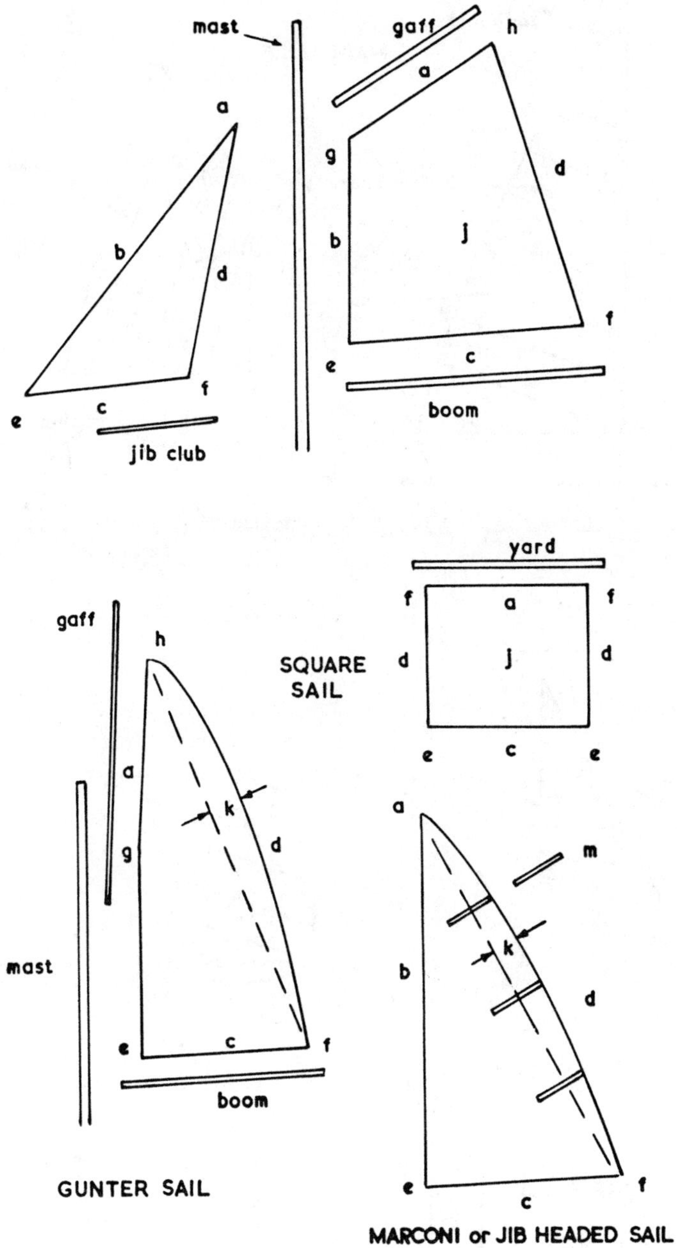

Fig. 2-10. The commonly used names for parts of a sail are: a - head, b - luff, c - foot, d - leech, e - tack, f - clew, g - throat, h - peak, j - bunt or belly, k - roach, m - battens.

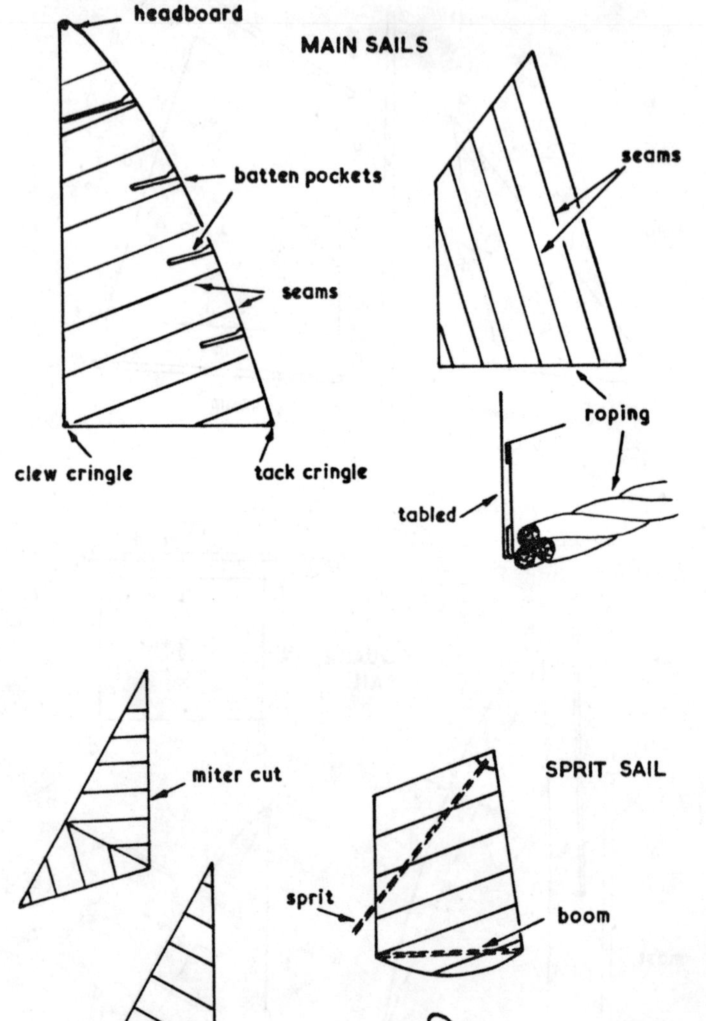

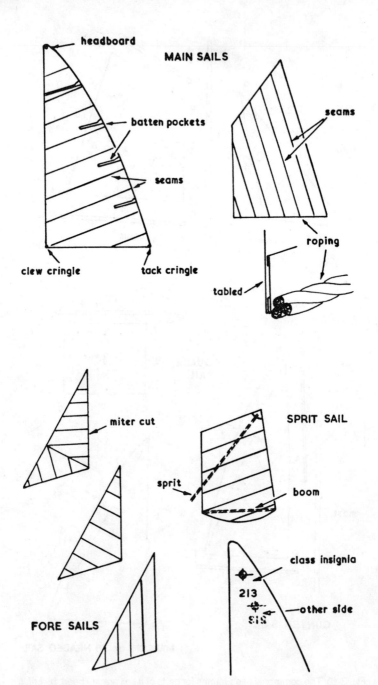

Fig. 2-11. Fittings, attachments, and constructional details have the usual names shown.

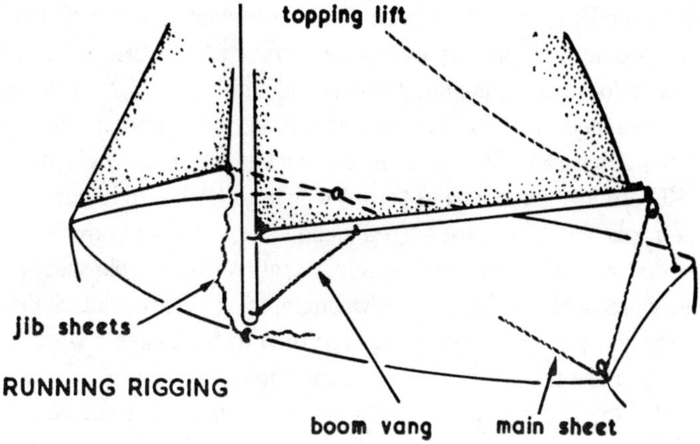

Fig. 2-12. Running rigging hoists and controls sails.

SAIL TERMS

The language of the sea has become complex and often more of a mystery than it should be. In the days before rapid communications around the world, local terms developed and these might not be

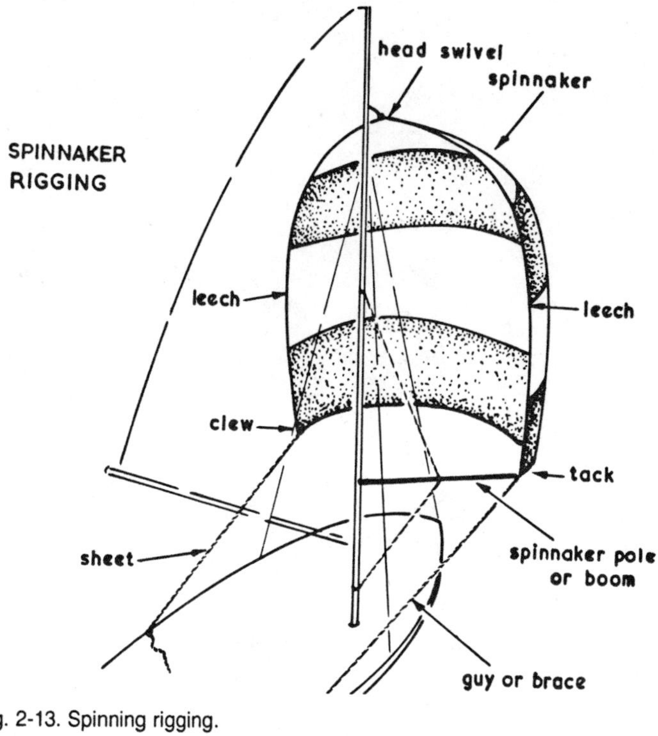

Fig. 2-13. Spinning rigging.

understood by people elsewhere. This has meant that names, even today, are not accepted by everyone and it could be that even with new parts of sailing equipment terms will differ, as with *boom vang*, just mentioned. This is of comparatively recent adoption, but that name is American. The term used is *kicking strap* in England.

There are some sailing terms which go back into history and were applicable to square-rigged sailing ships, but are now better regarded as archaic. Unfortunately, some sailing people discover these words and use them, often wrongly, to show how nautical they are. It is better to use plain language than to try to use a word for which you are unsure of the exact meaning.

However, it is important that anyone who wants to make sails know the more common terms. The majority of names applied to sails and related equipment are now mostly universally used. A knowledge of them is worth having so you can talk enough of the language when discussing sails with others. A selection of names as applied to various rigs is shown in Figs. 2-10, 2-11, 2-12, and 2-13.

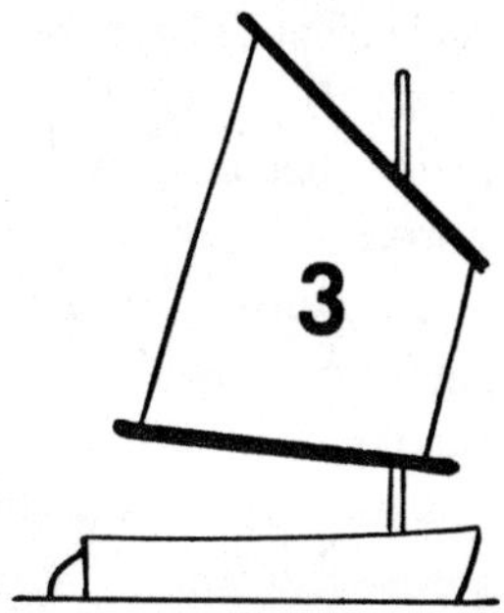

Rig and Boat

The large variety of sailing rigs used in many parts of the world shows that there can be no finality in design. All of this can be very bewildering to anyone choosing, for the first time, a new or used boat. Most modern yachts have a simple one-mast rig with a jib-headed main sail and one working head sail. Although this may be regarded as the norm, a flick through the pages of any yachting magazine will show that many other sail arrangements are still used.

It is not easy to say why any rig is chosen. There may be convincing arguments that show one rig is superior to another, yet there will still be yachtsmen who prefer an allegedly discredited rig. The reason for some of this choice is tradition and nostalgia. There are very few working sailing craft today, so if we are sailing for pleasure, why not have the rig of our choice?

There are a few broad principles to consider when trying to match a sail plan and a boat. The most efficient use of a given sail area can be made when it is in one sail, providing that it is properly designed. Efficiency then means driving power. If that means a very large sail, there may be practical problems of supporting it, and it may be more than the available crew can handle. Although it may drive the boat fast, it may not be amenable to maneuvering. You may want to change direction, but the sail may not. At one time the sail plan was broken down into several sails for ease of handling and to allow for manipulating in order to maneuver the boat. Today it is acceptable to have two sails on most craft, with a selection of different sizes and types for use forward of the mast; but only one of these sails is normally hoisted at a time.

If the sail plan for a new boat has to be chosen, a *sloop* should be considered first. If there are bridges to pass or it would be more convenient to keep the spars short for storage or trailing, maybe a *gunter sloop* would be better, but other things being equal, having the mast in one piece will probably give a better performance to windward.

For utter simplicity in the smallest boat, a balanced or standing lug has possibilities, with the balanced lug requiring the minimum number of fittings. With both rigs, all spars will stow inside the boat. A small sprit rig is comparable for simplicity and performance. However, even a small dinghy may benefit from having another sail forward of the mast.

As the number of sails and the number of masts increase, so does the number of ropes to be handled; the effort of sail handling calls for a larger crew. The *schooner* may appeal to traditionalists. The *ketch* is generally accepted as being outclassed by other ways of using the same sail area. The *yawl* may have advantages in maneuvering, but the little mizzen sail is not much use as a part of the wind power system.

Modern rigs tend to be higher and narrower—because of lessons learned from aeronautics. A lower spread-out rig may have traditional appeal, but for efficiency it falls behind the tall rig.

Lateen and junk sails may appeal to those who like experimenting. You may even want to try wing sails, but for the owner who merely wants to cruise or race, the more conventional sail arrangements are the ones to consider.

SAIL AREAS

There is no easy way of relating the area of sail to a particular hull. There are too many unknowns, imponderables, and requirements. Formulas have been devised that take into account length, beam, draft, weight, and other things, but a hull/rig relationship cannot be brought down to a mathematical equation. A hull with a wide beam should be able to carry more sail than one with a narrow beam on a given length, but the cross-section of the hull and the amount and disposition of ballast affect stability, so many more things besides beam have to be considered.

If the center of effort of the sail plan is low it will have less capsizing effect than if it is high. This means that more area could be carried in a low rig than in a high one, but the tall one will probably be more efficient, even with the lesser area.

Another problem is how much sail area to have in each of two or more sails. With a sloop rig, the mast position affects this. If it is about one-quarter of the length of the boat back from the stem head, as it often is, about three-quarters of the working sail area may go into the main sail to keep the center of effort correctly related to the center of lateral resistance.

Some designers advocate more area forward of the mast. This means bringing the mast farther aft. Quite often, practical considerations dictate the mast position and the sail plan has to be designed accordingly. Except when experimental sailing is intended, it is wisest to locate a sloop mast not more than one-third of the boat length from the bow. In a cat boat the mast goes very close to the bow, but for the other single-sail rigs one-fifth of the boat length from the bow is a reasonable location for the first sketching of the rig.

The actual amount of canvas to use is probably better related to experience than to any calculations. An examination of boats of similar specifications, either in catalogs or actually on the water, will show what sail areas have been proven satisfactory. Collecting information on the sails of a selection of boats of apparently similar characteristics to yours will provide a guide to how best to arrange the area and layout of your little ship, in a much more positive way than covering paper with calculations. It is the way most sail plans have been designed.

The conditions in which a boat is to be used also affect its sail needs. A yacht that will spend all its life in sheltered inland waters may need a higher and larger rig, to catch winds above trees and banks, than a yacht of similar size that is used for ocean cruising, where stronger and steadier winds may be expected. A racing yacht may carry much more sail area than would be wise for the family man whose main interest is in getting from A to B comfortably and at no great speed. This applies to dinghies as well as large yachts. The racing man may be prepared for and expect capsizes when using a comparatively vast sail area, yet the man who takes the family for a sail around the bay with a picnic en route, will regard half that area as adequate. Table 3-1 shows some examples of typical sail areas related to the main dimensions of the hull. There could be many

TYPICAL SAIL SIZES

Craft			Sails	
Type	Length ft.	Beam ft.	Number	Area s.ft.
General-purpose dinghy	11	5	2	70
Medium racing dinghy	12 1/2	5	2	90
Sailing surfboard	14	4	1	60
Fast racing dinghy	14	5 1/2	2	140
Cruising dinghy	16	6	2	125
Cruiser	17	7	2	125
Half-deck keelboat	19	6	2	175
Cruiser	21	7	2	230
Cruiser	24	8	2	250
Motor sailer	35	11 1/2	3	450
Catamaran	26	14	2	350
Trimaran	30	19	3	320
Older faff-rigged cruiser	30	8	4	425
Spritsail barge	79	18	5	2600
Sail training three-masted schooner	135	25	10	7100

more and anyone trying to relate a rig to a hull will have to search for them, but we have to start somewhere. Sail areas are usually quoted as the working rig or *all plain canvas.* There may be larger and smaller jibs, genoas and even spinnakers of a size to double the total area. At the other extreme there may be foul weather sails of very much smaller area, and the normal area may be reduced in steps by reefing.

AUXILIARY SAILS

Another use for sail is in steadying. A power boat can have its rolling reduced by hoisting a comparatively small area of sail. Whether the center of effort of the sail plan bears a correct relationship to the center of lateral resistance or not depends to a certain extent on the amount of sail in relation to the speed of the boat under power. Not much area of canvas is needed to give a more comfortable motion and this should have negligible effect on steering and control in the average power boat. The sails can then be arranged almost anywhere convenient, depending on how the mast can be located. This may lead to rigs that would not be much use on a purely sailing craft, but they serve their steadying purpose well (Fig. 3-1A).

Another use for a steadying sail is when the power craft is to heave to or ride to an anchor for fishing. Some power craft will yaw about under these circumstances. If a mizzen mast can carry a small sail sheeted centrally (Fig. 3-1B) there is a weather vane effect and the boat is kept fairly steadily head to wind. Such a sail also has some steadying effect when used under way.

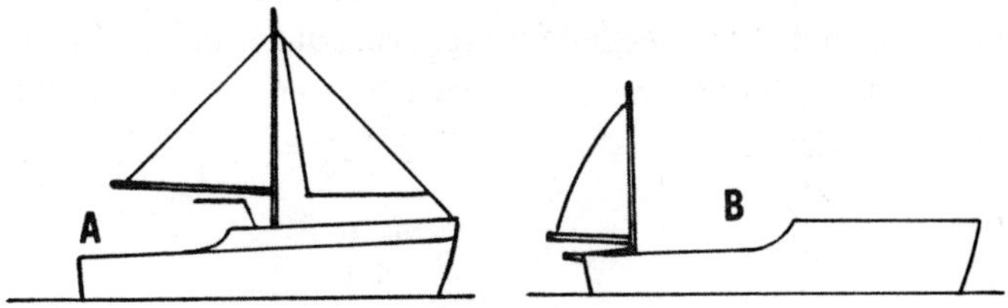

Fig. 3-1. Sail may be added to power craft for steadying purposes.

A further step in putting on a sailing rig is to consider it as a second means of propulsion if the engine fails. The average power boat does not have an underwater shape that would allow it to sail properly to windward, but sufficient sail area to work the boat might allow it to reach a haven downwind or in a direction approaching reaching. The amount of superstructure on many power craft militates against successful sailing, so don't expect too much of a sailing rig. The top hamper of deck houses, cabin tops, and other projections of hull above the waterline make up a total fixed area exposed to the wind and trying to push the boat sideways. Nothing can be done about this and it is one reason why an auxiliary sailing rig should only be expected to drive the boat within certain limits each side of downwind.

How much working sail is put on a motor cruiser or other power craft will depend on practical considerations. A tall single-masted arrangement may not be possible, or if it is, the amount of gear required would occupy far more space than could be allowed for what is intended to be only emergency equipment. The original design may not have allowed sufficient strength anywhere to take a mast in the usual forward position, either through the cabin or deck to the keel or in a tabernacle on deck. If there is an aft cockpit or wheelhouse, the bulkhead position may be the strong point. A mast there may require an unconventional rig (Fig. 3-2A), but it could be as effective as any other arrangement.

It may be better to divide the rig between two masts with modified yawl or ketch rigs (Fig. 3-2B). A mast right aft is out of the way and a mizzen sail on it has the secondary use of keeping a heaved-to boat head into wind. If there is a wheelhouse, the boom from a forward mast cannot be very low (Fig. 3-2C) and this is another reason for dividing the sail plan. Another consideration is obstruction of view under power. With a divided rig, the mizzen and jib may be all that are needed for steadying under power, and they should not impede the helmsman's view, then the main could be added for sailing only.

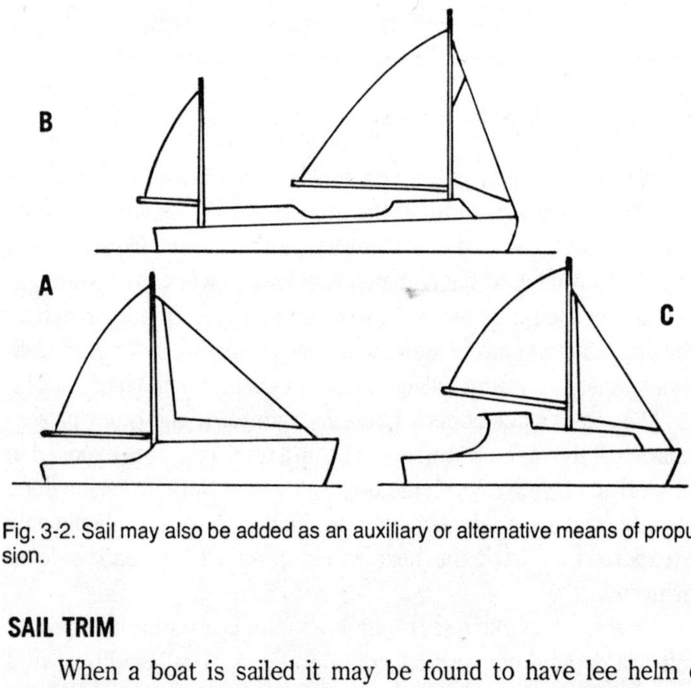

Fig. 3-2. Sail may also be added as an auxiliary or alternative means of propulsion.

SAIL TRIM

When a boat is sailed it may be found to have lee helm or excessive weather helm—slight weather helm is desirable, as already explained. If there is a lee helm—a tendency for the boat to run off the wind if the helm is released—the center of effort of the sail plan is too far forward in relation to the center of lateral resistance of the hull. Of course, a major fault can only be corrected by redesigning, but there are several things that can be done to reduce or correct lee helm.

If it is a dinghy or other boat small enough for the disposition of its crew to affect trim, moving people forward a little may be all that is needed. This puts more of the hull into the water forward, so moving the *c*enter of *l*ateral *r*esistance forward (Fig. 3-3). If there is

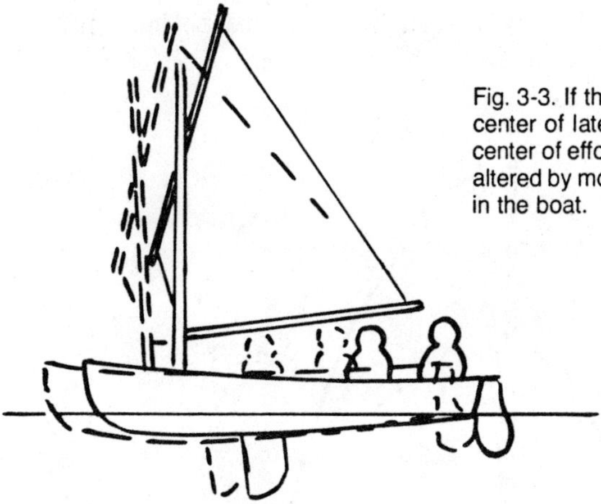

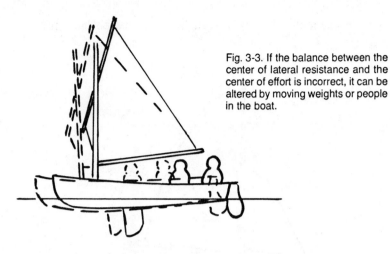

Fig. 3-3. If the balance between the center of lateral resistance and the center of effort is incorrect, it can be altered by moving weights or people in the boat.

a centerboard, dropping it fully down from a partly-lowered position will also move c.l.r. forward (Fig. 3-4A).

If correction of lee helm is to be made with the sail plan, its *c*enter of *e*ffort has to be brought further aft. Reducing the sail area forward of the mast will help. There may be a smaller jib, or the normal one can be reefed or cut to a new shape (Fig. 3-4B). It is not usually possible to increase the size of the main sail to bring the center of effort aft, but if the mast angle can be altered by adjusting

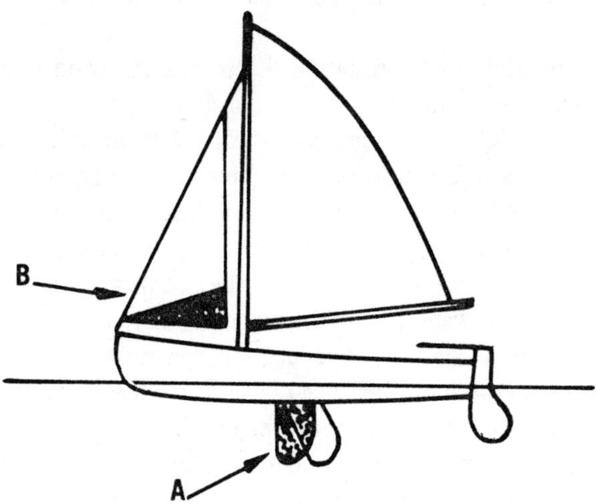

Fig. 3-4. Dropping the centerboard will also work, as will altering sail sizes.

stays, raking it aft will bring the center of effort back a little (Fig. 3-5).

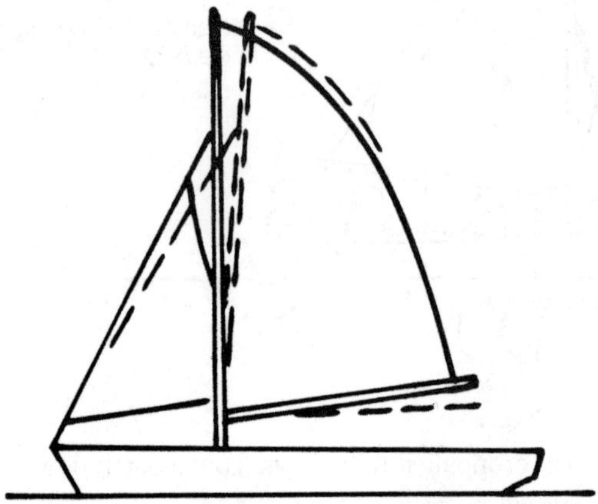

Fig. 3-5. Raking the mast is another way to achieve better balance.

Reduction of weather helm is mainly accomplished by reversing suggested actions for correcting lee helm. In a boat where crew weight has much effect, bringing people further aft will help (Fig. 3-6A). It may be inadvisable to reduce keel surface by partly raising a centerboard, but if this can be done, it will move c.l.r. a little aft (Fig. 3-6B).

Above the water, reducing the size of the main sail may be necessary for a permanent cure of considerably too much weather helm (Fig. 3-6C), but a larger sail forward of the mast (Fig. 3-6D) or raking the mast forward (Fig. 3-6E) may be all that is needed.

The rudder area is part of the total keel surface that affects c.l.r. Its normal area may be needed for effective steering and an alteration of size, because of this, may be inadvisable; but cutting the size of the underwater part of the rudder would help to cure lee helm or increasing its size would reduce weather helm.

Larger craft have their mast position fixed and any adjustment to it is restricted to small alterations of rake. In some dinghies the position of the mast foot can be altered fore and aft. This allows greater correction than raking the mast, because the whole rig can be moved aft to reduce lee helm, or forward to reduce weather helm.

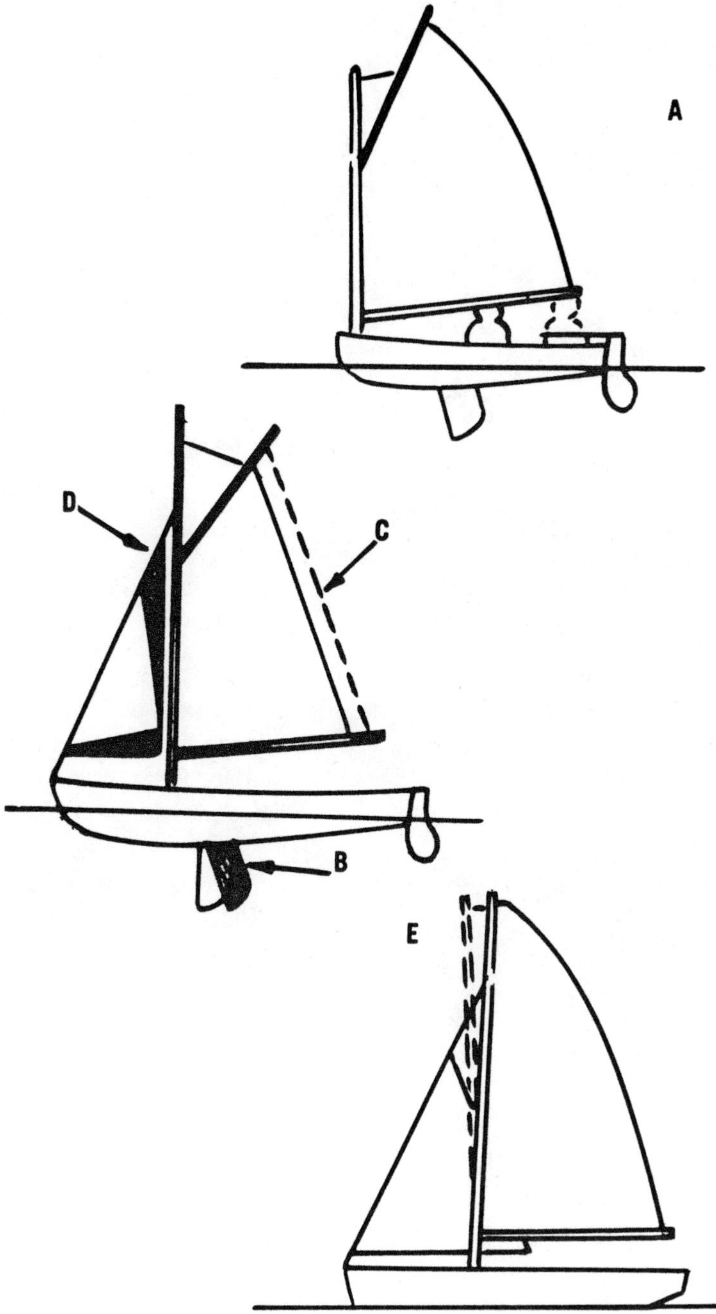

Fig. 3-6. Reduction of weather helm is accomplished by reversing actions taken for correcting less helm.

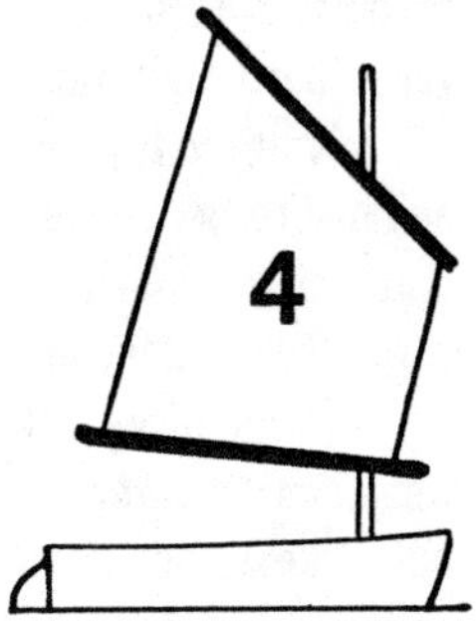

Materials and Tools

A sail has to offer a resistance to wind. It is this resistance to the passage of air that takes wind power and converts it through spars and rigging to the hull, which is shaped to accept the power in a way that drives the hull forward. Sails have been made of absolutely impervious materials, sometimes rigid in fixed aerofoil section or flexible in the form of manufactured plastic or other non-woven sheeting. Early examples of this latter type were leather sails. There are many practical problems with non-woven sails, particularly their lack of sufficient flexibility and compactness for stowing.

Most sails have been made of woven fabric. Various basic natural materials have been used, depending on local supply. Flax and hemp were used for the heavy sails of ships before the days of steam. Cotton was a better material for lighter and smaller sails. Until comparatively recent times, cotton has been the accepted material for the sails of pleasure craft. Sails made from cotton may still be found, but all of the natural fibers have been superseded by synthetic fibers and almost all new sails will be made in these materials.

Cloth woven from natural fibers suffers from the ever-present risk of rot. This meant that traditional sails had to be treated to make them water- and rot-proof. Because the treatments would not last indefinitely there had to be periodic reproofing. An excess of proofing solution in a lightweight sail affected its performance, though, so sails for dinghies and other small craft were not always adequately proofed and there was a constant struggle to dry them before stowing or have them out to dry as soon as possible after stowing. If this were not done rot started, usually first as the disfiguring spots of mildew. Heavier working sails were treated with solutions that left them hard and stiff as well as dark.

Another problem with natural-material sails is stretch. A new sail had to be carefully used so it did not distort. Any stretch had to conform to what was planned and the final shape had to be satisfactory. Even then, an old sail might lose its shape.

The synthetic materials used for most sails today are polyesters (Dacron, Terylene) and nylon. Nylon is elastic and is suitable for spinnakers, but unsuitable for most other sails. Much experiment and research has gone into the production of modern sail cloths and there are many types available. All are closely-woven to prevent much air from passing through. The method of weaving gives a stable form with a good resistance to distortion, so the sail keeps its shape for a long time. This cloth also needs little or no stretching when a sail is new, so preliminary breaking in of the sail is not critical. The material is also immune to the effects of dampness. This means a modern sail can be stowed wet without much risk of it being damaged, although it's obviously better to dry it or avoid long stowage while wet.

Some cloths are treated with resins and other fillers to stop them from stretching or from letting air through. A close weave without this is better for a long-lasting sail. Coloring of polyesters is best done during manufacture. The material is not absorbent to common coloring or proofing solutions applied by hand after manufacture, although there are special coloring agents which can be used. Most owners find it is better to leave the sail finish as supplied.

Sail cloth is graded in several ways. Most suppliers of synthetic sail cloth follow traditional ways of grading, but not necessarily with the same standards. The weight per yard is commonly used. In the case of cotton cloths, this is the weight before proofing, so the cloth may actually be heavier than specified. Synthetic material in the grades likely to be needed for pleasure craft is comparatively light, so grades may be only a few ounces for many small craft sails, with differences to two decimal places in some cases.

The weight is not always computed per square yard, as it is with most fabric imported from Britain. Some American grading is computed per yard length on a width of 28 1/2 inch. As there is less cloth in the narrower width, this means, for example, that 4 ounces American grade is equivalent to 5 ounces imported grade. (The proportion 4:5 is useful for conversion). Table 4-1 shows some typical examples, but there are many things affecting the choice of sail cloth besides size of boat, so the figures quoted should only be regarded as an approximate indication. With the coming of metrication, grades will have to be revised.

Table 4-1. Typical Polyester Sail Cloth Weights.

Craft	Individual sail area s.ft.	Weight (ounces)	
		American	Imported
Dinghy	50	2.4 - 3.2	3.0 - 4.0
Open keel boat	80	3.2 - 4.8	4.0 - 6.0
Cruiser to 25ft.	100	4.0 - 5.3	5.0 - 7.0
Cruiser to 30ft.	180	4.8 - 6.4	6.0 - 8.0
Cruiser to 40ft.	300	6.4 - 8.0	8.0 - 10.0

Much heavier sailing ship canvas was graded by number. Some synthetic sail cloth suppliers use a number grading, which should not be confused with that used for the older heavy natural fiber cloths. One range goes from 1 to 5, the numbers indicating the strength of wind the cloth is intended for.

When considering making a sail for a particular boat, it is probably wiser to seek the advice of the cloth supplier after giving him full details of the size of sail, the type of boat, and the expected conditions, than to go to buy sail cloth with fixed ideas about the grade. Besides weights there are variations in hardness (favored for racing) and softness (favored for cruising).

ROPE AND HARDWARE

Rope has gone through similar changes to sail cloth. At one time hemp, manila, cotton, and other natural fibers were the usual ropemaking materials, but nearly all rope now is synthetic and it would be unwise to incorporate natural fiber rope in a synthetic fiber sail. The man-made rope materials are mostly the same as those used for sail cloth, with polyester for the non-stretch rope and nylon where some elasticity is acceptable or desirable. Other synthetic materials are used for ropes but it is wisest to match the rope material to that of its sail.

This also applies to twine, thread, and any other light line used. There are natural fiber twines and threads available and these are sometimes used on synthetic fabricis. Even if the thread is waxed or proofed it is liable to fail through rot before the sail itself wears out, so it is better to use synthetic threads.

Traditionally, rope has been made three-stranded, with the fibers laid up into yarns twisted together one way to form strands which are twisted the other way (Fig. 4-1A). Synthetic fiber rope is made in this way and much of it commonly available is of this type and the usual rope is laid right-handed, meaning that as you look along the rope the twist is clockwise away from you.

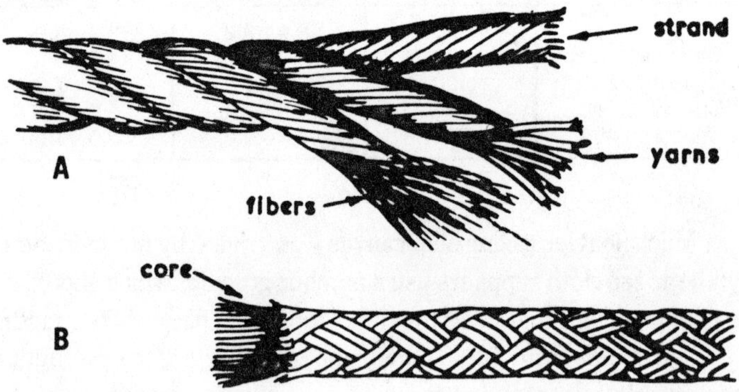

Fig. 4-1. Stranded rope is made of fibers twisted into yarns. Braided rope is made by weaving yarns around a core.

Ropemakers have used synthetic fibers to produce ropes with special qualities. Many sheets and halliards are made of braided rope (Fig. 4-1B). This is more comfortable to handle, less liable to kink or tangle, and often stronger. The braiding may be around internal fibers laid lengthwise, or laid up like a three-stranded rope, and there may be a second braided sheath. A number of special lays of rope are used. These bring their own problems of splicing. Many of these specially-laid ropes are associated with sails, but most actually built into sails are three-stranded.

At one time there was little but cloth and rope in a sail, with attachment points, reefing arrangements, and anything special made by reinforcing and sewing. In modern sails there are many metal and plastic items. These provide strong points and are more convenient to use. Also, they are usually simpler and quicker to fit. Grommets are included where attached ropes or other fittings put a local strain. There may be slides on a main sail or snaps to fit the forestay on a jib. A metal or wood head board may be built in.

Metal hardware should be stronger than the equivalent plastic fittings, but particularly for smaller sails, nylon and other plastics have been found to be strong enough. Plastic is kinder to the sail cloth than metal. Any metal used should be of a salt-water resistance type and intended for use afloat. Corrosion of the metal may discolor nearby fabric. Some hardware is also used with canvas ashore and it is advisable to check that such things as grommets are of a type intended for use afloat, otherwise common brass may corrode and leave a blue-green stain on the fabric. Stainless steel is acceptable and strong for some hardware, but ordinary iron or steel is more appropriate to sails of working craft than to those on a yacht. If iron or steel is used it should be adequately protected by plating or other coating—galvanizing (coating with zinc) was the method used on older fittings.

Although galvanic action is unlikely to be a serious problem with the metalwork associated with sails, it should be kept in mind. If widely different metals are in contact with each other in a salt-laden atmosphere, one metal will be eaten away. For instance, copper rivets through a galvanized steel fitting would cause the zinc coating to disappear.

Further information on sail hardware is given in the appropriate places concerned with tools or making sails.

TOOLS

Most cutting of sail cloth can be done with scissors, but they should be sharp, have tight joints, and preferably be rather larger than those used for domestic purposes. A sharp knife is also worth having. In the past this sharp kinife has been a fairly large sheath knife with a thin blade; but one of the modern general-purpose type with replaceable blades is probably just as useful.

Polyester and nylon can be melted by heat. For rope-cutting you can use appliances that are basically knives brought to a sufficient heat to cause the cut ends to melt and flow together as the knife goes through. This seals each end and prevents unlaying. Although the sealed end may seem as secure as if whipped, it is usual to add a whipping if no splice or other work is to be done on the end. The same effect may be obtained after cutting with an ordinary knife if the rope's end is heated with a flame from a match or cigarette lighter, then the end is rolled with the moistened finger and thumb.

If cloth is to be cut and left without the edge being turned in or otherwise protected, this can also be heat sealed. Instead of a knife a heated electric soldering gun is used, which will sever the cloth by heat and cause the fibers to run together so the threads do not fray. Pinking shears can be used to give a fray-resistant zig-zag edge.

Most sewing is done with a sewing machine, although almost every sail will need some hand sewing. The sewing machine may be the ordinary domestic type, as most modern sail material for the average boat is little heavier than the cloth used for normal home sewing. However, if a heavier machine can be used it will be better able to cope with multiple thicknesses and deal with some parts that would otherwise have to be handsewn. A machine that will sew with a zig-zag stitch is preferable to one that only does straight stitching, but straight stitching can be used, if that is the only method available.

Except for sewing by machine, there is very little else that can be done mechanically and sails are largely the products of hand craftsmanship.

Traditionally, a sailmaker sits on a long low bench or stool without a back to do hand work. Many of his tools are pushed into holes in the end of the stool. With the stool located on a floor large enough for a sail to be spread over, he can pull the canvas about and move himself and the sail as he progresses. The part being worked on is usually placed over his thighs, which are protected by a stout apron. The apron may be made of canvas or leather and usually has a pocket, as well as a patch of cloth into which spare needles are stuck.

An amateur sailmaker may not need a special seat, but if an expert chooses this mode of working it is obviously the best way to proceed. Some sort of low seat is advisable. Good protection over the legs is needed to guard against pricks with the point of the needle.

Although it is possible to sew light sail cloths with almost any type of needle, proper sail needles are better and are essential for heavier materials. The thread or twine used is comparatively thick and a parallel needle would not open a large enough hole to allow this and the eye end of the needle to pass through easily. Sail needles are made with a triangular section, reducing to round at the eye end (Fig. 4-2). This has the effect of pushing open a gap of sufficient size in the weave of the cloth to make passage of needle and thread thickness easy.

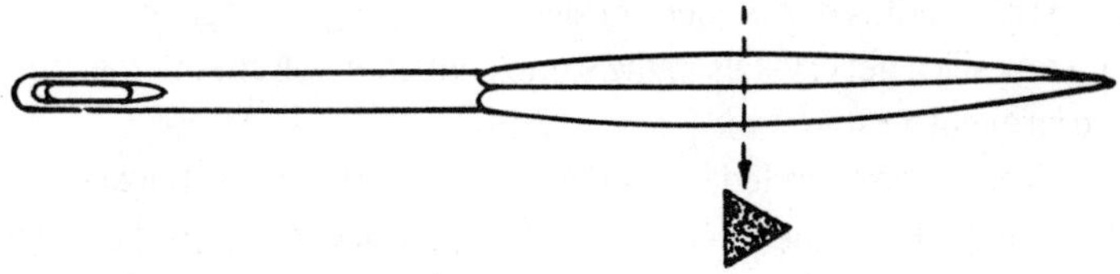

Fig. 4-2. Sail needles are shaped to force open the weave. They have a triangular cross section.

Needles are made of steel and are supplied highly polished with sharp points. For most purposes the points need to be kept sharp, although for roping and a few other purposes a slightly blunted end may be preferred. A needle with a very blunted end may serve as a bodkin for leading a cord through a seam at the neck of a bat or similar purpose. Needles should be protected from rust as the roughness this causes interferes with easy passage through canvas. There are needle cases (Fig. 4-3A). One way of protecting the points is to push them into a cork (Fig. 4-3B), which is then pushed into a glass tube or bottle. As a glass tube is liable to break, an alternative used by some traditional sailmakers is a section of cane or bamboo (Fig. 4-3C) with the cork pushed into its end.

Needles may be pushed into a piece of cloth, which is then closed over them and wrapped. With natural fiber cloth there is a risk

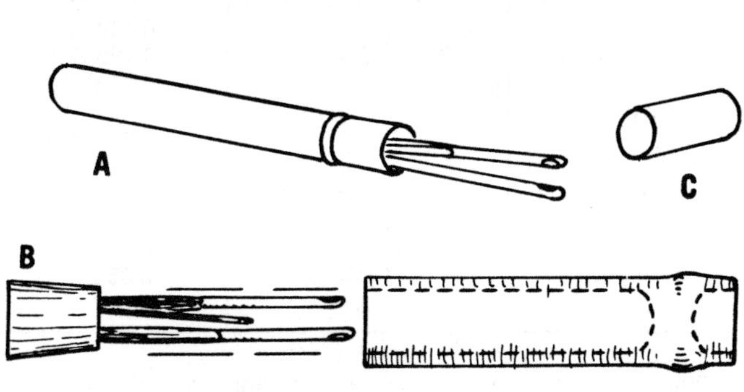

Fig. 4-3. Needles should be protected when out of use, as with this case, or by pushing them into cork.

that this will absorb moisture from the atmosphere and cause the needles to rust, but if synthetic fiber cloth is used, this problem should not arise. Needles may be coated with oil to prevent rust, but as oil is best kept away from sail cloth, they would have to be thoroughly wiped before use. It is better to rely on a container to keep the needles dry. A piece of silica gel impregnated paper or cloth or a few silica gel crystals in the same container will absorb moisture and prevent rust.

Needles are graded by number, which is the gauge thickness of the round part of the needle. Lengths vary according to the gauge size. Sizes are in inverse proportion to the gauge size—the higher the number, the smaller the needle. The usual range is from 4 to 18, with a few half sizes in the smaller needles. For most small craft sails it is only the smaller needles (higher gauge numbers) that have much use.

Table 4-2 shows the approximate sizes of the usual sail needles. The thicker needles are rarely used and it is the range from 9 to 18 that are commonly made. Of these, an amateur sailmaker is likely to find all he wants in the range between 13 and 16. Covers, awnings, bags, and other canvas goods generally need needles larger than those used for modern sails. Shorter needles have been offered as roping needles, but roping can be done with ordinary sail needles.

Table 4-2. Needle Sizes.

Needle number (gauge)	Length (inches)	Thickness (inches)
9	4	0.144
10	3 3/4	0.128 (1/8)
11	3 1/2	0.116
12	3 1/4	0.104
13	3	0.092 (3/32)
14	2 3/4	0.080
14 1/2	2 5/8	0.076
15	2 1/2	0.072
16	2 3/8	0.064 (1/16)
17	2 1/4	0.056
18	2 1/8	0.048

Almost all hand sewing of sails can be done with the normal sail needles, but it is likely that other canvas work will be undertaken, when other needles may have their uses. Packing or bagging needles

(Fig. 4-4A) are fairly large and used for sewing coarse fabrics such as burlap, particularly for making large stitches with cord, as when sealing package or drawing a wrapping around something temporarily.

Curved needles (Fig. 4-4B) are used in several trades. They are useful when only one side of the work can be reached. Leatherworkers favor an oval section to push aside a hole large enough to clear the eye end and double thickness of thread. For use in upholstery the needle usually has a round section and some have points at both ends. An upholsterer also uses some very long straight needles. Any of these special needles may have occasional uses for the sailmaker who does other canvas work or makes cushions as well.

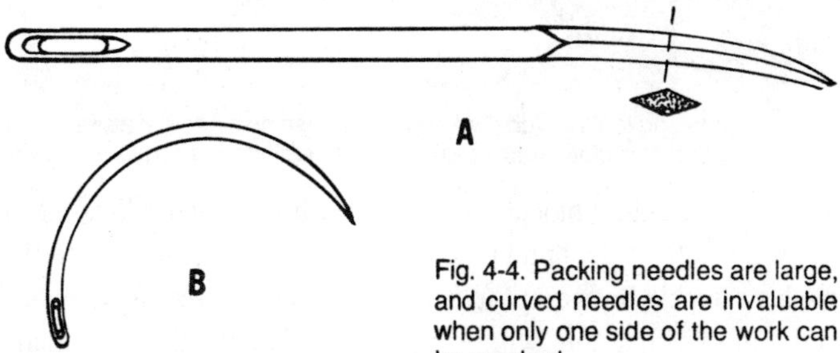

Fig. 4-4. Packing needles are large, and curved needles are invaluable when only one side of the work can be reached.

Besides needles there are needle-like pins, prickers, and spikes, which are used to hold cloth over a laid-out pattern, make or mark holes, or to temporarily hold cloths together for sewing. These may be simple steel pins or they may be handled. One- or two-handled spikes are worth having, ranging from ice pick size down to some that are little more than handled needles (Fig. 4-5).

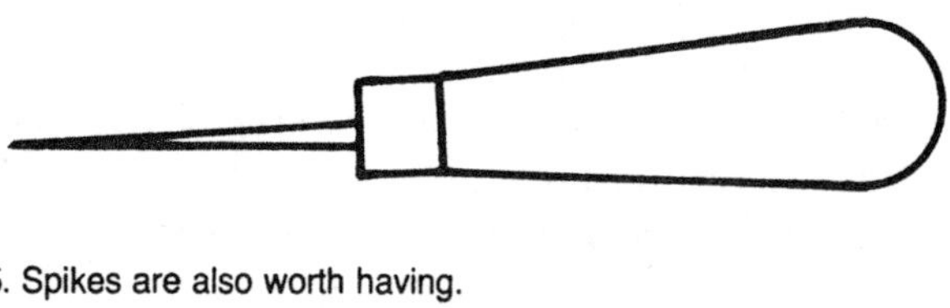

Fig. 4-5. Spikes are also worth having.

The tool that has evolved for pushing the needle through fabric is a palm. Basically, this is a leather strap with a hole for the thumb and a means of fastening it around the hand. Over the center of the

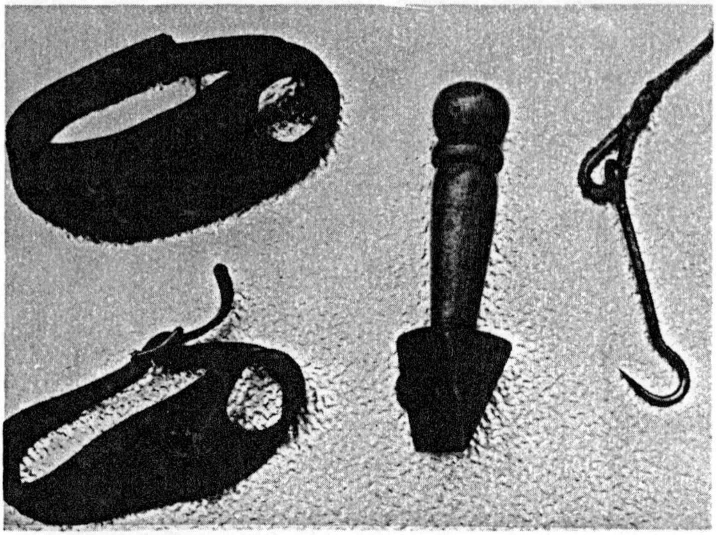

Fig. 4-6. Sailmaking tools include two palms for pushing a needle, a seam rubber for sharpening folds in cloth, and a sail hook for stretching a seam while sewing.

hand comes a metal block (Fig. 4-6). With the needle head against this, the whole of the hand provides thrust. To adjust for size there may be a buckle between the ends of the palm over the back of the hand; but it is common, where the palm will be used by one man, to adjust the size and trim the ends, then join them with a few turns of thread through holes.

Palms are commonly available right-handed. There are left-handed palms, but their use is unusual. As sewing in this way is a new skill for most people, the average left-hander usually finds he can adapt to right-handed sewing with a palm. In emergency a needle might be thrust through a few stitches by bearing down on a bench, but a palm is essential for anything more than this.

One palm may serve for all hand sewing, but there are some variations. A maker may describe his strongest palms as sailmakers' palms, while a lighter version is called a sailors' palm. To take care of the slightly different, and often heavier, push needed, there are roping palms with more protection around the needle end, for use when sewing a rope on the edge of a sail.

It is unlikely that there will be much choice of palms, but one should be tried for fit. A new one may feel stiff and awkward, but this will improve with use. The metal pad that pushes the needle should have a pattern that reduces any tendency for the needle end to slip and be set fairly deeply in the leather so the needle is unlikely to jump out.

Besides the lighter and finer spikes there are uses for rather thicker pointed tools. A steel marline spike (Fig. 4-7A) is used for rope splicing and for pushing through holes in canvas to enlarge them. A larger and thicker spike made of hard wood is called a fid (Fig. 4-7B). Wood is felt to be kinder to fabric and rope than metal, so wooden tools are often favored. A fid can be used for forcing a grommet into shape, enlarging a hole, or for splicing larger ropes.

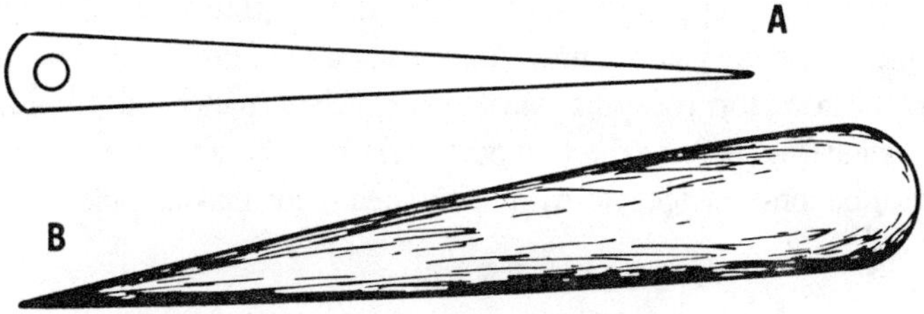

Fig. 4-7. A steel point is a marline spike. A wooden point is a fid.

Stitching for much length by hand is more easily made even and true if the fabric being sewn is stretched as it is stitched. This is best done with a sail hook (see Fig. 4-6), which is a long steel hook, usually with a swivel eye. There is a lanyard to tie or loop over a peg or the end of the stool.

Seams to be sewn often have to be rubbed down to a tight crease and this is done with a seam rubber or creasing stick. Some traditional seam rubbers have been elaborately carved in wood, bone, and other materials. These are attractive, but the important part is a rounded bevelled end that can be drawn along the seam. To stand up to wear the tool should be made of close-grained hardwood or bone. It is unlikely that one will be found for sale; it will have to be made.

Many holes in canvas are cut with a knife or made with a spike, but there are occasions when it is better to punch out a circle. This can be done with a hollow steel punch (Fig. 4-8), used with a hammer over a piece of wood. There has to be a separate punch for each size hole. For light fabrics there are punches that work with a plier action. A brass pad may act as a die, then punches can be changed to suit the

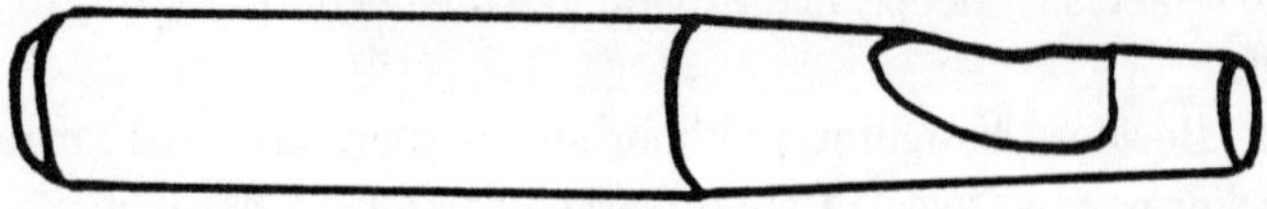

Fig. 4-8. A hollow punch makes holes.

size of hole needed. As this type of tool relies on the strength of a hand grip, it can only be used for light work.

Grommets (eyelets) are mostly of metal in two parts, with a simple ring at one side and a tubular piece from the other side, which has to be turned over it. These are best closed with a die that matches and supports the underside so the metal turns neatly over. A punch and die pair are needed for each size of grommet. The die may be in the form of a small anvil over which the punch is used with a hammer (Fig. 4-9) or the two parts may be in a plier-type tool and could be interchangeable with punch heads for making holes.

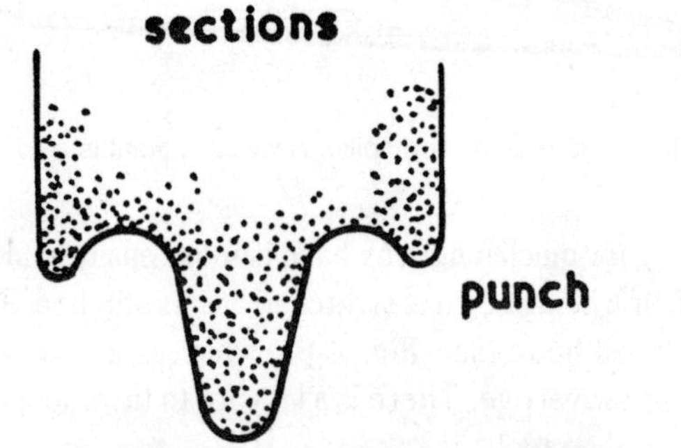

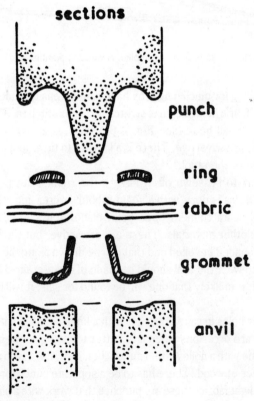

Fig. 4-9. A punch and die sets grommets.

Although sailmaking is primarily fabricwork with some associated fiber ropework, there are often other processes involved in completing a sail so many other tools may be needed. A wooden-jawed vise is less likely to damage fabric when parts have to be held or squeezed on a sail. It may be satisfactory to make wooden covers for the jaws of a metalworking vise, which will be needed if wire splicing is involved or if there are metal fittings and attachments to fit, alter, or adjust. Similarly, if metal parts have to be hit, a hammer is the right tool, but if it is wood or fabric that has to be hit, it is better to use a wooden or plastic-faced mallet.

Screwdrivers, pliers and saws for wood or metal are sometimes needed. Plastic fittings are being increasingly used on sails. These may have to be sawn, filed, and sanded. There may have to be holes drilled. A small hand drill is usually all that is needed.

A sail shape has to be *lofted*, which means drawn full-size on the floor. How to do this is described in the next chapter, but a long piece of wood to use as a straightedge is worth having, although longer straight lines are made with a chalk line. This is merely a long strong thin cord. A chalk line used by builders is really too coarse. Crochet cotton makes a good sailmakers' chalk line as it is fine yet strong. A spike is used at one end. The line has to be coated with chalk, which can be merely pieces of the school variety. Wind the chalk line on a reel, preferably with hollows for finger and thumb (Fig. 4-10). Other marks may be made on the floor with pencils, but it is useful to have a piece of french chalk (talc) sharpened to a chisel edge by rubbing on a file (Fig. 4-11).

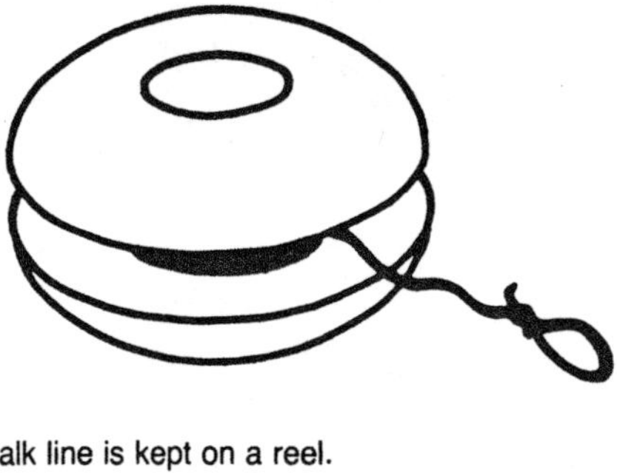

Fig. 4-10. A chalk line is kept on a reel.

A steel tape measure or an expanding rule will mark out sizes, but errors can be avoided if this is long enough to measure the greatest lengths required without having to do it in steps.

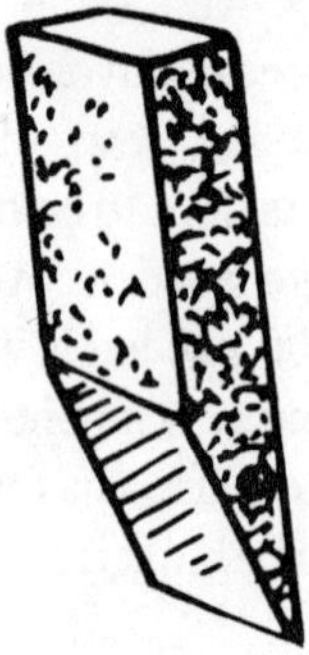

Fig. 4-11. Flat chalk draws lines.

There are many curves to be marked and these are often comparatively slight although it is important that they should be "fair." A kink or discrepancy in a curved edge will be very apparent to any viewer and may affect the performance of the sail. Curves are best marked with battens. These are long flexible strips of wood. They should have even grain and be free from knots or flaws that would cause uneveness when they are bent. A batten should be longer than the curve it is to mark, so the shape can follow through past what will be the ends of the drawn part and thus produce a fair curve all the way. The exact size of a batten is not important. A section about 1 inch by 1/2 inch might be about right for a 15 foot batten, but it could be greater and would have to be much greater for a very long batten. The important thing is the ability to flex fairly over all its length.

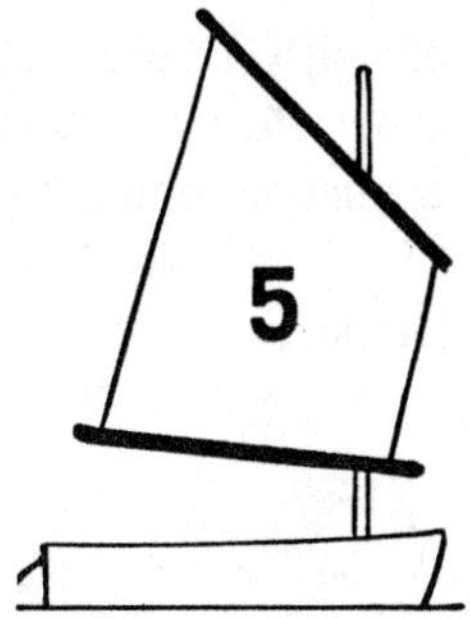

Lofting

An important step in the production of a sail is the setting out of its shape. Errors at this stage could result in a sail that did not match its spars, conform to class rules, or perform properly. Usually the information has to be taken from a sketch or scale drawing and reproduced full-size on the floor. There is really no alternative to this reproduction, so you will need a floor area big enough to take a drawing of the largest sail, preferably with some space for walking around, rather than over, a sail laid on the floor.

Any floor will do, but a wood surface that is reasonably smooth with a matt dark surface is best. Any gloss on the surface makes marking difficult. Most marking can then be done in chalk, but pencil can be used. Much of the setting out is fairly straightforward geometry, but at a size with which the amateur sailmaker is probably unfamiliar.

Long straight lines are best made with a chalk line. A wooden straightedge may be used for 8 feet or perhaps more, but there is always the risk of warping. A stretched cord is always straight. Have a loop in the end of the chalk line and use a spike to the floor. Walk backwards from this, letting the line run off the reel while you rub chalk on the line. Do this without jerks, otherwise the chalk dust will be dislodged. When sufficient length has been chalked, stretch the line and hold it with your thumb to the floor. Get an assistant to lift the middle of the line a few inches and strike it (Fig. 5-1). This will produce a fine line of chalk on the floor. If you are working alone you may be able to reach from the end you are holding and strike the line yourself with the other hand, but on a long line it is better for someone else to do it.

You will have to mark right angles. A piece cut from the corner of a plywood sheet can be used as a set square for distances up to about 4 feet. If a line has to be drawn at right angles to another, and extend more than this, there is a risk of error. Right angles with larger sides are better marked geometrically. There are several methods.

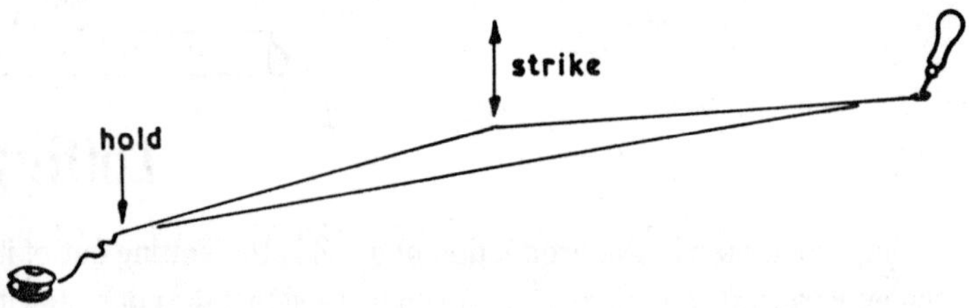

Fig. 5-1. Chalk a string and strike it.

The 3:4:5 method is commonly used. This makes use of the fact that in a triangle with sides in that proportion the angle between the short sides must be a right angle. Choose units that will let the '3' side extend more than the length of line you want. For example, if the length is to be about 9 feet, choose 3 feet as a unit. From the point where the right angle is to come on the base line measure 4 units (12 feet) to another point (Fig. 5-2A). Use a tape measure swinging on a spike or have a piece of wood 3 units (9 feet) long and mark a short arc that would obviously contain a right angle (Fig. 5-2B). This can be done with a pencil or a piece of sharpened french chalk. From the other point on the base line measure 5 units (15 feet) to a point on the arc (Fig. 5-2C). Use your chalk line and strike a line on the floor through this point.

If the line composing the right angle is to connect to the base line, use a strip of wood and a spike as a compass. Measure positions for the spike at equal distances from each side of the point where the line is to come at a right angle and draw arcs from these points (Fig. 5-2D). A line struck through their crossings will be at a right angle to the base. To reduce any risk of error, have the arcs themselves cross at about right angles to each other. This means choosing a distance each side of the base point that will let the 'compass' be at about 45° to the base line when it makes the arc. For this sort of 'striking a line' it is useful to have an assistant hold the end of the line, instead of pushing in a spike. He can hold the chalk line past the arcs, but watch that it cuts the crossing when it is struck.

An alternative to the first method, used when the line intended to cross the base line at a right angle on one side, uses the fact that when a triangle is drawn with its apex on the circumference of a circle and its base is a diameter, the angle at the apex is a right angle. From the point where the line is to come, make a mark that is about 45° from it (there is no need for precision). Use a piece of wood and a spike as a compass or have a tape measure swinging on a spike. Set this to the distance between the two marks (Fig. 5-2E). Swing the compass and make a mark on the base line, then draw an arc that will obviously contain the right angle (Fig. 5-2F). Use the chalk line through the compass center mark and the mark on the base line. Make a mark where this crosses the arc (Fig. 5-2G). A line struck between the base mark and this will be at right angles to the base line (Fig. 5-2H).

Although right angles are needed in many places, much of the drawing of sail shapes consists of making triangles, for which the lengths of the sides are known, but which may not contain a right angled corner. Even when the sail has a curved edge, the first setting out is with straight lines and the curves are added afterwards.

Strike a base line. If there is no reason for doing otherwise, let this be the longest edge of the triangle. It makes for greater accuracy to produce two shorter sides on a long side, than to work from a short side (although this may sometimes have to be done). In any case, let the base line be longer than the sail edge that is to be marked on it. Mark two points on the line at the correct distance apart. It is not always easy to see a small mark. It may be just a line across or it can be 'pecked' on one side (Fig. 5-2J). In any case it helps to draw attention to the exact location by making a freehand ring around the point (Fig. 5-2K).

From one point use a tape on a spike or a strip wood compass and make an arc (Fig. 5-2L). From the other point measure the appropriate distance to make a mark on the arc. This is the point of

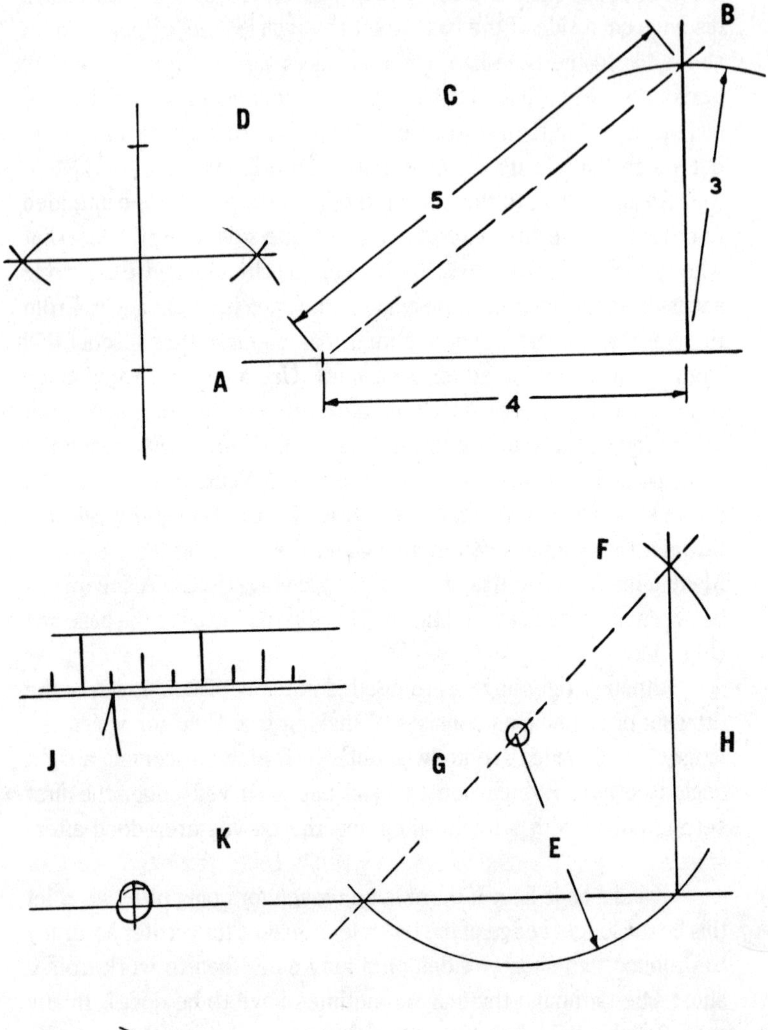

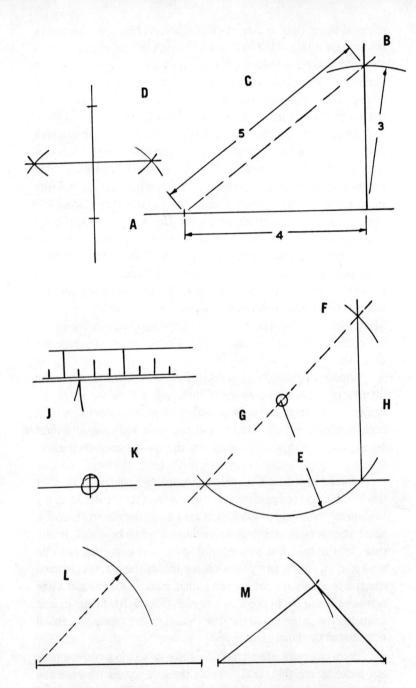

Fig. 5-2. Setting out lines and angles on the floor is the application of geometry on a large scale.

the triangle and lines can be drawn (Fig. 5-2M). If two tape measures can be used on spikes they can be manipulated so the two correct distances meet; then there is no need to use an arc.

There are not many right-angled corners in sail outlines, although there may appear to be. The tack corner may be a right angle, but it is more likely to be slightly less—possibly 87°. A right angle might be just as efficient, assuming there is adequate clearance at the other end of the boom, but it is largely considerations of appearance that explain the reduced angle. A right angle may make the sail appear to sag away towards the clew and this is aesthetically unattractive. Lifting the angle a few degrees makes it appear to be no more than a right angle (which it is not) and this is more pleasing.

Fortunately, one of the problems associated with natural fiber fabrics does not have to be considered. There is no stretching of Dacron sails to be taken into account and the drawing on the floor can therefore be full size. With natural material cloths there had to be a proportionate allowance, which varied according to direction of *warp* (yarns lengthwise) and *weft* (yarns crosswise). This was particularly important with class sails, where the finished sail had to be no bigger than specified by the class rules. If sails are made of cotton, or other natural material, and are to be altered or repaired, stretch should be allowed for.

When a curve has to be drawn with a batten there may be ordinates that give the height of curve above a base line at several points. This may be necessary if the curve is not part of the circumference of a circle, but is a tighter curve at one end than the other, as it is on luff and foot of some sails. Otherwise, the only height may be that at the point of greatest curvature.

In that case, the height is marked at the center of the straight line. A spike or nail can be pushed into the floor there. The batten is pulled around this until it passes through the end points. Let some excess length go past at each end and drive nails or spikes outside the batten to hold it to shape and position (Fig. 5-3A). It is important not to try to manipulate the batten. Let it follow a natural curve. The line that is wanted is on the inside of the batten and this can be drawn around with pencil or chalk. However, a very flexible batten may spring. Make a few key marks on the floor around the curve drawing all round, in case the batten moves. It may be necessary to locate a few more nails inside and out to steady the batten, but be careful that nothing is done to move it from its natural curve.

If the curve required varies and ordinates are provided by the designer, draw them along the straight line and put nails at the correct distances. Pull the batten around them and fix with nails outside the ends (Fig. 5-3B). It may be necessary to use a few nails outside the batten elsewhere. Sometimes the ordinate heights provided are not as accurate as they should be, particularly if they have been obtained from a small-scale drawing. In that case it may be necessary to let the batten take an average path that will follow a fair curve, even if some measurements do not come out exactly as expected.

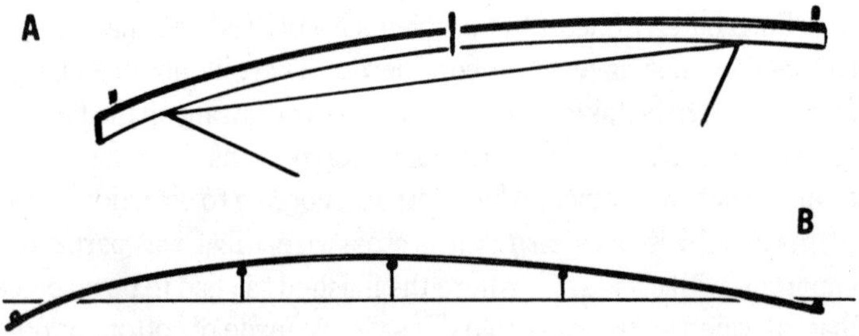

Fig. 5-3. Curves are drawn around wooden laths.

Many apparently straight edges are cut with a slight curve. This controls fullness of the sail, as described later. For instance, in a head sail the greatest curve of luff and foot may be at one-third the length of each side from the tack (Fig. 5-4A). A possible amount may be 1 inch for every 5 feet of luff and 2 inches for every 5 feet or foot. This may not be much, but the curve must be fair. Mark the height and pull a batten around through this and the corner points. Because the greater curve is at one end, you and an assistant may have to use a little force at that end to get a satisfactory shape. If working alone, it may be necessary to use several nails, each side of the batten at one end, while the other end is manipulated to get a curve you like the look of. This is the art part of sail design.

When the roach is put into a main sail, the resulting curve may be the final shape of the leech, but in some sails it is customary to cut the edge straight between battens. To arrange this, the curve is drawn, then the batten positions marked. Usually there are three or four positions spaced evenly, and at right angles to the straight line between head and clew. The exception is roller reefing where the bottom batten may be parallel with the boom, for ease in rolling without removing the batten. With the batten positions marked, join their ends with straight lines (Fig. 5-4B) and use these lines as the sail outline (Fig. 5-5).

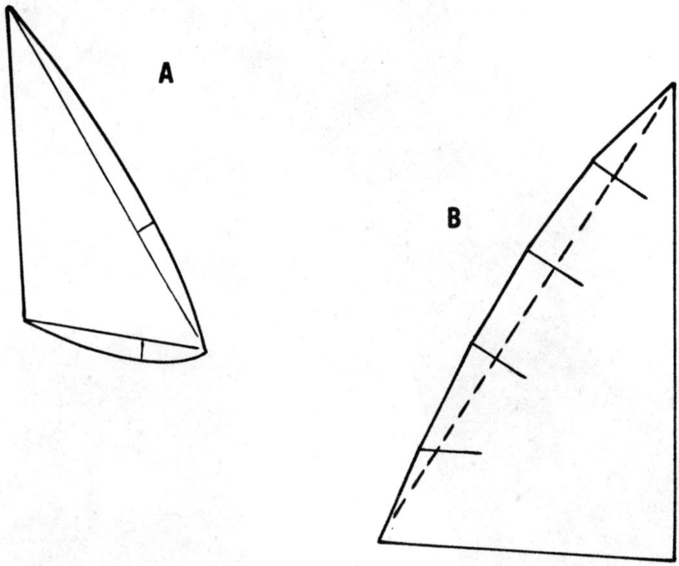

Fig. 5-4. Batten positions are marked.

In many sails the seams between cloths have to be arranged at right angles to an edge. In a main sail they may be at right angles to the leech and one seam comes at or near the tack corner. Even if the seam does not have to come at the corner, it is convenient to arrange a right angled line there and measure the actual seam position parallel to it (Fig. 5-6A). The right angle is arranged to the straight line across the leech, not to the curved edge.

One way of drawing this right-angled line is to use one of the methods already described to get a line in the vicinity of the tack corner, then measure the final line parallel to it (Fig. 5-6B). The basic methods do not allow for dropping the line to the base line from a point away from it. A method that does this uses a tape measure or strip wood and spike compass to swing arcs on the base line with the center at the tack (Fig. 5-6C). If the distance between these crossings is halved, this gives a point through which the line to the tack should be drawn (Fig. 5-6D). If the arcs cross the base line at a flat

Fig. 5-5. The way the battens hold out the leech can be seen in this side view, with the top full-length batten pushing out further and the cloth out straight between the batten positions.

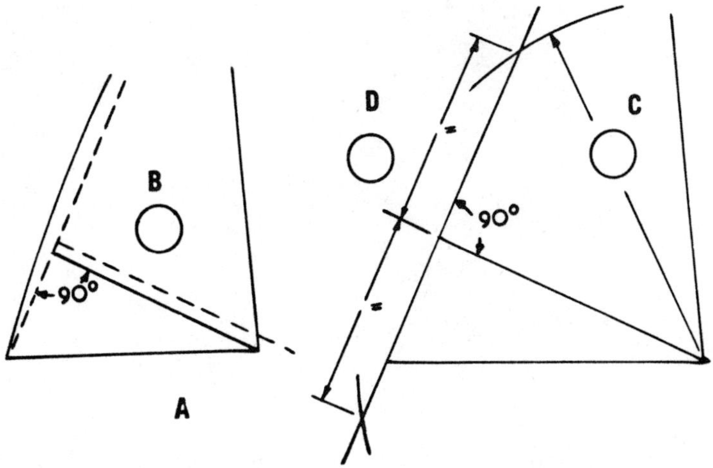

Fig. 5-6. Cloth edges are arranged at right angles to edges.

angle, it may be difficult to locate the crossing points exactly, so it helps to choose a setting that puts the arcs as far as possible along the base line.

6

Sailmaking Details

Nearly all work on a sail involves sewing. Details of design have changed with the coming of synthetic materials, particularly towards constructional methods that can be done with a sewing machine, where some of them previously involved hand sewing. There will continue to be a need for some hand stitching and any sailmaker should be able to do this competently.

The sewing machine should be treated as a tool under the control of the operator and not as something that can get out of hand due to ignorance of its functions. Under most circumstances the sewing machine chosen will be driven by an electric motor, but if a machine has to be used away from a power source it could be hand or treadle operated. A hand machine may be the only type suitable for taking afloat.

Zig-zag (cross) stitching looks better and the slight stretch it permits allows you to even the cloth and stitch after sewing; but there are parts of a sail where straight stitching is preferable. Adjustments that should be understood are: *tension*, which can be regulated so the knot comes in the middle of the cloth instead of on the top or bottom surface; and *stitch length*, which will be fairly consistent with zig-zag parts of a stitch at about right angles to each other for most parts of the sail.

A domestic sewing machine should deal with small sails without difficulty, but there is an advantage in having the greater capacity of a heavier tailor's machine, if varied sailmaking is to be tackled. The needle must be sharp, particularly if the cloth or its many thicknesses are coming near the capacity of the machine.

The needle has to be related to the thickness of thread and will usually be the heaviest a domestic machine will take. The thread color usually matches the sail, but a different color may be chosen. In any case, the dye should be fast to prevent unsightly runs.

Practice on scrap material is advisable. Even if the machine is already understood, practice on sail cloth—making the seams and other constructions involved—will be time well spent.

MACHINE SEWING

Cloths are joined edge to edge by overlapping in a flat seam. If the manufactured edge (selvedge) is used, it will not fray (Fig. 6-1A). If cut edges are joined in this way, they should be heat sealed to prevent fraying. There would usually be two lines of stitches on a straight seam. With small sails the seam width is about 1/2 inch. With larger and heavier sails it is more convenient to make the seams wider. What is important is that the two lines of stitches are far enough apart not to interfere with each other.

Zig-zag stitches can be taken over a cut edge (Fig. 6-1B) and this helps to hold down the edge and prevent fraying, but only half of each stitch is holding the joint. The method has uses in fixing insignia and numbers, but is not recommended for parts of the sail that will take a load.

It is more usual for cut edges to be turned under (Fig. 6-1C). This protects an unsealed edge and provides an extra thickness of cloth for stitching, thereby increasing strength.

A seam across a sail is a strength line. In natural fiber sails seams were kept 12 inches or so apart so as to use them to reduce stretch and distortion. The problem is not so acute with synthetic materials, but if wide cloths are used there is still some advantage in including false seams to make the apparent width of cloth in the sail less.

A false seam has the cloth closed over to give a similar appearance to the flat seams used (Fig. 6-1D). Pencil a line where the false seam is to come and fold the cloth along it, rubbing down to make a tight crease. At a distance equal to the intended width of the seam, stitch the cloth with straight stitches (Fig. 6-1E). The cloth is folded back and two lines of stitching similar to that of the ordinary seams are made. If colored thread is being used for ordinary sewing, the first straight stitches, which are only there to hold the seam in shape before final stitching, should be the same color as the fabric so they do not show in the finished false seam.

If an edge has to be strengthened it is *tabled*. A straight selvedge may be merely turned over and fixed with two rows of stitches (Fig. 6-1F). A cut edge is turned under (Fig. 6-1G), while greater strength for the fitting of grommets or other attachments comes from a full-width turn in (Fig. 6-1H).

On a curved edge, turning in the cloth would result in puckers. With only a slight curve in relation to the length of the edge there may be sufficient pliability in the cloth to allow careful manipulation and the avoidance of creases and puckers, but if there is much curve, it is better to table by sewing on a strip (Fig. 6-1J). This may be a piece of sail cloth turned under, but a similar method is used to sew on tape.

At one time much use was made of roped edges, with the rope hand-sewn. This is time-consuming work and difficult to do so that tensions are correct. With Dacron's better resistance to stretch, simpler methods of strengthening edges can be used. Besides sewing tape on one side, a wider piece may be wrapped over the edge and fixed with two rows of stitches (Fig. 6-1K). Further strength may be obtained by using two tapes (Fig. 6-1L).

Roped edges are still needed, but it is more usual to enclose the rope in fabric, usually tape. Tape is folded over the rope and large straight stitches are made close to the rope (Fig. 6-1M). The tape is taken over the edge of the sail and fixed with two rows of stitches (Fig. 6-1N). With a heavy machine it may be possible to first sew through the rope and the center of the tape, but this is not essential and is impossible with a light machine.

Rope can be included in the tabling of the sail material itself. It is unwise to enclose it in the single thickness as the edge is tabled, but a double thickness should be turned back (Fig. 6-1P), the rope placed near the turned edge (Fig. 6-1Q), then the edge turned over, followed by straight stitches near the rope and two rows of zig-zag stitches over the tabling (Fig. 6-1R).

The rope may be fiber or wire. The method of sewing is the same, but tension has to be regulated and information on this is given with the instructions for particular sails.

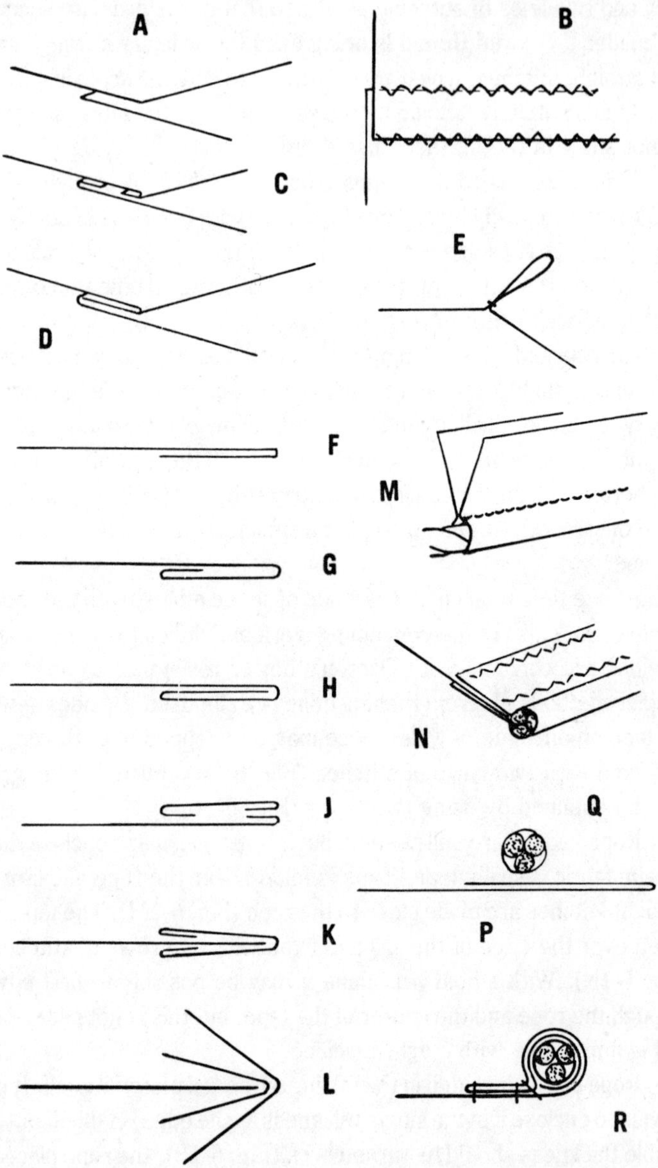

Fig. 6-1. Seams are made by overlapping edges of cloths. Edges of sails are strengthened by turning them in, adding other pieces and tapes or by joining on rope.

HAND SEWING

Repairs to a sail on board will almost certainly have to be done by hand. Only a large yacht is likely to carry a sewing machine. There are several ocean-going yachtsmen who have been glad of their ability to sew by hand, when repairs have been needed on a voyage to keep the sails working and the vessel going. Several trans-Atlantic single-handers seem to have spent most of the crossing sewing sails that were in to poor condition when they started.

It was usual to draw natural fiber threads through a block of wax or a piece of candle. This reduces the hairiness of natural fibers and waterproofs the threads. Neither of these problems occur with synthetic fiber threads, but it is still worthwhile waxing them before use as the wax helps in making the stitches stay put as they are made.

The needle used should be as fine as can be conveniently handled and pushed with a palm. A newcomer to sewing may find a palm rather clumsy at first, but it is essential to master it if much sewing has to be done. There is no other way of pushing the needle through that can be kept up for the length of a seam, without risk of damage to the hands and awkwardly shaped and uneven stitches. If more than a few inches have to be sewn along a seam, a sail hook with a lanyard to a convenient point should be used to stretch the seam as it is worked on.

Hold the needle between finger and thumb, with the eye end resting on the pad of the palm (Fig. 6-2A). As the needle point is inserted in the canvas thrust with the palm (Fig. 6-2B). Once it has entered and the point is protruding, release the hold on the needle and concentrate on the push (Fig. 6-2C). When most of the needle is entered, grip it again and pull it and the thread through to complete the stitch and be ready for the next. This will soon develop into a smooth almost continuous action. There is some advantage in giving the needle a slight counter-clockwise twist (looking towards the point). This has the effect of preventing the thread from becoming twisted.

For nearly all hand work thread is used double and the ends are not knotted together. How much thread to use at a time is a matter of personal preference. If a long piece is used, joints are less frequent, but time is taken up in pulling through the considerable amount of thread. If a shorter piece is used, pulling through is quicker so more stitches can be made in a given time, but joints are more frequent. Probably the best compromise is to choose a double length that allows the thread to be pulled through completely before the arm with the needle is fully extended.

If two edges have to be joined, the quickest way of sewing is to use a round seam. This is not the best seam, but when speed is important this is the seam to choose. It is not much used in sailmaking, except for quick emergency repairs, but it is sometimes employed in making bags and covers. Raw cut edges of canvas are left and only one line of stitches takes the strain. The two meeting edges are turned back about 1/2 inch and rubbed down. If there is a front and back, as in some treated fabrics, the folds are made towards the back surface and the folds brought together (Fig. 6-2D).

Sew the meeting edges together with a simple over and over action and aim to have the stitches about 5 or 6 per inch. This is the spacing for most types of hand stitching, with average materials. Small reasonably close stitches are not only neat, but they are stronger than coarse stitches. At the start, pull through all but about 1 1/2 inch of the double end of thread. Lay this along the seam and sew over it as stitches are made (Fig. 6-2E). At the end of a seam take the needle back under the last three or four stitches to get the same effect there before cutting off (Fig. 6-2F). If the thread used is not long enough to complete a seam twist about 1 1/2 inch of the old and the new ends together, lay them along the seam and sew over them (Fig. 6-2G).

After a round seam has been sewn, pull the pieces in line with each other. The amount of tension in the stitching should not be excessive or the seam will not pull out flat. Experience will show how tight to pull each stitch.

A better way to join two cloths edge to edge is to use a flat seam. It may be possible to use the selvedges without turning in (Fig. 6-1A). If cut edges are to be joined they should be turned under and rubbed down (Fig. 6-1C). An overlap of about 3/4 inch is satisfactory for many jobs. This should be marked with pencil or chalk so seams are completed evenly. For a long seam it is important to pull with one hand against a sail hook while sewing with the other.

Most seaming of this type is done by a right-handed sailmaker from right to left. Lay the thread ends along the seam, in the same way as described for a round seam, so they are sewn over. If the end of the seam is not to be supported by another joint or seam it can be strengthened by taking a few turns over the end before working along the seam. Work back from the end which is held by the sail hook, along the far edge so the needle point comes towards you (Fig.

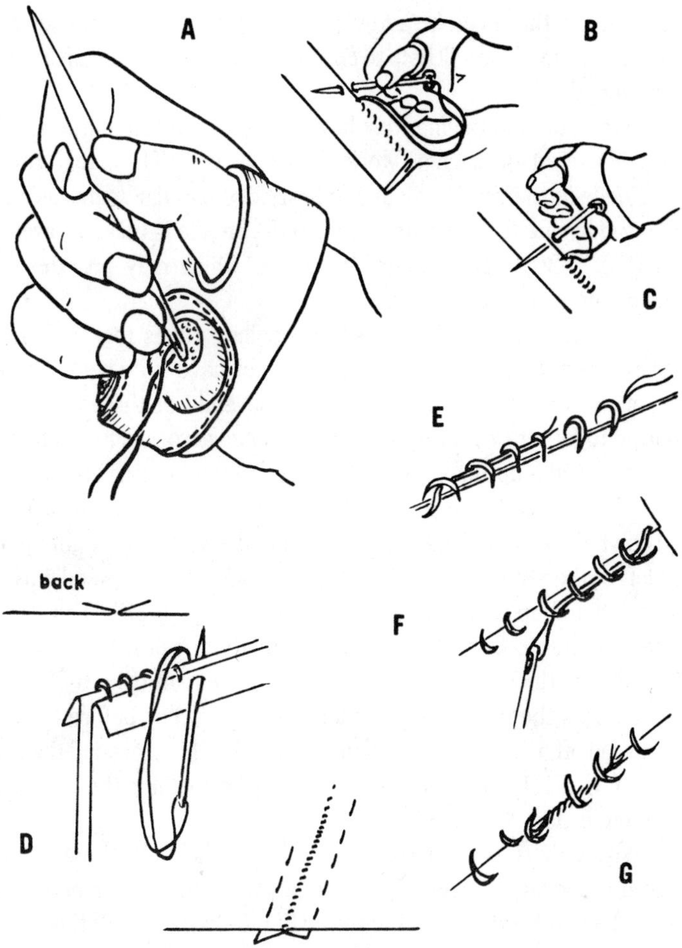

Fig. 6-2. A needle is held with its eye end against the block of a palm to thrust the point through a seam. Hand stitching is done with double thread and the simplest joint is a round seam.

6-3A), making 5 or 6 stitches per inch. Take in new thread and finish the edge in the same way as described for a round seam. To complete the flat seam turn the work over and sew the other edge in the same way (Fig. 6-3B).

A problem with a long hand-sewn flat seam is for one cloth to move in relation to the other. As the first edge is sewn there may be a tendency for the lower cloth to shorten slightly. If cutting to length can be delayed until the seam is sewn, this can be corrected.

Alternatively there can be a few temporary big tacking stitches put along the seam. This will help to control the width of the seam as well as its length.

Hand-stitched tabling may have the edge turned in one of the ways described for machine work. Rub down well. The actual stitching is done in the same way as the first edge of a flat seam, using a hook and having the work arranged so the needle is tucked towards you (Fig. 6-3C). Avoid over-tensioning, which may pull the flat canvas into a crease.

Herringbone stitching is used for pulling edges together. In a repair it takes the strain where ripped edges have to be held. This is one of the few cases where the doubled ends of thread may be knotted together. With the edges to be joined across in front of you, take the needle up through the far side, so the knot will be underneath (Nig. 6-3D) towards the left-hand end of the rip. Come across and down through the nearside, so the needle point is brought up on the left of the stitch (Fig. 6-3E). Pull tight and take the needle over the stitch and up through the far side again (Fig. 6-3F). This completes one stitch. Continue in this way and the result will be a series of stitches with crossing threads laid along the joint (Fig. 6-3G). At the end pass the needle back under several stitches before cutting the thread off, or for greater security, put a half hitch around the last stitch (Fig. 6-3H) and a second one locking against it in the form of a clove hitch (Fig. 6-3J).

Where there is considerable strain to be held and the greatest degree of locking is needed there is a variation, but the needle is entered on both sides from the front (Fig. 6-3K) and both times the point is brought up through the space (Fig. 6-3L). The finished appearance is very similar to the first method, but tends to be more lumpy along the center.

Either variation of the herringbone stitch can be used to pull together a canvas covering on a spar, such as on a handrail or tiller. The canvas edges are turned under and herringbone stitches made through the folded edges (Fig. 6-3M), which can be progressively adjusted in the amount turned under to give the desired tension.

Herringbone stitches are certainly the best for pulling edges together and resisting the strain of them trying to pull apart again in use, but the lumps along the center may be undesirable if they will show through a patch. A simple zig-zag stitch can be used (Fig.

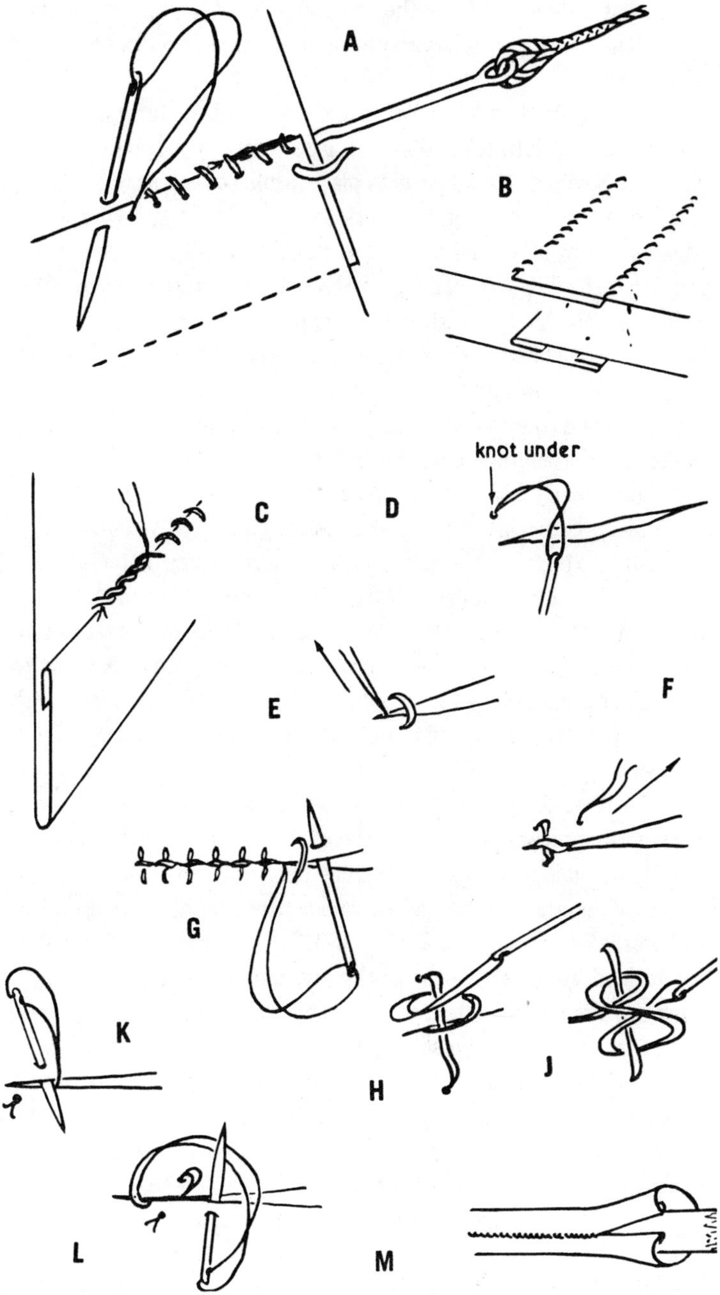

Fig. 6-3. For hand sewing a flat seam a sail hook tensions the cloth. A rip is pulled together by herringbone stitches.

6-4A), but it does not have the tensioning quality of a herringbone stitch. The baseball stitch is another one for drawing edges together (Fig. 6-4B).

Sticking stitch is a simple up and down action through several thicknesses of cloth (Fig. 6-4C). Large temporary stitches of this type may be used to hold parts in place while sewing seams. Closer sticking stitches are used for work such as retaining a wire in the edge of a sail (Fig. 6-4D). If the needle is inserted diagonally, pointing in the direction of progress the effect is of small stitches and wide intervals due to the thread moving forward in the thickness of the joint. Much hand sewing of leather is done with two needles from opposite sides through the same holes (Fig. 6-4E). This stitch may not be needed often in sailmaking, but it is worth knowing because leather reinforcing is sometimes used.

Traditionally hand-sewn roping was done on the port (left) side of the sail. The edge to be roped is strengthtened by tabling. The needle has to be taken through the rope in such a way that it takes up one strand at a time, preferably going around this strand and between it and the other two strands of the usual three-strand rope. In practice it is difficult to avoid the needle entering strands so as to break fibers, but dulling the needle point reduces this risk, although blunting too much may make it difficult to pass the needle through the canvas.

The rope should be in a relaxed state, free from kinks and with any twists or curves shaken out. Have the rope across in front of you and lay the tabling on top. Stitch away from you, going under a rope strand and up through the canvas, so as to come down ready to go around the next rope strand (Fig. 6-4F). The size of each stitch is determined by the thickness of the strands. A hook should keep a strain on the canvas while roping. The rope may tend to stretch more than the canvas, so slightly more canvas should be taken in at each stitch by working the needle point slightly more to the right as it comes up to the canvas. At a point of extra strain or near an end there may be two or more stitches around the same rope strand, but let the needle point enter the canvas at a slightly different point of the canvas so as to spread the load on the weave.

ROPEWORK

When natural fiber ropes were used with natural fiber sail cloths there were many knots, splices, and other rope formations that

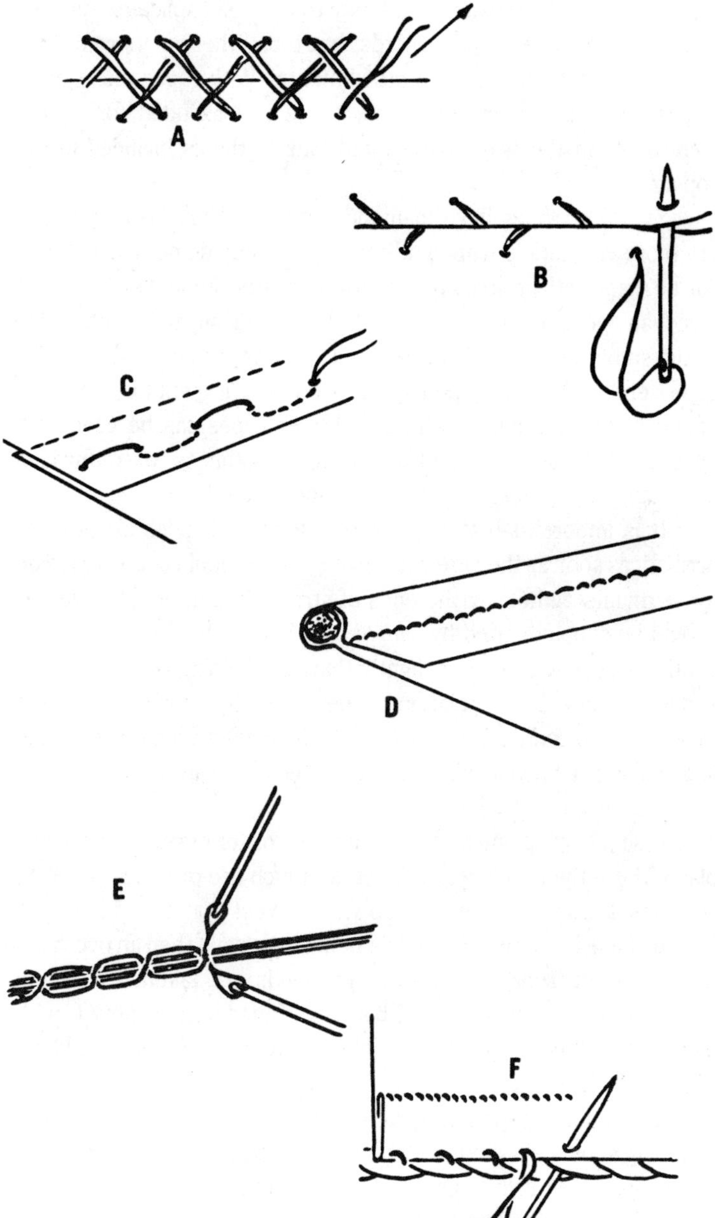

Fig. 6-4. Edges can be pulled together with zig-zag or baseball stitches. Leatherworking and sticking stitches are up and down. A roping stitch is regulated by the size of rope strands.

were needed. There was a tendency to knot and splice extraneous ropes used as sheets and halliards, but today there is more use for metal and plastic fittings and attachments. With ropes enclosed at edges instead of being sewn on, there is less need for special treatments in the way of eyes and similar things included in the roping.

Synthetic ropes have many advantages. Their characteristics are more compatible with synthetic cloth. They do not rot and they can be made with no stretch or with a calculated amount of stretch. A disadvantage is the greater care needed in splicing and knotting due to the smoothness of the strands and the way the lay can be lost if a rope's end is allowed to open up out of control. Except for this, most of the techniques used with natural fiber ropes can be used with synthetics. As grip may be less due to smoothness, extra turns in knots and extra tucks in splices may be needed.

It is important that ends of ropes be sealed, as already described, as soon as they are cut. Sealing alone should not be relied on for permanently holding the ends of strands together, however. It should be supplemented by *whipping*. This can be done with stout synthetic sewing thread or slightly thicker whipping twine. The line should be quite fine in relation to the rope. Heavy whipping line is more likely to come away in use. It is a help in forming the whipping and making it stay in place to draw the line through a piece of beeswax or a candle, just before applying.

A simple whipping for temporary use or for permanent use in a place where the rope's end will not get much use or where it will be sewn inside a sail, is generally known as a West Country whipping. A length of line is put with its middle behind the rope then an overhand knot made in front (Fig. 6-5A). The ends are taken behind and another overhand knot made. This is continued back and front, with each knot pulled as tight as possible and kept close to its neighbor, until a sufficient length has been whipped, then the last knot is made into a reef knot and spare line cut off (Fig. 6-5B). For small ropes the whipping should be about as long as the diameter of the rope. For large ropes, 1/2 inch is usually long enough.

A better whipping in areas where the greatest strength is needed is called a sailmaker's or palm-and-needle whipping. It is particularly appropriate to the ends of reef pendants, which may flap like whiplashes on occasion. There are two ways of making the whipping on three-strand rope. The first does not need any special equipment. The other requires a needle and a palm to push it through the rope.

For the first method, open the strands for a short distance (seal each strand end) and put the line in so a loop encircles one strand loosely and the ends extend together from the opposite space. A long end will make the whipping, while the short end need only be a few inches long (Fig. 6-5C). Lay the strands together again. Hold the loop and the short end down the rope and put on some tight turns with the long end (Fig. 6-5D). When a sufficient number of turns have been put on, hold them tight, lift the loop over the end of the strand it is already encircling (Fig. 6-5E), and pull the short end to tighten it. This will put two *snaking turns* outside the whipping and following up two spaces between strands. Take the short end up to make the third snaking turn and lead it into the center of the rope, where it is joined tightly to the long end with a reef knot (Fig. 6-5F).

If a needle is used on the whipping line there is no need to unlay the end of the rope. This method can also be used on braided rope. Put the needle through the rope and leave a short end of line projecting (Fig. 6-5G). Lay this end up the rope and put on whipping turns over it, using the end with the needle on. After sufficient length, push the needle through the rope again (Fig. 6-5H), preferably so it emerges in a space between strands. Use the needle to take the line over the whipping turns in the form of snaking turns following spaces between strands, or straight along braided rope. If the needle is taken lengthwise through the whipping, the ends can be cut off and the whipping should be secure. Alternatively, with three-strand rope, bring the ends together in the middle of the end of the rope and knot them together.

Some sailmakers put a second whipping an inch or so behind the first on reef pendants, as an insurance if the end one comes adrift. However, a properly heat-sealed end serves something of the same purpose as an extra whipping on synthetic fiber ropes, so the second whipping is not as important.

Few splices are needed in the ropes of a modern sail, but it is useful to know two versions of the eye splice. The strongest one, and the one to be chosen except in the special circumstances requiring the other, has the end strands tucked against the lay of the rope.

Unlay sufficient sealed end strands to be handled. This will be more than actually used up in splicing, but a few extra inches make

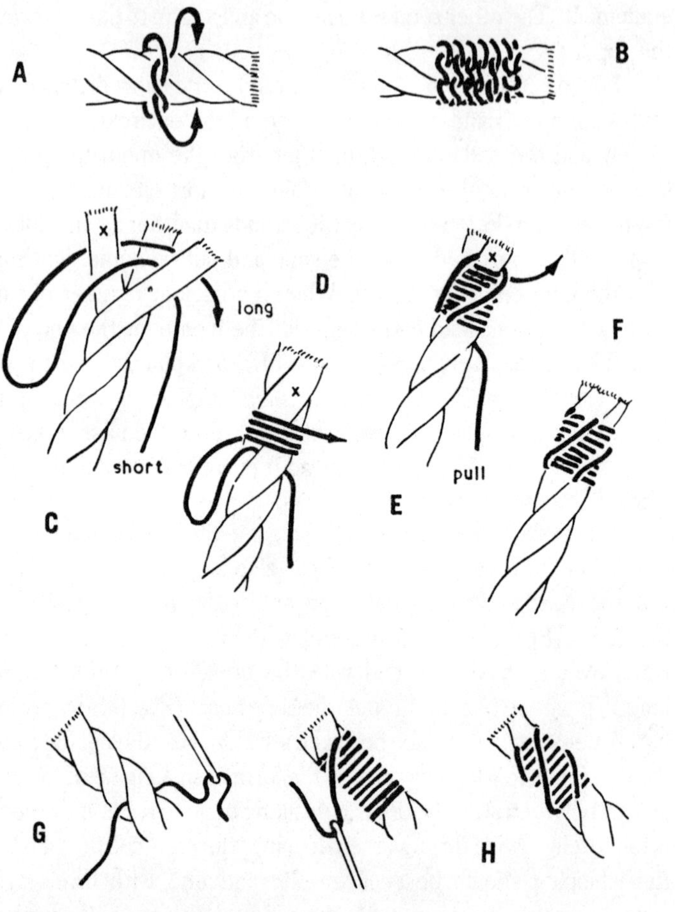

Fig. 6-5. A West Country whipping is knotted around. Sailmaker's and palm-and-needle whippings pass through the rope.

neat splicing easier (about 7 inches on a 1/2 inch diameter rope is reasonable). Put on a temporary whipping to prevent further unlaying and seal the ends of the strands. Bend the rope into the size eye required and arrange the end strands so two are across the lay of the main part of the rope and the third is behind out of the way (Fig. 6-6A). Lift a main strand. This may need a spike or some rope can be twisted open with the hands. Tuck the upper front end strand under this main strand (Fig. 6-6B). Lift the next main strand and tuck the other front end strand under it. This will go in at the space where the other end strand comes out (Fig. 6-6C).

Turn the splice over and find the main strand that does not yet have an end strand under it. Lift it and tuck the remaining end strand under it, but take this in the same way as the others (Fig. 6-6D). Pull the ends tight in turn. You should now have one end strand projecting from each space in the main part of the rope (Fig. 6-6E). Further tucking consists of taking each end strand in turn and continuing to tuck it against the lay around the rope, going over the main strand it adjoins and under the next (Fig. 6-6F).

In natural fiber rope tucking three times in this way was sufficient, but five tucks are better in synthetic rope. The last tuck can be halved: use a knife to scrape away about half the thickness of the strand before tucking it, to give a taper to the splice before cutting off surplus ends. Rolling the splice will get it into a good shape. The ends may be heated to seal them, but be careful not to weaken any part of the rope by melting it.

The common eye splice is thicker than the rest of the rope and it has a woven form. If a rope has to be sewn to a sail right up to the eye, it is better if the splice can keep the laid form of the rope as far as possible. The sailmaker's splice is designed to give the laid form specially for this advantage in sailmaking. While it has adequate strength when sewn to a sail, it is not as strong as the common eye splice and should not be used for a free eye or any place where it is not sewn in place.

A sailmaker's splice is prepared like a common eye splice, but the parts are brought together so the front end strands are in the same direction as the lay of the main part of the rope (Fig. 6-6G), instead of across them. Tucking is done in the same sequence, but the other way, with the lay. One strand goes under (Fig. 6-6H) and the one nearer the eye goes in where that one comes out (Fig. 6-6J). When the splice is turned over, the third end goes under the remaining main strand (Fig. 6-6K). There should now be one end projecting from each space.

Further tucks are made under the strand the end is already under, wrapping it around it. After another complete tuck in this way, the end strands may be tapered and tucked at least twice more, so the outline of the splice comes down to the ordinary rope diameter in a neat slope (Fig. 6-6L). Sewing around strands can then be taken right up to the eye.

One rope can be spliced into another in the same way as common eye splicing (Fig. 6-7A). This makes a *cringle* on the side of

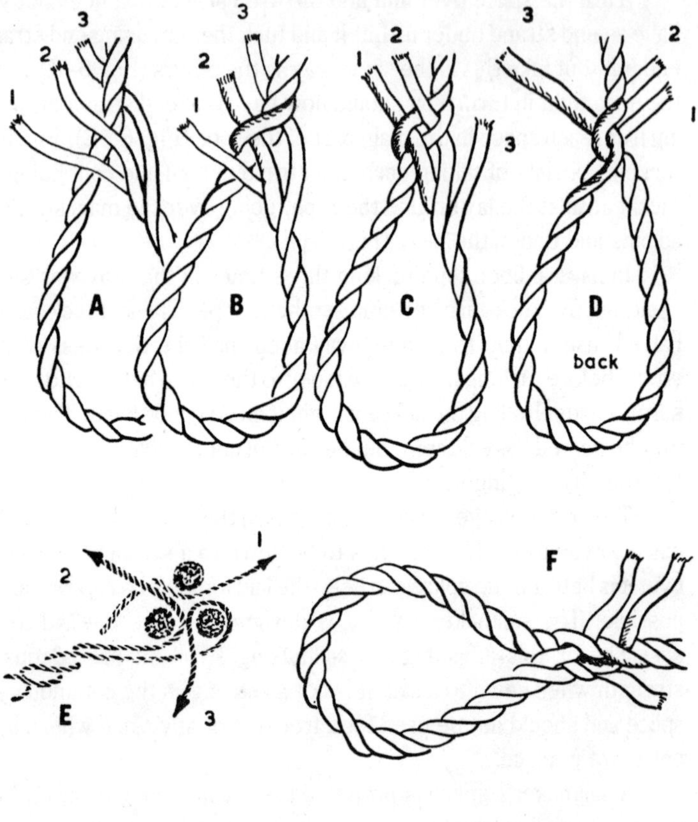

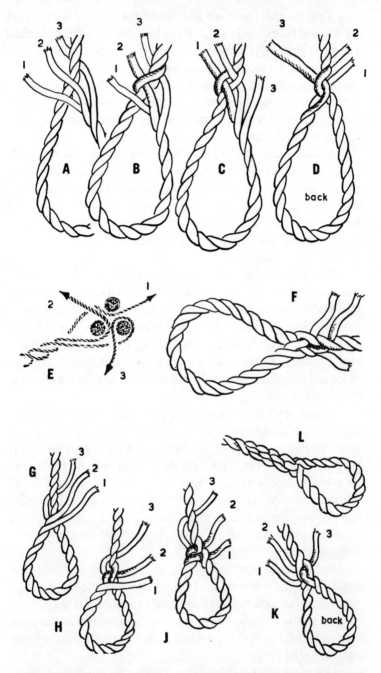

Fig. 6-6. An ordinary eye splice (top) is tucked against the lay. A sailmaker's eye splice (bottom) is tucked with the lay.

the rope. Today a cringle is more likely to be needed through grommets in the sail. A neat way of doing this is to take one strand from a rope, without disturbing any lay or twist in it. This needs to be about four times as long as the cringle is to be.

Put the strand through one cringle and let one part be about twice as long as the other (Fig. 6-7B). Twist the strands together and take the long end through the second grommet (Fig. 6-7C). Lay it back around to make a three-strand rope (Fig. 6-7D). Adjust the parts to an even tension. Take the ends through the grommets and tuck them back into the cringle, over and under as in making the eye splice, tapering after the first tuck (Fig. 6-7E).

This can be done with more than three parts or the cringle may be made with many turns of light line instead of the strand of rope. A thimble or other fitting may be secured to the edge or corner of a sail in this way.

GROMMETS

Metal washer grommets (eyelets) have many uses and when fixed so as to include turned-over fabric edges, can be very strong. Some extra strength comes from using grommets, which have teeth to penetrate the cloth under the washers. Their method of fixing was described in Chapter 4.

There are occasions when a different method of including a hole or ring in a sail is required. A plain metal grommet may not be strong enough or suitable for an attachment to the corner of a sail, such as where a sheet may pull quite hard at the clew.

The sewn grommet may be hard or soft. A hard one includes a metal ring of round section, which is sewn over. It could be a large tool-fixed grommet, but a round-sectioned ring is better. For a soft eye a rope ring is used.

The rope grommet is made by taking one strand of suitable rope, which has been carefully unlaid so its natural twist is undisturbed. A length about four times the intended diameter is needed. Lay this up in a ring (Fig. 6-8A) and continue to fit the rope together in its natural lay until there are a full three strands all round (Fig. 6-8B). Cut off any surplus. This is sufficient for a rope grommet that is to be sewn over, but if the grommet is being made for use as a free ring, the meeting ends may be tapered, twisted together, and tucked.

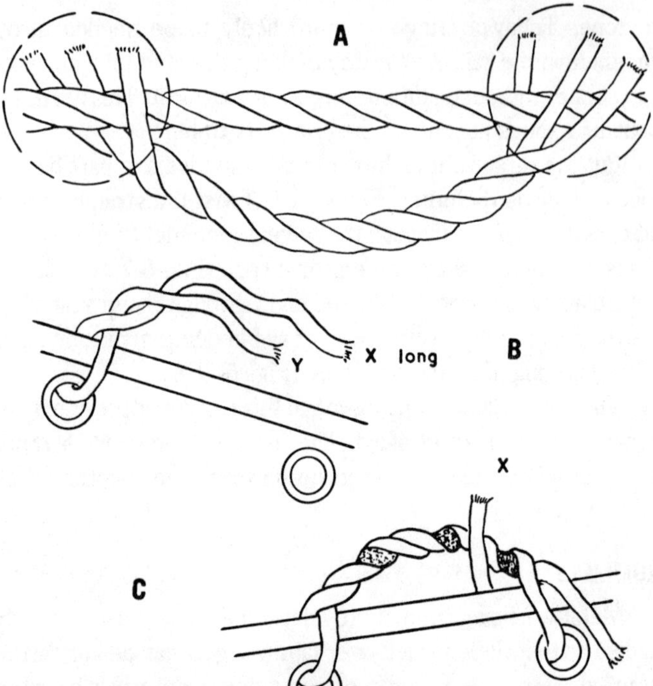

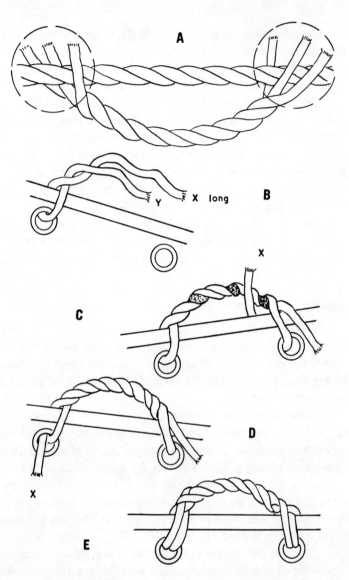

Fig. 6-7. A cringle may be spliced into the side of a rope or worked with a single strand through grommets.

Lay the metal or rope ring over the fabric, which may have been punched, but is better with crossing cuts so the points can be turned up as sewing progresses. Use double thread and go all round sewing with stitches close enough to meet inside the hole. Although stitches look neatest if taken through the cloth close to the outside of the ring, it is better to make occasional stitches longer, so as to spread the strain over different parts of the weave (Fig. 6-8C).

The strain may be further shared if additional small grommets are made and several turns of line are taken from the main grommet to them (Fig. 6-8D). Further help is given by the roping, if the grommet pulls against it and some stitches go through the cloth and rope.

Of course, there is a risk of the stitches wearing away inside the hole if they are not protected. One method of protection is to include a round thimble or liner. The problem is to make this a tight fit, so a soft grommet has to be made the right size to fit closely in the bottom of the hollow of the thimble. After sewing, use a fid or spike through the hole to force it open. Have the thimble ready to jump it into the hole as soon as the fid is withdrawn and before the stitched edges have shrunk back to size (Fig. 6-8E). If a brass thimble is used, it may be further tightened by light hammering.

RINGS AND SLIDES

Another method of providing an attachment point is to use a metal ring and tapes. In a simple small sail a round ring can have three or more tapes taken along the edges of the sail and in the direction of pull. This suits a taped-edge sail with a reinforced corner (Fig. 6-8F).

For a more substantial attachment a metal D-ring is lashed to the corner of the sail, using a number of small grommets through the reinforced sail (Fig. 6-8G). The amount of lashing depends on the strain that has to be taken, but there should be sufficient lashing to spread the load over the corner of the sail.

The corner of the sail may be shaped to match the flat edge of the D-ring or the corner cloth may be wrapped around the ring. As the stitches might be chafed by any metal fitting engaging with the D-ring, a piece of canvas or, preferably, leather should be arranged through the ring and sewn to the sail (Fig. 6-8H).

Sail slides and other attachments needed on the edge of a sail can be fitted in several ways. Twine or stout thread may be taken around the bolt rope (Fig. 6-9A). For rather more strain it is better to use a grommet through the tabled edge of the sail, fairly close to the roping, if any (Fig. 6-9B). It helps to keep the slide or slug in line, as well as making a tighter attachment, if a few turns of line are taken

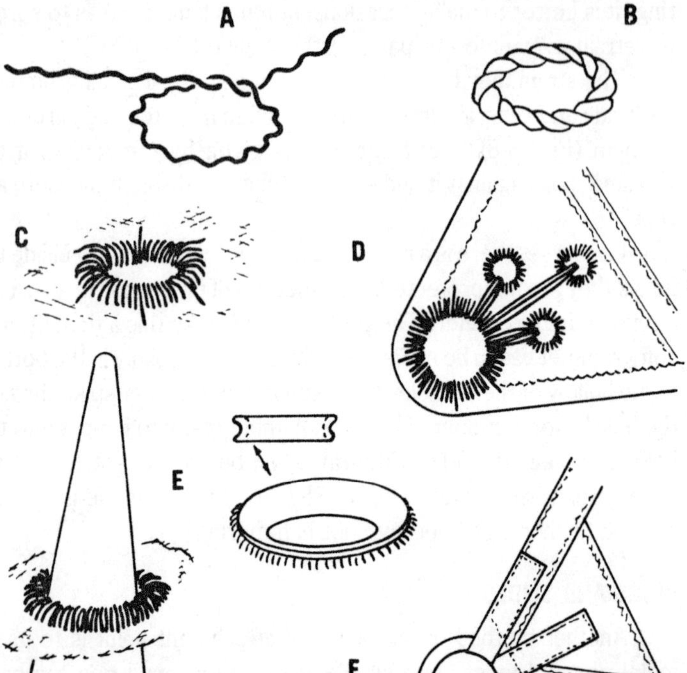

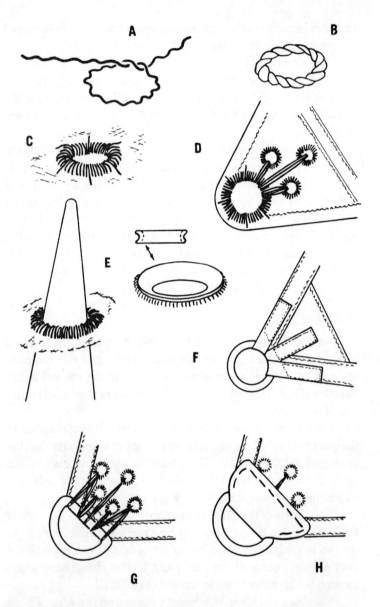

Fig. 6-8. A sewn grommet may be made over a rope ring. Metal rings may be sewn or taped into the corner of a sail.

around between the metal loop and the sail edge (Fig. 6-9C). The grommet may be a metal type fixed with tools or, for a heavier load, a hand-worked grommet.

There are sail slides and other edge fittings with clip-on arrangements (*bodger clips*). Others have parts to fit each side with a screw to go through the sail behind the bolt rope. Some have a projecting part like a shackle, which has a screw to go through a grommet.

The head of a sail is usually provided with a headboard and similar strengthening may be used at tack and clew. The headboard is metal or plastic and it may be a single piece included within the cloth reinforcing patches or there may be a pair of boards arranged on opposite sides of the sail. A pair of boards may be riveted through the sail, but it is more usual to hand sew with double twine from both sides (Fig. 6-9D). The hoisting holes in a pair of boards may need no further treatment, but with a single board between cloths a metal grommet may be fixed through the hole.

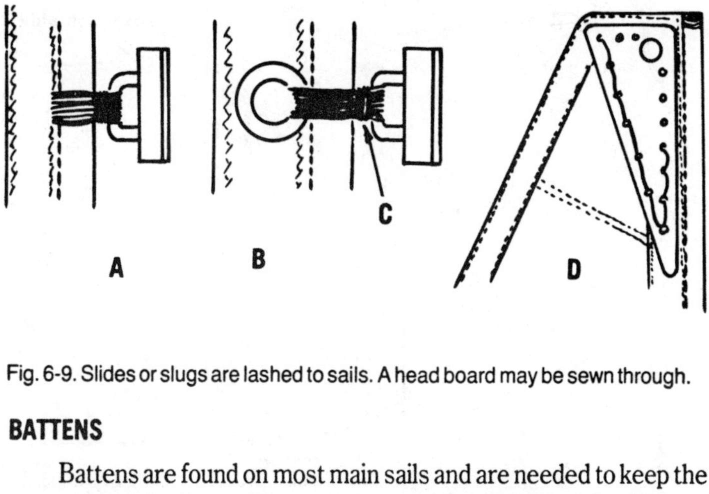

Fig. 6-9. Slides or slugs are lashed to sails. A head board may be sewn through.

BATTENS

Battens are found on most main sails and are needed to keep the curved leech in shape. They take many forms and may be made of wood, plastic, or combinations of these materials. They may be tapered, parallel, or specially shaped. A pocket has to be sewn to the sail for each batten.

The basic type of pocket is parallel right to the edge. Double stitching is advisable along the edges and further reinforcing may be advisable at the end where the batten will thrust (Fig. 6-10A). At the leech edge there may be a grommet in the sail and in the pocket cloth to take a cord for securing the batten. The batten may have a matching hole (Fig. 6-10B) or the cord may go over the end of the batten (Fig. 6-10C). Lines may be sewn each side so no grommets are needed, or a double-ended line may be sewn at one side, to pass through a pair of grommets to knot outside (Fig. 6-10D).

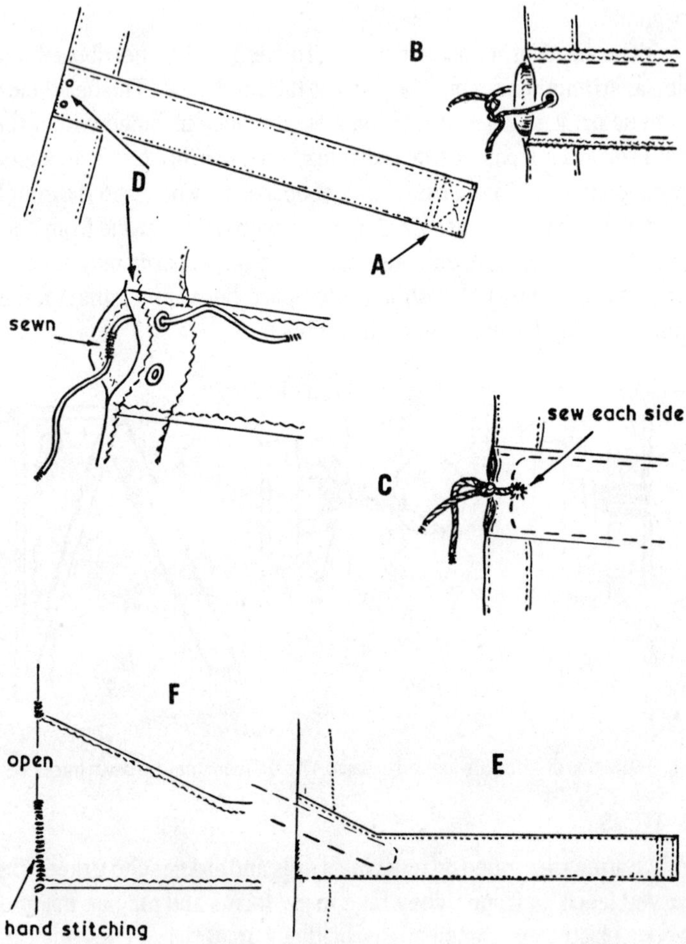

Fig. 6-10. Batten pockets are sewn on and the batten retained by cords or by offset fitting.

With tie-in battens there is a risk of the tie coming loose and the batten being lost. The use of knots can be avoided with an offset batten pocket (Fig. 6-10E and 6-11). The offset piece should have an opening wide enough to pass the batten, but with no more space than is needed for that. As the batten has to be a tight fit in the length of the pocket, stitching along the leech should be strong and hand

Fig. 6-11. The construction and cut of the sails can be seen as the sun shines through them. The main sail has one row of reef points as well as facility for roller reefing. The bottom of the four batten pockets is arranged nearly parallel with the boom for reefing without removing the batten. The genoa head sail is miter cut.

stitching is advisable (Fig. 6-10F). There are pocket end protectors available, which can be fitted in and will give a small amount of elasticity to help spring in and secure the batten.

Jib-Headed Main Sails

The sail hoisted aft of a mast in a normal rig is the principal driver. This applies whether it is the only sail in this position on a single-mast rig or mizzen or other sail additionally on a multi-mast rig. The majority of these sails today are jib-headed (Bermudan) and are basically made in the same way.

Although the shape is apparently a triangle, each edge is actually cut on a curve. The curve along the leech is there for appearance (a straight edge will appear hollow when sailing) and for giving extra sail area. The curves along luff and foot control the draft (fullness) of the sail. When these curved edges are pulled straight, the body of the sail will take a curve. The amount of this fullness is controlled by the amount of initial curve in the edges (Fig. 7-1A).

Another way of making a full sail is to cut the seams curved (Fig. 7-1B), so when they are sewn together the cloth is pulled to a curve. Although it should be possible to give a straight-edged sail a predetermined curvature by this means, it is not a method recommended for amateur use in making normal main sails. It is better left to the experienced professionals, and even they make most cruising and general-purpose sails with parallel cloths and the draft imparted by curving the edges.

The method of drawing the shape, including the curves, was given in Chapter 5. The greatest curve is usually one-third of the length of the edge from the tack corner (Fig. 7-1C). How much curve is given is largely a matter of experience, but 1 inch depth of curve for each 5 feet of luff and 1 inch for each 3 feet of foot are reasonable figures to consider. Less depth gives a flatter sail; more depth gives more fullness. In a two-masted rig, the sail on the aft mast may be made slightly flatter than the other.

There are other ways of arriving at the amount of curve to be given to luff and foot, but the above figures give an average draft for a cruising sail. Variations are largely the result of experience because there are so many unknown factors that it is difficult to use any mathematical method of deciding on the curves. How the cloths are laid has a bearing on the fullness, but nearly all sails of this type are normally cut with the cloths at or near right angles to the leech. Unless there is a special reason for doing otherwise, this is the recommended practice.

When setting out the shape full-size on the floor, tack and clew may be taken to points, but there will usually be a head board and the sail should be made a suitable width or shape there to match it and the leech curve drawn to allow for this (Fig. 7-1D). There will usually be three or four battens. Draw their locations along the leech. Usually, they are at right angles to the straight line representing the leech, but the bottom one could be parallel to the boom if it is likely to be taken in to roller reefing. The "curve" of the leech may actually be straight lines between the ends of battens (Fig. 7-1E).

Although many of the problems that were inherent in the variable stretch of cotton and other natural materials are not so apparent in Dacron, it is still necessary to reinforce edges, particularly where cuts come diagonally across cloths, in order to keep the sail in the intended shape. This is also done to provide strength, particularly at points where local loads come from the attachment of slides. Strengthening is required at each corner, where there is particular strain. This may vary from a simple triangle of cloth sewn on to many patches, roping and other reinforcing.

The steps in making a main sail, after it is drawn full-size are: sewing together sufficient cloths, trimming and strengthening their edges and corners, and making attachments and fittings.

The sail cloth used will almost certainly be wide. It may be used as it is or it can be divided by false seams to reduce the width between all seams in the sail to the region of 12 inches. This means one false seam along the center of a 28 inch cloth or two seams dividing equally the width of a 36 inch cloth. Lay the cloth along the floor and pencil the seam positions. Sew these false seams as described in Chapter 6. The cloth may be rolled and fed to the sewing machine by an assistant, then rolled again as it comes off the machine. To avoid too great and heavy a roll to handle, approximate lengths may be cut first, but all false seams should at least have their first line of stitching before cloths are joined at the edges.

How the seams are spaced across the sail is not too important, but laying out the cloths on the full-size drawing has to start somewhere and it is usual to make the first seam through the tack corner. It is then positioned at right angles to the straight line across the leech. Set out this line on the floor, then unroll the cloth along it (Fig. 7-1F). Allow some surplus at the ends, for tabling and other purposes (5 inches would be enough on a small cruising main sail).

When cutting and laying other cloths, keep the false seams upwards and do not turn cloths over. It is unwise to depend on sight for making seams so pencil the amount of overlap on the edge of the cloth. It may be a continuous line or marks at frequent intervals. Although you will need to see the marks when sewing, avoid using a marker that makes a prominent or indelible line that will show in the finished sail. Soft pencil should be satisfactory.

Seams for smaller sails may be 1/2 inch and rather wider for large sails. With cotton sails, seams in the vicinity of the tack corner were widened as they approached luff or foot. This was for stretch control and is unnecessary with Dacron.

Lay the next cloth up to the first. By turning end-for-end (not over) diagonally-cut ends can be fitted in with little waste (Fig. 7-1G).

Another carry-over from the days of cotton sails is the use of *strike-up* marks (Fig. 7-2). These are pencil marks across seams at intervals of 12 inches or so, to register the meeting edges as they pass through the sewing machine. With natural materials there was a tendency for one piece to "grow" in relation to the other as it was sewn. This is less of a problem with synthetic fibers, but strike-up marks are probably still worth using for early attempts at sail making.

It is a help to use weights to keep the cloths in position as they are laid and cut. Avoid treading on the cloths, if possible. If you need to walk on the cloth, use stockinged feet.

Before removing the cloths from the floor, transfer the outline of the sail to the cloths, but do not cut. Fold up so the outline drawn

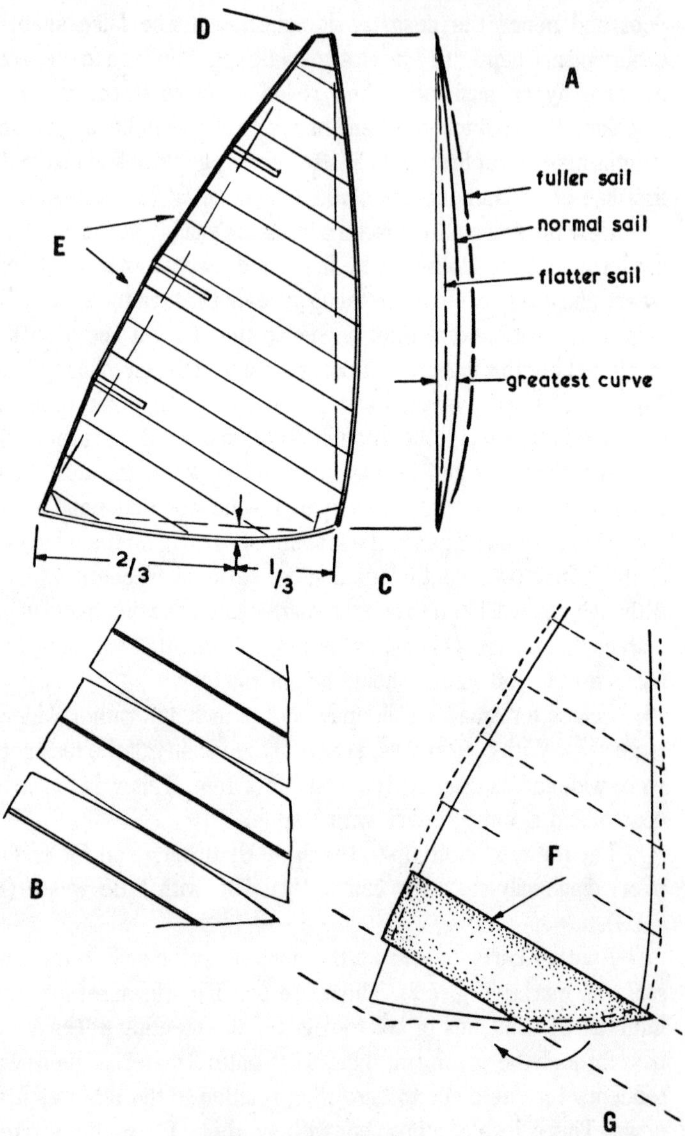

Fig. 7-1. Shape of a main sail comes from the curved edges or may be by shaped seams. The first cloth may be through the tack.

on the floor shows and mark with a pencil at close intervals within the fold. In particular, mark the outline where cloths meet.

Lift the cloths in turn, putting the first on top of the second, and so on, without turning any over or round. If you have doubts about keeping them in order, number the ends in the waste parts. At the sewing machine, take the first two cloths and bring them together exactly as they were on the floor. Sew along the upper cloth a short distance in from its edge. Watch that strike-up marks match. Turn the job over and do the same from the other side. The two lines of stitching should be no more than 1/8 inch from the edges.

If any false seams have not yet been sewn down, do them in turn with the main seams. Make each joint the same way. Establish a sequence of sewing operations so the seams are all alike. As a normal sewing machine has its opening and operating part at the left, work so the bulk of the sail is to the left and the minimum amount has to be passed under the arm and upright.

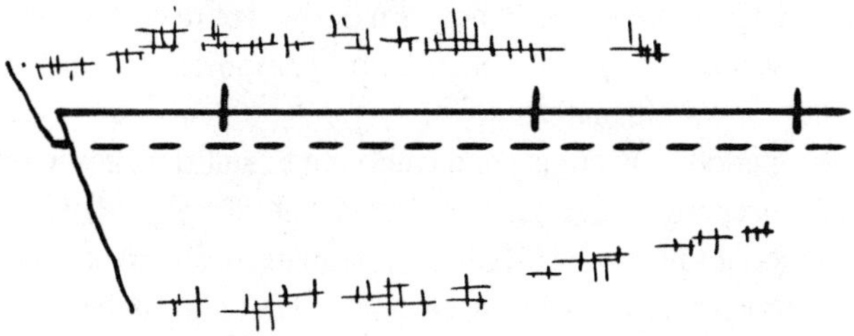

Fig. 7-2. Strike-up marks insure seams registering when sewn.

An assistant is useful on a sail of any size, as are extensions to the platform of the sewing machine. The large expanse of fabric will drag and cause uneven stitching if it has to be picked up and lowered again around the limited flat area of a domestic sewing machine. An assistant can manipulate the mass of cloth so it feeds on and off and the operator works without having to strain the material. A very large table extension on the machine will keep the level area of cloth large and avoid distortion. Sewing machines have been let into the floor to give this effect, but such an arrangement has a few drawbacks.

You now have a sewn assembly of cloths bigger than the sail is to be. Lay it on the floor over the full-size drawing. There will almost certainly be some discrepancies around the outline, due to cloths being joined slightly out of register. This does not matter, as there is spare cloth to allow for this. Go around the edges and rub down a fold hard on the final curves. Where you cut the cloth depends on how each edge is to be finished.

The leech edge crosses the cloths at close to a right angle. This means that tabling by turning the edge under (see Fig. 6-1G and H) brings the strands of warp and weft close to the same way as in the unfolded cloth, and there should be little risk of creases or puckers. On an average sail allow a tabling width of more than 1 inch. If the leech is to be roped, the rope can be included in a wider tabling (Fig. 6-1P, Q, and R) or it may be taped (Fig. 6-1M and N) over the single thickness of a small sail or over a tabled edge. Do not sew yet—only cut to suit.

Although the curves of foot and luff are slight, tabling by turning them in would bring warp and weft diagonal to the main weave, with a risk of distortion. Instead, allow for using a cut-off piece as separate tabling (Fig. 6-1J) to strengthen the edge, but do not sew it yet. Use a piece from the same edge; do not turn it round or over and arrange any seams slightly staggered from their original positions. Doing this keeps warp and weft matching.

After marking the outline and trimming to suit the chosen edge treatment, prepare corner patches. Individual sailmakers have their own ideas about the shapes of patches, so an examination of sails will show several patterns that can be used. There must be enough extension of patches to take in a good length of edge stitching as well as stitches across the corner. Much of the strain should be taken by the reinforced edges and not by the body of the sail.

In a typical arrangement there should be a patch considerably bigger than the head board (Fig. 7-3A), the tack corner might be four-sided or curved (Fig. 7-3B), while the clew corner could have similar patches or long liners carried along leech and foot (Fig. 7-3C). For a large sail or one expected to take considerable strain, there can be two or more patches on each side, overlapped so an outer patch does not extend quite as far on to the sail as an inner one. Alternatively, let there be an outer and an inner patch on each side, with the outer patch turned under the inner patch (Fig. 7-3D) and sewn through. Patches are normally made from the same cloth as the sail, so strength is obtained by using extra thicknesses.

Sew on the patches where they cross the body of the sail. The edges will be sewn with the same stitches as the tabling or other sail edge treatment. If an internal head board is being used, remember to include this before edges are sewn at that corner.

Sew the edges in the method selected. If roping is taped on, the tape is made from strips of sail cloth or may be special Dacron tape.

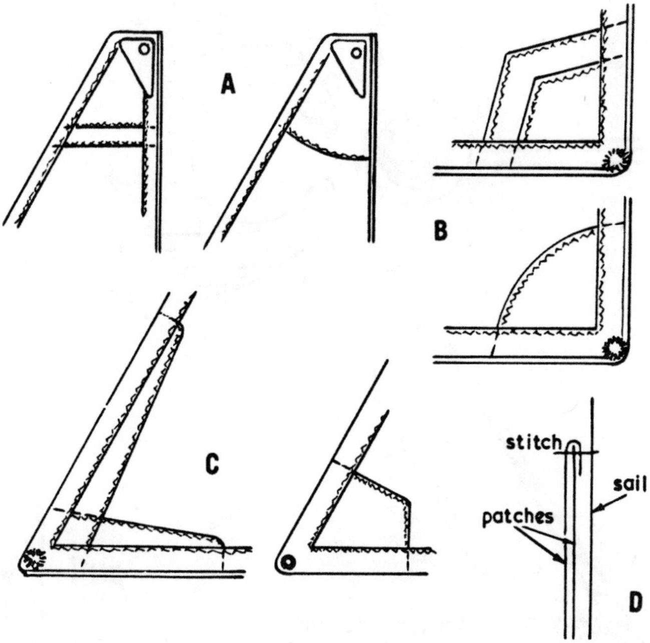

Fig. 7-3. Patches in the corners of a sail may be in several shapes and can be in several thicknesses.

The edges of cut cloth may be heat sealed or turned under when sewn to the sail. Sew with straight stitches close to the rope, whatever method is used, but use zig-zag stitches elsewhere.

If the roped edge is to slide in a mast groove, the rope size used will have to be chosen to suit this (Fig. 7-4A). Elsewhere the rope need not be very thick, as Dacron rope is much stronger for its size than natural fiber rope. In the first assembly, it is usual for one rope to go from head to clew around the tack corner and be free to slide in its tape or pocket. Do not fix its ends until the tack corner can be held while the rope's ends are pulled. In the finished sail the rope should be taking the load when the sail is stretched along its foot and luff, so tension on the rope should be very slightly more than on the canvas. As there is very little stretch in the rope or fabric, do not allow for much difference, but get a good pull on the rope, while the edge of the sail is also held taut, then put some hand stitches through at head and clew so rope and fabric cannot move in relation to each other (Fig. 7-4B).

At the head the bolt rope may be cut off and sealed to finish straight up (Fig. 7-4C). This can be done to the foot at the clew,

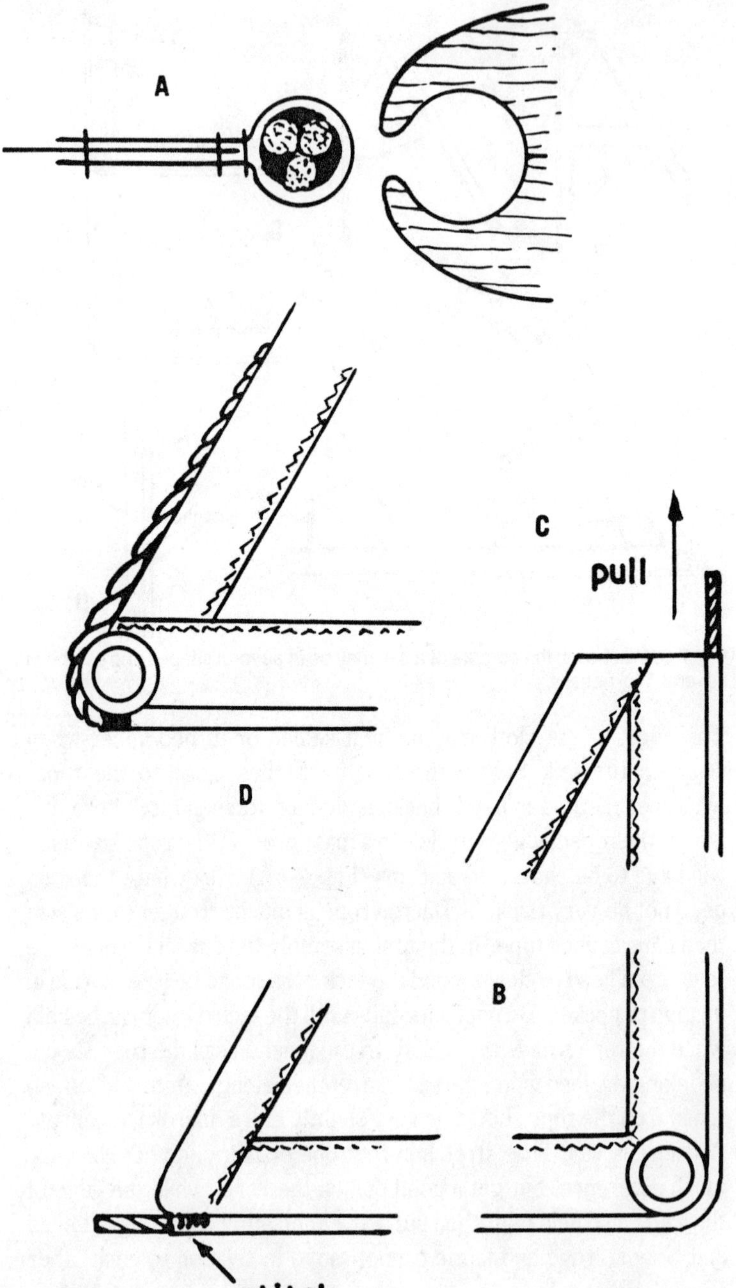

Fig. 7-4. Roping may be arranged to suit a groove or it may be taken around on to the leech.

particularly if the roped edge is to go in a grooved boom. Where the edge is laced or loose-footed, some strength may be given to the clew corner by following traditional practice and carrying the tapered roping a short distance up the leech. The rope's end is opened and some of the fibers scraped away with a sharp knife, so the strands become tapered. These are laid up again and hand-sewn up the edge of the sail (Fig. 7-4D).

Batten pockets (see Fig. 6-10) should be cut from sail cloth with warp and weft the same way as the sail. As they will be in line with the seams, or very nearly so, they can be cut economically from strips off the roll. At the open end of the pocket turn the cloth under in a narrow tabling. Stitching near the opening may be strained so make sure it is tied or there are hand stitches.

The tack corner is often made to a simple angle, but there is the complication of the gooseneck, which may extend several inches, particularly if there is roller reefing gear. In that case the sail can be made to set better by cutting back or offsetting the tack (Fig. 7-5A). Except for the change in outline, this does not affect the method of constructing the sail.

Many racing classes permit the use of Cunningham control to adjust flatness or fullness of a sail. For the sailmaker this only means the provision of an extra grommet some way above the tack corner—how far will depend on the class or size of sail, but it is likely to be somewhere between 6 inches and 20 inches. If the roped edge goes in a grooved mast, the grommet must be in the tabling far enough away to clear the mast. It may be advisable to include a reinforcing patch (Fig. 7-5B). If the sail edge does not go in a grooved mast, the grommet can be strengthened by being attached to the bolt rope.

In the simplest Cunningham arrangement a loose line is used to haul down on the grommet when required. In a more elaborate arrangement a line from it goes around a pulley lower on the mast to somewhere convenient for the crew. Tightening moves the draft, or fullness, of the sail forward.

Allied to the control at the tack is the use of a leech line to vary the tension along the leech. A light line is enclosed within the leech and secured at the head end. Near the clew corner it emerges through a small grommet and there is a plastic button sewn on below it (Fig. 7-5C). The line varies the tension along the leech and provides roach control. When the desired setting is obtained, the line is twisted around the button. There should be a knot in the end of the line, large enough to prevent the line from passing back through the grommet.

If a leech line is fitted care is needed when sewing on batten pockets to avoid sewing in the leech line or prevent it from working.

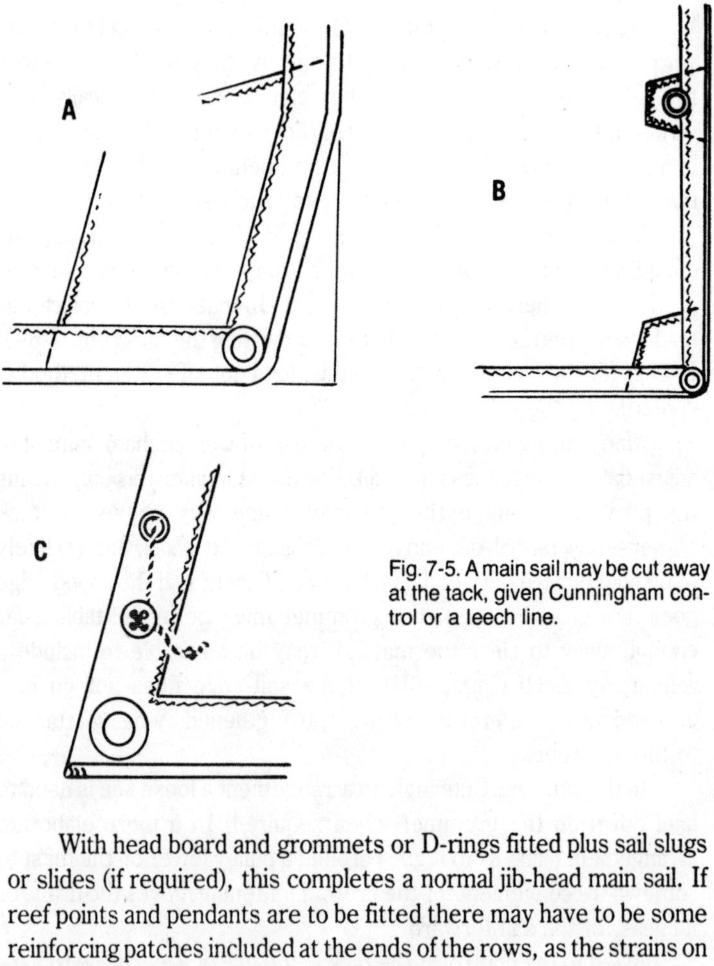

Fig. 7-5. A main sail may be cut away at the tack, given Cunningham control or a leech line.

With head board and grommets or D-rings fitted plus sail slugs or slides (if required), this completes a normal jib-head main sail. If reef points and pendants are to be fitted there may have to be some reinforcing patches included at the ends of the rows, as the strains on the grommets there when a sail is reefed are comparable to those on tack and clew in normal sailing. These patches should be included before the edges are sewn.

For some smaller and simpler sails, particularly for the general purpose small play boat, beach catamaran, and craft not intended for very serious sailing, a main sail may be taped all round without the use of rope anywhere. The leech may be simply tabled, then single or double tape put around the other edges (see Fig. 6-1K and L). Such a sail is not usually given much curve to foot and luff, so it sets fairly flat.

Some simply-rigged dinghies have a single sail on an unstayed mast, with the sail sleeved over it. The sleeve does not have to make a tight fit on the mast. It is made in the same way as taping rope to a sail, but cut larger to suit the mast. Many of these masts are parallel aluminum tubes, so the sleeve is a parallel piece of sail cloth, cut wide enough to easily fit the mast and having enough at the edge to sew to the sail (Fig. 7-6A). For a tapered mast the sleeve should be cut with about the same taper (Fig. 7-6B).

If the foot of the sail is to be laced to the boom, instead of sliding in a groove, the tabled edge should be wide enough to provide a

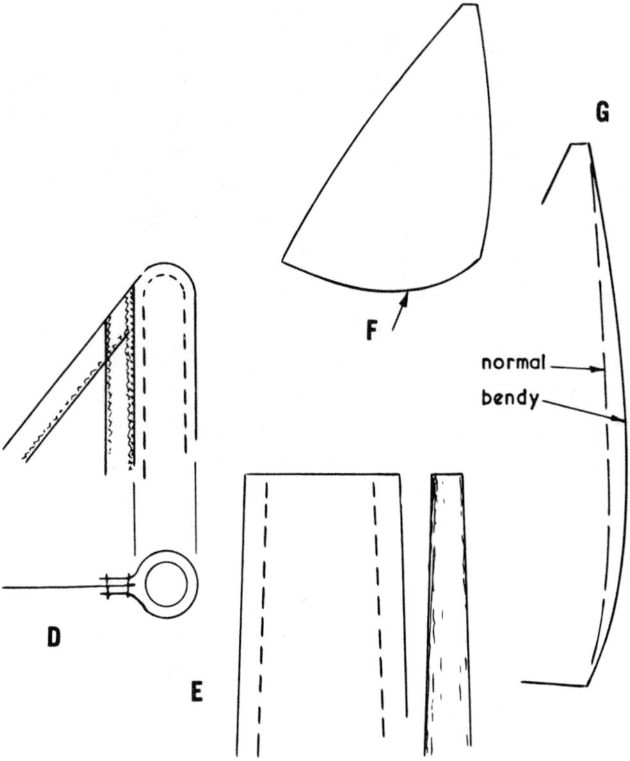

Fig. 7-6. A main sail may be adapted to be sleeved or fitted to a bendy mast.

Fig. 7-7. The foot of the sail of this board boat is loose and only attached to the boom at tack and clew. The luff is laced to the mast.

secure fixing for a row of grommets. If the sail is loose-footed, there will be nothing along the foot to share any of the strain of sailing, so reinforcement at the clew should take this into account and both patching and the fitting of the grommet be adequate.

A loose-footed main sail (Fig. 7-7) is often given considerably more curve than one attached at intervals to a boom (Fig. 7-6C). This is cut like the roach, but as the edge is diagonal to the weave, an applied tabling should be used. Turning in the material itself would lead to creasing and poor setting.

A main sail for a bendy mast needs more luff curve, otherwise it is made in the same way as a standard jib-headed sail. How much curve to allow depends on many factors. With too little extra curve the flattening sail will develop creases running from the clew corner to the luff. The amount of flexing of the mast has to be considered—the more it will flex, the more luff curve there should be. If the standard amount of curve, already suggested, is taken and then doubled, that is the sort of thing to consider (Fig. 7-6D), but it may be advisable to try flexing the mast and measuring the amount of this at several points to get a better indication of what to allow.

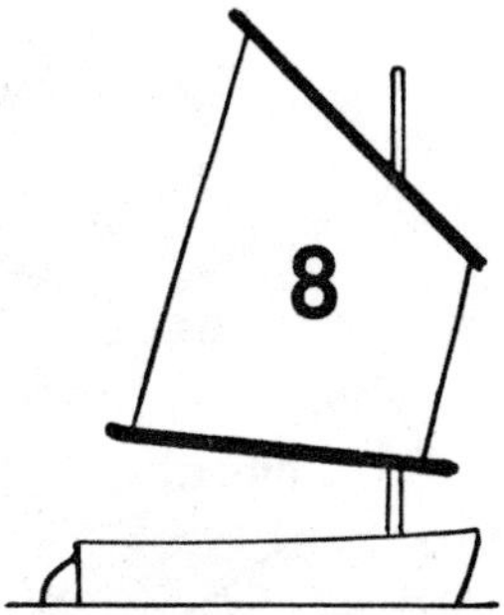

Head Sails

There can be a great variety in the types and sizes of sails set forward of the mast. In some rigs there are several used at one time. In other rigs there may only be one head sail in use, but several others are available for frequent changes. A cruising yacht may only have one main sail, but she may carry several head sails for use in different weather conditions. A main sail can be reduced in area by reefing. Although some head sails can be reefed, it is more usual to change the sail when a different size is required. Because of this, a newcomer to sailmaking may decide to first make a head sail to add to those he already has.

The name "head sail" is probably the safest choice of description, but they are also collectively called *fore sails*. "Jib" is a convenient short word that is now sometimes used for sails other than the first of the possible three head sails of a cutter. The one above it is correctly called a *jib topsail* (sometimes *flying jib*), while the one aft of it is a *stay sail*, (see Fig. 1-2F).

Additionally there are larger head sails that overlap the main sail and are given a variety of names, some of which change according to locality. *Reachers* and *drifters* are quite large for use in light airs. A *genoa* is just as large, and is used when something more than the ordinary head sail area is required. The normal working jib may have its clew no further aft than the mast, although there may be an overlapping working jib that is not as large as a genoa (Fig. 8-1).

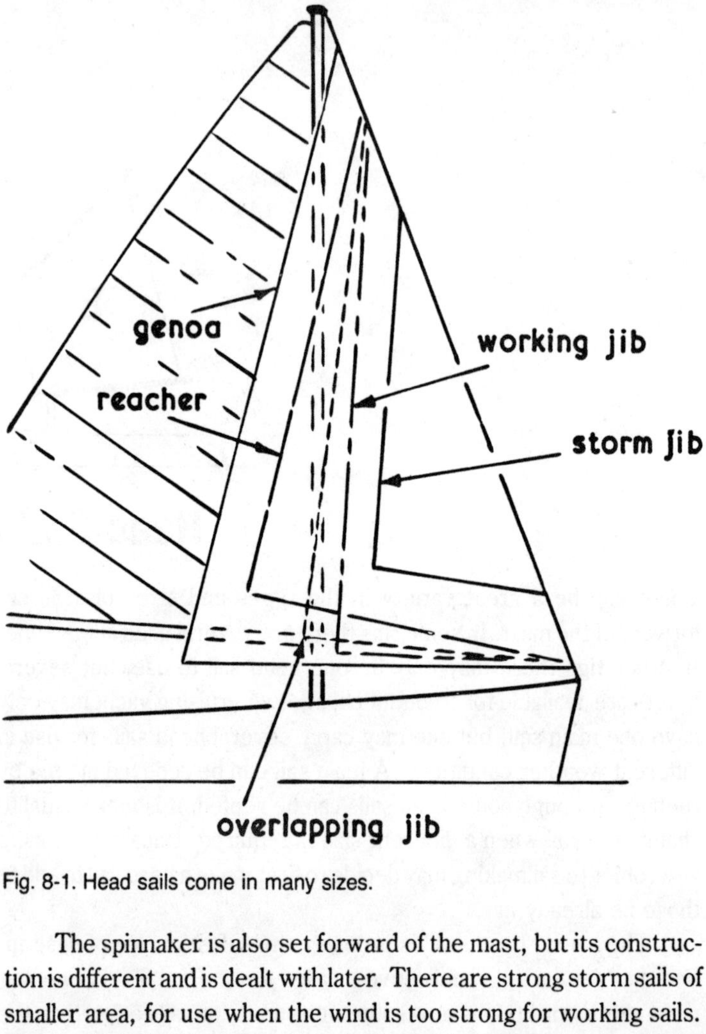

Fig. 8-1. Head sails come in many sizes.

The spinnaker is also set forward of the mast, but its construction is different and is dealt with later. There are strong storm sails of smaller area, for use when the wind is too strong for working sails. Head sail design is open to experiment, but most head sails for dinghies and cruising yachts are likely to be made conventional in shape and cross cut or miter cut, as described below.

At one time in a single-masted rig a very large proportion of the total sail area was always in the main sail. In some rigs the mast is now stepped further aft and more area goes into the head sail. This means that some head sails are quite large and, as they play a greater part in driving the yacht, they may need stronger construction with more reinforcements, than similar, but smaller, sails for older yachts (Fig. 8-2).

Almost all ways of arranging the cloths on a head sail have been used, so almost all constructions might be found. Heavy natural fiber sails of working craft were often cut parallel with the leech (Fig. 8-3A). Having the cloths parallel with the foot was less common, but might be found when the jib was given a boom (Fig. 8-3B). A variation on this was to arrange the cloths more nearly at right angles to the leech and this cross cut is found suitable for sails made of synthetic fiber cloths (Fig. 8-3C).

The better and later sails in natural fibers were miter cut, with the miter bisecting the angle at the clew and so coming approxi-

Fig. 8-2. The mast of this yacht is stepped further aft than was usual a few years ago, so more of the total sail area comes in the head sail, which is a miter-cut genoa. Unusually, the main sail is also miter-cut.

mately in line with the pull of the sheet (Fig. 8-3D). Sails have been made with the cloths of such an arrangement laid parallel with leech and foot, but this is more suitable for a broader angle (Fig. 8-3E) than is found in the head sail of a sloop. It is more usual with a miter cut to have the cloths at right angles to leech and foot (Fig. 8-3F).

It is important for efficient sailing to windward that the leading edge of any sail should be as taut and straight as possible. The mast keeps the leading edge of the main sail straight, but head sails are kept in shape in two ways. The luff of the sail usually comes immediately aft of a stay, and it may be attached to it with snaps at fairly close intervals. As the stay has to be tight to do its job of supporting the mast, it also helps to keep the sail edge straight. It is usual to also include a fiber or, preferably, wire rope in the edge of the sail, so this can be pulled straight and hold the sail edge taut.

The foot and leech are not normally supported in any way, although some rigs call for a boom along part or all of the foot. Some head sails have reef points so some of the area at the bottom of the sail can be gathered up. Where reefing is required, it is more likely to be by roller, with a line around a drum causing the luff to roll to any area up to completely furled. There may be a tube or light spar over a wire cable, on which the sail rolls, or it may roll around a cable, light chain, or rod. A sail for this type of reefing (see Fig. 2-5H) may be made in the normal way, but provision will have to be made for attaching to the reefing arrangement.

Draft in a head sail is controlled mostly by outlining it with straight seams. Draft could also be arranged with curved seams, but this is more the method of the specialist racing sailmaker. No matter how tight the head stay or luff of a head sail, there will be some sag. Most sails are designed for this sag to be kept to a minimum. Increase in sag causes increase in draft, making the sail fuller due to stronger winds. Flatter sails are wanted for strong winds, though. A large sail tends to cause more sag than a small one. Opinion varies on the way to cut head sails to get the desirable draft. Another consideration with an overlapping sail is control of back-winding the main sail.

For a general-purpose head sail, all forward of the mast and for cruising, rather than racing, the layout has a straight leech, but curves at luff and foot. The basic shape is a triangle (Fig. 8-4A). The final edge of the leech follows the line of the triangle, but curves are

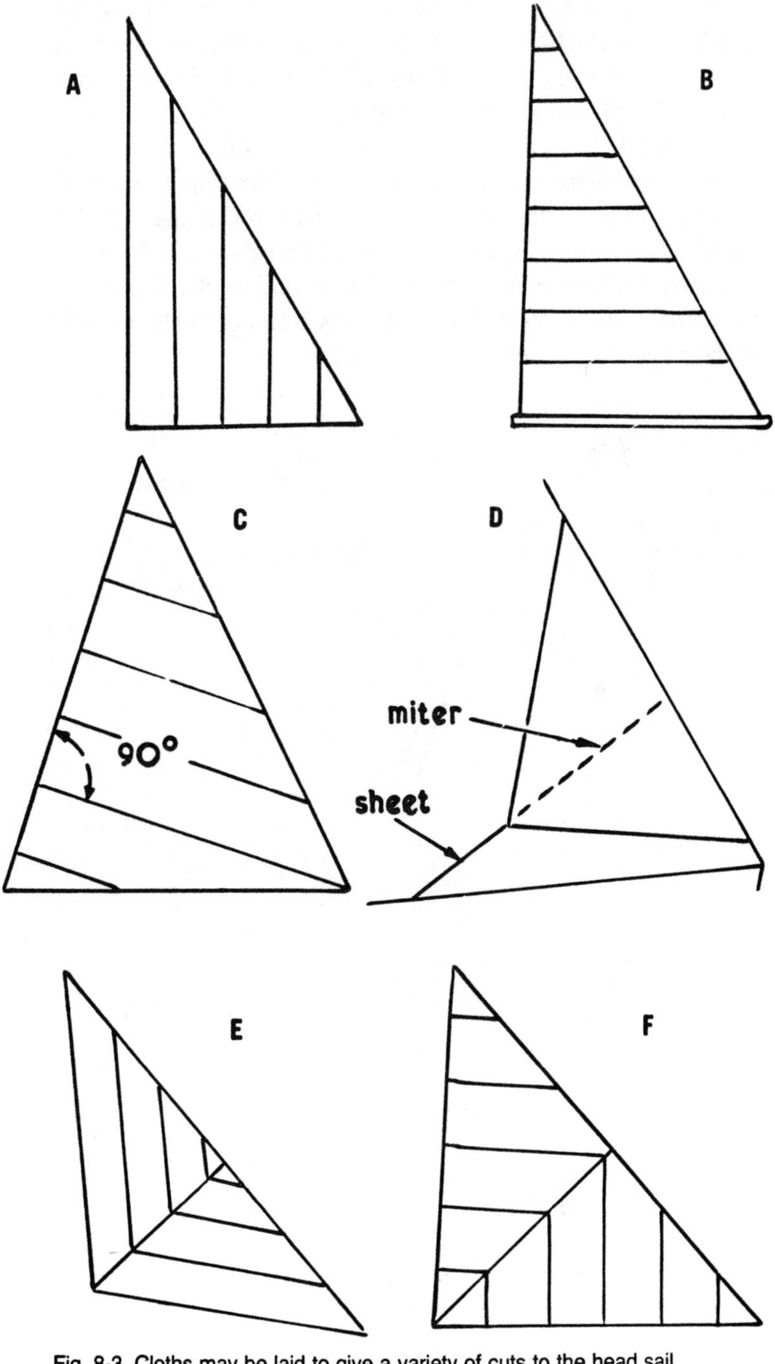

Fig. 8-3. Cloths may be laid to give a variety of cuts to the head sail.

given to foot and luff, with the greatest curvature one-third of the length from the tack (Fig. 8-4B). Determining the amount of curve is a matter of experience, but 2 inches in 5 feet along the foot and 1 inch in 5 feet for the luff should be suitable.

A straight leech does nothing for the draft of the sail when it is tensioned and there could be too much fullness develop. One way of reducing this is to cut the leech hollow, so a load trying to pull it straight flattens the cloth. A sail intended for light airs may have a straighter leech than one intended for strong winds. A possible amount of hollow is about 1 inch for every 3 feet of leech, with the deepest part near its center (Fig. 8-4C).

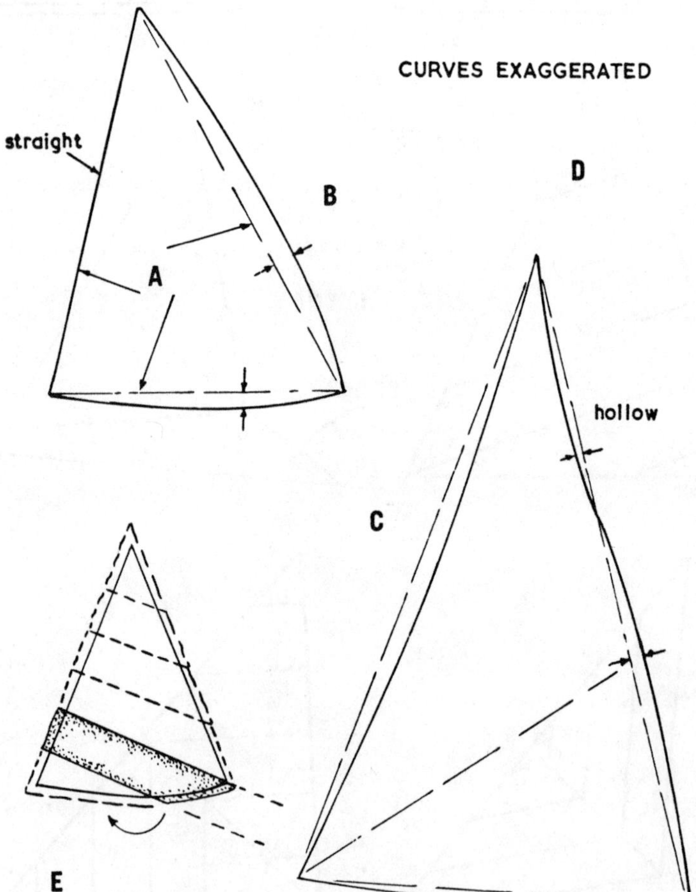

Fig. 8-4. Edges of head sails are curved to give the desired draft.

A sail performs best when its set is approximately the same for its whole depth. There is a tendency for this to fall off towards the top, so the angle of attack when close-hauled is greater at the top of the sail than at the bottom. This tendency can be reduced if the luff is cut slightly S-shaped, so straightening of the luff pulls some of the draft out of the top of the sail. How much this is done is a matter of experience, but whatever is included, the luff should not be cut far off a straight line.

As a guide to drawing a luff line, the greatest curve may come where the miter line bisecting the clew crosses the luff. Here, the depth of curve may be about 1/2 inch for every 6 feet of luff. The hollow of the upper part can be about half this at about halfway between this point and the head. With these two points marked, a batten is twisted through them and the corners, to draw the line (Fig. 8-4D). If the sail is intended for roller reefing and furling, the luff is better kept straight, otherwise unevenness and creasing may develop as the sail is rolled.

If the cloths are to be laid cross-cut the early stage is the same as those described for making jib-headed main sails. Cloths are false-seamed if required. Many head sails have full-width cloths without false seams. The first joining seam is through the tack at right-angles to the straight line of the leech (Fig. 8-3E). Let the cloths overlap the final outline sufficiently to allow for turning in or to allow for the cut-off strip being used for tabling. Use strike-up marks, then gather up the cloths and sew them in the same way as in making a main sail.

If the sail is to be miter-cut, bisect the clew angle and draw a line from the corner to the luff (Fig. 8-5A). With a correct miter, cloths laid exactly at right angles to the straight lines of the edges should meet. Bringing seams together in this way may not be absolutely essential, except for appearance (Fig. 8-5B).

It is possible to start at the clew corner (Fig. 8-5C), but accuracy is more easily obtained if the longer cloths are dealt with first (Fig. 8-5D). If a start is made at the clew there can be whole-width cloths there and the seam towards the luff can come as it will. If the longest cloths are laid first, there may only be part-width cloths at the clew, but this does not matter. Either method of working is acceptable.

Mark out the cloths in both directions, treating the parts each side of the miter line as if they were separate sails at first. Allow surplus along the miter line for making a seam, as well as plenty around the side for tabling or other treatment. By turning cloth around, the piece cut off each time along the miter should match for the next piece without further trimming.

With the two parts of the sail sewn, lay them over the drawing again to check and mark the miter seam. Because this is cut diagonally across the weave, turn the edges under as the seam is made up. Although the seams on the two parts apparently meet, bulk can be reduced if they are moved enough to be slightly staggered, then excessive bulk does not have to be taken in as the needle travels along the miter seam. Seams between cloth edges about 1/2 inch wide should suit all but very large sails, although sewing may be easier if the miter seam is a little wider.

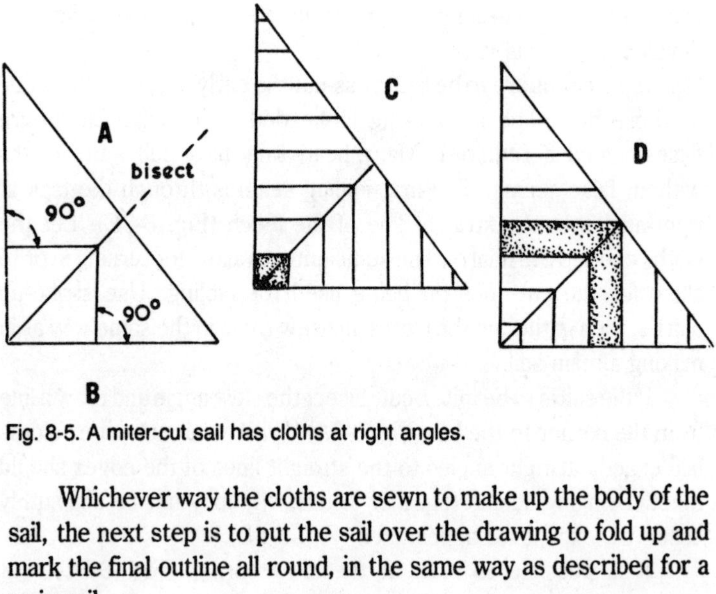

Fig. 8-5. A miter-cut sail has cloths at right angles.

Whichever way the cloths are sewn to make up the body of the sail, the next step is to put the sail over the drawing to fold up and mark the final outline all round, in the same way as described for a main sail.

As with main sails, individual sailmakers have their own ideas about the corner patches. The important thing is to ensure that loads are taken along the strengthened edges of the sail as well as by the main part of the cloth. The actual outlines of the patches are not so important. In general, the patch shapes should match those of the main sail, but as they are not very obvious, this is not important. Simple triangles will do, and there may be several arranged in steps

(Fig. 8-6A). If the angle of a corner is wide, the patch may be four-sided or curped (Fig. 8-6B).

Much of the load at head and tack is taken by the luff wire or other strengthening, but at the clew the load from the sheets has to be taken by the sail alone. Instead of a single patch pattern there may be strips extending some way along leech and foot, as well as a general patch (Fig. 8-6C). Sew the patches across the sail, but leave their edges to be taken in by the stitching around the outline of the sail. Where there are several thicknesses of patches the outer one is sometimes left until after the edges of the sail have been dealt with, then its edges are turned under and it is sewn on outside everything else.

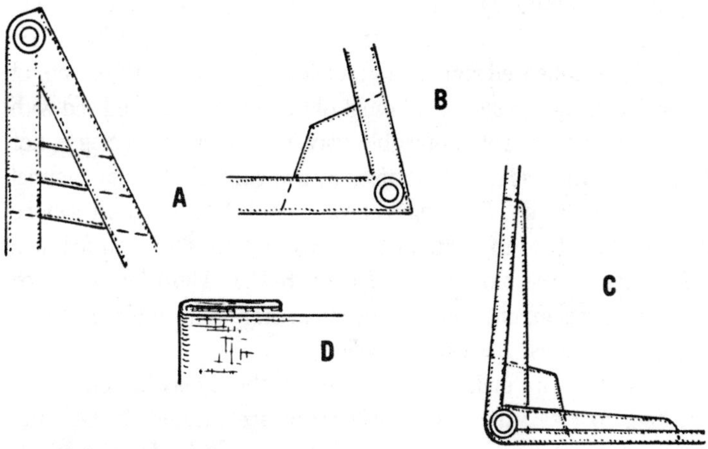

Fig. 8-6. Several corner patches are possible.

Because the weave of the cloth is at right angles to the leech in both methods, it is acceptable to treat that edge with ordinary tabling; but for strength, turn fully under to give three thicknesses for stitching (Fig. 8-5D). On a miter-cut sail the cloths are also at right angles to the foot and this can be treated in the same way.

The luffs of both sails and the foot of a cross-cut one are diagonal to the weave. Tabling with the uncut cloth would lead to trouble, as the resulting different directions of weave in the tabling would react differently to making up and the strain when sailing. Instead, cut a strip from the waste along the edge and use this for an applied tabling, without turning it around or over, so its weave is the same way as the main body of the sail (Fig. 8-7A). Move it in the length so seams are sufficiently staggered to allow for convenient sewing. One way of avoiding the difficulty of keeping the tabling accurate, with all edges having to be turned under, is to first put one turned-in edge of the tabling over the sail edge and sew through (Fig. 8-7B). With this line of stitches made, turn over the tabling to sew the other edge (Fig. 8-7C) and put another line of stitches near the first one.

In some sails there may be a length of fiber rope enclosed in the luff, but for most sails it is wire rope. The edge can be sewn with open ends, but without the rope, if a length of cord is enclosed in the tabling to pull the rope through later. For some roller reefing systems there has to be a roped edge, similar to that of a main sail, to engage with a groove in the fairing which fits around the head stay.

Traditional sails had the luff wire ends spliced and the splice sewn in so it appeared more like a cringle or grommet in the corner of the sail. It is more usual to let most of the eye be exposed and with modern high-tensile steel flexible wire rope tucked splicing is not practicable. Instead the eye is made by swaging or other commercial process (Fig. 8-7D). The length of wire should be such that it is more than the length of the luff. In the relaxed state it should follow a wandering course along the luff (Fig. 8-7E). There is not much stretch in Dacron, but there is more than there is in steel wire, so as the wire tensions, the cloth is pulled taut.

With the wire pulled through the luff, there may be some hand stitching to close the ends. Grommets are located through the patches fairly near the corners, then sail twine is used to secure the sail to the eye in the wire. The cloth may partly overlap the bottom of the eye, then stitches will take it into the opening for extra security. The sail twine may stitch through the cloth, but most of the load is taken by many turns through the grommet (Fig. 8-7F). Treat head and tack in the same way.

At the clew there may be a grommet or taped ring (see Fig. 6-8) to suit the method of attaching the double sheet. It is also possible to have taped D-rings at head and tack if the luff wire is attached to them instead of being spliced into eyes, but spliced eyes in the wire is generally considered the more seamanlike method.

Like main sails, it is possible to include a leech line in a head sail (see Fig. 7-5). There can also be a foot control line arranged in the same way and also emerging to a button near the clew of the sail.

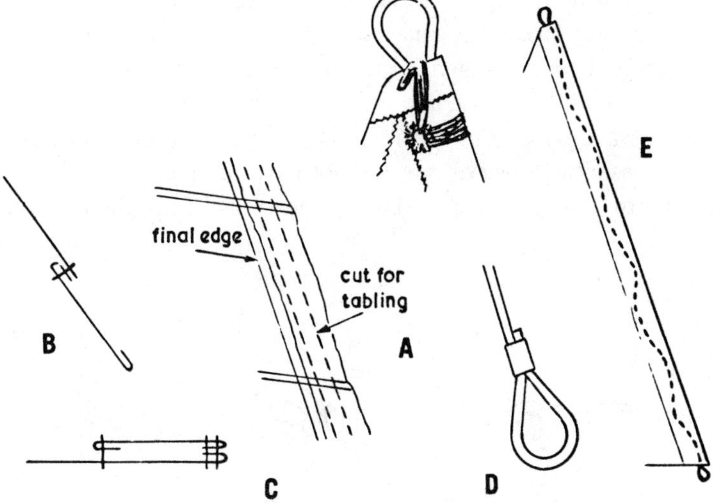

Fig. 8-7. The luff has a tabled edge and encloses a wire rope.

There have been many ways devised to attach the luff to a head stay. Although the luff wire should take much of the strain, there can sometimes be a considerable load placed on these little pieces of sailing hardware, so they should be strong enough in relation to the size of the sail. As the sail must be hoisted or lowered with the snaps on the head stay, they should be an easy fit. Although they must never come adrift when sailing, they should be easily cast off when necessary for quick changing of sails.

For a very small craft there may be strips of tape sewn on with press buttons (Fig. 8-8A), but this arrangement cannot be expected to be very strong. A common fitting, in many sizes, is a bronze jib snap or piston hank. This is sewn with sail twine through the sail and it is designed so it settles with the stay about in line with the sail (Fig. 8-8B). The knurled head is on a spring-loaded piston, which can be withdrawn to allow the stay to be released. There are plastic versions that use a similar idea. Instead of sewing, one type grips the sail with a screw (Fig. 8-8C). A simple type for smaller sails may be metal or plastic and is slipped on to the stay with a twisting action (Fig. 8-8D).

Snaps or hanks need to be fixed firmly to the sail, and arranged so the luff wire takes the strain, but is not trapped. When it takes up tension, it should be able to move within the cloth.

It is unusual, but not unknown, for the leech of a head sail to be given a curved roach like a main sail, and to require battens to hold it in shape. Treatment then is as described for main sails. The only reason for putting roach into the luff of a head sail is to gain some extra sail area, where this is permitted by class rules. However, aerodynamically, where rules do not have to be considered, it is better to have the area in the body of the sail and a straight or hollow leech.

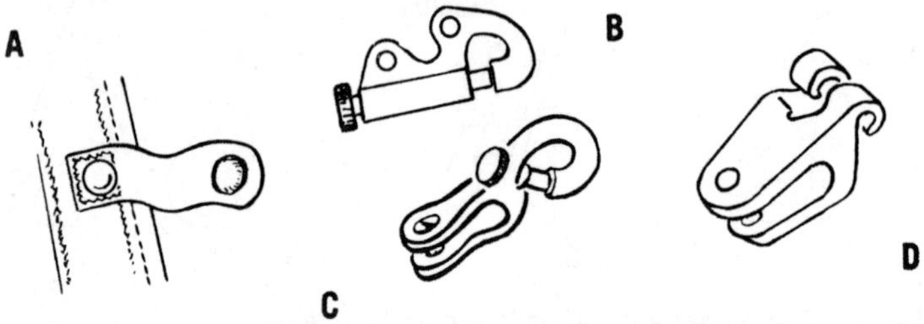

Fig. 8-8. Several types of hanks join the jib to the forestay.

The wider head sails, of the genoa type, are made in the same way as described for working head sails. The hollow leech is important, particularly if there is much overlap on the main sail. When planning a genoa for a particular yacht, the part that goes behind the main sail can be ignored in calculations of sail area and center of effort. Of course, that part of the sail is effective and the slot effect as it takes air behind the main sail contributes to the total drive. The arrangement of sheeting needs to be considered. A large overlapping sail may be planned, and then found to be incapable of being sheeted properly. If the clew is high, for example, it may need an angle of sheet that takes it somewhere aft of the transom!

There are some advantages in having the foot of a head sail low, but this obscures the forward view. Fortunately there are flexible transparent plastics that will make windows and fold or roll with a sail. They may not be as clear as glass, but they do allow enough visibility through a sail (Fig. 8-9).

Ths size of window may be controlled by class rules if it is a racing boat, otherwise one should be planned that will be large enough to see through, but no bigger than is practicable for that. An opening about 20 inches by 10 inches should do. It is advisable to compare the transparent plastic with the weight of cloth used in the sail—0.020 inches plastic would do for a small sail, but greater thicknesses would be chosen for larger sails.

Cut the opening. Heat seal the edges or allow for turning them under. Make the plastic about 1 inch larger all round. Fix it down

Fig. 8-9. The head sail of this gunter-rigged Mirror dinghy has a round plastic window. Otherwise the very low sail would blot out a wide angle of forward view.

temporarily with adhesive tape. Stitch around the cloth edges (Fig. 8-10A). It would be satisfactory to also stitch the plastic edges, but the appearance may be better if tape is used over the edge (Fig. 8-10B). Further strength then comes from using an adhesive inside the joint. There is no stretch in the transparent plastic. Although stretch in the sail cloth is almost negligible, there is a little and too lavish an arrangement of windows might affect the shape the sail takes under wind pressure.

If reef points are to be fitted, they are not really applicable to a head sail with a wire luff rope. They might be arranged diagonally, so the sheet is transferred to a cringle at the end of a row of reef points coming up from the tack (Fig. 8-10C). If there is no wire luff there can be reef points parallel to the foot and an additional place for the tack attachment provided.

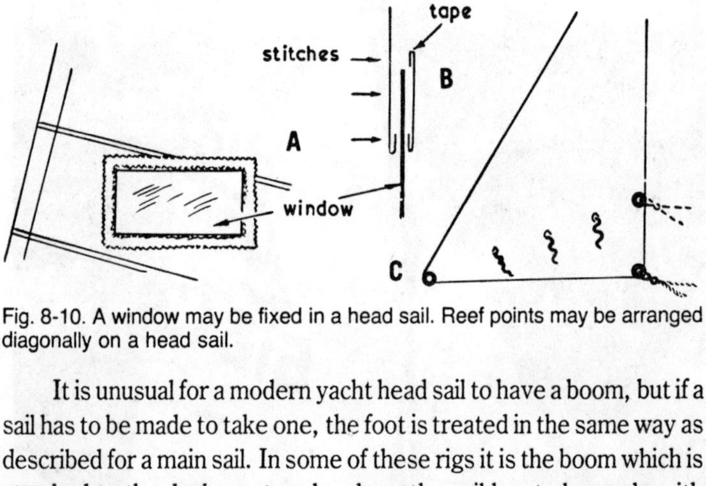

Fig. 8-10. A window may be fixed in a head sail. Reef points may be arranged diagonally on a head sail.

It is unusual for a modern yacht head sail to have a boom, but if a sail has to be made to take one, the foot is treated in the same way as described for a main sail. In some of these rigs it is the boom which is attached to the deck or stem head, so the sail has to be made with grommets or D-rings at tack and clew so the foot can be stretched along the boom, to which it is laced, arranged in a groove, or fitted with slides on a track. The sheet may also be attached to the boom instead of the sail, with a self-acting arrangement of sheet so the sail automatically changes sides. Sometimes the boom reaches from the clew only part of the way towards the tack and may then be called a club. In this case there should be reinforcement where the line at the end of the boom comes to a grommet, as well as the patch at the tack corner. Cross cut cloths are better able to take the different strains from a boom than are miter-cut head sails.

Gaff-Headed Sails

Increased knowledge of aerodynamics as they apply to sailing, particularly to windward, coupled with the improved technology that makes higher masts possible, has brought an almost complete change to the adoption of jib-headed main sails on modern yachts. In the days when masts were usually made from tree trunks and rigging was not as reliable as could be desired, having the required sail area low and spread out made for a safer rig. To get a sufficient area in the main sail without taking it high meant the use of a boom extending over the transom and a spar to support the head.

If the four-sided sail was used alone it usually crossed the mast and in its various versions (see Fig. 1-1) could be regarded as a development of the square sail, swung round from across the boat to fore and aft. It is usual to call the top spar crossing the mast a *yard*. If the sail and spar are wholly aft of the mast, as they usually are if there are head sails, the spar is called a *gaff*. The gaff may be at any angle to the mast between horizontal and vertical, when it becomes more of an extension of the mast, as with the gunter sail.

There is still a considerable interest in craft with gaff-headed sails, even to the extent of clubs and societies to keep alive the tradition. Some new craft are given gaff-headed sails. Although the demand may not be as great as for jib-headed sails, a sailmaker should know how to make these four-sided sails.

Most gaff-headed sails have a boom, but there are some which are completely loose-footed. With a boom, the sail may be laced to it, fitted to a track, or only attached at tack and clew, when it may also be described as loose-footed. Advocates of this last method claim it allows a better shape to the sail under wind pressure. A boomless sail performs well on the wind, but is difficult to set to the best advantage for sailing downwind without resorting to a spare spar to boom it out.

To get the shape of a four-sided sail correct it is necessary for the designer to provide a diagonal measurement, which divides the shape into two triangles. Many proportions are possible, mainly associated with the length of gaff. In some craft, such as Dutch yachts, the gaff is quite short and not always straight, so the sail may almost look jib-headed at a quick glance, while other yachts have a gaff longer than the boom. How steep the gaff is arranged depends on whether a topsail is to be set above it (this is unusual today). Without a topsail, a high-peaked gaff (steeply sloping) should give a better performance to windward. If no design is available, a first shape as a basis to work on can be drawn by letting the boom make an angle a few degrees less than a right angle to the mast, then have the throat of the sail at a height about three-quarters of the length of the boom up the mast, and the gaff about five-eights as long as the boom, set at a right angle to a diagonal line (Fig. 9-1A). An experimental layout, with the boom reaching the transom line, will show if this arrangement will give the intended area and position of center of effort. If not, further trail drawings must be made.

Traditionally, the cloths of gaff main sails were arrranged parallel with the leech (Fig. 9-1B). This is still often done, but with modern sail cloths, and their minimal stretch, the cloths may be laid at right angles to the leech (Fig. 9-1C), as is usual with jib-headed sails. Heavier booms were usual, and the shape of sail puts more load on the cloths, particularly if the gaff is angled steeper than intended when hoisting. Therefore, it was best with natural-fiber fabrics to have the strain taken in the length of the cloths.

For a gaff main sail, the plan is drawn on the floor with straight lines, then all edges are given curves. It is unusual, although not unknown, for the leech to be given enough roach to require battens. Normally, the curve there is only enough to look right by avoiding an apparent hollow and aid in providing fullness to the sail where needed as the load on it pulls the edge straight.

The amount of curve put into the edges depends on many factors and is largely a matter of experience. A comparatively short head or luff may need relatively less curving than if these edges are long. As with jib-headed sails, the greatest curve should be at about one-third of the length of the side from the tack. Along the head it may be between one-third and halfway along the edge from the throat, while the leech curve should be halfway. A curve of 1 inch in 4 feet is about right for each edge—possibly flatter on the luff and perhaps a little more on the foot (Fig. 9-1D).

Draw the edges with a strip of wood bent through the corners and the point of greatest curvature. Sight along to see that there is a fair curve.

Prepare cloths by false-seaming if required. It may be satisfactory to use 28 inch cloths without false seams, but cloth wider than that should have at least one false seam. If the cloths are to be laid parallel with the leech the first one will have to be laid so it overlaps the leech sufficiently to allow material for cutting off to make tabling after the curved outline has been cut (Fig. 9-1E). Allow sufficient spare at head and foot.

Place the other cloths in position, using pencilled marks to indicate the width of the seams and with strike-up marks, as described for making jib-headed main sails. Sew the cloths together, then return the sail to the floor for marking the final shape and preparing for patching.

If the cloths are to be laid at right angles to the leech, prepare them and put them down in a similar way to that described for the jib-headed main sail, with the first seam at right angles to the leech and passing through the tack corner (Fig. 9-1F). Sew the cloths together and return the sail to the floor. Whichever method of laying cloths is used, subsequent steps are the same.

The strain on patches will depend on the size of the sail and the weight of the boom. The actual shape of a patch is less important than it having a sufficient length along the edges to transfer loads to the strengthened seams along the sides of the sail. There should be several thicknesses of patching, either in steps or arranged with the outer layer turned under to cover one or more lower layers.

Simple triangles may be used (Fig. 9-1G). They may be extended at edges and center (Fig. 9-1H). Loads can be expected to be more vertical than horizontal, so four-sided patches may be deeper than they are wide (Fig. 9-1J). The clew may have extended patches

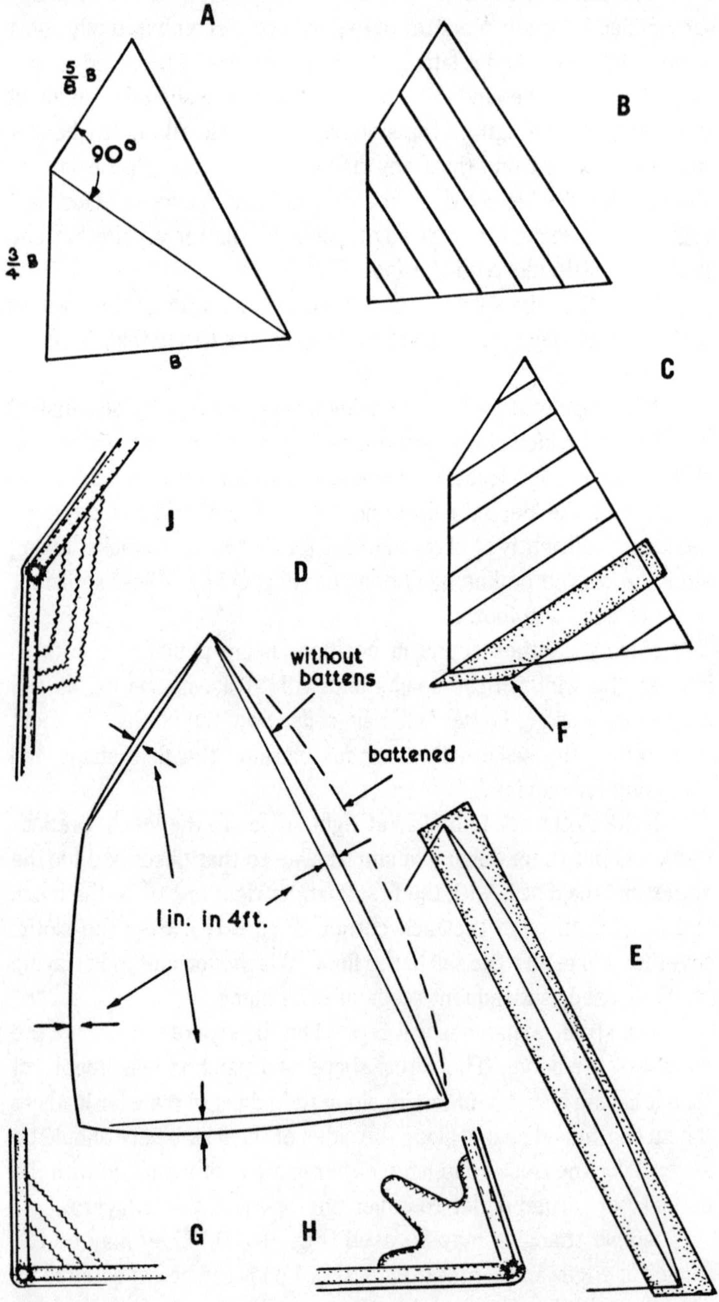

Fig. 9-1. A gaff-headed sail may be vertically or cross-cut, with curved edges to give draft, and reinforcing patches at the corners.

as described for head sails (see Fig. 8-4). The extension up the leech may go past the first reefing line, to give strength there if reef points are being used.

If the cloths are laid at right angles to the leech, that edge may be turned under for tabling, as described for other sails with similar edges. If the cloths are parallel to the leech and that edge is not given much curve, it may be tabled by turning under, but if there is much curve it is better to use applied tabling. The other edges cross the weave diagonally, so they should be tabled with strips cut from them and sewn on, to equalize strain and reduce any risk of distortion along the edges.

It is unusual in a traditional gaff rig for grooved spars to be used. The head may be lashed along the gaff, after grommets at the corners have been used with lines to haul the edge of the sail along the spar. Less commonly, there may be a track along the spar for slides lashed to the sail. The foot may be attached to the boom in one of these ways, or there may be no attachments except at tack and clew.

It is usual to rope head, luff, and foot. This is one piece of rope from peak to clew. If groved gaff and boom are used, the rope end should finish straight along the edge, tensioned and sewn as described for a jib-headed sail (Fig. 6-9D and 7-3F). Otherwise, it is much stronger to taper the projecting end of rope and sew it by hand along the leech (Fig. 7-3H). By doing this all four corner grommets have much of the load taken by the rope around them. The rope is most simply taped on (Fig. 6-1M and N).

In traditional sails roping was hand sewn on the side of tabling (Fig. 6-4F). This is a tedious and slow process, but if the sail is to match an otherwise traditionally-equipped craft, hand roping will preserve the character.

At the luff something has to be done to keep the sail to the mast. With a small sail there may be a lacing line fixed after the sail has been hoisted (Fig. 2-2C), but this is impractical when the throat is too high to reach. It is more usual then to use mast hoops or parrels (balls) at intervals (Fig. 2-2A and B). There may be one grommet at each position, although two close together are more usual. For a small sail metal eyelet grommets may be fixed with a tool, but for larger sails it is better to hand sew grommets with metal rings.

Larger grommets, with ample reinforcing stitching, as described in Chapter 6, should be sewn at the corners and other grommets arranged at intervals along head and foot for lashing to spars.

Reefing of gaff-headed sails is usually done with reef points. These sails were not usually taken off, except in real emergency, so provision had to be made for several rows of reef points, often to the stage where the gaff jaw was brought right down to the gooseneck.

The reef points may have their individual reinforcements or pass through reef bands taken right across the sail (Fig. 9-2A). With a traditionally roped sail, roping from the foot was taken up the leech at least as high as the highest reef position. Instead of grommets worked into the strengthened edge of the sail, cringles were spliced into the roping (Fig. 9-2B). Permanent *reef earings* were arranged through the cringles and *bee blocks* on the boom, so tackle could be used to haul down a reef (Fig. 9-2C). However, roller reefing dates as far back as the days when gaff-headed sails were most popular, so this may be used without spoiling the character of a boat of this vintage.

Other four-sided sails are made in a way broadly similar to the gaff-headed main sail. A square sail used with a following wind may be parallel. It is given a strong top edge for lacing to its yard, with patches at the corners for grommets (Fig. 9-3A). The top is cut straight, but the sides may be given slight convex curves to prevent them from looking hollow and to help give a good draft, which is an advantage when running before the wind. A hollow foot may improve draft.

If one square sail is set above another, it is likely to be tapered. This is best arranged with a seam down the center (Fig. 9-3B). The two parts are made with their cloths parallel with the sides, then cut to match and joined like a mitered sail.

A balanced lug sail or one of the variations on it is made very similar to a gaff sail. Although the yard may be arranged to be supported by its halliard at somewhere near the point of balance, considerable strain is sometimes put on the short leading edge luff while sailing. Even if there is no other roping in the sail, this edge should be roped and the ends taken at least a short distance along head and foot (Fig. 9-3C).

In all but the smallest lug sails the roping should go in one length along foot, luff and head, with the ends taken on to the leech. With some modern versions of these sails, the spars are grooved, but it is more usual to lash the sails to yard and boom, then stow them by

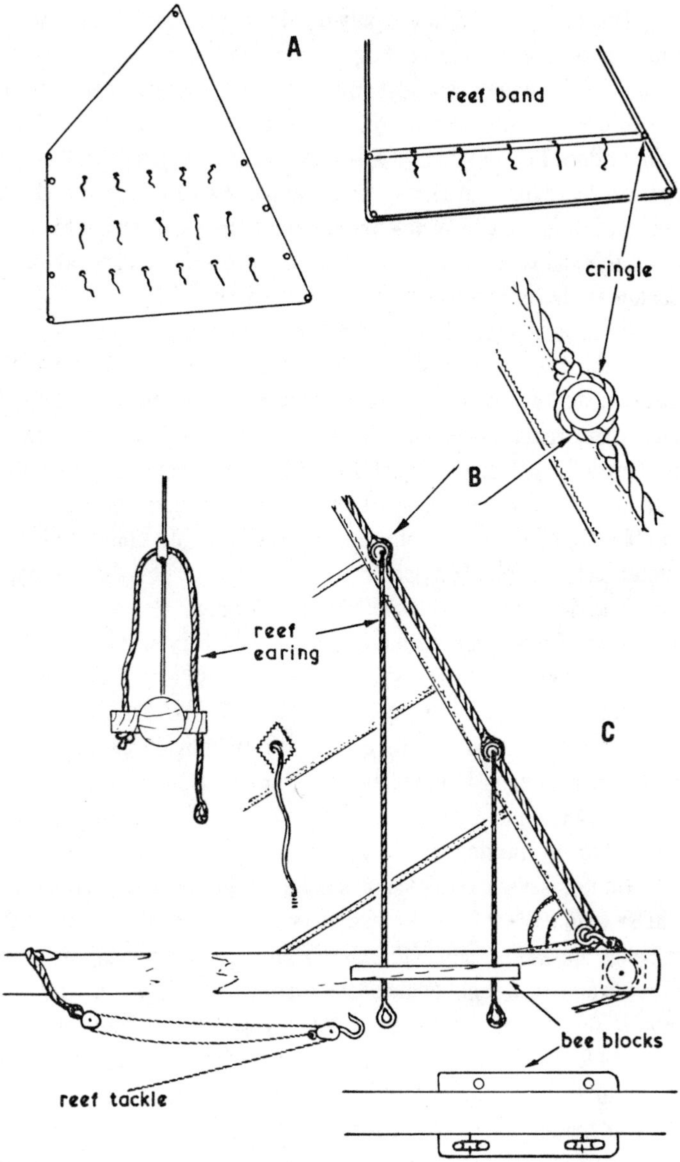

Fig. 9-2. Reef points may go almost to throat height on a gaff sail and there may be reef earings rove through cringles.

rolling them around them. Give head, foot, and leech similar curves to those described for gaff-head main sails, but let the luff be straight (Fig. 9-3D).

This type of sail today is only used for small open boats and it is unusual to provide any reefing arrangements. If the wind is too strong for the usually modest amount of sail, you lower the sail and row or use the outboard motor. However, a row of reef points may be provided. In a simple rig, where the yard is only held to the mast by the halliard through a mast sheave and not with a metal traveler on the mast, this brings a problem of keeping the yard against the mast when the sail is reefed, but the consequent spilling of wind due to slackness there might be regarded as a safety factor.

If the yard or gaff is so high-peaked that it follows nearly up the line of the mast the head and luff of the sail become one and the resulting gunter sail is very nearly the same as a jib-headed main sail. There are practical problems that limit the size of gunter sails, as the overlap of the gaff on the top of the mast has to be enough to maintain stiffness of the projecting part, which cannot have the stays that would be used on a mast of the same total height. This means that gunter sails are found on open boats and cabin yachts of only modest size. The rig made too large puts too much weight aloft and is difficult to support. For smaller craft it is quite satisfactory particularly when problems of storage or transport make having all spars shorter than the boat desirable.

It is difficult to make the gaff remain tight against the mast and follow its line exactly and still be able to move from side to side with the sail. Consequently, there is a slight slope aft, and this has to be allowed for in the design of the sail.

Gunter sails are similar in design to jib-headed main sails of similar size, except for their leading edges. In the simplest form the sail edge appears straight (Fig. 9-3E). In fact, it is not made straight. There would be a slight angle at the throat if the edges were straight (Fig. 9-3F). The part along the gaff is given a curve about 1 inch in 3 foot or 4 foot at the center of the gaff. A line drawn around a piece of wood through the peak and this point to the tack corner should just about eliminate the angle at the throat (Fig. 9-3G).

Some gunter gaffs are hoisted from a wire span. These tend to fall off more from the mast and their sail may need a definite angle at the throat.

Some small gunter sails are made without battens on the leech. If so, the amount of roach should be only enough to eliminate an appearance of hollowness in the edge—about 1 inch in 20 foot may be

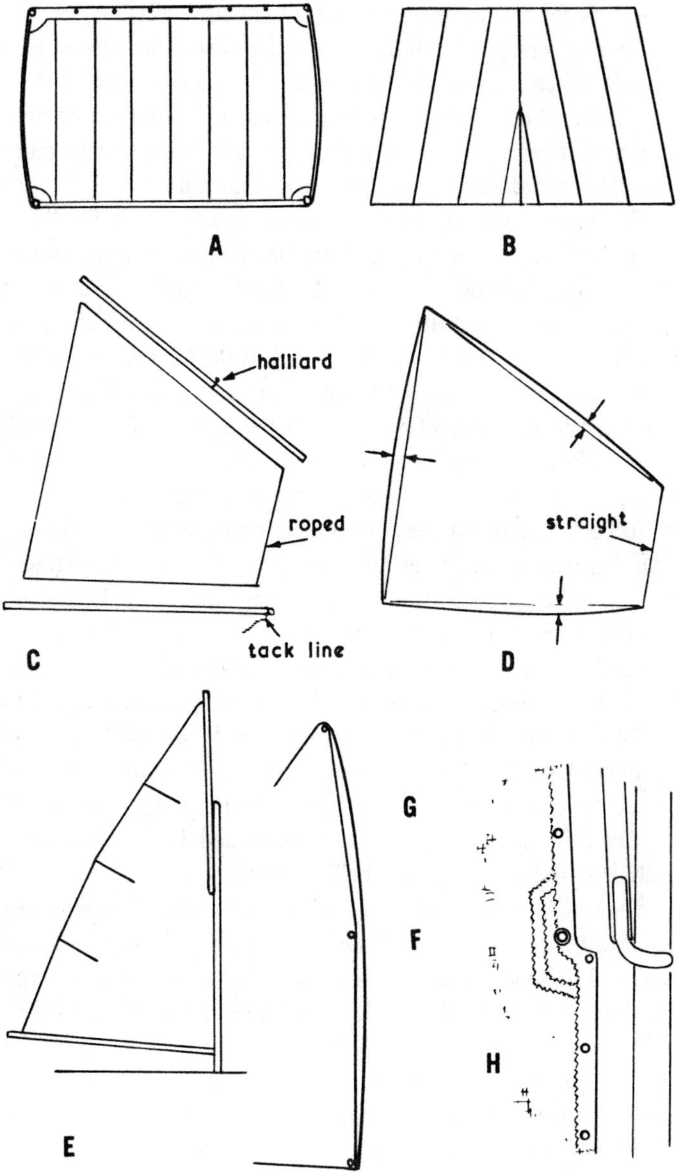

Fig. 9-3. Square and lug sails are given shape by curved edges.

enough. If battens are to be used, treat the roach in the same way as for a jib-headed sail.

The gaff may be fitted to the mast with jaws or it may slide on a track, but whatever arrangement is used there is a step of several inches at the joint. An alternative to the "straight" sail is to offset the sail edge at this point (Fig. 9-3H). From the offset down the edge of the sail is straight. Along the head there may be a curve of about 1 inch in 3 feet. Making the sail this way should let it set better and put less of a bending strain on the top of the gaff. It will remain more upright and therefore more efficient to windward.

The foot of a gunter sail may be laced, loose-footed, fitted to a track, or slid in a groove. The head may be attached to the gaff in any of these ways, but the relation to the wind is similar to that of a jib-headed main sail and the more the sail blends into the spar, the better it should perform to windward, so a well-rounded spar with a groove for the roped edge of the sail makes the most efficient rig.

If the gaff jaw is still within reach when the sail is hoisted, the luff may have a lacing line taken through grommets and around the mast. This is probably best for a small sail, but for a larger sail there will have to be hoops or parrels. If there is much length of sail edge behind the mast blending this into the mast with fairly close attachments, so there is a smooth air flow, will make the sail set better and give a better performance to windward.

A fault with a gunter sail is its unsuitability for easy reefing, due to the inefficient position of the gaff if it is merely partly lowered to allow for roller or other reefing to the boom. When partly lowered the gaff will flog about due to the length of halliard between it and the mast sheave. There can be a second higher attachment point for the halliard on the gaff for use when the sail is reefed, but the gaff has to be fully lowered to change the halliard over.

When replacing sails for an old gaff-rigged yacht, there may be a need for a main top sail to set above the gaff. This was always a difficult sail to hoist and set properly. Its effect is to put more area above the gaff so the total effect is something like a jib-headed sail or one with the gaff crossing like a sprit. As there is so much rigging and extraneous lumps to affect air flow, it is understandable that this sail arrangement was abandoned in favor of the aerodynamically cleaner single jib-headed sail on a smooth single-piece mast.

If a main top sail has to be made, the old one will serve as a pattern, but if the new one has to be made without reference to a similar one, it is made in the same way as head sail. In some cases the cloths were arranged parallel to an edge, but it is more usual to use a miter cut (Fig. 9-4A). The sail may come entirely between mast and gaff. In that case construction is just like a head sail, with wire or fiber rope along the luff, so it can be tensioned to give a straight leading edge behind the mast (Fig. 9-4B). Attaching to the mast along the luff would only be possible by going up there to lash or fix in some other way.

For some rigs the top sail area is increased with spars. There may be a top sail yard extending above the mast and a jack yard

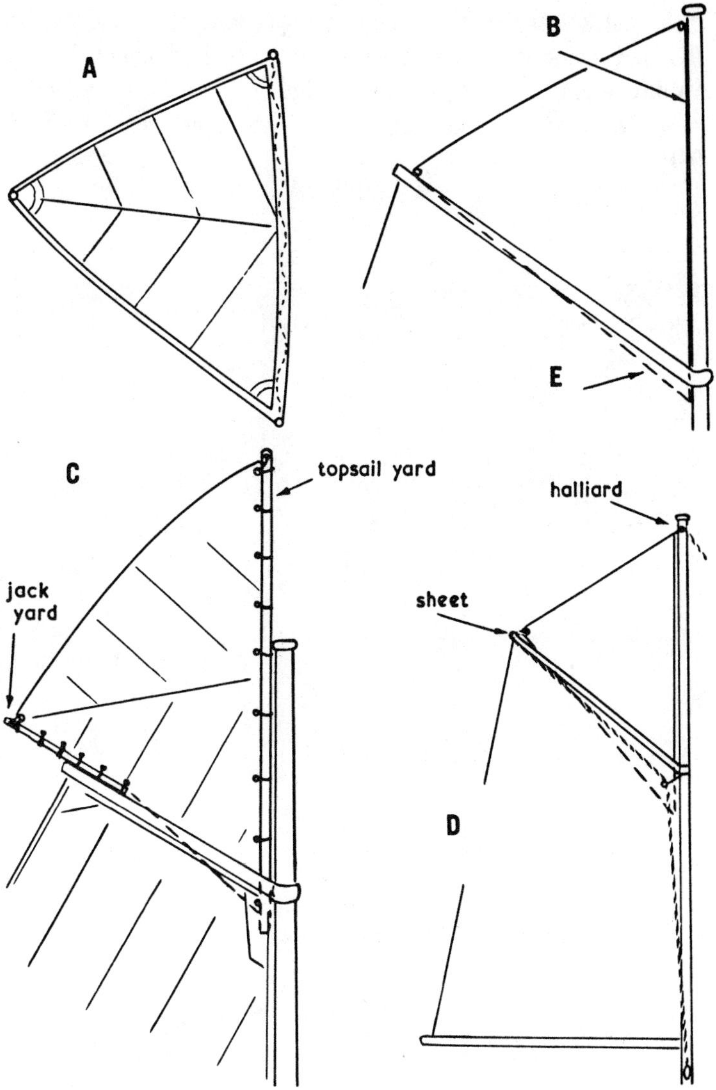

Fig. 9-4. A main top sail gives extra area above a gaff-headed main sail.

extending the boom (Fig. 9-4C). The top sail yard may extend the full length of the luff, so that edge can be equipped with plenty of grommets for lashing to give the leading edge of the sail the most efficient form. It could be sleeved on the yard, with a gap in the sleeving for the halliard attachment. The jack yard should overlap the end of the gaff enough to keep it in shape. It is hauled there by a sheet through a block on the end of the gaff, which is then led via another pulley block near the throat of the main sail down to deck level (Fig. 9-4D). Provide grommets along the edge that will meet the jack yard. It was usual to let the lower edge of the top sail overlap the main sail so as to avoid a gap through which air could pass (Fig. 9-4E).

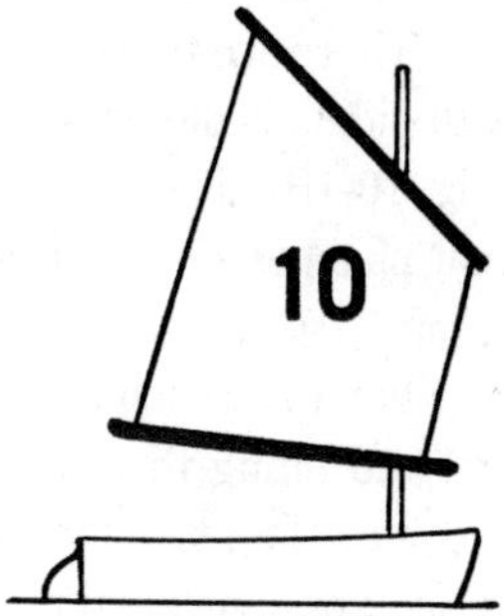

Other Sails

The majority of modern boats are rigged as sloops and most of those that are not use similar sails, so the making of sails for them involves processes and designs similar to those already described. Some specialized craft, particularly those of foreign origin or influence, may have other sorts of sails. It is possible to get a sailing performance of some sort by supporting a sufficient area of canvas of almost any shape and trimming it to suit the wind. It is understandable, therefore, that not all boat-building nations of the world have followed the conventions that have become usual amongst the Western yachting nations.

Not so many larger craft have unusual rigs, although some may be met and sails have to be made for them, but these less common variations are often found on small craft, where they may have some advantage of novelty appeal. A boat that is intended to be seriously raced, whatever its size, will almost certainly have a conventional rig, but where the ability to point that bit higher into the wind or gain just that little more speed over a competitor is not an overriding consideration, the sail plan may be simpler for family sailing off the beach, lazing around a lake, or letting the children learn to sail in a safely-rigged boat. Of course, any rig should be capable of sailing on all the usual points, otherwise it could be dangerous if it would not sail back to shore.

LATEEN SAILS

The lateen sail, or variations on it, is found on board boats and other small craft. Many rigs tend to push the bow down when driving hard. The lateen sail can have a lifting action, so with a small or shallow boat that could be sailed under with some rigs, it helps to keep the bow up and give an exciting sail.

There are two versions: one that gives a high peak (Fig. 10-1A) with sides of different length, and one that has equal lower sides (Fig. 10-1B). The first type is always used the same way round—the boat changes direction in the usual way by going about. In some original Pacific Islands craft the boat changes from a reach in one direction to a reach the other way by taking the rudder to the other end and tilting the sail on a central mast, so what was the peak becomes the tack. Of course, this sail has to be symmetrical. The method of construction of both sails is the same.

Cloths may be at right angles to the head (Fig. 10-1C), parallel to it, or at right angles to one edge. The last type may be preferable if one side (leech) is longer than the other (foot). If the clew is a right angle or close to it, this puts the cloths near to parallel to the foot (Fig. 10-1D).

A simple straight-sided triangle would give a poor shape and the unsupported sides would look hollow. Draft is best given to the sail by curving the head, with the greatest curve somewhere between one-third and one-half the distance along the edge from the forward corner. About 1 inch in 3 feet should be right (Fig. 10-1E).

The other edges may be given about the same amount of curve, but with the greatest curve towards the spar (Fig. 10-1F). If it is a high-peaked lateen rig, with a long leech, it may be given enough curve for a roach, to be supported by battens like the leech of a normal jib-headed sail, but that is unusual.

If the cloths are at right angles to the long edge, make the first cloth through the clew (Fig. 10-1G), otherwise make the first cloth along the edge, with enough overlap to allow for the curve (Fig. 10-1H). Mark and join the other cloths in the usual way, then mark the exact outline of the finished sail from the drawing on the floor.

Patches should be ample. The edge along the spar will receive fairly evenly distributed support, but all of the load along the free edges is concentrated at the clew. Patches there should build up several thicknesses with varying degrees of overlap, so there is a

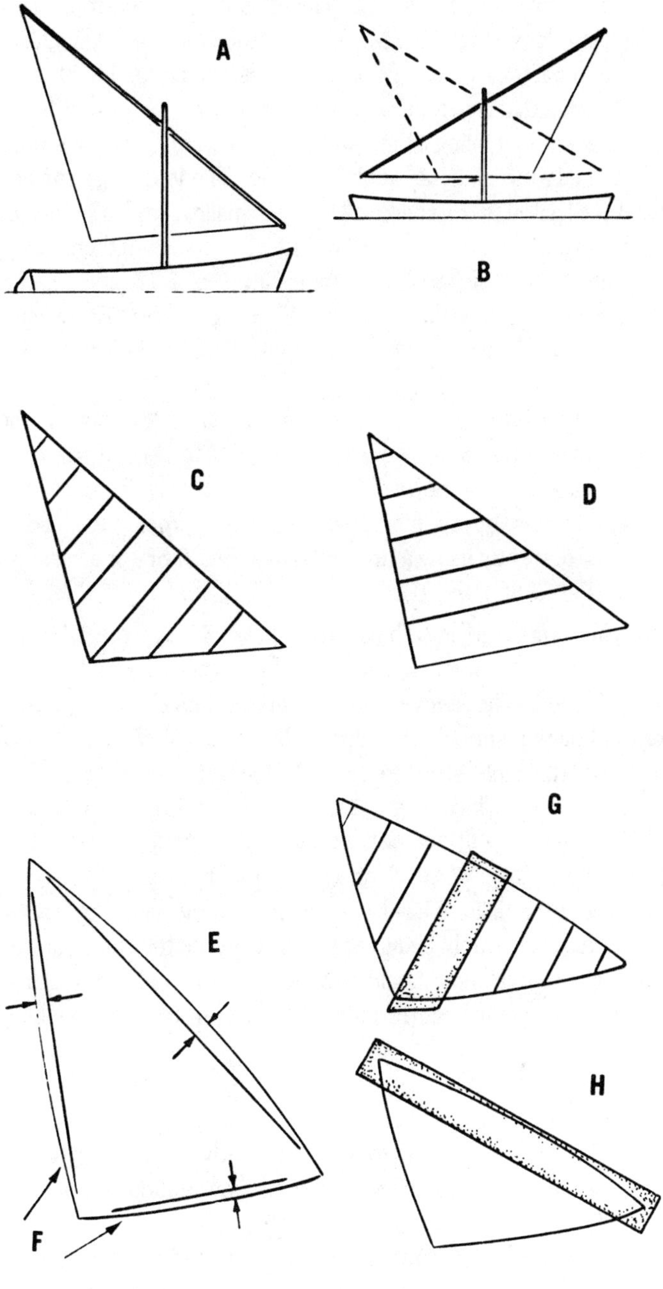

Fig. 10-1. A lateen sail may have its cloths laid any way and is given shape by curving the edges.

graduated spread of the strain. There could also be strips carried along the edges (Fig. 10-2A). At the other corners, triangular or four-sided patches in several thicknesses should be adequate.

An edge that is parallel to a line of weave may be turned in with a three-thickness tabling (Fig. 10-2B). Elsewhere, use a strip cut from the edge to make an applied tabling. The long edge should be roped and lashed to the spar in all but the smallest sails. For the small play boats and board boats it will be sufficient to strengthen the edge with one or two thicknesses of tape (see Fig. 6-1K and L). If the edge is roped it can be included in a tabled edge (Fig. 6-1P, Q, and R) if this is parallel with the weave, or applied in a tape (Fig. 6-1M and N).

Roping of a large sail is best tapered and hand-sewn a short distance along the other edges (Fig. 7-2H) to relieve the corner grommets of some of the load. The clew corner may have a grommet through patches, but as the corner is not usually roped, the load may be spread better by using a ring and tapes (Fig. 6-8F) or a reinforced D-ring (Fig. 6-8G) and H).

The long edge may have grommets through the tabling for lacing to the spar, but in smaller versions of this sail it is more likely to be sleeved. The sleeve does not provide much strength to the edge although it spreads the support better than lacing, so the edge should still be tabled for strength. The spar for small sails may be aluminum tube, which is parallel and may be jointed. The sleeve should be an easy fit and carried far enough over the sail edge to allow several rows of stitching (Fig. 10-2C).

Where the halliard has to be attached to the spar, cut away the sleeve. It will probably be advisable to reinforce the sail edge with a patch. The sleeve ends should be tabled, but to avoid this catching on the spar being pushed through, it is better to turn the tabling outwards (Fig. 10-2D).

If the spar is much longer than the edge of the sail, the sleeve may be taken to the corner of the sail, but if there is little length exposed, it may be better to keep the sleeve short (Fig. 10-2E). Table the sleeve end outward in the same way as at the cut-out part.

The lateen sail is an easy one to spill wind in an emergency, so ordinary reefing arrangements are not often provided. Where it is used on a small pleasure boat, it is unlikely to be hoisted when winds are strong. If anyone is caught out in a strengthening wind, easing the sheet may be all that is needed to continue sailing safely.

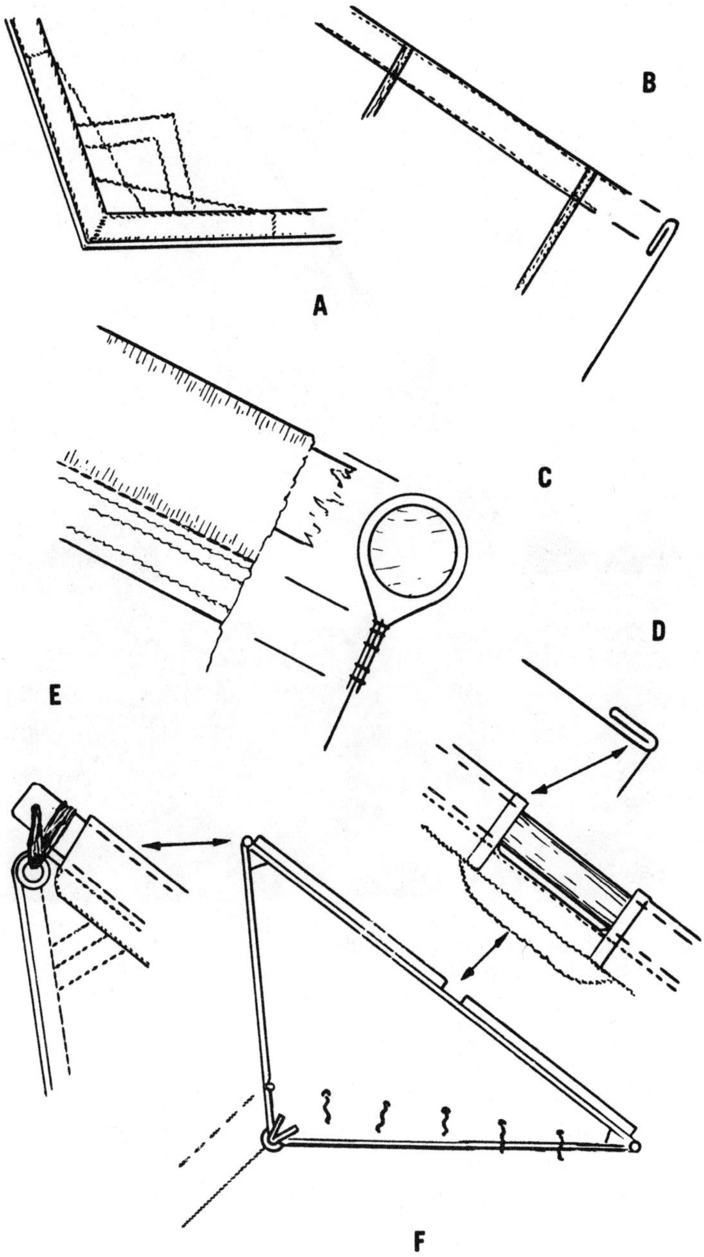

Fig. 10-2. The long edge and clew of a lateen sail must be strong. If the edge is sleeved there must be a gap for attaching the halliard.

Fig. 10-3. A sail more usually seen on a canoe than a dinghy. The aluminum tubes are hinged at their forward ends and supported by a tube mast. The sail is lashed to the spars and is cut with the cloths parallel to the leech.

If reefing is required, there can be a row of reef points running diagonally from the tack (Fig. 10-2F), with another grommet for attaching the sheet. This alters the angle of the sheet, but in strong winds that call for reefing, a slightly inefficient set of the sail may not matter. If a better angle of the sheet is required from this higher position, it can be led further aft on the deck.

CANOE SAILS

What is in effect a lateen sail with a boom has been used as an auxiliary sail for canoes, but the same type is found on board boats and other small pleasure craft (Fig. 10-3). Compared with a lateen sail with a loose foot it has the advantage of keeping the sail more manageable, particularly when being hoisted or lowered, as there is no free canvas flapping awkwardly and possibly dangerously in what may be an unstable craft. Whether it is as efficient in use may be debatable, but although a loose-footed lateen sail may be better for a long reach, the boomed sail gains when there are frequent changes in sailing direction.

For a traditional canoe sail, the spars are wood and the sail is laced to them (Fig. 10-4A). The mast is comparatively short (about half the length of the other spars) and the yard is hoisted by a halliard well forward of the point of balance. A tack line hauling back the forward end of the boom, or a lashing between boom and mast, is needed to keep the sail in the required attitude. The spars are hinged

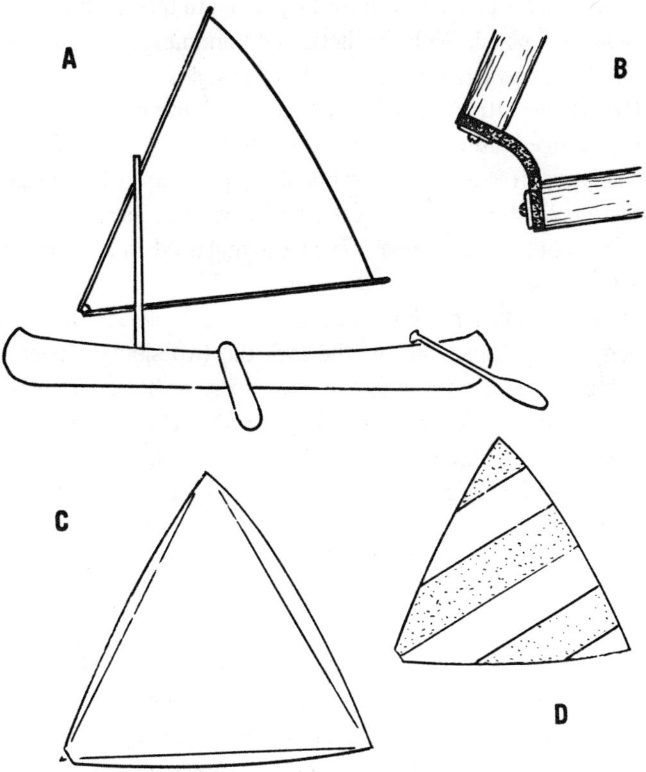

Fig. 10-4. A canoe sail is attached to two spars hinged together. It may be lashed or sleeved with gaps for attaching lines.

together, either with a metal fitting or, traditionally, by a strip of leather (Fig. 10-4B).

A typical canoe sail is equal-sided, so all corners are at 60 degrees. This is not essential, but it is a convenient layout. For an 18 foot canoe the sail sides could be about 11 feet. (Fig. 10-4C). The long light spars tend to bend and they put some curve into the edge of the sail to increase draft, so edges may be satisfactory if straight. However, a slight edge curve is usual, probably 1 inch in 3 feet with the greatest curve at the center of a side. On the leech there should be enough curve to prevent a hollow appearance—4 inch or 5 inch in an 11 foot edge should be satisfactory. Battens would be a nuisance in such a sail that should be kept simple for easy stowage when not needed to provide a break from paddling.

In natural fiber cloth a canoe sail was made of the lightest material available and to allow for its tendency to stretch and lose its shape, the sail was made with cloths parallel to the leech so distortion was minimized. With synthetic cloth and negligible stretch, it may be better to have the cloths at right angles to the leech (Fig. 10-4D). Some attractive sails of this type have been made with cloths arranged alternately in different colors.

This type of sail on a board boat or other craft than a canoe, usually has jointed aluminum tube spars, with the sail sleeved on them. Except for this, the sail is similar to that used on a canoe and an equilateral triangle is a common shape.

Constructional methods are generally similar to those described for the lateen sail. At the tack the two sleeves meet and there must be some space to allow the spars to be slid into them. This means cutting away the sail (Fig. 10-5A). The short edge may be taped, or even roped. There should also be adequate patching, as it is unusual to have a grommet or other means of securing the sail at this point—the angle made by the spars being considered enough to keep the sail in place. For the best set it may be better to provide one or a pair of grommets so there can be a lashing or a clip to the hinge (Fig. 10-5B).

The sleeve on the yard must be cut away for the halliard attachment. At the peak it may be cut back or taken to the end of the sail edge, depending on the amount of spar projecting. On the boom there will have to be a cut away part of the sleeve for the tack line to the mast (Fig. 10-5C). In both cases, the only adjustment to sail angle is to move the halliard or tack line along the spar, so the cut-away sleeves should not be too narrow. There should be space for a few inches of adjustment. This means having a strengthened edge, either by extra taping along the open part with an overlap of the sleeving, or by patches (Fig. 10-5D).

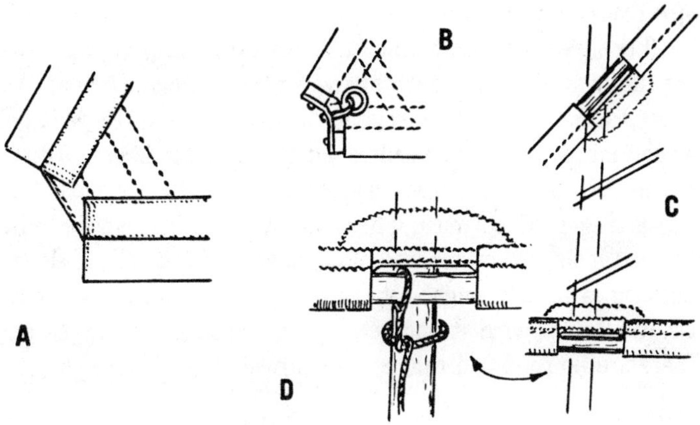

Fig. 10-5. Construction methods.

If the sheet is attached to the end of the boom, this will not affect the sail construction, but to get sufficient sail area the boom may extend over the transom, then the sheet has to be attached forward of the end. There has to be another cut away part of the sleeve to allow the sheet to be attached (Fig. 10-6A).

With some rigs of this type the sheet is arranged through pulley blocks at more than one point on the boom. If several cut-away parts of the sleeve are to be avoided, it might be better to lash the boom to the sail with grommets instead of using any sleeving, or there may be sleeving for the forward part, then lacing used for the part of the sail aft of where the furthest forward block comes (Fig. 10-6B).

There are sleeved main sails of the jib-head type, which have family likenesses in construction to the canoe sail. There is a very loose pocket to fit over the mast, which is unstayed and therefore liable to bend, and a boom which may be fitted into the foot pocket after the sail has been fitted to the mast, then coupled to its gooseneck. The boom may be more permanently attached to the mast and hinged parallel to it for fitting into the two pockets at the same time. In a simple form the boom may be given a jaw to loosely fit the mast, then a down-haul is used after the sail has been assembled on the spars, or this may serve as a boom vang as well, by being taken through a grommet in the sleeve (Fig. 10-6C). In any case there should be a sufficient cut-away part in the corner and this should be taped and patched (Fig. 10-6D), with the patch extended as far as the boom vang attachment if this is not too distant, otherwise that can have its own patch.

For sheeting other than at the end of the boom there will have to be a cut-away part in the boom sleeve for the sheet attachment. With sleeved sails there is no satisfactory way of reefing, so they are only suitable for use in settled weather and moderate conditions. With the lateen-type canoe sail it is possible to lower the sail while afloat, but if the sail is sleeved to a mast, it has to be attached and removed when the boat is ashore or moored alongside. Consequently, a sleeved mast rig is usually under-canvased so its use does not become hazardous if the wind strengthens before the shore can be reached. There are no reefing arrangements provided for these rigs.

SPRIT SAILS

The alternative to using a gaff at the top of a four-sided sail is to use a spar called a *sprit* diagonally across it to keep the peak aloft and the sail in shape. Although there have been some very large sprit sails on working craft and a few of these survive, the sprit sail is met now in small dinghies for training young people and in some modernized versions of sailing rowboats.

There may be a boom, or the sail may be loose-footed. The sprit may be taken from the tack corner of the sail or may be attached to the mast at a higher point. Probably, theoretically, it should bisect the angle of the sail at the peak, but a very exact angle does not seem to be important (Fig. 10-7A).

Set of the sail is dependent on the upward push of the sprit, so this has to be allowed some adjustment and it is usually lashed to a cleat on the mast. Security here is important and there may be something provided to limit movement if the lashing comes away, as the pressure on a sprit suddenly released could force it down quickly, not only collapsing the sail, but doing damage to deck or hull.

A sprit sail has much in common with a gaff-headed sail. The outline is drawn with straight lines (Fig. 10-7B). The luff has a curve with its greatest amount about one-third up from the tack—1 inch in

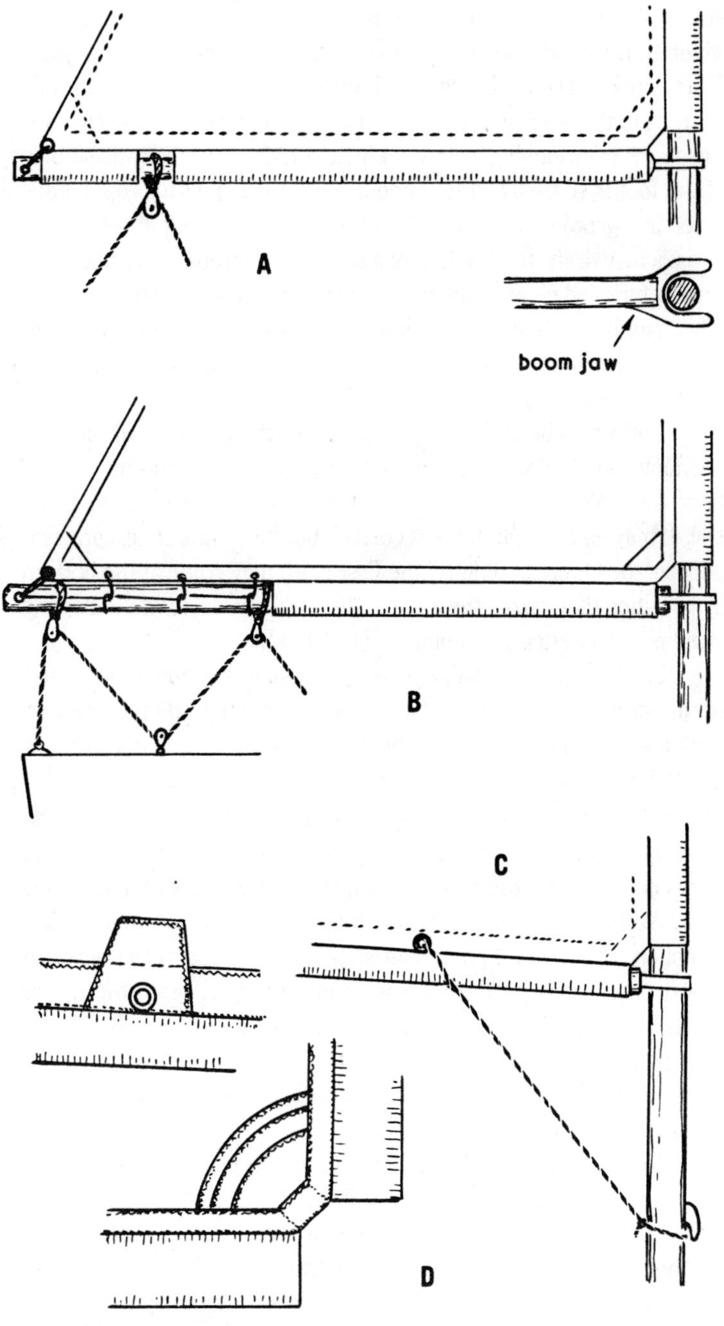

Fig. 10-6. A sail may be sleeved to mast and boom with provision for sheets and vangs.

5 feet should be enough. About the same amount of curve may be given to the head, although in some sails it may be almost straight. This type of sail does not always have enough curve to justify fitting battens to the leech, so that edge may be given just enough curve to prevent it from looking hollow—1 inch in 15 feet may be satisfactory. If the foot is to be laced to a boom, or provided with a roped edge fitted in a groove, a curve of 1 inch in 3 feet or 4 feet should give a satisfactory draft, but the foot of a sprit sail is often held to the boom only at tack and clew. Then it is better to give the edge more curve. This may be as much as 1 inch in 2 feet with the greatest curve at halfway, but some experimenting may be needed to get a pleasing shape (Fig. 10-7C).

Cloths may be at right angles to the leech. There should be false seaming of wide cloths, but for widths up to 28 inches this may not be necessary. Where the first cloth is laid depends on the shape of the sail. It may go through the tack corner; but for a quite small sprit sail, such as the Optimist dinghy, the first cloth may come at the bottom in a position that makes the most of the width available while allowing surplus at the edge for tabling (Fig. 10-7D).

It is the top edge that gets the greatest strain, due to the thrust of the sprit, so allow for this being roped, even if no other part is. With a sprit sail intended for a boat bigger than a small open one, it would be better to rope all round, except the leech.

Having decided on the edge treatment to be used, take off the true shape from the floor and prepare patches. Those at tack and clew can be similar to those used on the foot corners of most other sails. At the throat the strain is not likely to be greater in a vertical direction, as it is with some gaff sails, but because of the outward thrust of the sprit on the otherwise unsupported head, the throat patch may be expected to have to resist greater loads in that direction. It may be as good there to take patch extensions along the edges as well as to provide several thicknesses of patching cloth across the corner (Fig. 10-7E).

How the peak is dealt with depends on the class. If the sail is not for a particular class and the method is not specified, there are two ways of attaching it to the sprit. The corner may be reinforced with patches, then a grommet used to lash the sail to the end of the spar (Fig. 10-7F). The alternative for a small sail is to have a pocket in the corner of the sail and let the rounded end of the spar thrust into it

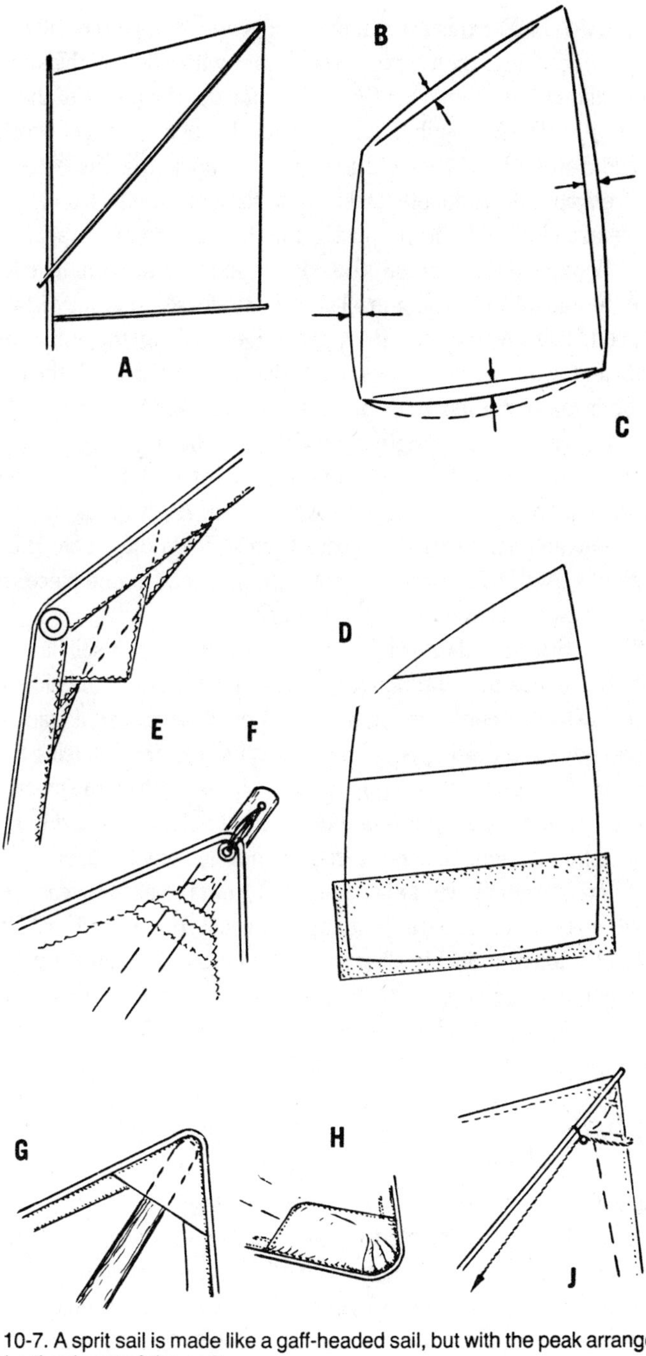

Fig. 10-7. A sprit sail is made like a gaff-headed sail, but with the peak arranged to take the thrust of the sprit.

(Fig. 10-7G). For this arrangement, it is best to give the sail corner suitable patching, then arrange the pocket with a double thickness of cloth and gusset it sufficiently to allow for the thickness of the sprit (Fig. 10-7H). Although a flatter patchlike pocket might work, it would distort the corner of the sail. If the pocket is gussetted, the sail remains flat. A double thickness of sail cloth should be adequate, but extra cloth may be put inside for the sprit to press against.

With patches sewn on, the edges can be dealt with. The leech may be tabled by turning in. The other edges should have tabling applied, using strips cut from the edges. Along the luff allow a sufficient width for grommets to take lacing to the mast. If the foot is to be laced to the boom, make a similar allowance there.

Edges can be strengthened with tape, but for larger sails it is better to tape on rope. If only the head is roped, let this go around the throat and a short distance down the luff. At the peak, taper the rope end and hand sew it a short distance down the leech. If more roping is used, take it around foot, luff, and head in one piece, with tapered ends carried over to the leech.

As with any other sail, it is important that a sprit sail has a taut luff that blends into the mast, to give the best aerodynamic shape when sailing to windward. It would be possible to use a track or a roped edge in a mast groove, but this is not common. Lacing to the mast is satisfactory, providing it is possible to reach up the mast. It is usual to provide lacing grommets for the full length of the luff, but where this is high, the top ones may not actually be used.

In emergency wind may be spilled from the sails by easing the sprit, so the greater part of the top of the sail ceases to draw. There could be conventional reefing along the bottom of a sprit sail, with reef points or even roller reefing, but the small craft with sprit sails are usually very modestly canvased so it is unlikely they will be sailing in conditions where reefing becomes necessary.

Commercial sprit sail craft never lowered their loose-footed sail. Instead, there were brailing lines permanently installed, that would gather in the sail to the sprit and mast. To reduce sail a little, the top brailing line was hauled in (Fig. 10-7J). With other brailing lines used, it was possible to gather up the heavy canvas so there was none left to draw. This method of reefing is completely unsuitable for small craft. Instead of having reef points, there could be lines that gathered up the top of the sail around the sprit and reduced area in that way.

FULLY-BATTENED SAILS

Battens across sails give a positive control of shape (Fig. 10-8). They are used in some sails of otherwise conventional shape, over part or all of the area. The International 10 square metre Sailing

Fig. 10-8. The main sail of this Tornado catamaran is very fully battened, with ten battens across the sail and tensioning lines at their protruding ends.

Canoe, which was the fastest sailing machine afloat for a very long time, uses a fully-battened sail. Some jib-headed main sails have a top batten that is full width and pushes the leech out to get a little extra area near the top. The sail which makes most use of full battens is that of the Chinese junk. This is being increasingly used on yachts that are otherwise more in keeping with Western ideas, so junk sails may be required for new craft.

A junk sail is something like a balanced lug with battens (Fig. 10-9A). The battens may be in pockets, but are more likely to be external. The sail then comes between a stout batten against the mast and a lighter one on the other side. In a full-battened sail of more conventional type the battens are in pockets, for the most part parallel with the boom (Fig. 10-9B).

For full battens, the sail may be made without the seams having regard to the directions of the battens, then batten pockets are fixed as required (Fig. 10-9C). With the negligible stretch of synthetic materials this should result in a sail which keeps its shape, but such a sail cannot get its draft from the shaping of edges only because the battens restrict the curving of the bunt of the sail and the resulting shape may not be what you intended.

It is better to have the cloth seams and the battens parallel and to rely on cutting the seams curved to shape the sail. The outline of the sail is then straight at the mast and boom—although some designers favor some slight curve along the foot. The battens going right across the sail permit any amount of roach and the upper battens may have different angles so they can hold a considerable curve towards the top (Fig. 10-9D).

For this arrangement it may be possible to have the battens and seams coinciding, but if the class rules specify batten spacing that cannot be made to match the cloth widths, the batten pockets may have to be arranged as they come and seams as they will.

The sail plan is laid out, with the location of all battens marked. Cloths have to be cut to get the required draft of the sail. The amount of curve to be cut is only slight and should follow a fair curve for the length of the seam, although if the center one-third is straight there will be little difference in the sail draft. It is useful to be able to seal the edge at the same time as it is cut. This can be done with a specially heated knife, or an electric soldering bit, with its end filed to a knife shape.

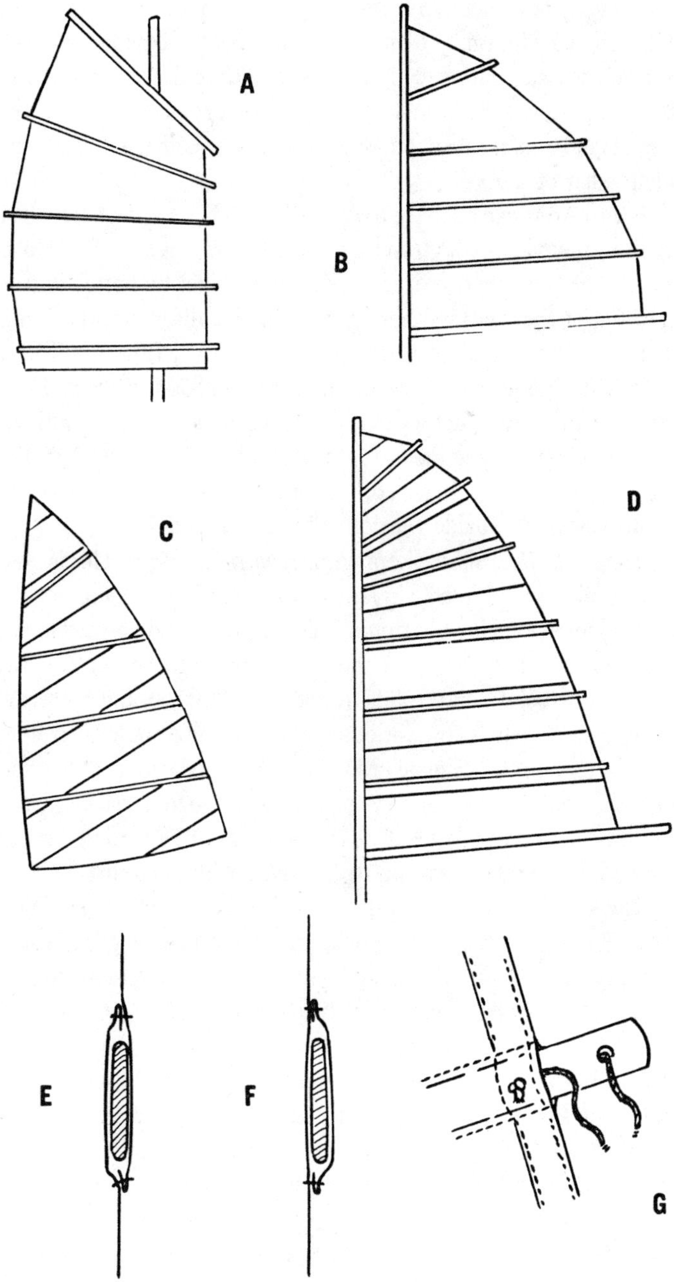

Fig. 10-9. A junk sail is fully battened. The battens may be sleeved.

Deciding how much to curve an edge is a matter of experience, but 1 inch in 10 feet might be considered. As the amount of curve required in a sail varies with wind strength and the direction of sailing, any curve built in must be a compromise. Ideally, the greatest curve should be about one-third of the seam length from the leading edge of the sail.

If the seams can be made to coincide with batten positions, they may be made wide enough to take the battens (Fig. 10-9E). However, the battens impose extra loads and it might be better to sew the cloths of the sail together first, then add the batten pockets, either over the seams or at the designed spacing (Fig. 10-9F).

It is desirable to be able to adjust the tension of the sail and batten, so it is unsatisfactory to try to fix battens in pockets without lacing. A batten may come within the length of a pocket, but it is more likely to project, then a cord through a hole near the end of the batten is used to provide tension (Fig. 10-9G and 10-8).

The lower battens are kept parallel with the boom. This is best aerodynamically and is convenient if roller reefing is used.

The edges of a fully-battened sail are tabled and finished in the same way as other sails, but there may need to be some extra reinforcing at points on the luff to take the thrust of the battens.

A junk sail may follow various outlines. There are local preferences for use on the original craft, but for a modern yacht the sail may have the bulk of the battens parallel with the foot, or nearly so, then an increase in angle towards the head, where a yard that is set fairly high-peaked is drawn up to the mast with a halliard.

The sail may be made with vertical or horizontal cloths. With natural fiber cloths there was some advantage in strength in using vertical cloths, but with synthetic fiber cloths it may be more convenient to use horizontal cloths. It is convenient to regard the leading edge of the sail as vertical and the foot at right angles to this (Fig. 10-10A). Both edge and foot may be cut to curves, but their original design lines are straight. The head is comparatively short and tilted to rather more upright than 45 degrees. The other edge starts near parallel to the leading edge, then curves around to the yard (Fig. 10-10B). This may be treated like a roach and the "curve" becomes straight lines between batten positions (Fig. 10-10C). There is no boom and the bottom of the sail projects loose-footed below the lowest batten.

With the sail shape set out on the floor, make up with cloths starting at the bottom. Seams may remain parallel with the bottom right to the top, but there may be some advantage in cutting the top seams so they approximate to the angles of the battens. The curved edges will cause some draft in the sail, but it is usual for them to be kept fairly flat by the battens.

The battens may be flat wood, they could be plastic, or they may be stout bamboo canes on the mast side of the sail and rather lighter ones on the other side. These are secured by lashings at their ends and by intermediate lashings through the sail. An alternative would be to have the light batten in a pocket and only the stout batten external. The external batten is needed to bear against the mast and be attached to it with parrels.

The leading edge of the sail and the foot may be tabled by turning in the cloth. The head and the other edge are better tabled with applied pieces cut from the edges. The sail is kept up by the yard. There should be large corner grommets through patches and more grommets for lacing along that edge (Fig. 10-10D).

A junk sail is sheeted to the ends of the battens. There are usually no sheets to the bottom corners of the sail, so there is no need for much patching there.

There should be patches at each batten position, with one or a pair of grommets for lashing to the battens. There may be individual patches across the sail for more grommets that will take the lashings through the sail, but it will probably be better to sew on a tape (Fig. 10-10E). Even if the lighter batten is inside a pocket, these grommets will still be needed to secure the external batten (Fig. 10-10F).

There are no reefing arrangements, as such, on the sail itself. Instead, reefing is done by lines which gather up the bottom of the sail, one batten at a time, until the required reduction in area has been achieved.

In practice there may be need for more patches at points of strain or wear, as in the vicinity of the parrels to the mast. In such a sail which is not allowed much movement between battens, local stresses may cause loads of stitching, grommets, and other attachments.

OTHER RIGS

Much experimenting is always taking place to make sailing boats more efficient or faster. There are double sails. Others are

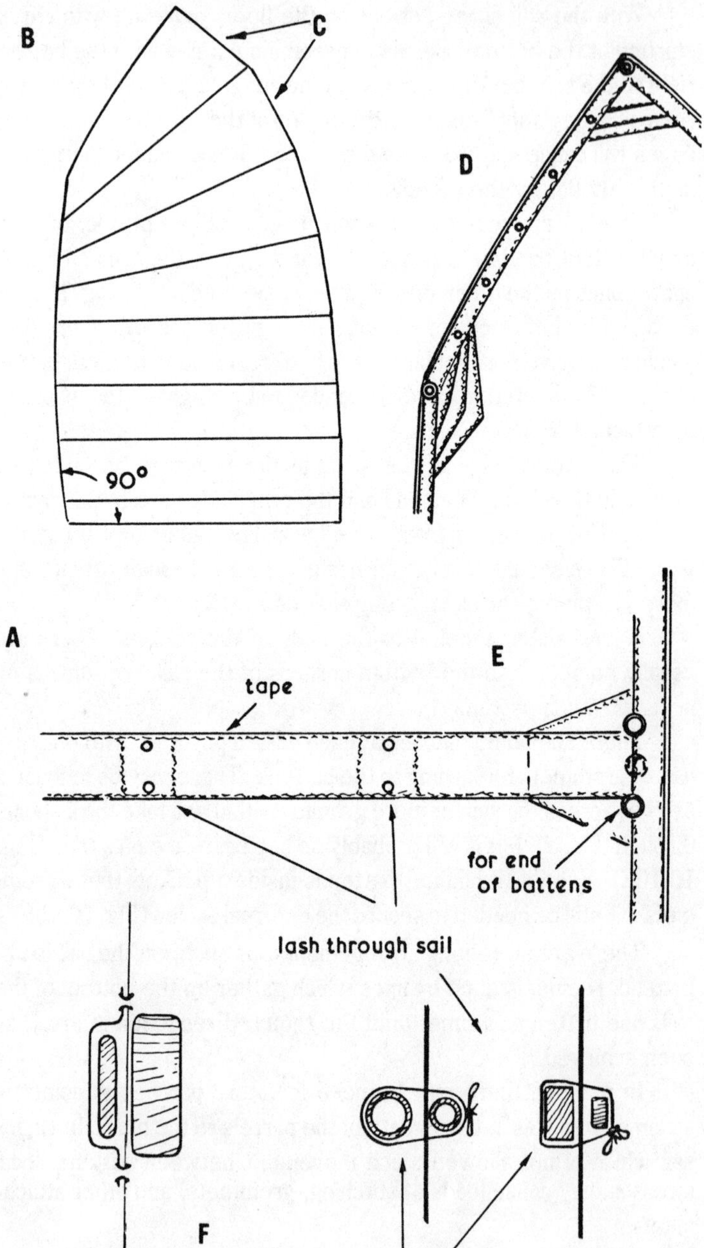

Fig. 10-10. Battens of a junk sail may be each side of the sail and arranged at angles to give shape at the top.

arranged in a series of slots so air from the inside of one part goes over the outside of another part. When making sails for this sort of thing, where original concepts are sketchy and uncertain, there are a few points to watch that are applicable, whatever the overall design of the sail.

If a sail is to go to windward properly, its leading edge must be as taut as possible. If the sail comes aft of a mast, that keeps it stiff. If there is a stay to which the sail is fastened, that keeps it tight. If the tautness has to be provided by the sail itself, a wire rope along the luff or equivalent part of the sail is almost essential.

The sail should set into an aerodynamically correct curve. This normally has its greatest curve nearer the leading edge than the trailing edge. This is much more efficient if the same angle of attack to the wind, when going to windward, can be maintained throughout the whole height of the sail than if the top of the sail falls off the wind. Maintaining an equal angle of attack is one of the reasons for experimenting and the best that can be done may be far from perfect.

If details of construction are left to the sailmaker, an abrupt change of section should be avoided. Several overlapping patches in decreasing sizes are better, both for strength, and for the set of the sail, than having several patches all the same size. Edges may be tabled or taped. Roping is often necessary for strength. If it comes on an edge over which the air flows, there will be a slight turbulence as the air leaves the edge. It may be preferable, therefore, to strengthen in some way other than roping a trailing edge, although any difference in performance is not likely to be very marked. However, for experimental work, which may be tested in a wind tunnel, every little bit helps.

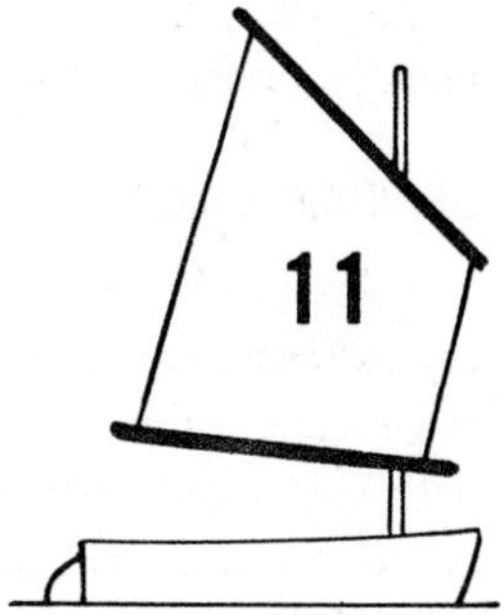

Light Weather Sails

The normal rig of a yacht will be suitable for use over a large range of wind strengths. When the wind strengthens it is possible to reduce the sail area by reefing and by changing head sails for smaller ones. When the wind is light there may be larger head sails replacing the working ones.

For a great part of the time a yacht is sailed there will be no need for any other sails. On rare occasions a yacht may be caught out in winds so strong that the yacht becomes unsafe, even with fully reefed normal sails, yet it is necessary to continue sailing to make port or get off a lee shore. (Otherwise, all sail could be lowered and the yacht allowed to drift under bare piles.) More often in the usual yachting conditions winds are so light they are almost non-existent and there is a need for sails that will make the most of what air can be found. In the days of commercial sail, there were extra sails to hang below square sails or extend them outwards. Fore and aft sails could have pieces added, and the top sails already described might only be used in light airs.

Such methods of increasing sail area are not applicable to modern yachts. The techniques used to add more canvas were really only applicable to occasions when the wind was aft of the beam. Extra canvas, added where convenient and not necessarily aerodynamically applicable, worked for downwind sailing. But it would not be very effective on a reach or with the wind forward of the beam, unless it was more scientifically designed than it usually was.

It is unusual to do anything to increase the size of a main sail for light airs, but with more of the total sail area in the fore triangle it can be effective to use reacher or genoa instead of the working jib. The further step, however, used on many racing craft and used increasingly by cruisers, is to hoist a *spinnaker*.

SPINNAKER RIGGING

A spinnaker is a very light sail, used outside all stays to catch and use as much of the lightest breeze it can and convert it to forward movement of the boat. Spinnakers have developed from being sails with little more curve than some of the larger head sails, to very deeply curved shapes. These latter were once called *parachute spinnakers* to distinguish them from the flatter ones, but now that all spinnakers are this shape, the word "parachute" is rarely used.

A spinnaker is used with the wind aft to billow out ahead and pull the boat along. It can be set with the wind on the beam or forward of it, when it acts in much the same way as a jib, but its curve makes management difficult and care is needed to make the sail draw the boat forward instead of part of the sail tending to blow it back.

The method of hoisting a spinnaker allows it to be used with another head sail, or for it to be gotten into position before the other head sail is lowered. Normally the main sail is in use and in a following wind sheets have to be manipulated so the main sail does not blanket the spinnaker and keep air from it. With the wind abeam, the spinnaker directs a considerable amount of air to the back of the main sail, which has to be adjusted accordingly.

There have been many ideas about how spinnakers are made and used, but the majority follow a common method of rigging, even if there are peculiarities about the way cloths are made up. The head is hoisted with a swivel. If the sail is used for racing, quick action is important and clips or other attachments are permanently fixed to the sail. The head clip engages with one on a halliard (Fig. 11-1A). The bottom corners may both be called clews, but the one to windward, to which a spinnaker pile is attached, is better called a *tack*. The other corner takes a sheet and the name clew agrees with this point of other sails.

The spinnaker pole has a clip to the mast and the outboard end engages with a ring on the sail. Also at that corner is a clip to a guy or brace (Fig. 11-1B). The pole is also regulated by an uphaul and

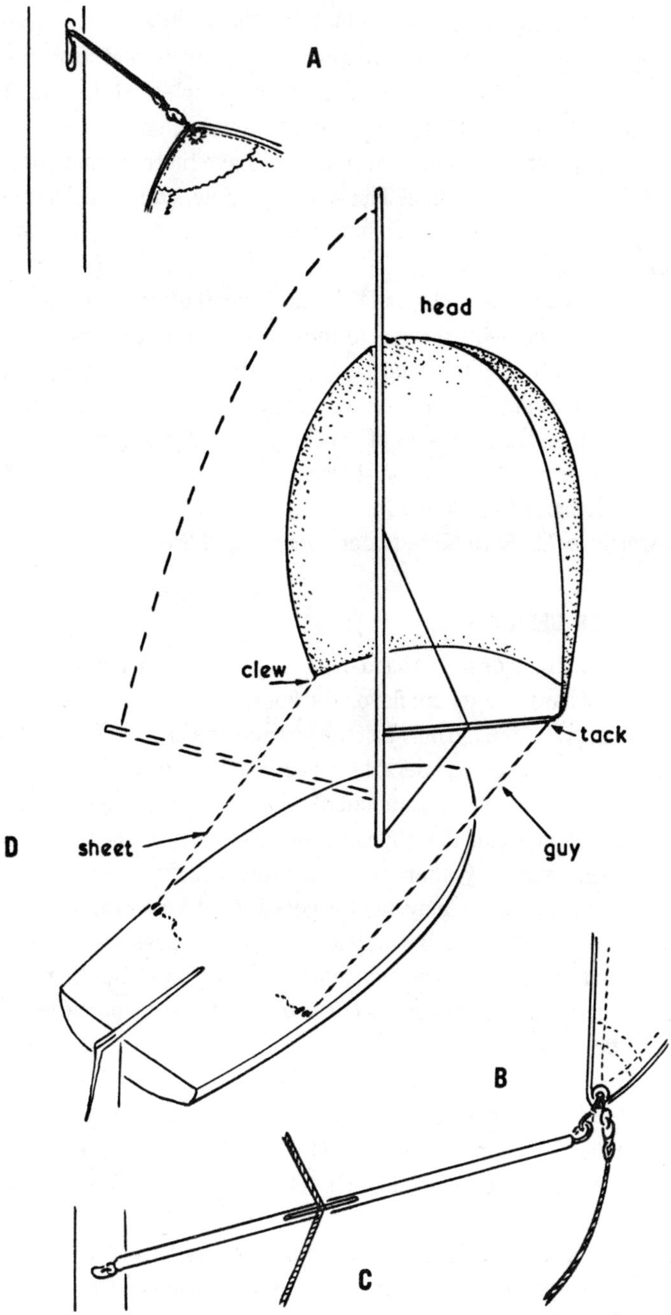

Fig. 11-1. A spinnaker has considerable curve and is hoisted outside of other sails and rigging.

downhaul line to the mast (Fig. 11-1C). These allow the tack to be raised or lowered, and the guy moves it backward and forwards.

At the other side the arrangements are simpler, with a sheet to control the sail (Fig. 11-1D). Tack and clew may change functions when the yacht goes about, so the sail is symmetrical and corner arrangements are the same. The spinnaker pole, with its uphaul and downhaul may change over, but the sail remains the same way round.

Spinnakers are never used in heavy weather. They come into their own in the lightest airs, so they have to be made as light as possible for a wind of minimum strength to blow them into shape and set them working. Consequently, spinnaker cloth is always much lighter than that of other sails of a yacht and the elasticity of nylon has advantages over the more usual Dacron for this particular sail. The type of cloth used will depend on the size of the sail and the craft, but its weight is likely to be between 1/2 oz. and 2 oz.

SPINNAKER DESIGN

Although the desired shape of spinnakers is almost hemispherical, the sail has to be set out flat on the floor. This is normally done by using a central seam, so only half the sail need be drawn. The central joint needs to have considerable curve when developed to the flat outline on the floor and the amount of this curve is the major factor in determining the shape the spinnaker will take when it fills with a light breeze. Unfortunately, there is no easy way of arriving at a curve. A professional sailmaker may say he gets the curve as the result of experience, which is another way of saying it is a guess based on a lot of trail and error. This is not much use to a beginner, but there are some dimensions that will give a curve that may be acceptable as it is or can be modified.

Two base lines are laid down at right angles (Fig. 11-2A). These follow leech and foot. The foot curves downward with a symmetrical curve about 1 inch in 1 foot (Fig. 11-2B). The leech curve may be about 1 inch in 2 feet (Fig. 11-2C). The center of the foot is at the bottom of the center seam.

If the sailmaker does not have a design size to follow, the foot may be assumed to set as part of a circle when viewed from above, somewhere between one-third and one-half of a complete circumference. The width of sail to be set out on the floor is half of this

(Fig. 11-2D). The height of a leech is probably about the same as the luff of a normal head sail. This will be curved, but a spinnaker is used with its foot higher than the foot of a working sail.

Divide the set-out height into four with lines drawn across at right angles to the straight leech line. Mark the width of the foot on the bottom line. A reasonable curve can be drawn if points are marked on the other lines at distances from the straight leech line proportional to this. Suggested proportions are shown on the drawing (Fig. 11-2E). Bend a piece of wood through these points to get the curve. It is unlikely that a fair curve will come exactly through the points, but let the lath average out the positions so a smooth line can be drawn around it.

Laying the cloths across the sail is probably the best method to use for your first spinnaker. They can be in mixed or alternate colors. Even when other sails are fairly conservative in appearance the spinnaker may be decorative in bright colors, with emblems or motifs added.

SPINNAKER CONSTRUCTION

Lower seams may be made of full-width cloths laid at right angles to the leech (Fig. 11-2F). This arrangement can be continued right to the top, but the shape the sail sets may be improved by angling upper seams (Fig. 11-2G).

In the lower part of the sail there is less compound curvature required, as the bottom cloths do little more than wrap around as part of a circle. Further up the cloths may be cut to improve the curve in other directions. Edges, particularly of the angled cloths, are cut on a slight curve, preferably with a special electrically heated knife or a sharpened soldering bit, so edges are sealed automatically. Although a curve going the full length of a seam may be ideal, it should be sufficient to leave about half the length straight near the center and only curve the ends (Fig. 11-2H). Like other curves on the sail, determining how much to shape a seam is a matter of experience, but on a 5 foot length of seam the ends of each meeting panel may be curved back about 1/2 inch.

The sail is made up by sewing the seams. Strike-up marks may be important, if the light material is to be kept properly in register and one cloth is not to move on the other and finish with wrinkles or creases. When making the center seam the sail looks best if the

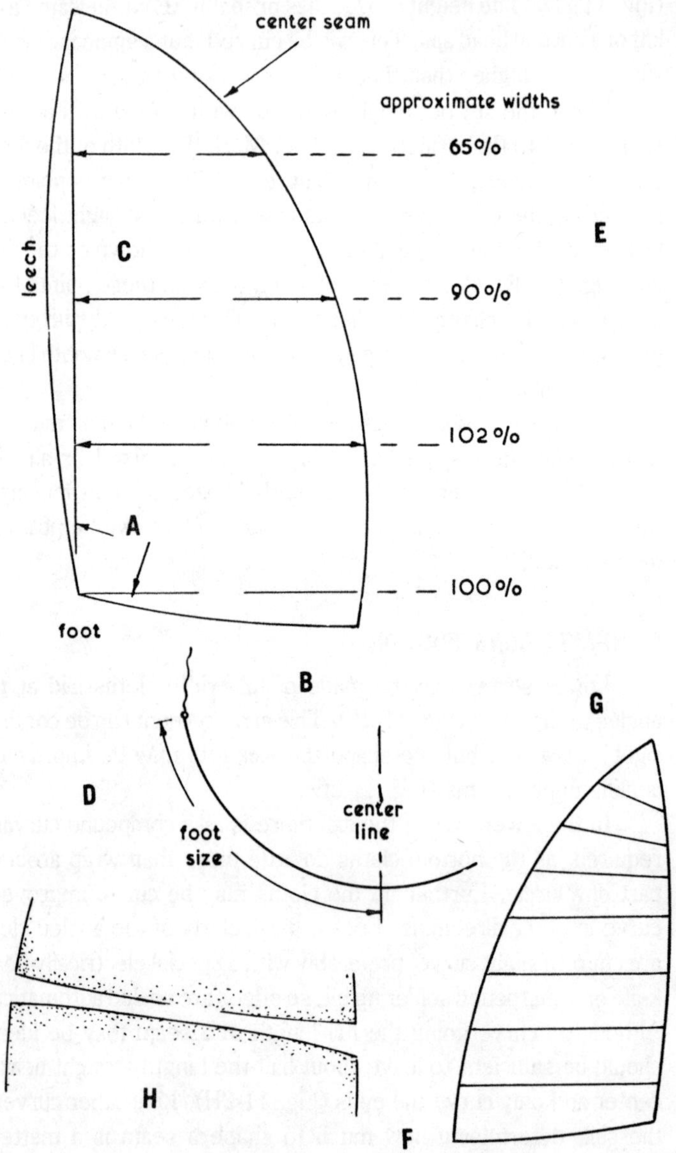

Fig. 11-2. The shape of a spinnaker is mainly due to the curve of the center seam, but there may also be some shaping of cloths.

horizontal seams meet, but sewing will be easier if they are staggered slightly so fewer thicknesses of cloth have to go through the machine.

Corner patches can be simple rounded triangles, with several thicknesses for a large sail. It is an advantage to let the weave of the patches be the same as that of the sail at the point they are fitted. Head patches will be fairly wide and may be rather bigger than those at the bottom corners (Fig. 11-3A). They may also contain a metal or plastic headboard, which helps in holding the sail to shape.

It should be satisfactory to merely table the three edges by turning in the cloth itself, although an applied tabling from the waste cut off could be used if preferred.

Additional taping of the edge may be advisable (Fig. 11-3B). On a large sail this may be doubled. Although some stretch in the body of the sail is desirable, there should be some restriction around the edges, but this should be the same material. There may be some advantage in using different colored tapes on the three edges for easy identification. A spinnaker is a large sail compared with others on the yacht and it is often needed to be hoisted quickly, so anything that helps in finding the correct sides and corners may be justified. If the sail is flaked down properly or it is stowed in a chute, it can be kept ready for hoisting, but there will still be occasions when it is helpful to be able to sort out parts of the sail without the need for opening it fully.

Some large spinnakers have the edges further strengthened by roping, which may be a quite light line or even a thin wire rope. This is included in the tabling or taping and should not be arranged so it restricts sail set by being fixed at intervals that prevent the sail from finding its own shape. However, once the sail has settled to its shape, it would be better to prevent the very light cloth sliding on the rope and assuming a creased and unsatisfactory shape after being lowered and hoisted again. It will probably be best to leave the ends of the line exposed so a first hoist can be made and the line adjusted before enclosing the ends and stitching at intervals to keep the roping in position.

SPINNAKER FITTINGS

At the corners of a spinnaker there should be secure grommets, which may be metal ones fixed with punch and die for small sails, but sewn ones are better for large spinnakers. The head may have a clip or other attachment to mate with the fitting on the halliard premanently fixed. This can be lashed on a small sail, or shackled to a large one. It is important to have a swivel in the system, usually in the halliard fitting, so any twist in the sail or halliard will unwind (Fig. 11-3C).

At the two lower corners, which may change from clew to tack, both should be equipped in the same way. There should be a ring to engage with the hook or other fitting on the spinnaker pole, as well as a quick-action clip to engage with the sheet or guy (Fig. 11-3D).

When the spinnaker is hoisted both it and all lines attached to it go outside all other rigging, with the pole set on the side of the mast opposite to the main sail.

The lowered spinnaker may be kept in a bucket or bin. In some cases it may be stowed under a net with a roller across its front edge. If the three corners project forward under the roller, the halliard, sheet and guy, as well as the end of the pole, can be attached before the halliard is pulled to bring the sail almost automatically into the set position (Fig. 11-3E). There are no modifications to the sail that the sailmaker need make for this method of stowing.

If a chute is used, the sail has to be pulled through a funnel on the deck and this may be done by letting the halliard be a continuous line, thus eliminating the risk of one end going adrift (Fig. 11-3F). The retrieving line has to be attached to a patch below the geometric center of the sail. Locating it about 9 inches below should be satisfactory for average-sized sails (Fig. 11-3G). The patching may be done on both sides, with a stout tape loop for the attachment on a small sail, or some grommets to allow lashing the attachment on a larger sail (Fig. 11-3H).

Guy and sheet may remain attached to the sail and follow it into the chute, then as the sail is hoisted the only extra work is attaching the pole as the tack emerges.

OTHER SPINNAKER PATTERNS

With the need to get a balloon or parachute form to the sail when it sets, it is obvious that there are a great many ways that cloths can be cut and arranged to produce the desired result. Very complex methods of cutting and seaming have been used, often with combinations of colored cloths to give rather startling effects.

It is possible to have the seams parallel with the leech and achieve a reasonable shape. This is probably the most economical way of making a spinnaker. The sail outline is the same as that for a

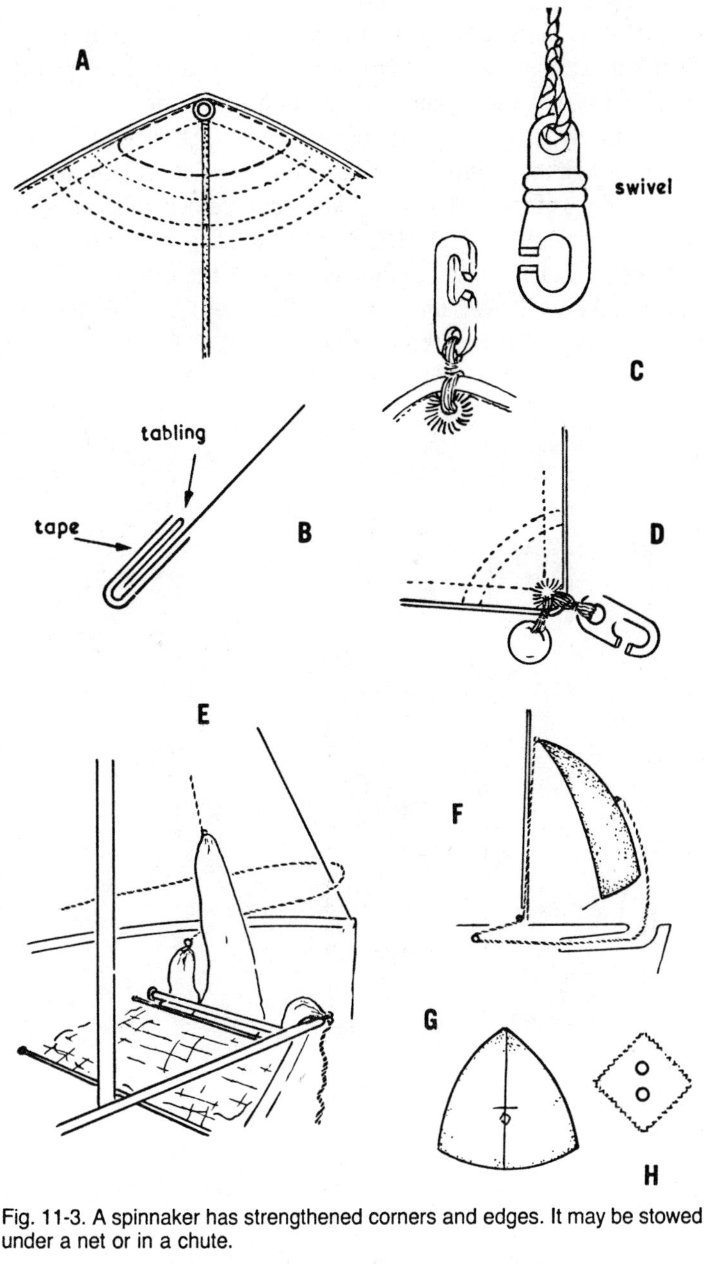

Fig. 11-3. A spinnaker has strengthened corners and edges. It may be stowed under a net or in a chute.

cross-cut sail. Have the first cloth parallel with the straight line which makes a chord of the leech curve, but with enough overlap to allow for tabling (Fig. 11-4A). Continue to mark more cloths across the sail

(Fig. 11-4B). Mark the seams in the usual way with strike-up marks. Even with straight seams and parallel cloths the final shape may be satisfactory, but there can be some shaping by curving meeting edges slightly towards the top of each seam (Fig. 11-4C).

Although the seams appear vertical on the floor plan, when the curved edges of the two parts are brought together, they will slope inwards and meet (Fig. 11-4D). Slight staggering of the seam ends will reduce their bulk where they go through the sewing machine. This should be allowed for when marking the outlines of the two halves of the sail flat on the floor before joining them.

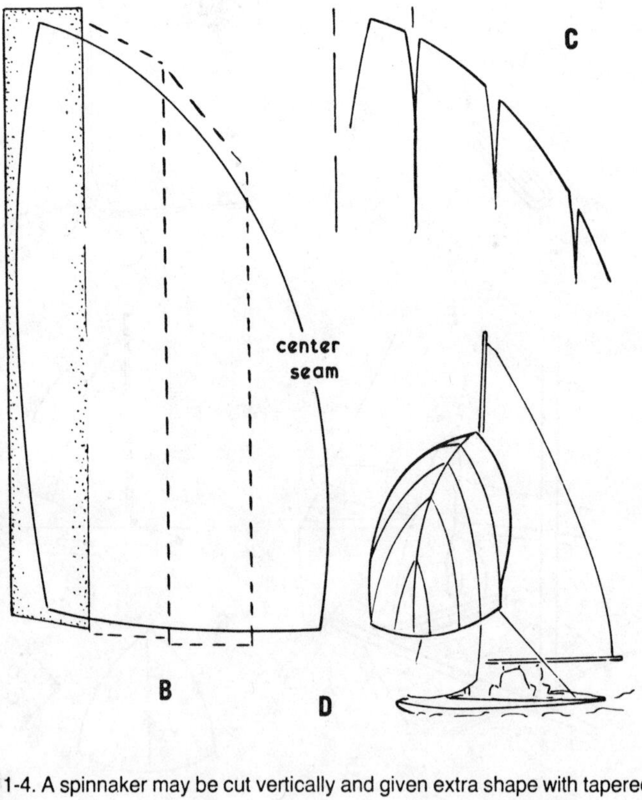

Fig. 11-4. A spinnaker may be cut vertically and given extra shape with tapered seams.

The obvious next step is a combination of vertical and cross-cut cloths. The lower part of a spinnaker has a mainly wrap-around curve, while the top needs more shaping to bring the pointed part into a compound curve. A spinnaker can be made with two or three lower cloths laid across, then the upper part laid with vertical cloths, given tapered seams towards the top (Fig. 11-5A) or with a series of cloths radiating from the head and cut with predetermined curves (Fig. 11-5B).

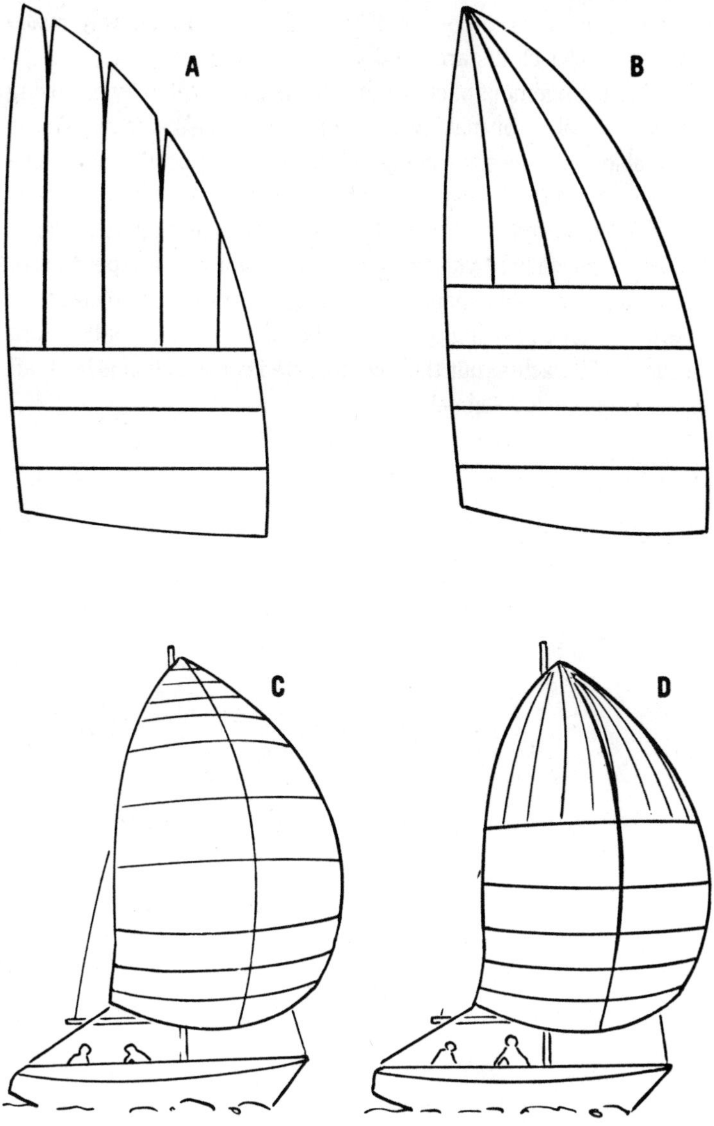

Fig. 11-5. Cloths may be laid in several directions and tapered to achieve the correct shape.

The width of a cloth does not provide much compound curvature, except for any elasticity in the cloth. The cloths may be full width across the middle part of the spinnaker, then more shaping above and below that becomes possible if narrower cloths are used and their edges are curved (Fig. 11-5C). This may have all the cloths cross-cut, or only the bottom of the sail treated in this way, while tapered upright cloths are used at the top (Fig. 11-5D).

The arrangement of cloths may be mainly for effect when using a variety of colors or making up a personal or class pattern. This is acceptable, but excessive complication does not necessarily mean a better spinnaker. The sailmaker should guard against cutting cloths into narrow pieces with curved edges so the sail requires a large number of carefully sewn seams, any one of which could spoil the set of the sail if errors in shaping or sewing were allowed to creep in. There are some pleasing patterns to be seen and some of them are on successful yachts, but their complicated construction is best left to the experienced sailmaker.

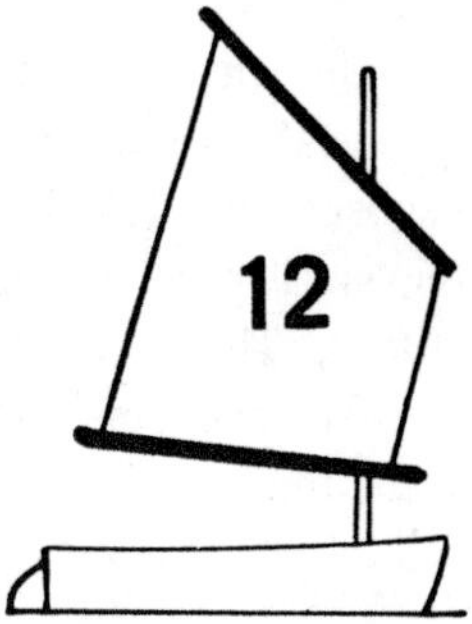

Heavy Weather Sails

The average yachtsman hopes he will never be caught out in winds of such velocity that conditions become hazardous. He hopes he can choose the occasions when he leaves port so he may have an enjoyable sail without risk. He is usually more concerned with light weather sails when planning how to equip his yacht. If his yachting is confined to local sailing for not more than day at a time or to brief coastal cruises with a port as haven every night, he may never need to consider how he will cope with really bad weather, unless he is extremely careless in interpreting weather forecasts or is very unlucky.

The yachtsman who is more ambitious and plans cruises that take him offshore for several days cannot run for port in time to always avoid bad weather, and he should know how he would deal with high winds and the sea conditions they produce. This may mean the provision of special sails kept for these conditions.

Of course progressive reduction of the area of working sails will take care of deteriorating conditions to a certain point. A main sail reefed down to its normal limit and the smallest working head sail, may deal with all but the worst conditions. At one time the grade of natural fiber canvas used for working sails might have been suspect in storm conditions, but Dacron has strength far beyond the needs of fair weather sailing and working sails may now be trusted in winds up to considerable strength.

There is one problem in using maximum main sail reefing and a small jib. The sail balance may be affected so steering becomes difficult if a course is to be maintained. As the main sail is reefed, its center of effort moves forward (Fig. 12-1A). The use of a jib much smaller than usual does something to correct this, but if the smaller area there has its tack in the usual place, the center of effort ahead of the mast is also further forward than when the working area is exposed (Fig. 12-1B). Some improvement can be obtained by using this smaller sail higher (Fig. 12-1C), bringing its center of effort a little aft. This also helps keep the bow up by giving a little more lift.

The effect of moving the center of effort forward is to make the yacht tend to turn downwind if left unattended, which is almost

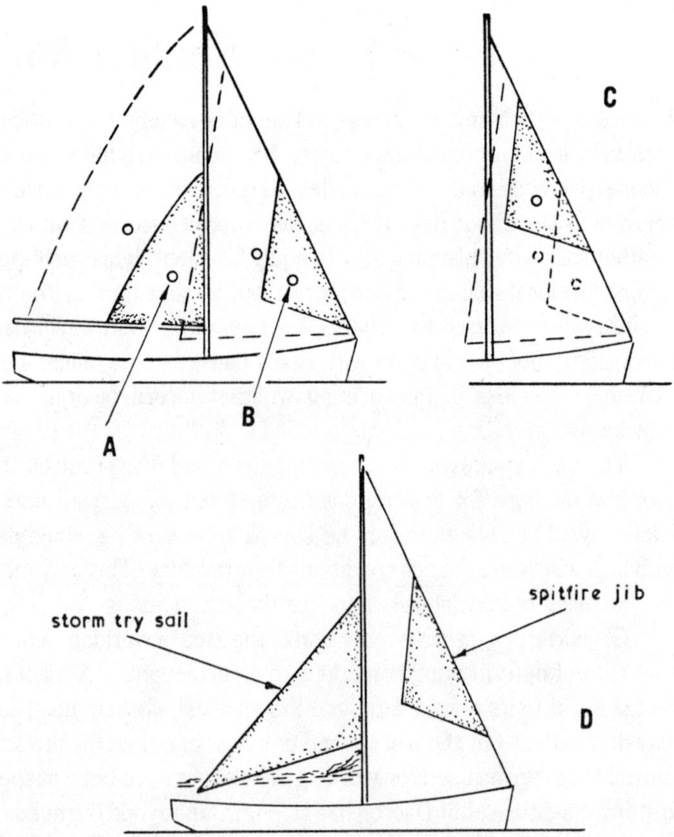

Fig. 12-1. Heavy weather sails have to be arranged so the combined center of effort is as close as possible to that of the working sails.

always dangerous, as progress that way might be impossible to stop if the yacht resisted the use of the helm to turn into wind. If there is plenty of sea room, running before the wind might be the best thing to do with some craft, but if there is a lee shore ahead, the yacht could be heading for disaster.

If a yacht is to be kept under control in heavy weather it is better to lower the main sail completely and replace it with a smaller sail that has its center of effort further aft than that of the fully reefed main sail. This is a *storm try sail*, and the small head sail used with it is usually called a *spitfire jib* (Fig. 12-1D).

STORM TRY SAIL

A storm try sail has to be hoisted without taking the main sail off—something that could be impossible in storm conditions. Instead, the main sail is brought down to the boom and gathered to it. If there is a track on the mast the main sail may be lowered far enough to disengage from this so the try sail can be hoisted with its own slides engaging the same track from the bottom. In a better arrangement there is either a completely separate track for the try sail or a short length of track, enough to take all the slides of the try sail, alongside the bottom of the main track, then a switch leading into the main track a short distance up the mast. The alternative is to use *parallels* at intervals, with toggles and eyes to go around the mast (Fig. 12-2A).

The try sail is normally loose-footed and without a boom. When set, it should have its foot high enough above the gathered main sail, so there is a tack line, possibly permanently spliced to the sail and with a shackle or other fitting to engage with the gooseneck fitting (Fig. 12-2B). Its length is already fixed so it acts as a downhaul to keep the tack at the intended height.

There are two ways of sheeting the try sail. There may be a clew line to attach it to the boom, then the normal sheeting is used to control the sail. Some of the weight of the boom should be taken by the topping lift. It may be given a pair of sheets like a head sail. In that case the boom is lashed down and not used, but the sheets go to blocks at each side of the deck.

Try sail and spitfire jib need to be made of much heavier cloth than that used for working sails. The weight to choose depends on the size of the sail and the yacht, but half as heavy again or double the weight. For a small yacht using 4 oz. cloth for working sails, 6 oz. or 7 oz. would be suitable. The thread used should be proportionately stronger and grommets, metal eyelets and anything else attached to the sail should be about twice the size and strength normally used.

The foot of a try sail should be a little less than that of the main sail. The distance up the mast may be about the same as the foot, or somewhat less. The clew should be lower than the tack so it is at a suitable height for attaching to the boom, if that method is used, or below the level of the boom in its crutch if it is sheeted independently (Fig. 12-2C).

Cloths are usually laid parallel with the leech (Fig. 12-2D). Include enough false seams to give a spacing no more than 12 inches. The sail needs to set fairly flat, so only slight curves are given to leech and luff (Fig. 12-2E), but the foot may be given more curve (Fig. 12-2F).

Patches may be basically triangular, but at clew and possibly head, extension patches may pass some of the strain along the edges (Fig. 12-2G). Use several thicknesses at each corner with sizes in steps, and several rows of stitching, so the load is shared and transferred without abrupt changes of section.

Allow for roping all around. The leech may be tabled by turning in the cloth, but at the other two edges apply tabling using strips cut from the edges. Although roping may be included in the tabling along the leech, it is probably better to enclose the rope in tape for this as well as the other edges (Fig. 12-2H). Traditionally, roping would have been hand sewn to one side of tabling, and this may have to be the method used if the many thicknesses of cloth and the stout thread are more than the available sewing machine can manage.

Whatever method of roping is used, the greatest strength is obtained if there is a continuous rope around the sail. The ends can be spliced together along one edge. Alternatively, they may overlap and be sewn to each other before covering with tape. Some reinforcing at the clew, where the greatest strain may be expected, can be obtained by overlapping the rope's ends there sufficiently to go around the corner with the double rope extending a few inches along each side, with ample hand stitches through the rope.

Grommets should be of the sewn type, using substantial rings, through which the cloth can be turned and adequately sewn over, with stitches of varying lengths and probably with reinforcing stitches to other back-up grommets (Fig. 6-8D). Rings and tapes

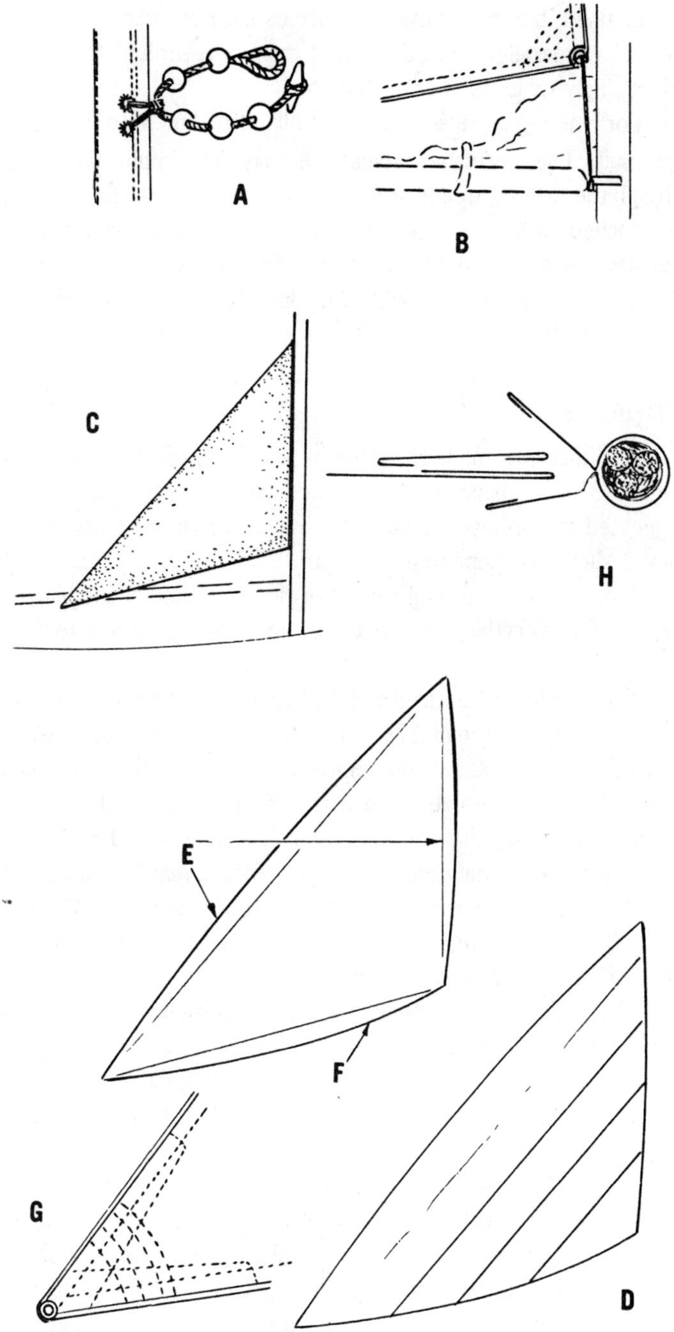

Fig. 12-2. A try sail sets above the furled main sail and is of strong construction.

may be used, but grommets are more usual. For the attachment of sail slides or parallels along the luff, fit grommets through the tabling, either singly or in pairs at each point.

For hoisting there should be a similar attachment to that on the main sail. The permanent tack line may be simply eye-spliced through the tack grommet or there can be a shackle. The sheet can be attached to the clew in the same way. A try sail has to be prepared, attached to the mast and rigged ready for hoisting in difficult conditions, so it should be equipped and made as simple and robust as possible.

SPITFIRE JIB

A spitfire jib is made like other head sails and is usually miter cut (Fig. 12-3A). Its shape may be obtained with similar outlines to those suggested for ordinary head sails, but it has to set fairly flat, so curves should be kept to a minimum.

The points concerning weight of cloth, method of patching and the need for everything to be oversize are just as applicable to the jib as to the try sail.

The luff should be wired and the load taken by eyes that tension the wire, as in other head sails. Hanks to the fore stay should be easy to attach, but substantial enough to each take their share of what is likely to be a considerable strain in use. A rather closer spacing along the edge of the sail than on working sails is advisable (Fig. 12-3B). Hank attachments that embrace the wired edge may be expected to be stronger than hanks of similar size that rely on lashings. Whatever the method of attachments, have the luff sufficiently reinforced to a good width with enough tabling.

The tack line or pendant should be permanently spliced or shackled to the tack grommet. At its other end there should be a similar fitting to that used for normal jib attachment to the stem or deck fitting (Fig. 12-3C). Hoisting is done with the normal halliard. Adjust the length of tack line so the sail comes at a suitable height, but this may have to be related to the run of the sheets.

Normal head sail sheets may be used, but if the spitfire jib is being used in place of the single head sail of a sloop, the usual sheets may not lead far enough aft, and there will either have to be more fairleads located so the sheets can be moved, or there may be a second set of sheets provided.

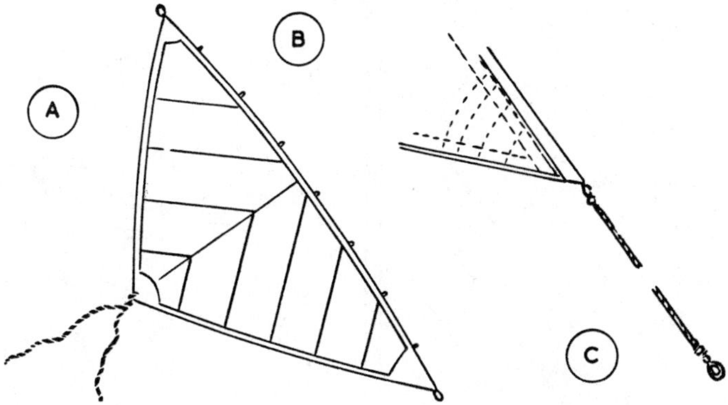

Fig. 12-3. A heavy weather head sail is made like a working jib, but stronger and with a tack line.

MIZZEN SAIL

In conditions so bad that maintaining a course becomes impossible or unwise, a yacht may heave to, using a reefed main sail or the try sail sheeted almost centrally and the spitfire jib backed, while the helm is lashed down. Different yachts behave in different ways and the best arrangement for a particular one has to be found. Craft which are primarily power-driven have a different problem when they meet similar weather conditions.

To keep a power boat head to wind, which is normally its safest position, in severe conditions, a small sail aft will have a weather vane effect. Ideally, this would be a mizzen mast (Fig. 12-4A). A boat used for fishing may have such a mast, but for other craft there may be a way devised to use existing superstructure or the signal mast (Fig. 12-4B).

Such a sail need not be very substantial for normal use in keeping the boat head to a light wind for fishing, but for storm conditions it needs to be substantial in the same way as a try sail. As the heavier sail would function in lighter airs, the one heavy sail need be the only one.

The actual sail area need not be very great as it is not intended to provide any propulsion. There should be enough curve to the leech for it not to look hollow and to take a head board, but the other edges may only have slight curves or be straight (Fig. 12-4C). Its function is as a vane and draft of any amount is not required.

Construction is similar to a storm try sail, with cloths parallel to the leech (Fig. 12-4D). The foot could be lashed to the boom, or

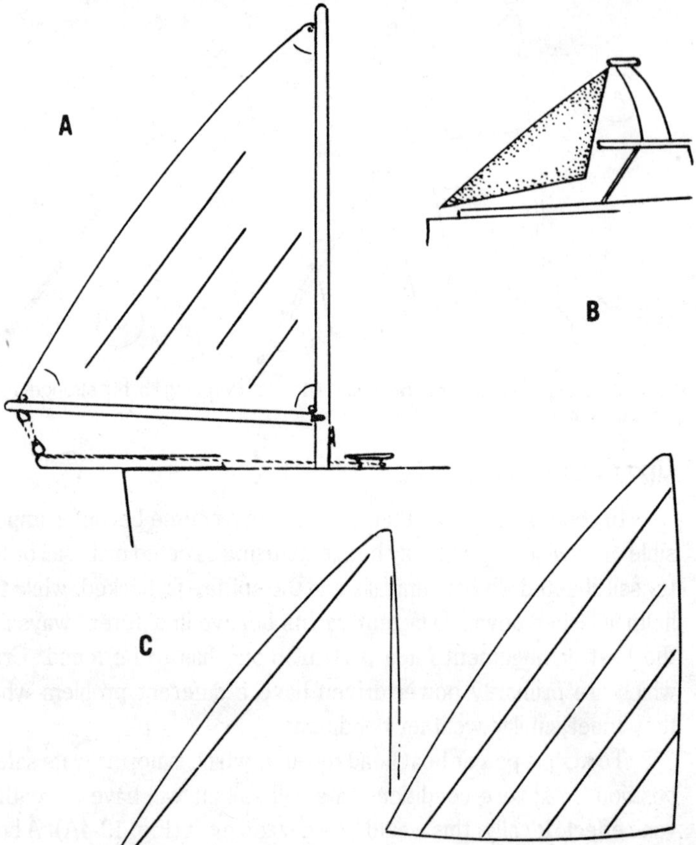

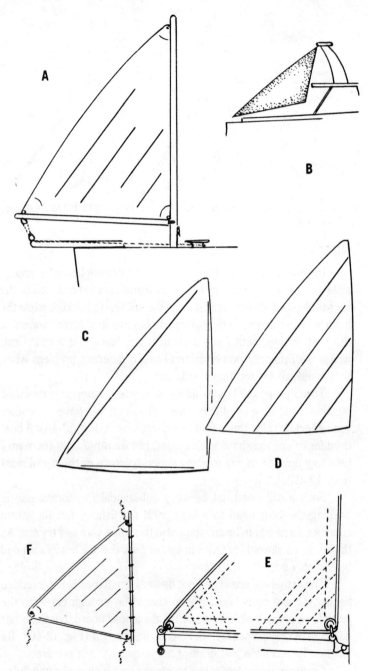

Fig. 12-4. A mizzen sail for heaving to in bad weather has to be designed to suit the boat and should be of strong construction.

merely attached at tack and clew (Fig. 12-4E). In a simple rig the luff may be lashed to the mast, providing this is within reach and it is possible for a man to do the job in bad conditions. Otherwise it may be better to use a track or have a roped edge in a grooved mast.

Roping all round is advisable. Clew and tack lines may be permanently spliced to the sail.

If an emergency mizzen sail is to be made for a boat without a suitable mast, where it has to be rigged with the aid of a shelter over a cockpit or something similar, the important thing is to have it vertical and central, as far aft as is practicable. The tack may be fixed to somewhere in the bottom of the boat, the head may be hauled to the top of the wheelhouse or shelter and the clew goes to a central point on the aft deck (Fig. 12-4F).

The sail has to be designed to suit the available space, but it becomes most effective if its leading edge can be as striaght and stiff as possible. The edge may be wired, so it can be tensioned as much as possible. It may be possible to include a light spar or piece of aluminum tube in the luff of the sail. The sail could be kept rolled around it ready for use. It may be possible to use a boathook or other spar, with the sail lashed to it through grommets. With the luff held stiff in this way and the clew pulled back to a central point, the best arrangement will have been made.

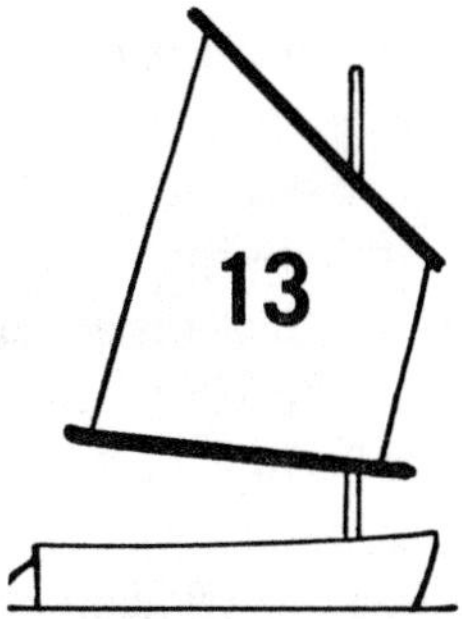

Reducing Sail Size

An introduction to sailmaking techniques for many amateurs may be the opportunity to adapt a discarded sail to suit a smaller craft. It may not be the best introduction, but it allows for professional methods to be examined and is an opportunity of learning techniques without the risk of damaging new materials. A sail that is no further use on a cruiser may appear to have possibilities in a reduced form for a dinghy or other small boat, or a large head sail that is being replaced may be retained in a smaller form as an addition to the suit of sails on the same yacht. Obviously, the idea of altering a sail that still has life in it, but is no longer needed for its original purpose, is attractive.

It can be done, but the limitations should be understood and any reduction of size carried out with these limitations in mind. A properly designed and made sail of a certain size will have its draft arranged by the curves of edges, the arrangement of tabling and roping, and possibly by shaping of panels. If the sail is made smaller, such built-in draft will be cut and the resulting draft of the new smaller sail may not be correctly proportioned to the new size. That does not mean the adapted sail would not work. It might still sail a boat, but it might not be quite as effective as a sail designed and made to the size. Sailing off the wind might not be affected appreciably, but a cut sail with the draft intended for a bigger one may not pull as well nor point as high when the wind is forward of the beam.

This means that a cut-down sail has its uses and it may be acceptable for a general-purpose small craft or as a reserve sail for a cruising yacht. It would not be satisfactory for racing or any occasion when nothing less than the best would be acceptable.

There are practical problems in cutting down a sail. It is no use merely drawing the new outline on the sail and cutting wherever these lines happen to come. It has probably been done, but this is not the method for anyone who claims to have some appreciation of sailmaking.

Note has to be taken of the direction of cloths in relation to edges. If cloths are at right angles to the leech or other edge, it is better to keep them this way in relation to a new leech. If they are parallel to an edge, the new outline should be arranged to keep them that way if at all possible. This was more important with cotton and other natural fibers, because serious distortion could occur due to changes in stretch. This is not such a problem with synthetic materials, but retaining the angles of the original sail will ensure the best chance of there still being a satisfactory draft.

What to do with edges also needs to be considered. If the length of edge has to be reduced something has to be done with tabling or other treatment and roping has to be altered. An added tabling strip could be cut and edges overlapped when the edge is reduced (Fig. 13-1A), but this is rather clumsy and it would be better to remove the tabling before reducing the edge, at least as far back as the cut, and sew it on again in one piece (Fig. 13-1B).

It is inadvisable to cut roping. If the rope does not have stitches through it, except at the ends, it will probably be possible to draw it out after the end stitches have been picked out. Much depends on the tightness of the stitching that forms the rope groove. If this can be done, a tabled edge can be cut and the new edges joined in a seam. A piece of thin line should be worked through the edge with a bodkin or blunt needle and this used to pull the rope through (Fig. 13-1C).

If it is a wired edge, the wire usually is slack in a wider pocket when the sail is not hoisted and the edge tensioned, so there should be no difficulty in withdrawing it, and pulling through the new shortened edge.

If the rope is taped to the edge it is better to unpick stitches and remove the roping as far as the cut, and sew it on again after making the reduction (Fig. 13-1D).

A roped edge is there to provide strength so it would be unsatisfactory to cut through roping as well as sail. When the shortened edge is sewn together again the cut rope would lack strength

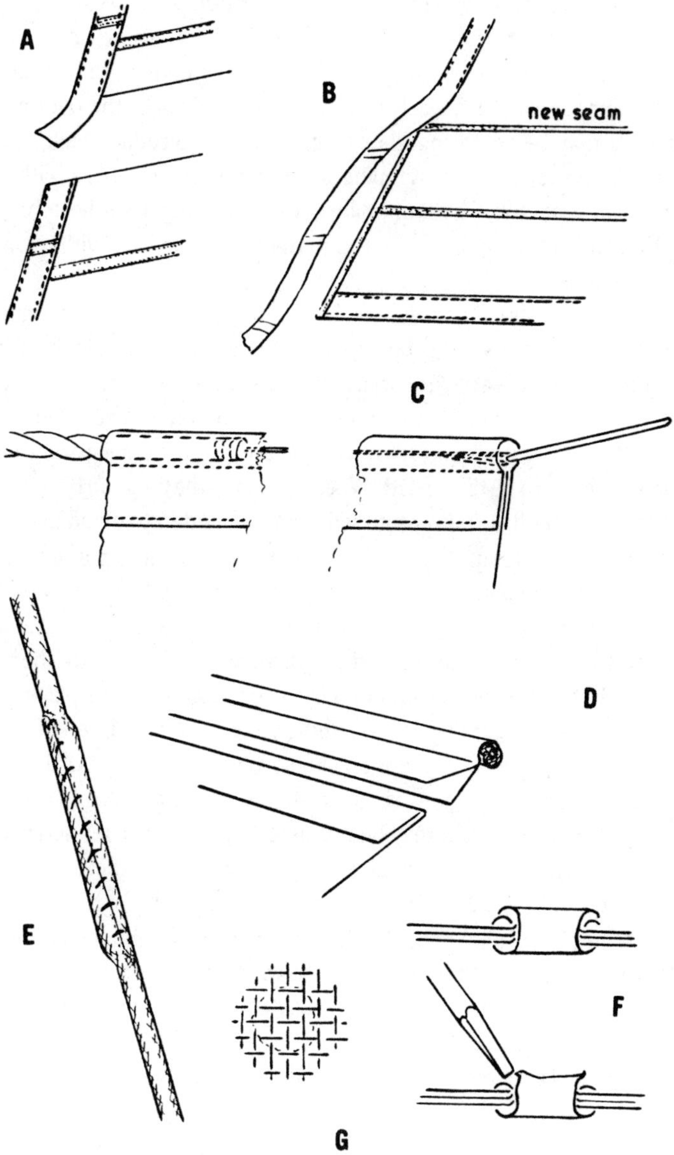

Fig. 13-1. When a sail is reduced in size tabling should be carried over, roping should be taken through without a joint, if possible, otherwise ends may be sewn. Old grommet holes should be darned.

to resist stretching along the edge. If roping is to be cut because it is impractical to remove and replace it in one length, the ends should be arranged to overlap in the remade sail. If the rope is large and three-stranded, it may be possible to splice the ends together, but for smaller ropes, particularly if they are braided rope, the overlapped ends may be sewn together (Fig. 13-1E). To reduce bulk, the ends may be tapered by scraping away some of the fibers with a sharp knife, but some bulk must be accepted, otherwise there may not be enough strength left. Arrange the tape or tabling with overlapping edges.

Things like head boards, sail hanks, and sewn grommets may have to be removed and repositioned. It is usually possible to pick out stitches and salvage these parts in a fit state to use again. Things that have to be expanded or shaped to fit are better discarded. In particular, metal eyelet grommets that are fitted by squeezing or punching, have to be discarded. Where possible they should be left in place, but if one has to be removed, care is needed to avoid undue damage to the surrounding fabric. With most types it is possible to use the end of a spike or thin screwdriver and coax back the metal that has been bent or expanded, so the parts can be separated and withdrawn without causing any more damage than is already there (Fig. 13-1F). If another grommet has to be put in the same place, it will have to be a larger one to have sufficient grip of what is left of the fabric edge, otherwise the edges should be darned (Fig. 13-1G).

When planning the new reduced shape, cuts may have to come in the body of a cloth or it may be possible to unpick stitches and use an edge again. If the stitched edge is a selvedge, there is the advantage that it is firm and will need no treatment before stitching again. A new edge should be sealed with heat, preferably by cutting with a heated knife, otherwise the edge will have to be turned under when a new seam is made. Stitches can be picked out with the point of a fine knife, although for the thin thread used for small sails a hook-type tool as used for unpicking domestic sewing may be useful.

Small reductions in size should be found to result in a new sail with satisfactory draft. If an edge is to be newly tabled or roped there may be some slight modification to the curve to suit the new size, but otherwise what shaping was already in the sail should suit the new size.

If a much smaller sail is made from a large one it may be found to have too little draft for its new purpose. Draft can be increased by tapering seams (Fig. 13-2A). Usually an increased shaping is needed in the leading part of the sail. Flatness towards the trailing part may be left. The length of tapering may be between one-third and one-half of the length of a seam from the forward edge.

If the amount of tapering needed is slight, the seam is unpicked and the edges given an increased overlap towards the edge (Fig. 13-2B). If much taper is required, it is better to cut the unpicked edges and sew them together again in a standard width seam (Fig. 13-2C). Making much of a taper without cutting the edges may cause puckering.

Tapering to get more fullness in the sail is obviously better done by slight tapering at many places than by too drastic tapering at a few places. If seams are few because cloths are wide, it may be advisable to cut intermediate darts between seams (Fig. 13-2D). Normally these should go as far as the tapered seams and have the same amount of taper. It would be less satisfactory to leave seams unaltered and depend only on darts.

It may be necessary to use darts along the foot of a cut-down sail to get satisfactory draft. This should be regarded as secondary to the use of tapered seams and darts towards the luff as cutting the cloths this way is less desirable, but they can be used. If possible, arrange the darts so seams are avoided (Fig. 13-2E), but if a seam has to be crossed, it may not matter except for the difficulty of keeping a smooth line to the taper when sewing the extra thicknesses.

It is easy to look at a sail obviously much bigger than the one to be cut from it and think that planning the shape will be easy. Besides the cut of the cloths in relation to the new shape, the pull of sheets, halliards, and other external items must be considered. Cutting down a head sail may alter the angle of the clew and the run of the seam if it is miter-cut. The pull of its sheet at an angle other than the ideal may have to be accepted, although it may be possible to manipulate the planned shape to keep discrepancies to a minimum.

With cutting down sails, the advice to measure twice before cutting once is very important. Make a drawing of the existing sail, with seams marked on it, and experiment with drawings of the intended sail superimposed on it to find the best way to lay out the new shape and cut so as to give the best results and be as economical in the work involved.

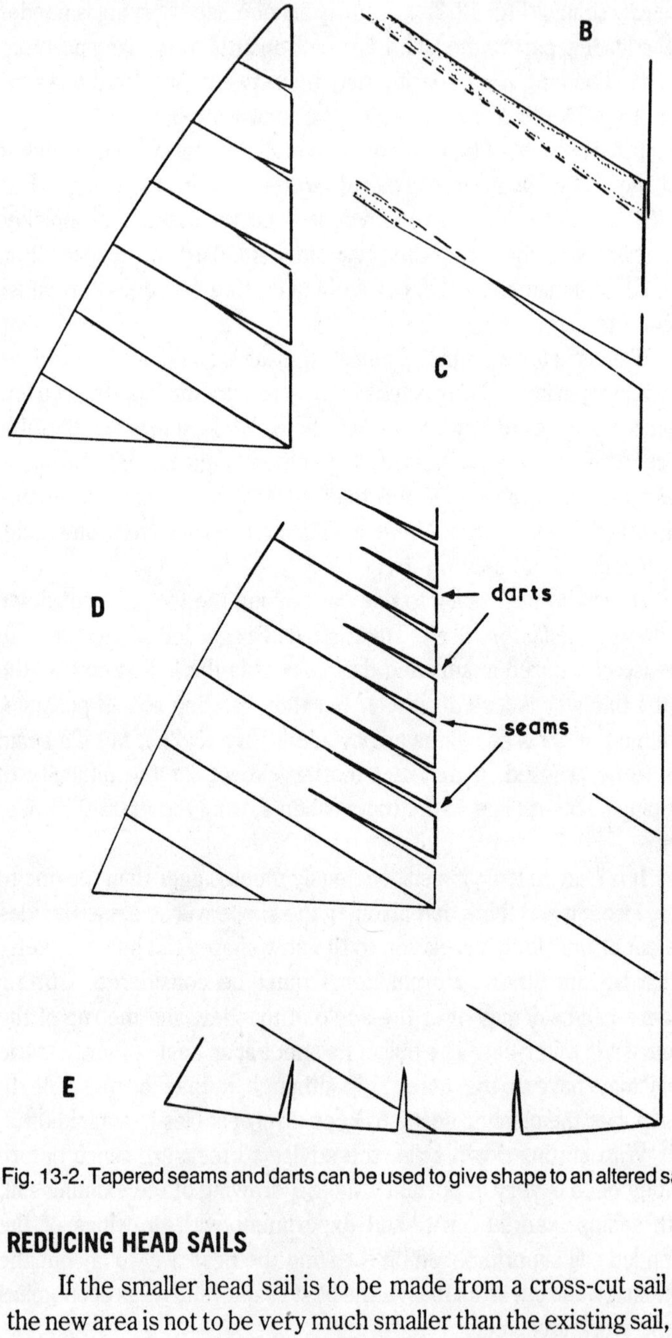

Fig. 13-2. Tapered seams and darts can be used to give shape to an altered sail.

REDUCING HEAD SAILS

If the smaller head sail is to be made from a cross-cut sail and the new area is not to be very much smaller than the existing sail, the angle of the clew and the direction of the pull of the sheet have to be considered. If the clew angle can be kept unaltered, reduction is made by cutting away the luff. A parallel cut (Fig. 13-3A) is simplest, but this has to be related to the pull of the sheet when the reduced sail is used, the clew can be raised by cutting the luff at an angle, either slightly out of parallel or from the existing tack to give a raised clew (Fig. 13-3B) or from the existing head to lower it (Fig. 13-3C).

These cuts also affect the lengths of leech and foot, which may have to be related to the available space in the fore triangle of the yacht. Tapering the cut from a corner may allow the use of existing corner grommets, but there will usually have to be some cutting and resewing of the edges in the vicinity.

The angle of the clew of a head sail may be very different on one yacht from on another, and the adaption of an old sail to another position on the same yacht may require a different angle. This means that planning cuts should start with the clew angle. If possible keep the same head angle, so the only alteration in shape comes at the foot.

The cut may be parallel with the old foot, but that would give the same clew angle as before and it might be better to reduce by cutting away the luff, as just described. To get a new clew angle draw the foot as needed. It is more likely to give a broader clew angle than previously (Fig. 13-3D) and will remove the intended amount of area. It is usually unwise to try to incorporate the existing tack and it is better to arrange a new one above it.

If it is thought preferable to reduce the area by cutting off the leech only, to retain the same tack angle, this should be done parallel to the existing leech to maintain the same angle of the edge to the seams (Fig. 13-3E).

Although the cuts are shown straight the usual curves should be drawn into the edges (Fig. 13-3F). These may be as suggested for making new sails, but it is advisable to check existing curved edges. They will give a clue to the way draft was worked into the sail originally. If the curves on the edges are much less than those described earlier, it is possible some of the draft has been obtained by shaping the edges of cloths. The new sail should only be given slightly curved edges if this is so. When the new outline is cut, make ample allowances for tabling, roping, and other edge treatments. Plan the finishing stages in the same way as for making a new sail.

Where there is sufficient waste it may be possible to cut new tabling strips, otherwise the stitches of old pieces may have to be

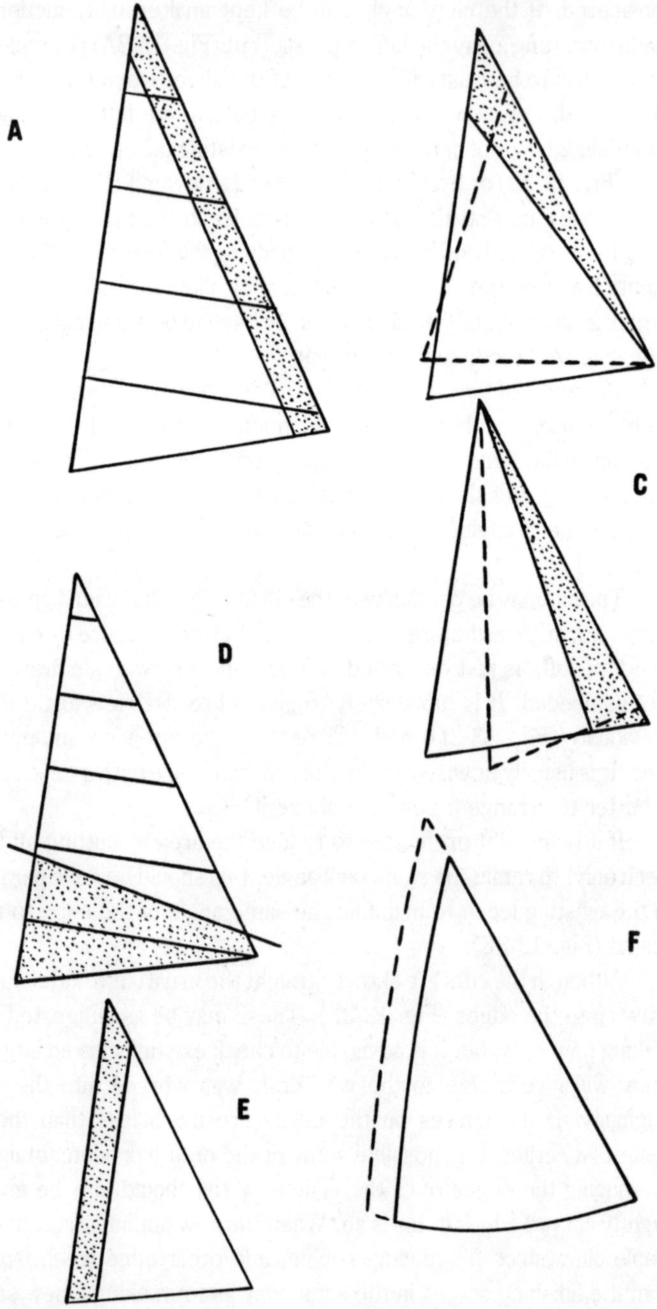

Fig. 13-3. Reducing the size of a head sail can affect shape and must be planned accordingly.

unpicked and the strips used again. If the new edge is at an appreciably different angle from the old one, the angle of the weave in the old strip may not match the new edge. If there is no more cloth to cut, this may have to be accepted, but if it is possible to make the applied tabling with a matching weave, this should be done.

There is very little stretch in Dacron and any stretch there was in a much-used sail will have been taken up, so no allowance need to be made in roping. The rope should be sewn into the cloth at the same tension as the cloth.

A miter-cut head sail does not offer as much scope for reducing. It is made with the cloths at right angles to leech and foot and it would be unwise to alter this. Consequently, any smaller sail should retain the same clew angle (Fig. 13-4A).

As the miter seam should also continue to pass through the clew corner, any reduction by cutting away leech or foot should be accompanied by cutting away a similar width from the other, as the miter seam bisects the corner angle (Fig. 13-4B).

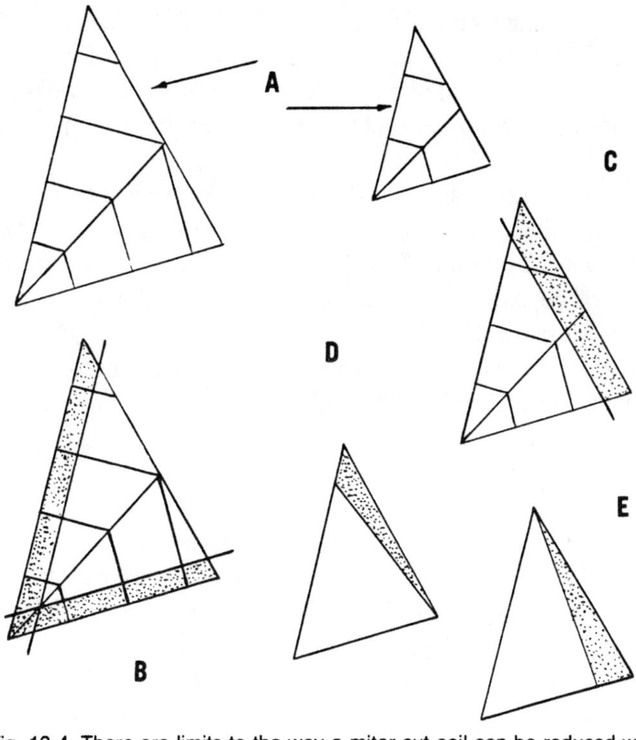

Fig. 13-4. There are limits to the way a miter-cut sail can be reduced without altering its character.

Cutting away in this manner retains the shape of the sail and its draft is likely to still be satisfactory. However, it means new work at all three corners as well as shortening the luff wire. It also assumes that the sheet angle will agree with the miter angle in the new situation.

A better way may be to cut away the luff. This can be a parallel cut (Fig. 13-4C) or it can be done by arranging the cuts at an angle to raise (Fig. 13-4D) or lower (Fig. 13-4E) the clew to suit sheeting. This will not affect the strength and set of the sail, as the cloths come diagonal to this edge in any case.

As with cross-cut head sails, leave ample allowances around edges, which are cut on the usual curves, and treat the edges with tabling and roping in the same way as new sails.

REDUCING MAIN SAILS

Nearly all main, mizzen and comparable sails are made with the cloths at right angles to the leech. This means that if area is to be reduced by cutting away the leech, this should only be done parallel to it (Fig. 13-5A). Because of the difference in the curve of the edge, depending on the amount of roach, there will have to be a modification of this and the curve will probably bend in more towards the head (Fig. 13-5B).

Foot and luff are diagonal to the weave so they may be cut in any way desired without affecting their relationship to the weave of the cloth in any significant way. It is unlikely that the angle between luff and foot will be altered, as on most craft this is a few degrees less than a right angle. However, the whole corner can be tilted if experimenting in this way would give a sail with the required foot and luff lengths (Fig. 13-5C). Although a seam may go through the existing tack corner, this is not an essential point in design.

If only luff (Fig. 13-5D) or foot (Fig. 13-5E) is cut away, these should be parallel with the existing sides to maintain the tack angle. Adjustment can be made to the angle by sloping one of these cuts. An old sail may have developed a sag, so there may be an advantage in making the tack angle slightly less than the existing one, which may have opened with age (Fig. 13-5F).

Nearly all main sails have head boards and battens. The head board can be taken out and replaced in a new position, but the leech will probably have to be reshaped to take it, even if reduction is not done by cutting away the leech. If the luff is shortened much, any existing curve in the leech is liable to produce too much roach in relation to the new length. This might necessitate longer battens in new positions, unless the new size is schemed to leave the remaining batten pockets evenly spaced.

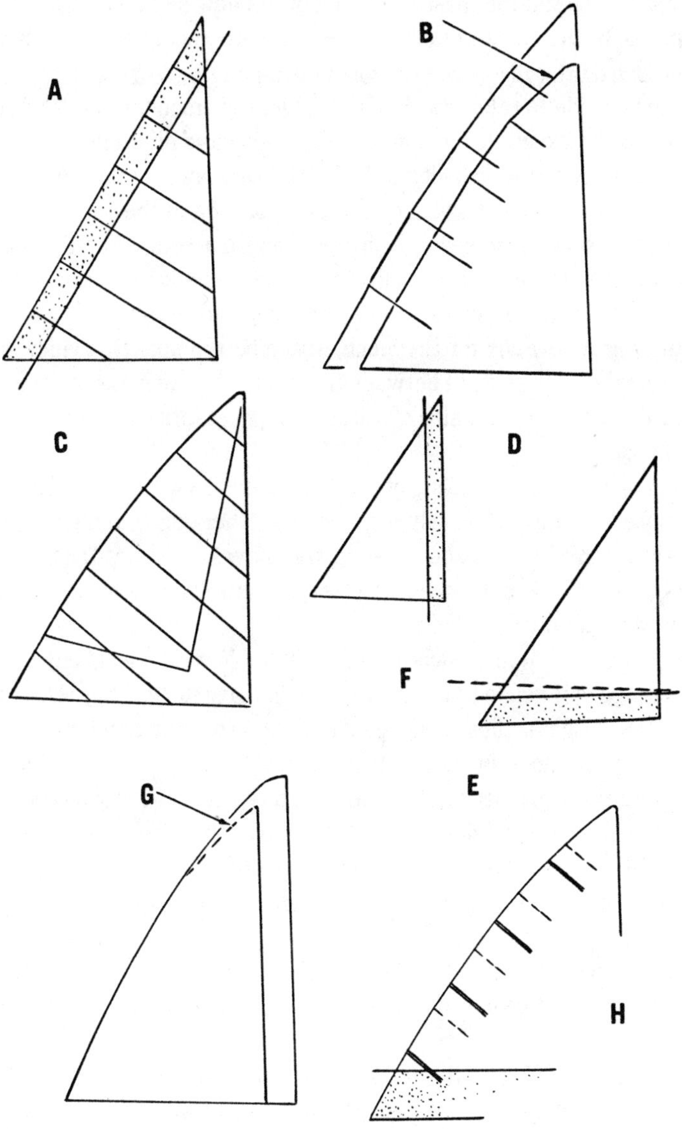

Fig. 13-5. Reducing a jib-headed sail may alter the shape of its leech and the spacing of battens. Smaller sails of new shape can be cut from an old sail.

Whatever method of reducing the size of a main sail is used, it is probable that some modification to the leech will be necessary, either cutting to a new curve (Fig. 13-5G) or repositioning batten pockets (Fig. 13-5H), with straightening of the edge between them.

Cuts will have to be related to the need for certain lengths of luff and foot to suit the mast and boom of the new situation. The luff is probably the most complicated edge, with roping to suit a mast groove or a large number of grommets for slides, so if the alterations can be made to retain much of this edge, the amount of work will be reduced. Of course, if the new sail location has a different method of attachment to the spars it may be better to cut away at the luff edge.

Finishing a cut sail should be approached in the same way as described for head sails. With the shape marked, allow the usual curves, but check on the curves of existing edges to see if they agree. If not, use similar curves or compromise between them. If there is a new line for the leech, space batten pockets evenly and make the edge straight between them, but allow an amount of roach applicable to the new size of sail and not necessarily the same as the old sail.

There may be tabling of the cloth itself along the leech, but use applied tabling, and usually reping on the other edges. If the new sail is much smaller it may be better to use a new smaller head board than previously to avoid a head which stands out excessively and might produce an unstable leech.

Jib-headed main sails are unlikely to have cloths laid any other way and gaff-headed sails of fairly recent construction may also have cloths at right angles to the leech. In that case, any reduction at the leech edge should be parallel to it to retain the angle (Fig. 13-6A). If it is more convenient to get the new shape by cutting away any one or more of the other sides, this can be done as they are all at a diagonal angle to the weave in any case (Fig. 13-6B). This gives scope for adapting an old gaff-headed sail to almost any other shape (Fig. 13-6C). It might be cut down to a dinghy balanced lug sail (Fig. 13-6D). Normally, there is little roach, but except for this it could be made into a jib-headed mizzen sail (Fig. 13-6E) or it might make a try sail.

Older-style gaff-headed sails have their cloths parallel with the leech. A simple method of reduction is to take away the outer cloth (Fig. 13-6F). This might be a good way to reduce area for use on the same spars. There is no control over the length of the head and the foot and these have to be accepted as they come.

As the other sides are diagonal to the weave, they can be cut in any way convenient. If the intended new sail is to have its leech at a

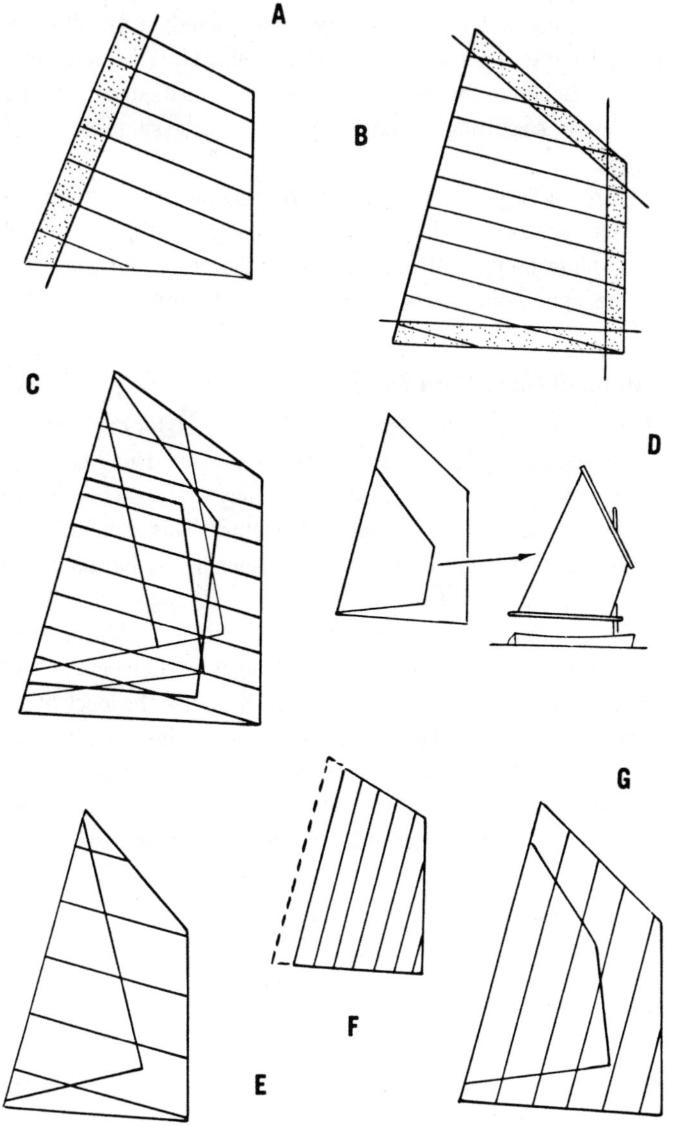

Fig. 13-6. A gaff-headed sail can be cut in many ways to reduce its size or to make another type of sail from an old one.

different angle to the other sides than the existing one, the new small sail may have to be cut on the skew to keep the leech the same in relation to the cloths (Fig. 13-6G).

Gaff-headed sails are usually strongly roped, so allow for this when cutting outside the lines. There is not usually much curve to the edges of a gaff sail. If existing edges can be used, grommets may be included in the new sail and some work reduced. If the new sail is only to be attached to the boom at clew and tack, that edge may need the least work, so cutting to size at that edge may be simplest, if that is possible.

If there are reef points on any type of main sail, they restrict the way the sail can be cut as they must remain parallel to the new foot, if they are still to be used. If they are to be discarded, stitching will have to be ripped out and the remaining holes darned.

MAKING HEAD FROM MAIN SAILS

It is not usually advisable to try to make a sail for one function from one originally intended for another function. Head sails are generally smaller than main sails, so there may be a wish to use up a discarded main sail by cutting a head sail from it. This may find a use for something that might otherwise be thrown away, but too much should not be expected from it.

The cut and method of making up one sail does not lend itself to adaption to another. A cross-cut head sail might be cut from the bunt of a main sail (Fig. 13-7A). It might be possible to use the leech of the main sail as the leech of the head sail, but usually there is too much curve in the roach and there may be unwanted batten pockets as well. If there is enough area, it is better to have all new edges, with existing tabling, roping, grommets and other of the main sail features cut away. What is left is similar to the sewn-up cloths of a new sail and further steps are the same as those for making new head sails (Fig. 13-7B).

REDUCING SPINNAKERS

The best advice on spinnakers is to leave them alone, unless they are no further use on the boat they were meant for or another of similar size, when their only future is to be cut down for a smaller boat. Nearly all spinnakers are made with a central seam, but the way the panels are laid each side of this varies. Although the seam

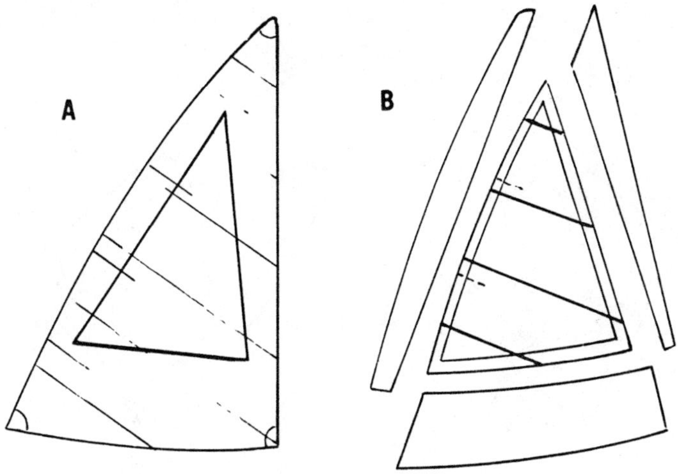

Fig. 13-7. It is possible to cut away the edges of an old sail and use the sewn cloths for a different sail.

looks straight, as made up, the two halves which are joined have considerable curve when they are flat (Figs. 11-2, 11-4, and 11-5).

If the spinnaker is too wide, rip the stitches out of the middle seam, after deciding how much has to be removed from the total width of the foot. Mark half this width from the seam edge and use a long batten to draw a new fair curve to the top (Fig. 13-8A). Cut this and use it as a pattern for marking out the other half. Unless a considerable amount is to be cut out it will probably be possible to leave the head, its patch and grommet undisturbed as the difference in curve will be negligible (Fig. 13-8B).

If the spinnaker is too high, the only simple way of reducing it is to cut a parallel band from the foot (Fig. 13-8C). This applies whatever the method of laying panels. The new edge is then finished in the same way as the original foot and corner grommets are worked again.

Some spinnakers are almost parallel for a short distance up from the foot. If one has to be opened for reduction in the width, it may be possible to alter the height by taking out a cloth or part of a cloth, so the existing bottom panel with its prepared edge and grommets may be used again by moving it up (Fig. 13-8D). As this affects the edge, it can only be done if the widths after cutting are the same. The tabling or taped edge of one part should be allowed to project a few

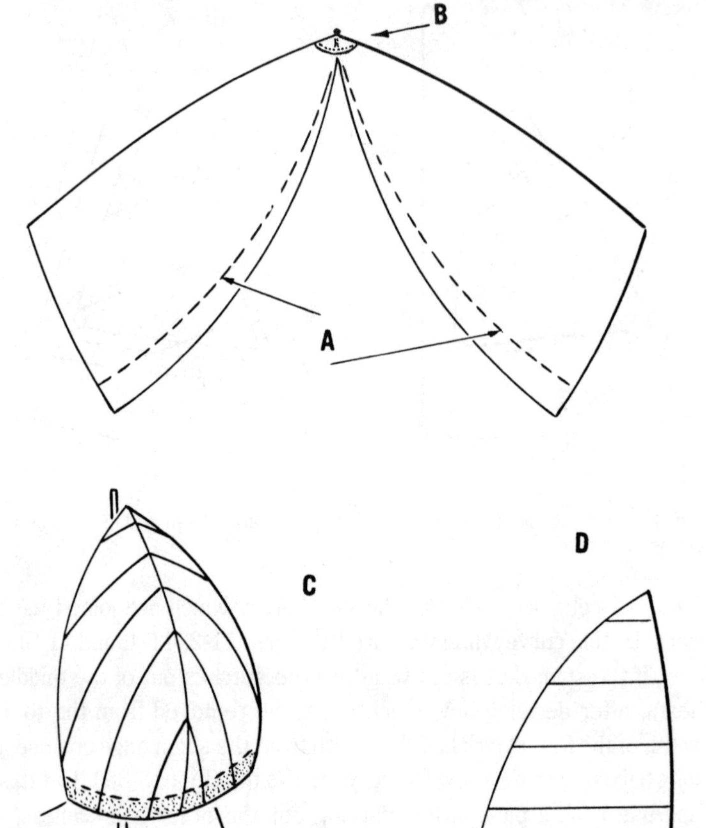

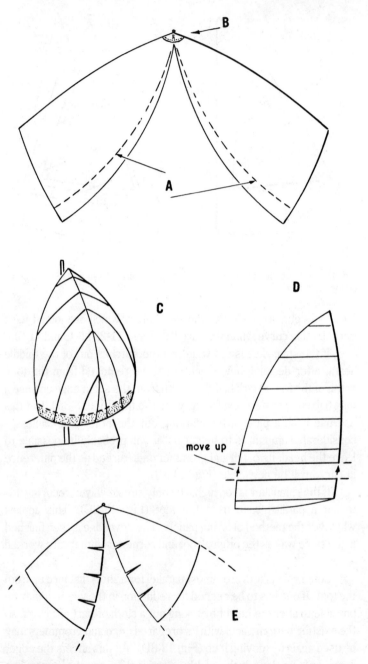

Fig. 13-8. A spinnaker can be reduced at the center seam, by cutting off the bottom or by cutting out part of a panel.

inches so it can be carried over the other part to strengthen the end of the new seam and provide continuity of load along the edge.

If a spinnaker is drastically reduced in size its shape may have insufficient curve for it to set properly, if nothing else is done to it. Greater fullness can be obtained by putting darts along the center seam edges before they are sewn up (Fig. 13-8E), or parts of seams that meet there can be opened and tapered. There may also be a need for darts along the leeches. Whatever is done should always be on both sides so the effect is symmetrical. The widths of tapers need only be slight, but it is the spoiling of spinnaker shape due to cutting down that is the main reason for leaving a spinnaker as it is unless the reasons for reducing its size are very convincing.

Enlarging Sails

Many of the considerations concerning reducing the size of sails also apply to efforts for increasing their area. A properly designed and constructed sail is related to the originally intended size and shape, so its cut and draft is planned. Such design work for one size is not always suitable for an altered size. Certainly, where the highest performance is required, as when racing, the sail should be designed for its size and an altered sail, whether enlarged or reduced, would not have as good a performance. However, for general sailing, moderate increase in area should be satisfactory.

A sail may be reduced in size because the area is too great for a particular craft as originally designed, but it is more likely to be cut down to be used for an entirely different purpose. Quite often, this cutting down may be quite drastic, as described in Chapter 13. Enlarging is not usually carried to such extremes. Indeed, it would be unwise to try to increase the size of a sail very much. As a rough guide, 10 percent is about the most that should be added to the area, and this is often the equivalent of one more width of cloth.

Whether enlarging is practicable or not depends on the design of the sail. It is no use merely adding a cloth, or part of a cloth,,along an edge, if this will be in a different direction to existing cloths. The added area might be there, but the sail would not set properly and the appearance would be wrong.

If there seems to be a prospect that enlarging will be an economic and satisfactory proposition, make a drawing of the existing sail, with seams shown and try cutting this and inserting cloths to see if what you have in mind is practicable. Sometimes adding or inserting cloth makes you see alterations to outlines that you did not anticipate before experimenting with a drawing.

Of course, it is important that any added cloth matches that of the existing sail. There are many weaves, and the weights of cloths vary in fractions of an ounce, so it may not be easy to identify the cloth originally used. The best plan is to let your supplier see the sail so the best match can be obtained. Fortunately, Dacron keeps its shape so differences in stretch of new and old cloths are not likely to matter. With natural fiber cloths there could be puckers develop due to the old cloths having stretched and reached their limit while the new cloth has yet to stretch.

ENLARGING HEAD SAILS

If a head sail is cross cut, its area can be increased by inserting a panel. How this is inserted affects the new outline as well as the area, and it is possible to increase on the leech and the luff, or all sides. If stitches are ripped from a seam and a cloth inserted, the new line will follow that of the leech, as the seams are at right angles to it (Fig. 14-1A), but any other edge crossed will have to be altered.

If the seam that passes through the tack is unpicked, the grommet or wire eye and patches there will have to be removed and probably discarded. But try to avoid damaging the cloths, which will be seamed to the new cloth. The joint will be neater if they are kept reasonably sound.

Join in the new panel with some surplus at each end (Fig. 14-1B). At the leech, turn in tabling to match the existing work. There should be no need for any special strengthening, but if there is a leech line, a new longer one will have to be included. Watch that the new edge follows any curve and is not merely straight between joins (Fig. 14-1C). The curve of the leech may be slight, but if it is not followed, appearance will be spoiled. Stretch the edge on the floor and sight along it, or bend a latch around the edge to mark the curve.

Continue the lines of the luff and foot to meet on the new cloth at the repositioned tack. This method of enlarging gives an increase on all three sides. Experimenting with a drawing will show if the new sizes are acceptable but this is the simplest enlargement and most likely to retain the sail in a good shape.

Fit new patches at the tack, repeating the pattern of the old corner. If there is a fiber rope along the luff, it may be possible to splice an additional length, but as this edge is often under considerable load, it is better to fit a new rope. If there is a wire rope along the luff, this will have to be replaced with a new longer one.

Treat the foot and luff in the same way as the old edges, but it is advisable to let any tape or applied tabling overlap the old edges (Fig. 14-1D), so it can be sewn to provide additional strength, but be careful that stitches do not interfere with the movement of roping or the luff wire, which may need to pull straight.

There is no satisfactory way of increasing a cross cut head sail area while retaining the original luff of the same length. It would have to be by sewing on to the leech, so seams bringing in extension cloths would cross the normal seams. This would result in a poorly setting sail. It may have been done, but is not advised.

If the foot is to remain the same length, the same seam through the tack corner is unpicked, but it may be possible to leave patches still attached to the lower cloth and its tabling or roping may remain intact almost to the corner, as the part of the sail below the ripped seam will be unaltered (Fig. 14-1E). A new cloth added above the old seam line, instead of partly above or below it, will necessitate a new luff line (Fig. 14-1F). Adding the new cloth entirely below the old seam line will result in a sail of similar shape and with the same amount of work along the luff.

Sew in the new cloth with some surplus at the ends (Fig. 14-1G). The leech can be tabled and finished as already described.

A new luff has to be made. The maximum increase in area is obtained by taking it to the new head position, but if a shorter luff is required the head can be brought further down the leech, but obviously bringing this too far down removes some of the benefits of the added area (Fig. 14-1H).

The luff is worked in the same way as for a new sail, repeating the edging as used previously and now cut off. Unfortunately, the old material will be too short and it is better to make a new full-length luff than to join tape or tabling. Refix patches, sail hanks and any grommets and sew in the eyes of any luff wire.

There is no satisfactory way of enlarging a miter cut head sail (Fig 14-1J). If sails are laid vertically, an additional cloth can be put along the leech, making both luff and foot longer (Fig. 14-1K). In a "scotch" cut sail with cloths parallel to foot and leech, the area can be

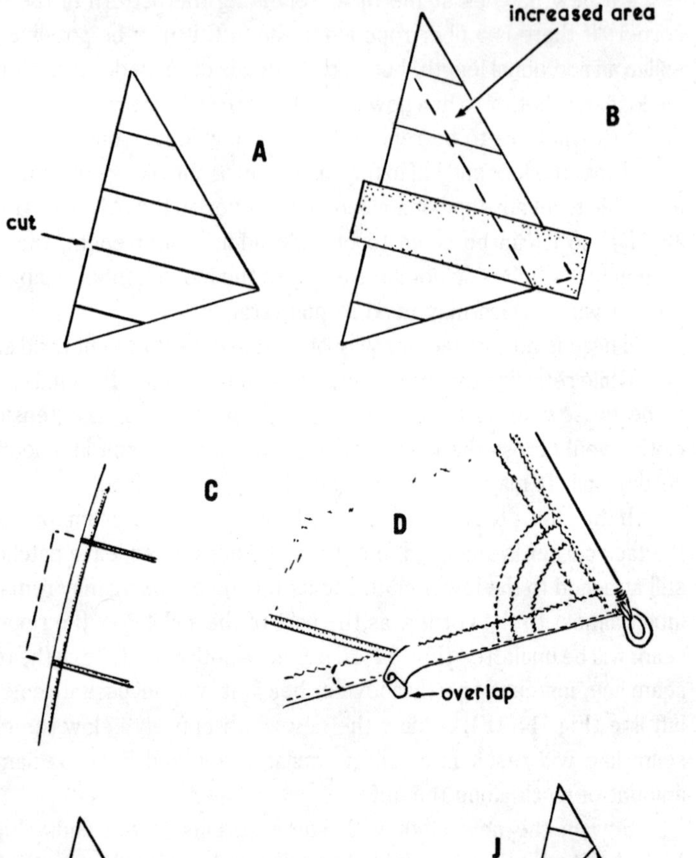

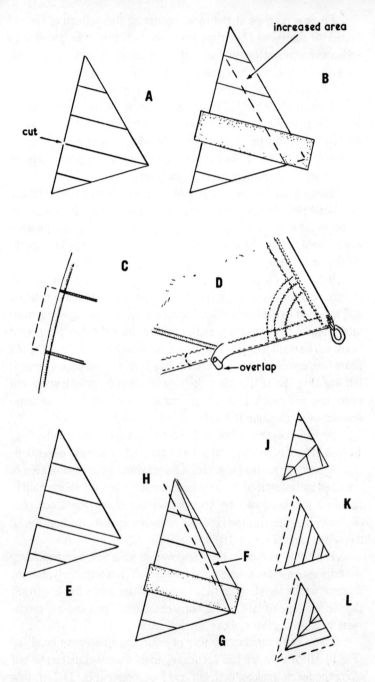

Fig. 14-1. Adding cloth to increase the size of a head sail has to be arranged to suit its cut.

increased by adding to these edges so the line of the miter continues (Fig. 14-1L). There cannot be an addition to only one of these sides.

ENLARGING MAIN SAILS

With the normal cross cut jib-headed main, mizzen, or similar sail, it is possible to insert a cloth in a similar way to that described for a head sail. Although the seams are at right angles to the leech it is usually better to let the luff line follow through and make adjustments to the line of the leech, although in some cases it may be better to match the leech and make a new luff. A drawing, which is cut and experimented with, will show how to arrange the additions to give the best effect and the minimum amount of work.

One method increases the length of all three sides. The other method keeps the foot the same length, but increases luff and leech. If the modification is to give extra area on a sail to suit an existing mast, but a longer boom, so the center of effort is brought further aft, the only satisfactory way that retains a good set is to use the method that lengthens all three edges, then cut down the luff at the head to give the right height and modify the shape of the leech to suit. This may not result in much greater area, but it will have the effect of moving the center of effort aft if this is required to achieve good sail balance.

For an increase that retains the same length foot, pick out the stitches in the seam that passes through the tack. Remove the patches and grommets. Loosen any roping for a short distance from the corner in each direction. Separate the parts and insert a new cloth (Fig. 14-2A). False seam it if that has been done to the other cloths. It may be possible to insert two cloths seamed together, but this will cause quite a lot of work achieving a good shape.

The inserted panel comes above the tack line and the foot can retain the existing clew and tack. The only time there may be difficulty at the clew will come when there is considerable curve to the leech and a satisfactory line cannot be followed. In that case it may be necessary to move the clew in a short distance to accommodate the new curve within the area of the existing cloth (Fig. 14-2B).

The tack patches can be refitted or new ones made and a grommet fitted. If the luff is roped and there are sail slides at intervals, it may be possible to splice in an extra length of rope, or a new piece may be sewn to the existing rope (Fig. 13-1E). If the roped edge has to slide in a mast groove, there will probably have to be a new full length piece of rope. Continue whatever method of edging is used on foot and luff, with some overlap for sewing, but avoid bulk anywhere if the part has to slide in a grooved boom or mast.

What is done to the leech depends on its shape. Although the seams are at right angles to the leech line, they do not allow for the amount of roach and there may be some alterations needed. The existing line can probably be followed through (Fig. 14-2C) and the edge tabled.

A complication comes if there appears to be too much cloth for the existing battens to support. If the edge is cut straight between batten pockets and not to a curve, any change of batten positions will necessitate remaking the edge if the best shape is to be obtained (Fig. 14-2D). In some cases it may be possible to retain existing batten positions and add an extra lower one, even if the final spacing is not even nor the edge shaped (Fig. 14-2E).

Roller reefing will be unaffected by increasing the area in this way, but if there are reef points the lower row will be divided, but it may be possible to use the parts in new lines (Fig. 14-2F).

If the seam through the tack is cut and the inserted panel is arranged to come partly below the tack (Fig. 14-3A), instead of entirely above it, as in the first method of enlarging, the separated parts have to be moved in relation to each other—how much depends on what cloth there is at the leech to allow for extension there (Fig. 14-3B). If the foot is moved too far aft there will not be enough of the old leech above the new panel to make a good shape (Fig. 14-3C). Sewing on pieces to lengthen the old panels would not produce a sail of good set. Consequently, the amount of movement of the foot section is the limiting factor that controls how much greater will be the lengths of the three sides (Fig. 14-3D).

With the possible shape decided, the actual constructional work is very much the same as just described. The new panel is false-seamed if that is necessary to match existing cloths, then it is sewn in, with enough spare material at the ends.

At the leech there will almost certainly have to be modificatons to the old edges above and below the new panel (Fig. 14-3E) to achieve a satisfactory shape and there may have to be a new batten pocket included, as well as others moved. Ideally, a new applied tabling strip will be put along the whole leech, but if the old strip is to

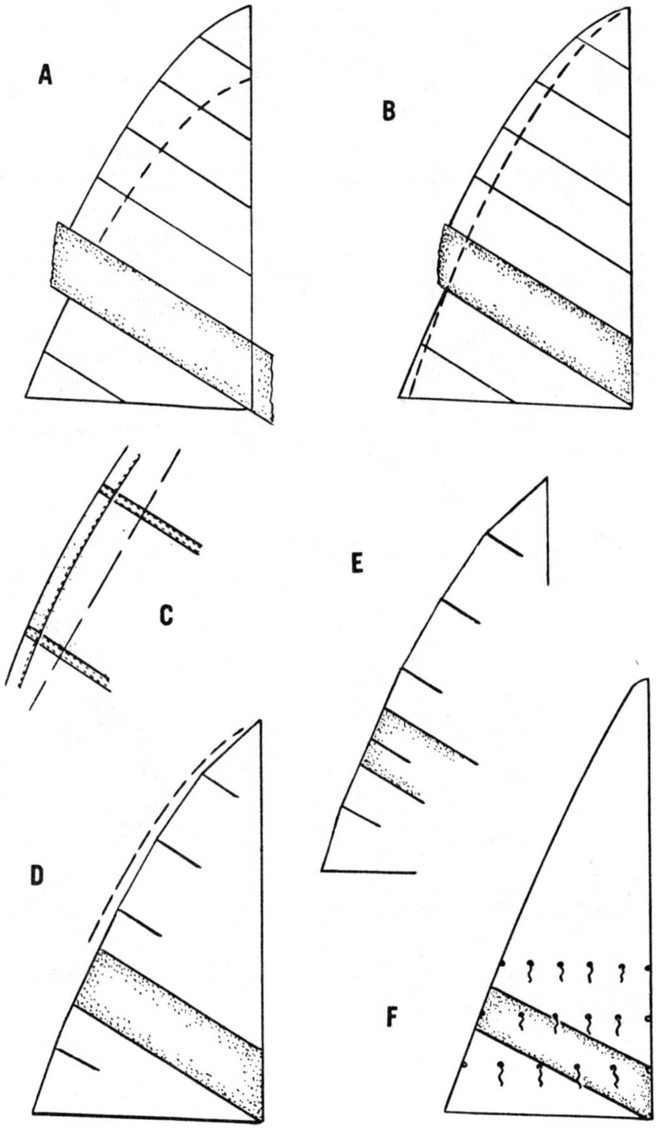

Fig. 14-2. Experimenting is needed when increasing the size of a main sail as the shape is altered, and the new arrangement of battens and reef points has to be considered.

be retained on the longer upper part, a new strip should be carried in one piece from the altered clew corner up the leech to past the new panel, so it can overlap on the existing strip above (Fig. 14-3F).

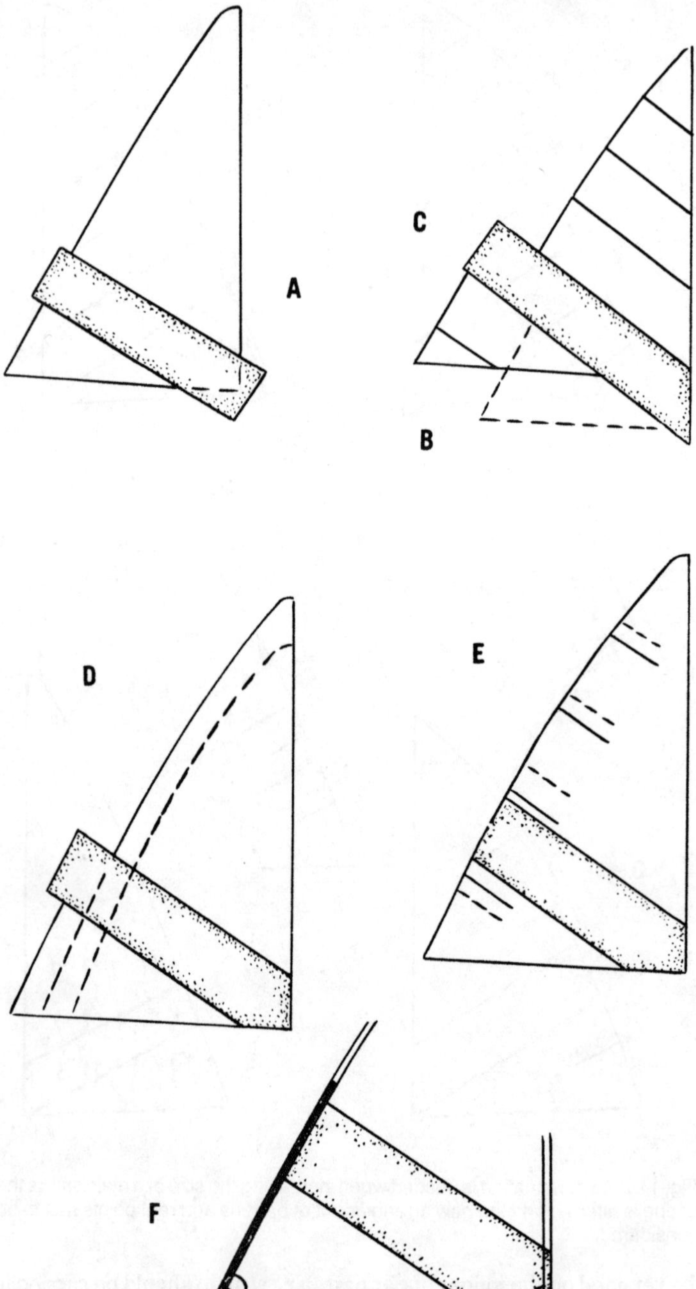

Fig. 14-3. A new panel in a main sail has to be arranged to suit the intended shape and to involve the minimum alterations.

At the tack corner the work is very much the same as when the panel comes entirely above the tack, but the new edging along the foot should be taken over as described for a head sail treated in a similar way (see Fig. 14-1D). There can be considerable load along the luff on a main sail, so ensure adequate strength in that direction. If there are reef points, they may have to be resited.

ENLARGING VERTICAL CUT SAILS

In general it is only advisable to enlarge a sail by putting new cloths beside and in the same direction as existing ones. It is unusual for jib-headed main sails today to have their cloths in any direction except at right angles to the leech, but sails on older working craft and more recent copies of them may have the cloths parallel to the leech. In that case, the only way to get a bigger area is to add a new cloth along the leech (Fig. 14-4A). These sails do not usually have much roach and they may even be merely straight, but it is more likely that there will be a moderate curve.

The shape of the edge should be checked with the sail stretched on the floor and a new straight line drawn (Fig. 14-4B). This is necessary to get a straight seam and a new edge that will set properly. As a check, see that the new line is parallel to the next seam (Fig. 14-4C). Remove patches, grommets, and any boards at clew and head. Unpick any stitches that will not be cut off in straightening the old leech. Sew on the new cloth and deal with its edges to give the leech shape required (Fig. 14-4D). This gives an opportunity to make the new area anything up to the maximum the full cloth will permit. So that loads on the weave of the new cloth will be comparable with those of the existing cloths it is best to keep the new cloth parallel, but if an increase in foot or luff only is required, this type of sail should still be satisfactory with a diagonal cut (Fig. 14-4E).

Deal with refinishing corners and extending edges in the same manner as already described. Working sails were often roped and tapered ends of the roping taken part way along the leech at the clew and head corners. It would be advisable to repeat this on the extension.

A cross cut gaff-headed sail can be enlarged by inserting a panel after the tack seam has been opened, in the same way as described for a jib headed sail. Doing this raises the gaff, as the luff is lengthened (Fig. 14-4F). If the angle of the gaff can be altered, it may be possible to increase the area by inserting a triangular panel (Fig. 14-4G). This gives the sail a higher peak, which should improve its performance to windward.

The more usual traditional gaff-head sail has its cloths parallel to the leech. The only way to increase the area satisfactorily is to put a new cloth on the leech (Fig. 14-4H).

The practical work then is similar to that described for the vertical cut jib-headed sail. New corners should be at least as strong as the original ones and roping carried around on to the leech is important, as the boom of a gaff rig is usually heavier than on a jib-headed rig, and much of the weight has to be taken by the cloth forming the leech edge.

ENLARGING SPINNAKERS

As was commented in the section on reducing the size of spinnakers, the best advice is to leave a spinnaker unaltered if possible. However, if the spinnaker is no further use for the boat as it is and cannot be passed on to another boat, the only alternative to discarding it is to enlarge it, and there are ways of doing this that should result in a satisfactory performance. Much depends on how the sail was made.

The majority of spinnakers have a central seam. One way of increasing the area without altering the height of the sail is to put in a wedge-shaped piece. Unpick the seam and open out the sail (Fig. 14-5A). Measure the length around the curved edge and make a wedge-shaped insert with a little to spare. It will probably be possible to leave the head patch connected, but with some stitches removed so the new piece can be arranged to come within the seam there (Fig. 14-5B). If the insert has to be made by joining in sections with seams across, this will not matter. Normally, the insert can have straight sides. If it is very wide, or the original sail was not full enough, the edges can be curved (Fig. 14-5C). Less probably would be a sail found to be too full. In that case the edges could be given hollow curves.

Sew in the insert. Finish the foot to match the existing edges. It may be satisfactory to rely on the seams for strength as a spinnaker is only used in light airs, but it sometimes gets rougher treatment when being handled than when sailing, so it may be advisable to take tape over the new joints.

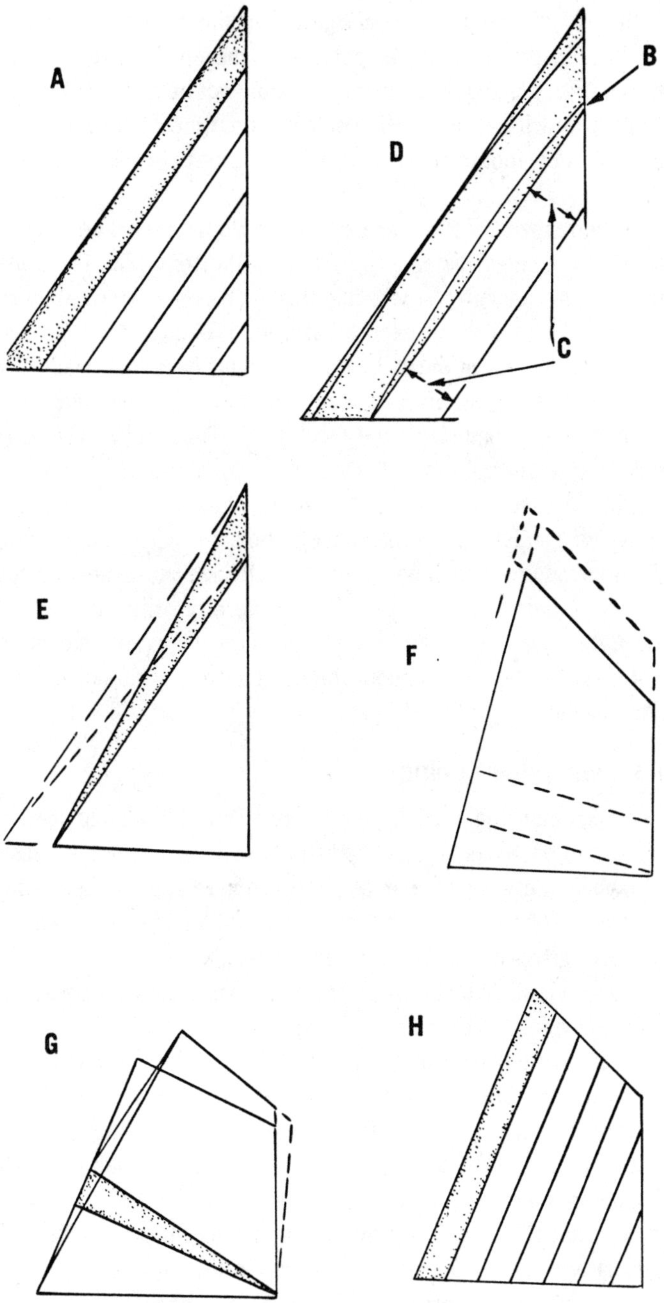

Fig. 14-4. A vertical-cut sail can have a whole or part cloth added to the leech. A gaff-headed sail can be altered in several ways depending on its cut.

If the spinnaker is to be enlarged by making it higher, cloths will have to be inserted. It may be possible to merely add a band around the foot (Fig. 14-5D), but too much should not be added in this way as the shape with a wide cloth would not be right. In any case there would be a new foot to be worked, with leeches to be faired in to new clews.

A better way, if there are cross-cut cloths, would be to insert new cloths a short distance up from the bottom. The compound curvature is not as great there and this allows the bottom panel and its foot and clews to be used unaltered. Whether this is feasible depends on the cut of the sail, and this probably cannot be checked until after opening the middle seam and flattening one side.

With many spinnakers the leech of the bottom cloth is nearly parallel to the central seam. In this case new panels can be inserted with the minimum alterations to leeches after opening the central seam (Fig. 14-5E). There may have to be some slight fairing above and below the new panel, but the new cloth edge can be near vertical and give a satisfactory shape. With some other arrangements of panels, it may be necessary to bring in a new one across higher up, but this can not be done without the need for more extensive fairing of the leeches.

ENLARGING AND REDUCING

Sometimes the sail shape required can only be obtained by enlarging in one direction and reducing in another. Whether this is worthwhile or not will have to be assessed in relation to the particular project. Too many alterations are likely to lead to a bad sail, that may never give satisfaction. It is often difficult to achieve perfection in an alteration. A build-up of slight discrepancies that may not matter individually could give an overall bad shape.

If the method of enlarging that has to be used will give increased lengths in more directions than are acceptable or can be made to suit existing spars, it may be necessary to carry out enlarging first, then reduce a part to suit. There are some cases where a reduction can be made before enlarging, but normally it is better to make a part bigger and see that the shape is right before taking off part of the sail, particularly if the reduction will overlap on the enlarged part.

Enlarging and reducing a sail may be a method of altering the location of the center of effort, even when no alteration in area is

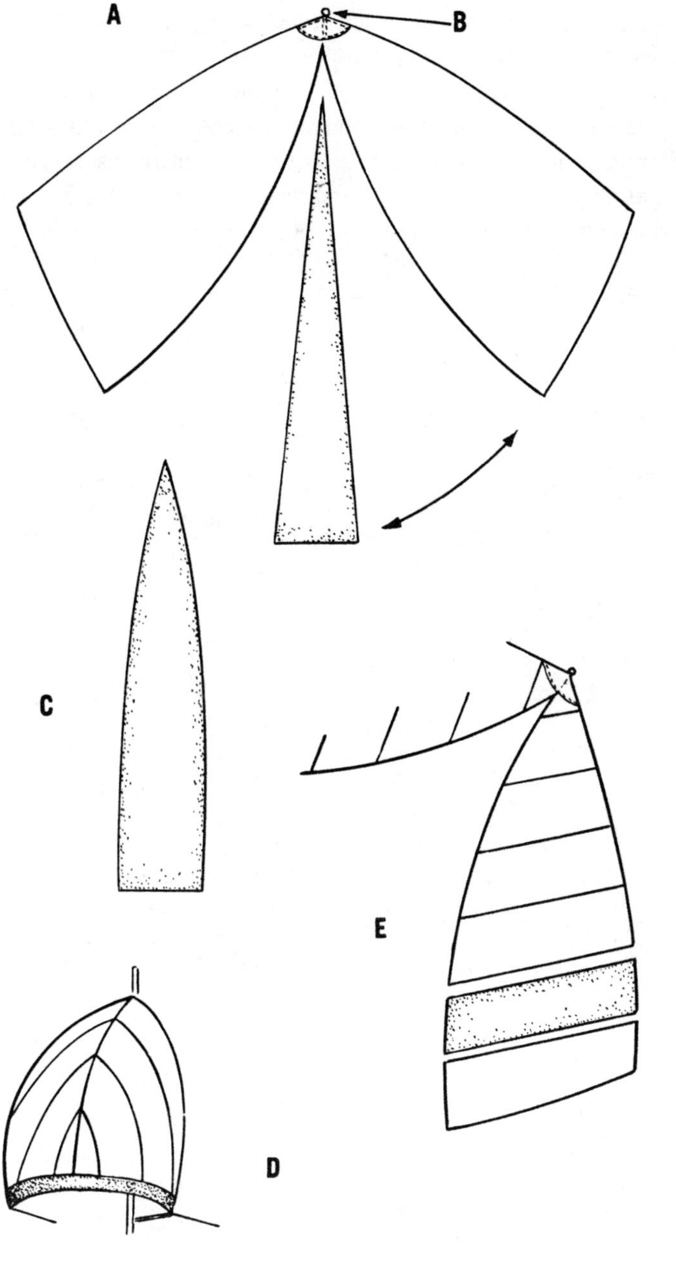

Fig. 14-5. A spinnaker may be enlarged by inserting a piece at center, adding a band at the bottom or taking in new panels.

desired. If the foot is made longer while the luff is reduced, the center of effort will be moved aft. Lengthening the luff, while shortening the foot, will move it the other way.

Apart from the practical considerations and the possibilities of the finished sail not being as good as expected, these complicated alterations involve considerable work, particularly as nearly all edges may have to be unpicked and remade, so economically a new sail may be more attractive.

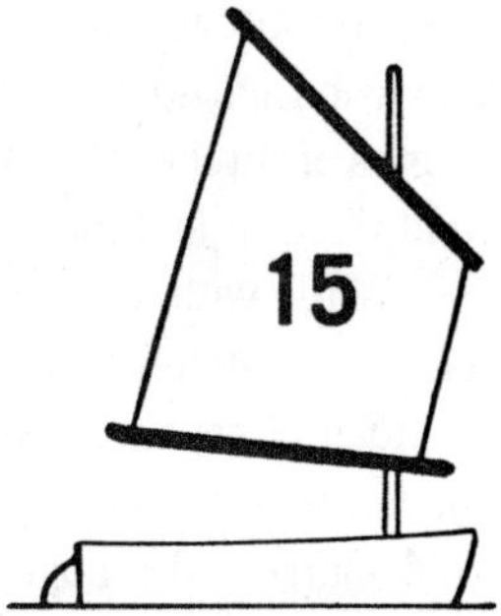

Repairs

Repairs to sails range from the *homeward bounder*, which is merely a very temporary repair at sea deemed sufficient to hold until port is reached, to a fairly comprehensive remake of part of a sail using full facilities ashore. There is also a broad division between those repairs that can be done entirely by machine and those in circumstances that require complete or partial hand work. An over-riding consideration is usually the need to do something. If a sail is suffering due to damage, wear, or just old age, it is very unwise to continue to use it without at least doing something to prevent the spread of the fault. Once cloth has torn or stitches have parted, further use will cause more repair work—hence the truth of the saying, 'A stitch in time saves nine.'

In the most basic repair at sea, a piece of cloth is placed over the damage and fixed with large sticking stitches (Fig. 15-1A) without bothering to seal or turn in edges or get the weaves matching. One advantage of this is that the appearance is so crude there will be no temptation to leave it, as there might have been with a neater temporary repair!

HERRINGBONING

Quite small rips can be repaired without adding a patch by using herringbone stitches (See Fig. 6-3). Instead of the widely spaced stitches used if there is to be a patch, the stitches are arranged as close together as is reasonably possible (Fig. 15-1B). To get them close and to spread the load, alternate stitches are made long and short, so different parts of the weave are penetrated. Such small rips are often right angled. The two straight sides may be sewn separately or stitches may be taken around the corner so they radiate. Confusion inside the bend is kept to a minimum by varying the lengths of stitches (Fig. 15-1C). Close herringboning does not let the wind through and may be regarded as a permanent repair.

Work with the cloth stretched flat and maintain a suitable tension of stitches to avoid bunching the fabric. This applies to other methods of repair as well. If the part being repaired is loose, the uneven tensions and spread of stitches may cause creases. Apart from marring the appearance of the sail, the creases can cause uneven loads which may lead to other trouble.

If a rip is along an edge or seam and is unsuitable for herringbone stitches it may be possible to pull the edges together temporarily and prevent further ripping by using round seam stitches (see Fig. 6-2D). This may distort the cloths in the vicinity, but this will not matter if a proper repair is made as soon as shore facilities become available.

Self-adhesive tape and cloth, such as is sometimes used for insignia and numbers on main sails, can be used for a temporary repair. With small damage, a patch made from this material and merely stuck on, may stand up to several days of use. It may be sufficient to prevent damage from spreading, and hold the cloth until facilities for a better repair can be reached. There are adhesives that will bond the cloths, but they are not so suitable for repairs. Self-adhesive cloth will peel off later wtihout leaving anything to spoil appearance or interfere with sewing, but many adhesives otherwise suitable cannot be removed completely. Do not use them for any occasion where the cloths have to be separated later for a different mode of repair.

A hole can be made in polyester (Dacron) or nylon by heat as well as by contact with something sharp. Consequently, a near-round hole may come from a dropped cigarette end or other carelessness with something hot, but not necessarily burning. If this is very large (much more than 1/2 inch) the better repair will be made by patching. A small hole needs treatment although another piece of cloth over it may not be justified.

If the hole was made by heat, its edges will be sealed, so there is little risk of the damage spreading, and the repair is done mainly to prevent wind from passing through. This can be done by darning. The finer the needle and thread, the neater will be the repair. For the lightest sails, ordinary domestic needles can be used, but for stouter materials small sail needles pushed by a palm will be needed.

Use the line double and start with a knot under the cloth. Lay on enough rows across the hole, but let the stitches pass through different lines of the weave and be only lightly tensioned (Fig. 15-1D), as stitches the other way will have the effect of tightening them. Put on similar stitches the other way, going alternately over and under the first stitches (Fig. 15-1E). There may be a need of a knot at the end, but it will probably be sufficient to pass the needle back under a few stitches before cutting off. Although there is no need for any waterproofing treatment of polyester thread, rubbing with wax before use helps to hold the threads in place as stitches are made, making neat work easier.

If a patch has to be applied, either temporarily or permanently, by hand or by machine, and something neater than the hasty homeward bounder is required, it is advisable to cut the patch so its weave matches the cloth being repaired—not only with threads in line, but with warp and waft the same ways (Fig. 15-1F).

PATCHING

The flattest and neatest repair by patching is made with the cloth and its patch heat-sealed around the edges. If this cannot be done, edges should be turned under. A simple straight or right-angled rip may have the edges drawn together by herringboning. These stitches should be enough to hold the edges together and share the strain of sailing with the stitches of the patch (Fig. 15-1G). They need not be as close as when no patch is to be used.

If the damage is more ragged or part of the cloth is actually broken away, it is better to trim the shape to a regular outline parallel with the weave. This applies whether it is a small hole or one that necessitates trimming a very large part of a panel. The patch should overlap by about 1 inch although for a very large repair a little more may be allowed.

If edges are sealed, patch and trimmed damage merely overlap (Fig. 15-1H). If the untreated edges have to be turned in, there must

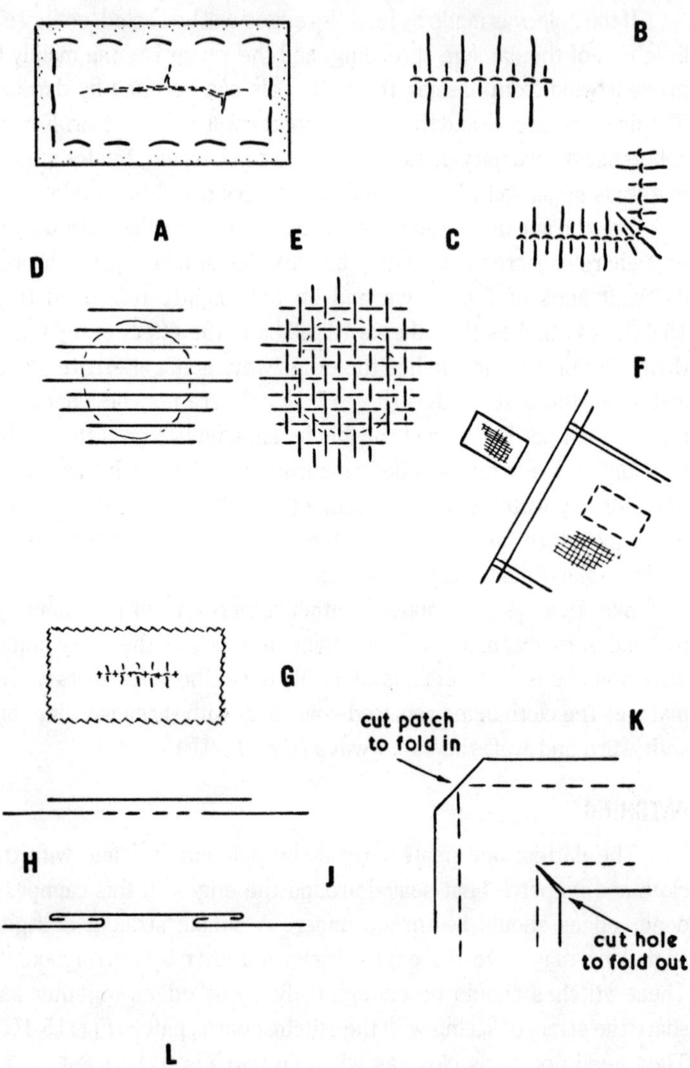

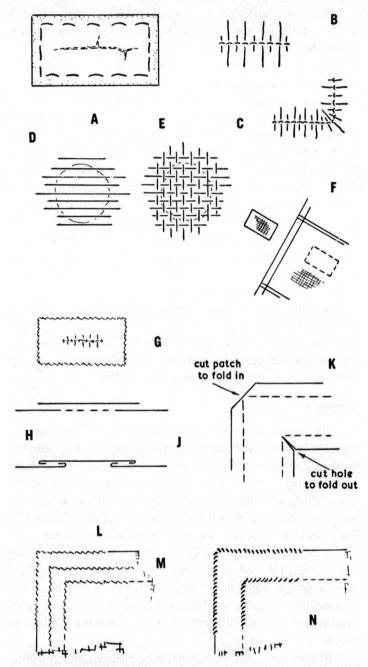

Fig. 15-1. Small repairs may be herringboned, darned, or sewn over with a patch by machine or hand stitching.

be an allowance for this (Fig. 15-1J). This means cutting corners of hole and patch to avoid unnecessary thicknesses there (Fig. 15-1K).

Machine sewing may be by zig-zag or straight stitches, through the double thickness of a turned-in edge, although with the flat cloth zig-zag stitches may go over the edges for a neat finish (Fig. 15-1L). Take additional rows of stitches around the patch after dealing with the edges (Fig. 15-1M).

For hand stitching the edges are treated in the same way as a flat seam (see Fig. 6-3), with stitches as close as convenient, but about six per inch is probably the most that can be fit in (Fig. 15-1N).

Whether the patch is hand or machine sewn, it may need to be positioned accurately before sewing. There may be little difficulty with a small patch, but it is possible to sew three sides of a large patch and find that the sail or the patch will finish loose and creased in relation to the other half of the seam, if sewing is freehand. There can be a few large sticking stitches up and down around the overlap, put in while the sail and patch are stretched flat, or it may be sufficient to use self-adhesive tape to hold the parts until one row of stitches has been taken around. Strike-up marks will also help in guarding against one piece "growing" on the other as stitches are made.

Stitching on sails made from man-made fibers does not pull into the weave as well as did the stitches on natural-fiber sails. This means that stitches are more exposed and therefore more likely to chafe. Sometimes the thread used in making a sail is a different color from the cloth. This may be regarded as decorative, but it also allows worn stitches to be identified easily by a break in the colored line of stitches.

Although there is a certain amount of interlocking in machine stitching, severed stitches will soon cause the thread to loosen and a seam gradually open, particularly in strong winds. In a bad case this could result in the sail blowing out, so a gaping hole appears. Apart from inconvenience or danger at the time, this sort of damage may be difficult to repair, so the sail is brought back to its original shape.

SEAMING

Seams should be examined frequently on a much-used sail, looking for worn or broken stitches. In some cases it may be advisable to rip out the damaged stitches and resew in the same way, but in many cases it is sufficient to put a new line of stitches over or alongside the old stitches, with sufficient overlap on to sound stitches to give enough strength.

If a seam has actually parted, the sail should be spread flat and evenly tensioned, while the edges are brought back into position and pinned or held with a few large sticking stitches in readiness for machine stitching (Fig. 15-2A). If the trouble has occured at sea or anywhere that machine sewing cannot be done, the edges must be hand sewn in the manner of a flat seam for a distance that overlaps slightly on the remaining sound original stitches (Fig. 15-2B).

If the trouble is at an edge, similar methods will have to be used. Many sails rely on the strength given by roped edges. Security of the roping is important. If the roping is enclosed in tabling or tape and stitches have parted locally, the cause should be explored. It will probably be chafe, but it may be due to uneven tensioning of cloth during the original sewing or distortion during use. So far as possible remove the cause of trouble or alleviate it. Sometimes trouble comes from attempts to over tension an edge, and this can be eased.

Failed stitches where roping is enclosed can be replaced by machine stitches over the broad part, but it may be better and stronger to use hand stitches close to the rope (Fig. 15-2C).

In older sails the roping may be external and hand sewn in any case (see Fig. 6-4F). Examine some of the old sound stitching before starting on a repair. Note that each stitch encloses one rope strand, so it is the size of the strand that determines the pitch of the stitches (Fig. 15-2D). With this method of roping there may have been a different tension on the rope and cloth along an edge. This was intentional. It may not be obvious or very much if only a short length of roping has come away, but if the repair is long, care is needed to spread the difference in tension as sewing proceeds. This is a case where the use of a sail hook is an advantage (Fig. 15-2E).

A sewn grommet that does not have a metal insert will suffer from chafed stitches. The pull usually comes mostly from one side, so damage may be localized. Any stitches completely severed may be pulled out, otherwise new stitches of similar waxed line may be put over them (Fig. 15-2F). If possible, take the new stitches through different parts of the weave, but this may not be possible in a corner. Look at the side of the grommet opposite to the load. Although there may be no chafe there, the stitches may be pulling excessively on the cloth and other stitches to different points may be advisable (Fig. 15-2G).

Letting the stitches take wear is not good practice, but it is unlikely that a metal thimble can be forced into an old grommet, so it

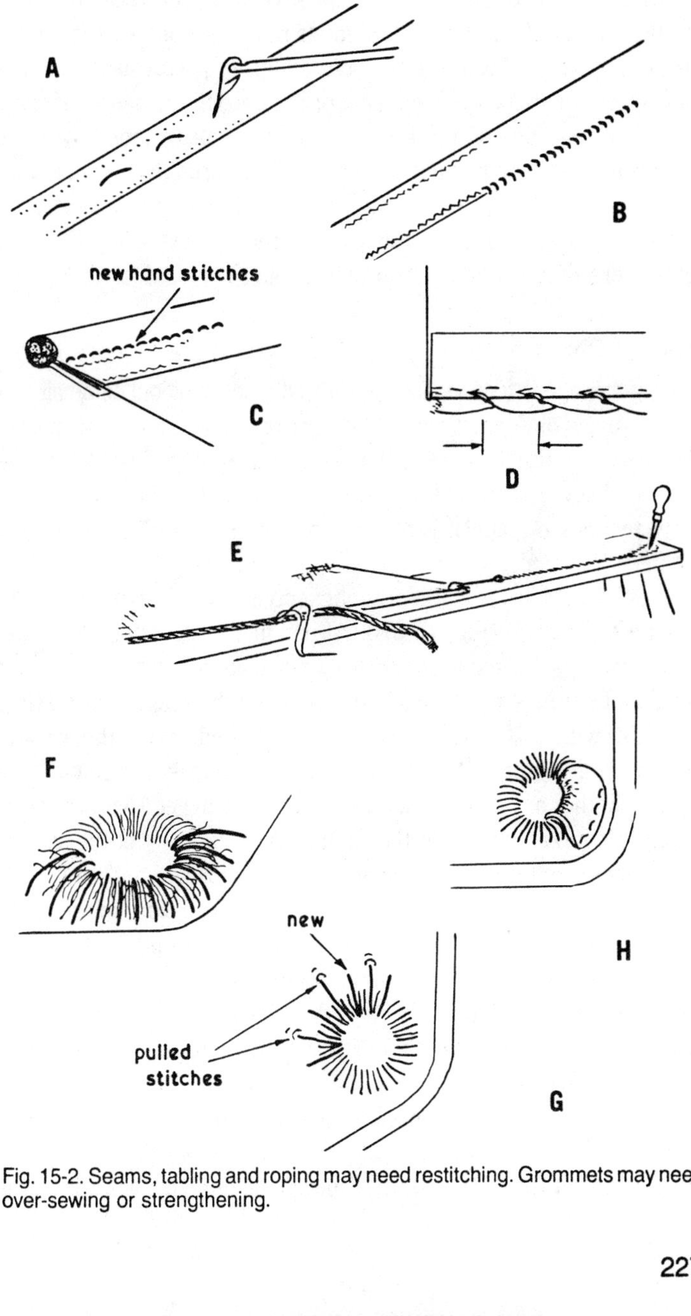

Fig. 15-2. Seams, tabling and roping may need restitching. Grommets may need over-sewing or strengthening.

may be possible to use leather, fabric, or plastic to cover the part that gets chafed. Flexible leather can be softened in water, then molded to shape while wet and sewn on (Fig. 15-2H).

Chafe is the enemy of sails. There are obviously two ways of preventing it. The cause of chafe can be removed or suitably padded or the sail itself can be protected. If much is done to the sail as protection against chafe, this could affect its preformance so it is always better to look to removing or minimizing the cause. If chafe comes at the edge of a sail, extra cloth may be wrapped over and sewn on, then renewed if it becomes chafed through. Leather has a much better resistance to chafe, so soft leather, molded to shape while wet, can be used at places like the throat of a gaff sail or elsewhere that a rubbing strip over roping seems desirable.

PANEL REPAIRS

If damage in a panel is so great that a patch would come almost to the seams or edge, it may be better to consider replacing a part of the panel to the full width between seams (Fig. 15-3A). If the damage is even more extensive there may have to be two or more new sections of panels, joined to each other as well as to the old cloths.

Joints could be made straight across a cloth, but this would create a hard line (Fig. 15-3B). Although the stretch of polyester fabric is slight, it exists, and this seam square across the weave might affect the sail set. It is better to make the seam diagonal (Fig. 15-3C), with adjoining panel joints staggered. With the greater stretch in nylon this is more important in spinnaker repairs.

Whether any of the existing edge can be salvaged will have to be decided by examination. If the damage is in the body of the sail and the edges need not be cut, seams can be unpicked and new joints made at both ends of the repair (Fig. 15-3D). The sides of the repair will be seamed as in the original sail, while the end joints can be treated as described for patching, either with heat-sealed edges or with cut edges turned in. Be careful to maintain an even tension by securing the parts correctly in relation to each other before commencing sewing.

More often it is better to let the repair coth go to an edge (Fig. 15-3E). This reduces by one the diagonal seaming and less care is needed to get the cloth setting properly. As the edge will still be the same size, it should be possible to retain any existing tabling or taped roping. Stitches can be removed and this eased away, so it is undamaged and can be replaced on the new cloth. It will have to be released a few inches each side of the seams to allow the new ones to be formed and the edge of the added cloth prepared in the same way as before (Fig. 15-3F).

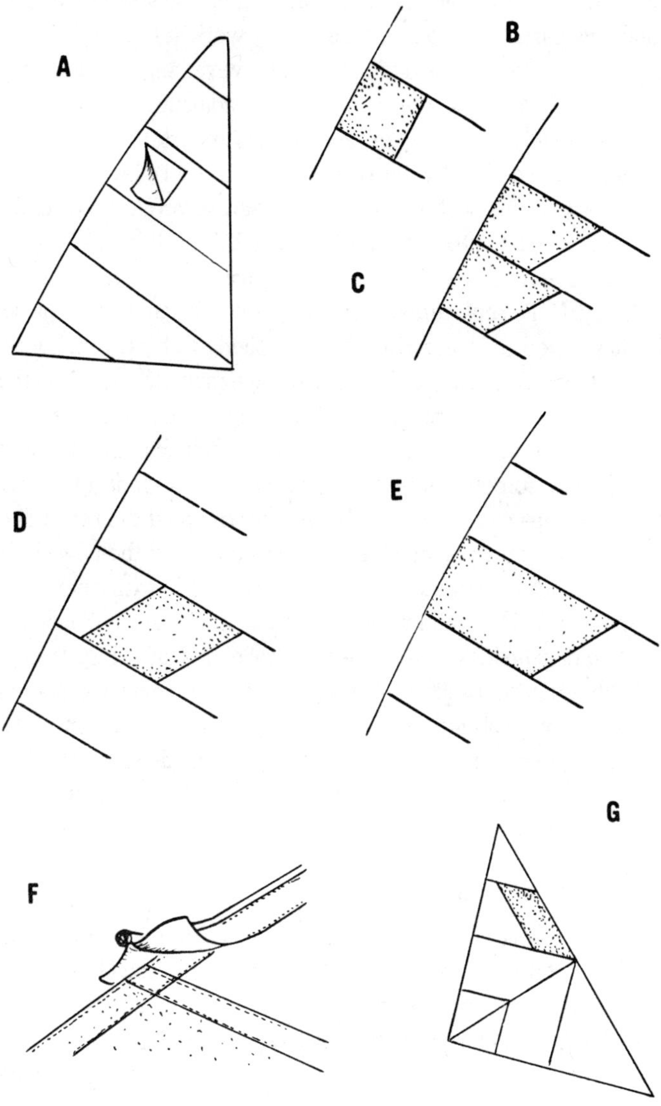

Fig. 15-3. Larger damage needs replacement or part panels.

In this sort of repair there is no need to keep the new panel down to a minimum size. It may only need to be big enough to replace the damage being cut out, but if a large panel would look better or give the sail a better shape, the additional material and amount of work are little more.

How the work is undertaken will depend on circumstances, but usually seams at each side are made first, then the seam joining the old and new parts of the panel, followed by work at the edge. Watch that the edge follows any existing curve, however slight. Turn it in or otherwise prepare it in the same way as adjoining panels before replacing the old tabling strip or tape. This is important if loads are to be evenly shared and the set of the sail is to be right.

Repairs of this sort may become progressively greater until a very large proportion of the sail is replaced. Whether this is worth doing or not will have to be assessed against replacing the sail completely. If the replacement runs over several panels, new pieces could be seamed and treated as a large applied patch, with staggered seams to the old cloths. A difficulty with such multiple patches is that cloth widths, that are not noticeably different for a single cloth repair, may produce seams that do not match exactly in a wide repair. It may sometimes be better to add one cloth at a time and build up the repair in steps, to achieve uniformity. If the repair is of such a size that much of an edge as well as an end of the new cloths have to be dealt with, it may be wiser to start again with a new sail.

Similar repairs to miter cut sails can be made. A cut diagonal to the weave may be less conspicuous if parallel to a side (Fig. 15-3G). Some old vertical cut sails may be seen to have so many repairs that there is little original cloth left and even repairs have apparently been repaired, so there is really no finish to what can be done in the way of replacing parts of panels. The limits are practicability and affordability of the obviously needed new sail.

BATTENS AND HEAD BOARDS

A place where stitches may chafe through without being noticed is inside batten pockets (Fig. 15-4A). The batten inside may rub against stitches, which may still look sound outside, but are thinned or completely broken inside. Battens have to be tight in their length, so the stitches at the bottom of the pocket may be worn, particularly if the end of the batten is rough.

As it is difficult to examine the stitches inside, a fine spike can be put under sample stitches outside. If any stitches break out, that is a sign of wear (Fig. 15-4B). Machine stitching can be put over the weakened stitches, backed up by more if there is room (Fig. 15-4C). If the repair has to be made afloat, some hand stitches can be used. These might be better, in any case, at the place where the thrust comes (Fig. 15-4D). There may have to be hand stitching along the sides of the pocket, and this may be best done with the batten in place (Fig. 15-4E) to tension the cloth, keep the stitches even and avoid stitching too far into the pocket.

The head board of a jib headed main sail exists to give shape to the head and to spread the lifting load. Wear may occur due to uneven loads or chafe. If there are a pair of boards outside the sail, they can be removed easily and resewn after repairs to patches or roping. If there is a single head board between patches, it is advisable to unpick any stitches through holes in the head board (Fig. 15-4F), then open the edge of the patch so the board can be taken out (Fig. 15-4G). If there is a grommet through the head board this will have to be removed.

Wear is likely to occur around the head and it will probably be necessary to restitch tabling and seams. Roping around the corner should be secured as this takes and spreads the load from the edge of the head board. It may be advisable to renew patches. Alternatively, add more patches outside the existing ones, if that can be expected to achieve a stronger head. Put the head board back in its pocket and resew the patches. If the head board has holes for stitches, they can be felt through the cloth. Sew through these as before, but it is usual to use a stouter sail twine than for normal sewing.

WIRING AND REEF POINTS

Metal and cloth do not go well together, particularly if there is movement. There may be even more trouble if the metal corrodes. This may lead to problems in the wired luff of a head sail.

Sea-water-resistant stainless steel should not lead to trouble, but in some older sails the flexible wire is galvanized steel. The galvanizing (zinc coating) is intended to protect the steel and prevent rusting, but this eventually breaks down and rust occurs. Rust may have little deteriorating effect on Dacron or nylon, but it roughens the metal and causes chafe, while brown stains will occur on the

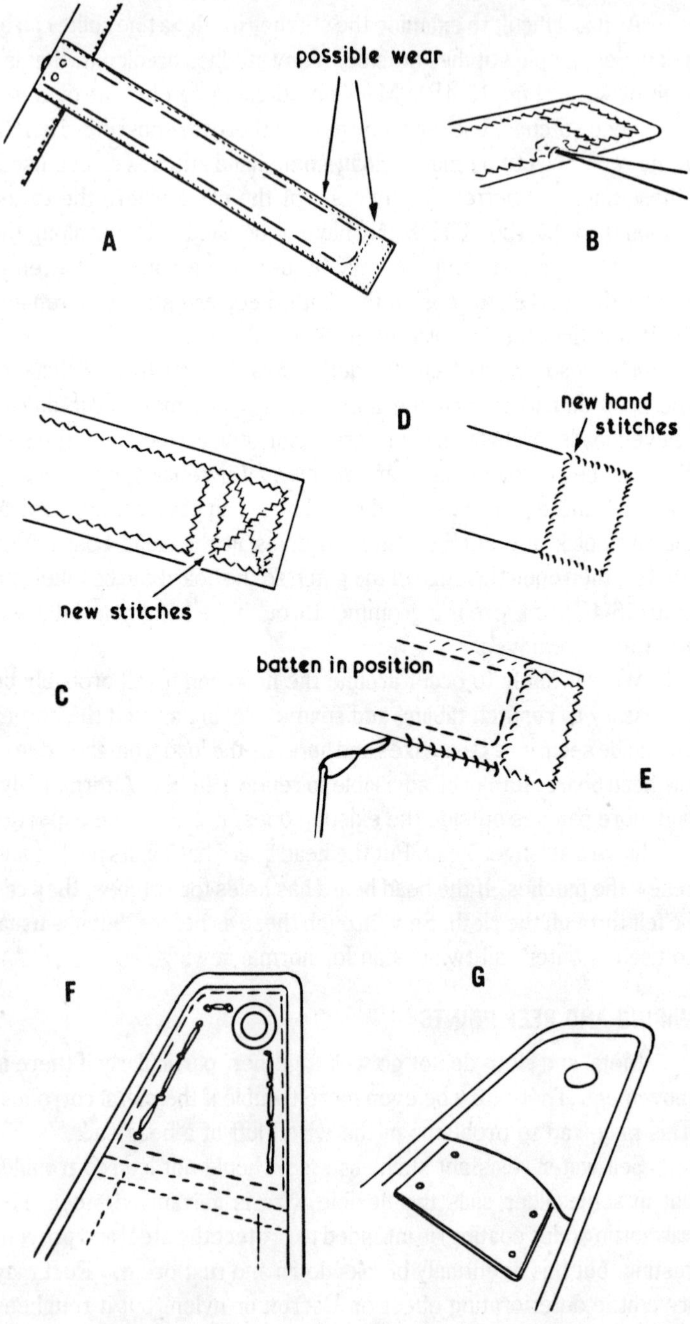

Fig. 15-4. Batten pockets may have worn stitching to repair. Head boards and patches may need strengthening and repairing.

cloth. Of course, rust eats away the steel, so the wire is weakened. With older natural fiber sails, rot will be encouraged and the fabric will break away.

Almost certainly, if the cloth around the wire has reached the stage of needing repairing, the wire itself should be replaced. If the wire is found to be sound a damaged sleeve may be repaired by covering with more cloth (Fig. 15-5A). Much depends on the way the sail edge was made. It may be better to cut out a section of tape or tabling and replace it with new. If the trouble is at head or tack, reinforcing followed by fresh lashing through the eye may be all that is needed (Fig. 15-5B).

If the wire is enclosed in a sleeve that is narrower than the eyes at the ends (Fig. 15-5C), the wire cannot be withdrawn and replaced in the existing sleeve, unless the new wires can have its second eye formed after the wire has been pulled through by a cord.

In this case, the old tape strip that encloses the wire can be removed and a new piece made up with the wire enclosed—either tightly, if that was the method first used (Fig. 15-5D), or with room for the wire to straighten under tension (Fig. 15-5E). Examine the method used in the existing sail edge before dismantling.

A simpler method is to cut down the side of the sleeve to release the old wire (Fig. 15-5F). Put the new wire back in the same place, but cover with a new tape outside the old one (Fig. 15-5G).

A roller furling head sail may deteriorate along the edge attached to the tube or other means of rolling. There are many different ways of securing the sail, but the simplest repair is usually to wrap a wide tape over the edge if this does not make it too thick for fitting.

If a sail is provided with reef points or there are grommets at the edge of the sail for other reasons, a repair at the edge is usually best made by removing the grommet then wrapping a patch over the edge, so it covers both sides (Fig. 15-6A). This thickness may be doubled if the sail is very weak. In any case, carry the patch far enough along the edge to reinforce it and spread the load. If it is a roped luff to slide in the mast groove, the part around the edge may have to be omitted, but the patches should be securely sewn through the tabled edge (Fig. 15-6B). The grommets can be resewn through the new patches.

When a main sail is reefed by the use of pendants, the end grommets should be pulled down and along the boom so the load is

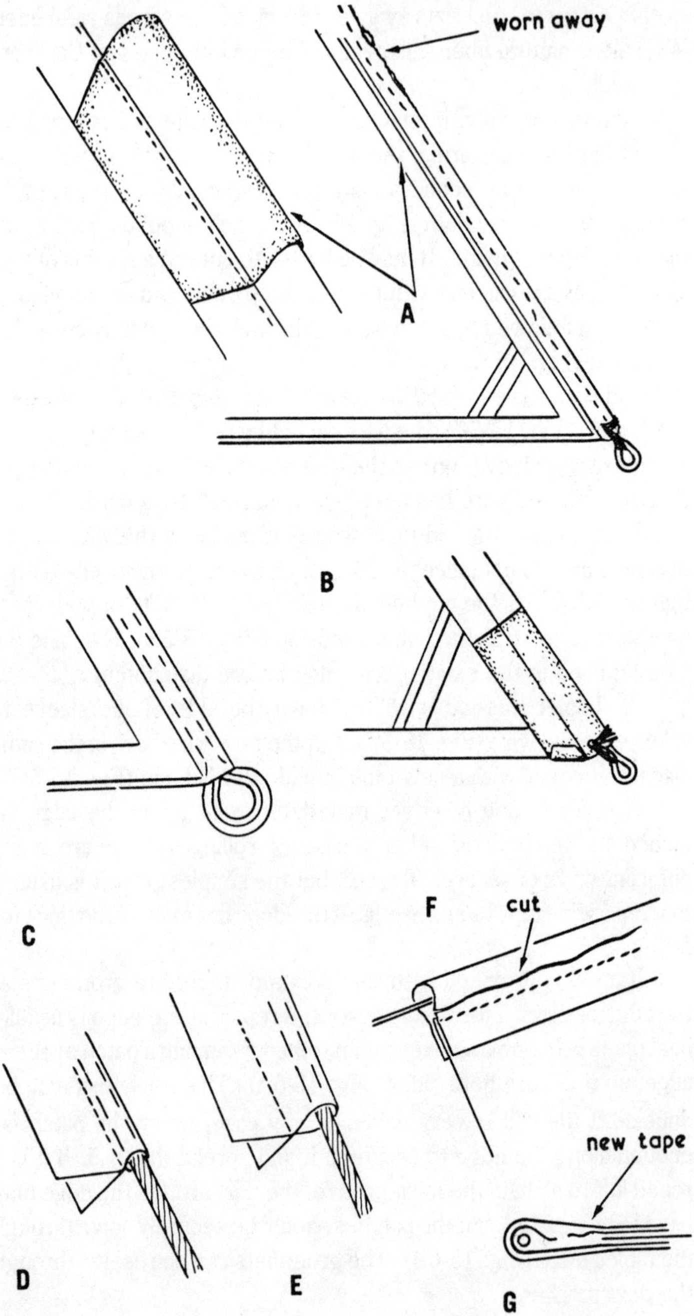

Fig. 15-5. Head sails suffer along a wire luff and parts of the tape may be reinforced.

taken by them. The pendants are then only required to gather up the slack of canvas. If the end grommets are not properly tensioned, too much load may be put on the pendants.

If a reef pendant has strained its attachment to the sail, examine how it was fixed. There is usually a patch or a band across the sail, then a worked grommet for the pendant, which is sewn in place. In a repair there may have to be a new patch, or new stitching through the old one and it maybe necessary to work a new grommet (Fig. 15-6C).

As the pull is downwards there may be some stitches through the pendants just below the grommet (Fig. 15-6D). Some of the

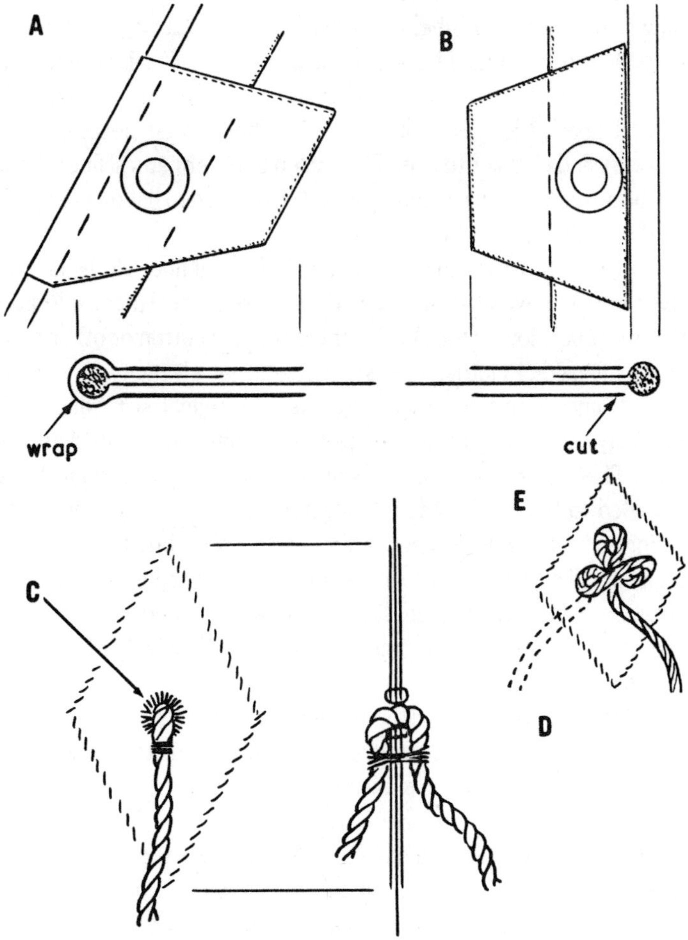

Fig. 15-6. Reef points and cringles may get hard wear and need strengthening.

pendant may be gathered up to allow for sewing around the grommet. With light flexible line this may be in a cloverleaf pattern (Fig. 15-6E), which helps to spread the load and looks neat.

NATURAL FIBER REPAIRS

Although it is unlikely that new sails will be made of anything but synthetic fiber materials, it is possible that cotton or other natural fiber sails will have to be repaired. Techniques are very similar and the actual work may be found to be easier. The softer fibrous cloths are easier to handle and they take stitches with less trouble.

The thread used should be of a matching type. It would be unwise to sew natural fiber cloths with synthetic fiber thread, mainly because the synthetic fibers lack the stretch which is inherent in the natural fiber cloth. It is also unwise to sew synthetic cloth with natural fiber thread, although this has been done because some workers find it easier to use. The cotton or other natural fiber thread will be susceptible to rot and cannot be expected to have as long a life as the cloth it is used on.

Although the techniques of sewing natural fiber cloths is much the same as sewing synthetics, there is one special consideration that must be allowed for. This is the stretch in cotton or other of the older sailmaking cloths. It is stretch and not elasticity. Nylon will stretch and return to something like its original size, due to its elasticity, but the natural fiber cloths stretch and do not return to size. This means that an old sail was made smaller than it was intended to be, to allow for its stretching. This was important for racing sails, which had to be within a certain size, but if the edge of a cruising sail attached to a spar was made to the finished size, it might stretch to be longer than the boom, or be impossible to hoist properly because no more space was left below the halliard sheave at the top of the mast.

This has to be allowed for in making a repair. The existing cloths of a much-used sail will have stretched and settled at their new size. It may be that cloth from a similar old sail can be used for a repair and this may be assumed to have stretched to its limit. In that case no stretch allowance need be made. If new cloth is used for a repair, it may be expected to stretch when the sail is put into use.

How much allowance is made for stretch and how this is arranged is largely a matter of experience, but the important thing is to allow something, unless the amount of new cloth used is quite tiny. If no allowance is made, the new part will become baggy after the sail has had some use. Its set and appearance will be spoiled. The amount of stretch to be expected varies between cloths of different weaves and weights, but it is always enough to take note of. A possible figure is elongation of about 6 in. in 20 ft. The repair may not be that length, but when brought down to 1 ft. it is about 1/3 inch stretch. In practice it seems wiser to allow proportionately more for a short distance and 1/4 inch in 6 inches is the sort of figure to consider.

This means that if a cotton patch with a 6 inch side is fixed to a cotton sail, it may be expected to stretch 1/4 inch along that edge, while the cloth it is attached to remains unaltered. As the patch is sewn on, the cloth of the sail should be allowed to be slack enough alongside the tighter patch, so it loses about 1/4 inch in the length of that seam. There will be a slight wrinkling of the sail cloth at first, but as the patch stretches in use, the final result should be smooth.

Patches and replacement panels should be cut with warp and weft matching the existing cloths. Diagonal cuts are best avoided where possible, as it is often difficult to arrive at a satisfactory assessment of relative stretch between new and old cotton cloths in these circumstances. There will have to be diagonal cuts at some edges. These are treated in the same way as synthetic materials, but size has to be regulated to allow for stretch.

Panels in the sail will have stretched in their width. If part of a panel has to be replaced and the new cloth is the same nominal width it will probably be found actually something like 3/4 inch narrower. It should be joined in at this width, which will mean some slackness where it comes against the cut old panel and this should adjust with stretch in use. Some allowance has to be made along the edge seams as well. The tabled edge should follow through, but stretch allowance is made along the seams.

New roping on a natural fiber sail ought to be made of natural fiber rope if possible. Cotton and hemp rope may be assumed to have about the same stretch as cotton fabric. So the roping takes more of the strain along an edge, it is usual to tension the rope very slightly more than the fabric it is sewn to. If it is new rope on new cotton cloth over only a shot distance, the difference in tension need only be slight, but if the new rope continues over already stretched old cloth, the cloth has to be gathered at about 1/2 inch in 1 foot to allow for the rope stretching. If the only rope available is synthetic, any stretch in it will be negligible. On old stretched canvas it can be fixed directly without any stretch allowance either way, but on a new cotton edge the cloth may be expected to stretch in relation to the rope, then the synthetic rope should be kept slack, so it is eventually tight when the cloth has stretched.

As can be seen, allowing for stretch in natural fibers requires experience or inspired guesswork. Fortunately none of this comes into the making of sails from synthetic materials, so success in the making of modern sails is easier to achieve.

REPAIR KIT

Any boat that is equipped with sails and is away for more than brief trips should carry a repair kit for sails and their associated ropes. If damage of any sort occurs, it is usually unwise to continue sailing without doing something to prevent the damage from spreading, if it is impossible to make a full repair on the spot. If the craft can be rowed or motored back to port there may be no danger, but the pleasure of sailing will have gone. If the cruise is of longer duration and there is more reliance on sails, the equipment needed for more extensive repairs should be carried. In a yacht you have to use your own resources, at least until your next visit ashore.

The extent of the repair kit will have to be adjusted to suit circumstances, but items should be drawn from those in the following notes. In a large sailing craft there may be a sewing machine, but most repairs anticipated will have to be done by hand methods.

Needles should be fairly plentiful in sizes that suit the sails. For the smallest and lightest sails domestic needles have their uses, but the triangular points of proper sail needles make pushing through cloths easier and will be appreciated after the first few inches of seam. Needles are necessarily made of hardened steel, which means they are brittle and may break, so have some spares in each size. Rusty needles are difficult to use, so keep needles in a case and oil them.

It may be worthwhile having more than one palm. If there is much sewing, you need to recruit all the help you can. It may be worth carrying a left-handed one, so a reluctant helper cannot get away with the excuse that he is left-handed!

Thread to suit the sails is best stored on reels. Hanks get tangled. Stouter thread or sail twine has uses in temporary lashings, in places where a grommet is coming away, roping is breaking, or something has to be bound in place. Although wax is not so essential with synthetic line, a ball of beeswax should be included. Thread pulled through it stays put better. If you have to make a darn or do some herringboning, rubbing wax over the repair consolidates the stitches.

You will almost certainly carry a knife for other purposes, but is it sharp enough for work on sail cloth? Synthetic ropes and cloths take the edge off a blade more than would natural fibers. It may be better to carry another knife in the repair kit and this could be one of the type with replaceable blades. There should also be a marline spike, which may be on the back of your normal knife or a separate one. When canvas was mostly heavy and stiff, a knife was the only sure cutting tool, but for the lighter cloths now used, scissors are often preferable and if your women crew are helping, they will prefer them.

How much actual sail cloth you carry for repairs is largely a matter of stowage space and what you have available, but it seems to be a fact that on most extensive voyages a point is reached where a piece of cloth just a little bigger than you have will be required. Have pieces that match the cloths of your various sails. For small patches the cloth may be lighter. Some stouter cloth may be carried for chafing pieces, but make sure you also have needles and thread stout enough to suit. Cloth tape is convenient and some self-adhesive tape may have uses.

You may be carrying spare rope for other purposes, but make sure you include some of the right size to match your sail roping or any other ropework associated with the sails. If there are metal eyelet grommets a repair afloat is usually better made with a sewn grommet over a ring. When eyelets pull out, the cloth around may be torn, so a similar eyelet cannot be inserted and it is not much use carrying spare ones and the tools to fix them.

Have spares for the hardware associated with your sails. Slides to match a track cannot be improvised so have spares. A cord loop might take the place of a hank to a forestay. A halliard might be tied to a sail head. Jib halliards do not have to join the sail with a metal fitting. Spares for most parts are convenient, but if you think ahead to possible improvisations, the number of things can be reduced. A few shackles of different sizes are useful in repairs.

There should be one or more spare sail battens. If yours are of different lengths, the spare should be for the longest, so you have something to cut down.

There are general tools you may be carrying for other purposes, but if you have pliers, screwdriver, hammer, and other tools that are used on an engine, beware of the dirt and grease they may transfer to your sails, if picked up for a job there in an emergency. Either clean them every time they are used or keep a different set for clean work.

The repair kit is better kept in a bag than a box. The container is liable to be put down on a sail spread out for repair and a fabric bag is less likely to do damage than a hard wooden or metal box, although compartments in such a box are convenient. One alternative might be a plastic box with rounded corners, but these are not usually big enough to hold rolled cloth or spare battens, and it is always better to pick up a complete package for a repair than to have to look for other things besides the tools.

Although tools and repair materials are often put in a round bag with a draw string at the end, this tends to mass everything together. What you want may not be easy to find, so you turn it all out on the deck, which is not a good idea if the yacht is rolling. It is better to have a side opening bag, with a special roll for smaller items or similar stowage arranged inside the bag (see Chapter 17).

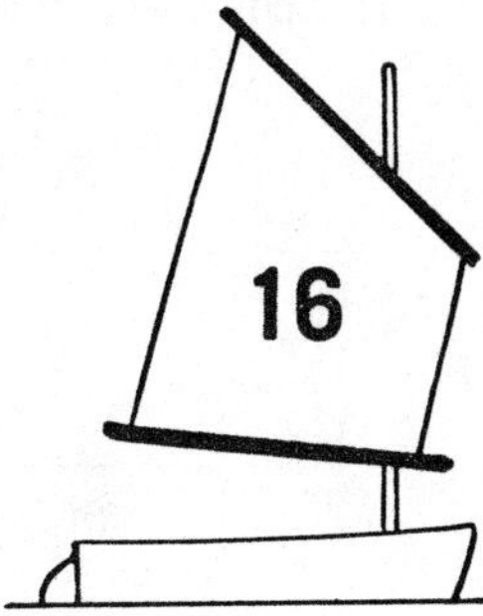

Maintenance of Sails

Although it is very true that nothing thrives on neglect, a surprising number of sails have a long and useful life despite the most casual treatment. Of course, this does not mean they would not have been kept in better condition for a longer time if some care had been lavished on them. Synthetic fiber sails do not need as much maintenance as those made of natural fibers, mainly because they are immune to rot, but abrasion and chafe or other mechanical damage may be more severe, so a carelessly used synthetic sail may not have as long a life as a more carefully maintained natural fiber one. However, on balance, Dacron and nylon sails can usually be expected to last much longer, given the usual treatment by an owner.

So far as possible, when a sail is out of use and taken off its spars it should be rolled or folded in such a way that sharp creases are avoided. Obviously, a large sail packed in a small bag will get creased, and some creasing cannot be avoided however the sail is stowed, but sharp folds can be avoided or minimized by using a large bag, even if this means the packed sail taking up more room.

If the sail has a window, try to pack the sail so the window is not creased. The transparent plastic used is surprisingly tough, but a sharp fold may break it. In any case, avoid a double fold across it (Fig. 16-1), where a fold in one direction is crossed by another. The plastic is much more brittle when cold, so a double folded window packed tightly when warm may crack later if stored in a cold place. The danger spot is at the crossing.

If there are persistent creases in a sail that do not disappear when the sail is used, they can be pressed out with a steam iron, set no hotter than is found necessary to do the job. This applies to natural and synthetic fibers.

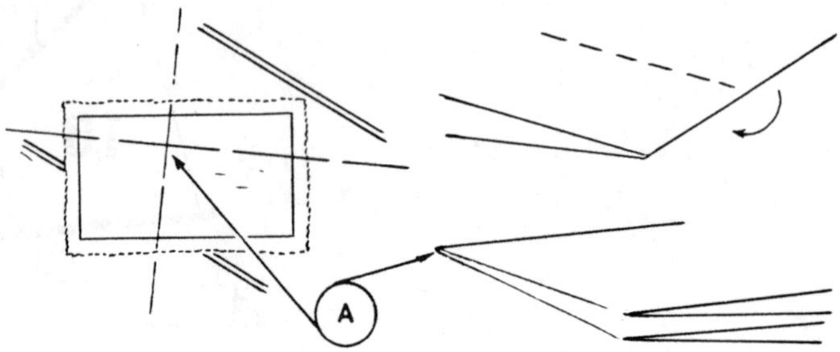

Fig. 16-1. Be careful how a window is folded.

CLEANING

If a sail has become generally dirty it can be washed in the same way as clothing made from similar materials. If the sail is small enough it can be washed in a tub. As a test for temperature, water as hot as the hand can stand is the maximum to use for most materials. Any detergent can be used in the strength the makers recommend. Alternatively, use soap and a little washing soda. For particularly dirty parts, stronger detergent can be applied and left for a while.

If a sail is too large to put in a tub it can be stretched on a flat clean surface, preferably big enough to take the whole sail in one piece. Washing can then be done with the aid of a scrubbing brush.

Follow washing with enough clean water to rinse out all detergent. The spread sail can be hosed. In itself, salt water does not do serious harm to synthetic cloths, but salt attracts moisture so dampness from the air may be attracted, causing the sail to be always slightly wet. A sail used at sea may benefit by an occasional hose down with fresh water.

Very soiled synthetic sails can be soaked overnight in a solution that will loosen the dirt prior to washing. This is a mixture of sodium metasilicate in water in the proportion of not more than 1 lb. to 1 gallon. The container should not be made of aluminum or galvanized iron. It may be made of stainless steel, procelain, or enamel. Check there are no aluminum alloy fittings or galvanized luff wire on the sail. After soaking, drain off surplus solution, but do not rinse, then continue with ordinary washing.

STAIN REMOVAL

There are many things that can stain sails, although some apparent stains on synthetic materials may be found to be only on the surface and they will come away with ordinary washing. Washing with clean water or with nothing more than mild detergent added should be tried before using more drastic treatment. Color on synthetic material may not have penetrated very deeply and any method tried for removing a stain may also remove dye from the sail. There are occasions where a stain on a colored sail may be less obvious than the uneven shades left after a treatment to remove it. Of course, a white sail has no color to lose, but then what has to be guarded against is dilution and spreading of the cause of the trouble, so there is a general marking over a larger area instead of a more concentrated dark mark.

Certain stain removers sold under trade names can be used on sails, but read the instructions, particularly noting if the makers include your materials in any they say are unsuitable. Fortunately, polyester fiber is unlikely to be damaged by the usual solvents in the strengths supplied.

Although polyester and nylon do not suffer from rot, they can be marked by mildew. This is a mold growth that develops in close damp conditions, which could happen when a sail is packed wet. It was one of the greatest problems with natural fiber sails (see the end of this chapter). Mildew leaves darkish black or green marks. It does not harm synthetic sails, but it spoils appearances.

A dry stiff brush will remove some of the looser mold growth (Fig. 16-2). What is left may be bleached. This is probably most conveniently done with a prepared domestic bleach. Steeping for maybe two hours in a weak solution, possibly 1 part bleach to 10 of water, would be more effective than a quicker treatment with a stronger solution. A bleach can be made up with a solution of sodium hypochlorite. After bleaching in either way, wash with clean water. If necessary, repeat the process. The bleach can be neutralized by a brief soak in a 1 percent solution of photographic hypo (sodium thiosulphate) followed by a clean water rinse.

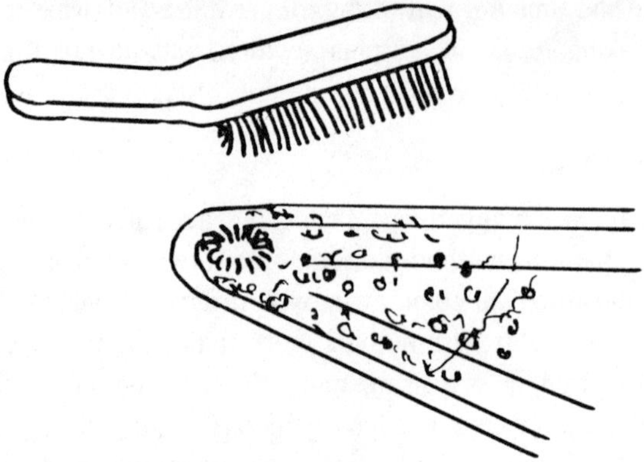

Fig. 16-2. Mildew can be brushed off.

Lubricating mixtures may get on to a sail from blocks or other gear. Such oil and grease may be removed if treated immediately by dabbing with a cloth soaked in a solvent or a degreasing fluid. Typewriter cleaning fluid can be used. Liquid intended for cleaning paint brushes may be effective.

If the oil or grease has been there longer and entered the weave to become completely or partly dry, trichlorethylene may be effective. This is the base of some commercial stain removers. Brush into the fabric and leave for a few minutes, then wash away with water. It may help to put a pad of cloth under the strain so the cleaner can take the dissolved grease through (Fig. 16-3). Most solvents are inflammable, so avoid naked flames in the vicinity and do not smoke. There may have to be more than one treatment. The last one, with clean cloth and fluid, will be used to remove dispersed dissolved grease that might leave a cloudy effect over a larger area. Follow with a wash using detergent and water, which is then rinsed away with clean water.

Tar, pitch, and their products that are sometimes used on the bottoms of boats or on docks, may leave stains very much like oil. Similar treatment can be used, but there are other solvents which are effective. Paint thinners, naphtha, and alcohol can be tried. Do not use paint stripper. As tar is a more intensive black stain than oil, try to localize the work and get as much as possible directly through to a pad of absorbent cloth on the other side without spreading the dissolved tar.

Sails which have come into contact with non-stainless iron or steel may get stained with rust. Contact with some varieties of brass may cause the green stains of verdigris. Oxalic acid is needed to remove these stains. This is a poison, so hands and sails should be thoroughly washed after use. Use a solution made by dissolving 1 oz. of oxalic acid in each pint of hot water. Soak the stained part in this, then wash with plenty of clean water. If necessary, repeat until the stain has gone. Do not re-use a solution and do not allow any awaitng use, or being applied, to come into contact with metal. Do not use a brush with metal binding. It is better to wear rubber gloves and use a cloth. Contamination with metal may *cause* staining instead of *removing* it.

Paint or varnish accidentally splashed onto sails can be a nuisance. With some modern paints it may be impossible to completely remove the marks they make. Trichlorethylene, paint brush cleaner and acetone can be tried. If the paint or varnish is known to have a spirit base, alcohol should dissolve it. If the paint is more on one side than the other, put the sail with the paint side downwards on a pad of absorbent cloth and use plenty of solvent from the other side. It is inadvisable to use any paint stripper, as this may have too violent an action, but in any case never use an alkaline stripper on polyester fabric.

It can be seen that removing stains from a sail brings many problems. Great care is needed and if there is any doubt about the cause of the stain or what the substance is, try a very small patch first. If it is dyed polyester be particularly cautious as the base color may come away with the stain. Many solvents are unpleasant, if not actually dangerous, to breathe, so work outdoors or in a well venti-

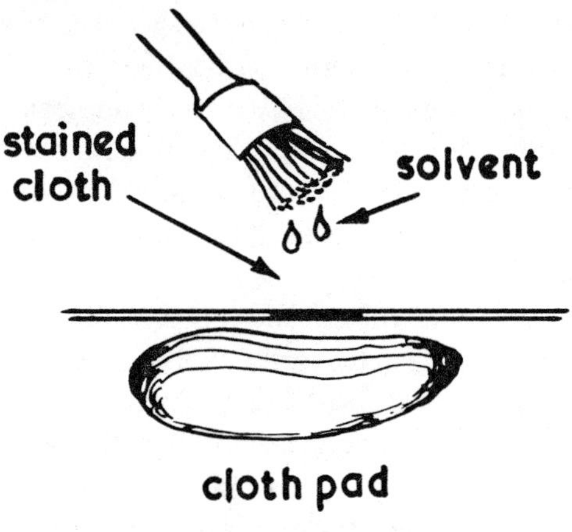

Fig. 16-3. Stain may be washed through to a pad.

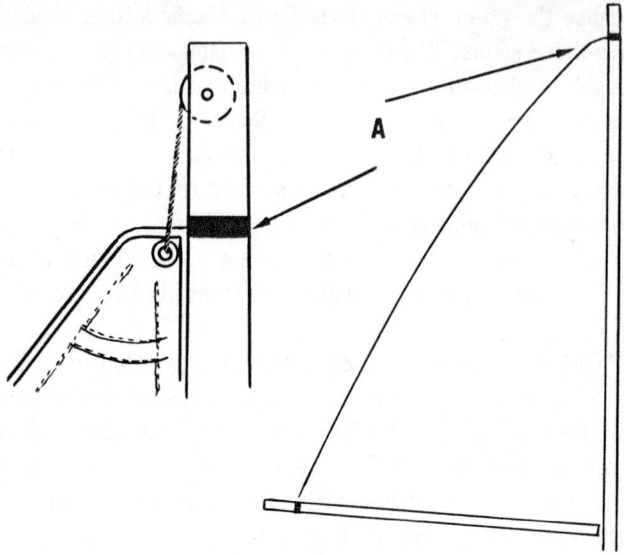

Fig. 16-4. Marked spars help prevent over-stretching.

lated place. Avoid contact with skin or clothing and take the obvious precautions with inflammable fluids.

SAIL SETTING

A polyester (Dacron, Terylene) sail is made in the correct size because there will be no stretch expected. However, it is possible to distort a sail. Head sails with wire luffs are unlikely to suffer because the wire length should be such as to properly tension the sail when it is hoisted, while in the other direction the sheet controls the sail.

When the sail is fixed to spars, such as the mast and boom of a main sail, care is needed to avoid excessively tensioning one way. There is often a means of gaining a purchase when hoisting the sail up the mast, but a direct hand pull may be all that is allowed for along the boom. Under these circumstances, it is possible to get a sail much tighter up the mast than along the boom. The sail was not made to take these uneven loads. An indication of this fault may be a crease crossing somewhere near the ends of the battens. Although a polyester sail has a good resistance to distortion, regular over-tightening in this way could permanently affect the set of the sail.

The black bands painted on spars of racing craft serve to show the limit to which the sail should go along the spar and this is a practice that might usefully be employed on cruising yachts to reduce the risk of over-stretching an edge (Fig. 16-4).

Most man-made fibers are affected by heat and light. Polyester fibers will deteriorate if exposed for long periods to very bright sunlight. For the average sail used in temperate waters this is not a serious problem but in more tropical climates sails out of use should be protected. If the sail is taken off it should be stowed in its bag. If a main sail is left on the boom, it should have a fitted cover (Fig. 16-5 and see Chapter 17). Apart from protection from the effects of the sun, using a cover is good practice in any case, as this keeps the sail clean and protects it from bird droppings.

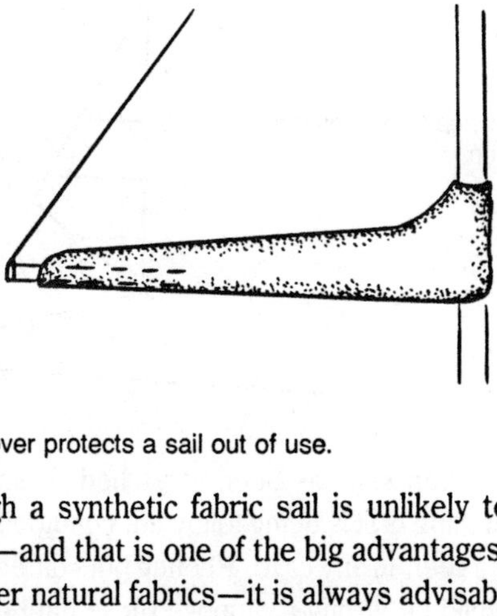

Fig. 16-5. A cover protects a sail out of use.

Although a synthetic fabric sail is unlikely to be damaged if stowed wet—and that is one of the big advantages of the synthetic materials over natural fabrics—it is always advisable to dry a sail at the first opportunity. Moisture brings insects, dirt, and probably mildew. If it is salt water, wash a sail with fresh water before drying it.

NATURAL FIBER SAILS

Much of what has been said about synthetic sail maintenance is also applicable to cotton and flax sails, but there are extra considerations because natural fiber sails are susceptible to rot and they tend to stretch. With a new sail there is a need for careful stretching before the sail is used seriously.

Head sails are not much of a problem. The wire luff preserves much of the shape, but the correct line of the sheet is important so the load comes along the miter (Fig. 16-6) and does not pull high or low and cause one part to stretch more than the other, making the sail distort and set badly always afterwards.

It is the main sail for which care is needed in the initial stretching. Choose a calm dry day. Natural fiber rope around the edge will be put on at a slightly tighter tension than that of the cloth. The first stretch along spars may tension the rope until it is the same as the cloth. Sail the yacht in this way, but apply a little more tension at intervals so foot and luff are gradually lengthened until they reach the indended size. The leech should have lengthened proportionately while the yacht sails in light winds.

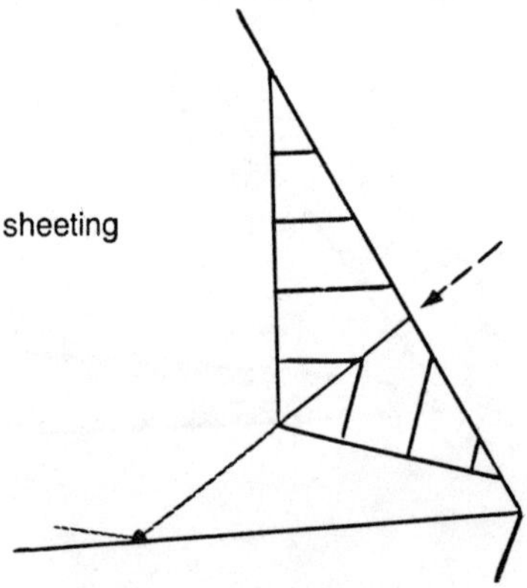

Fig. 16-6. Correct head sail sheeting prevents distortion.

Until a new cotton sail has been stretched, it should not be reefed. If the stretching drill is being followed, conditions will not be such as to require a reef, in any case, Reefing puts different loads on the cloth and it would be wrong to impose these until the cloth has been stretched.

Natural fibers tend to shrink when wetted. When they dry they should return to their normal length. However, if the fibers are held to their full length when wet, as they would be along the spars of a sail, there is a risk that they will then dry to a relaxed state that is longer than before. This is unlikely to be enough to matter with a small sail, but on a large yacht it may be better to loosen luff and foot while the sail is wet. Otherwise there is a risk of the sail becoming too big for its spars. Thick rope will stretch more than thin rope.

Because of the risk of rot, cotton and other natural fiber sail fabrics are treated with solutions that give them a resistance to the absorption of water and the onset of rot. Once rot has taken a hold, the process cannot be reversed. It may be disguised, but the weakening is still there. Mildew, which may be regarded as not very serious on synthetic fibers, is attacking natural fibers as a form of rot when dark spots show evidence of its presence.

Although there are formulas for making proofing solutions, it is simpler and usually preferable to buy a ready-made mixture. Some proofing solutions are colored, but in practice it is very difficult to get an even color on the sail. Even an uneven color may be preferable to the dirty and dishevelled appearance of an old cotton sail, but it is possible to use a clear solution on a sail where the existing appearance is satisfactory. The life and effectiveness of a proofing solution is not very long, so fairly frequent treatment is advisable if a natural fiber sail is to be preserved.

The best way to proof a sail is to soak it in the solution, and that is how it is done during manufacture, but the usual one-off method with a small quantity of solution is to brush it on. This should be done liberally, and the spread from a given amount is unlikely to be as much as optimistically stated on the can.

Even when the cloth is proofed, a sail should not be left long packed in a wet condition. It should be opened and dried as soon as possible. Frequent wetting will progressively reduce any water repellent qualities, and reproofing becomes necessary. Mildew seems to more readily attack new cloth than old, so particular care is needed with new cotton sails.

Salt has more tendency to attract moisture in natural fabrics than in synthetic ones, or it seems to. This means that washing with fresh water before drying is more important. Washing to clean should only be done with mild soap or detergents and not excessively hot water. There is a certain body or solidity put into the fabric during manufacture and powerful laundering or the use of chemicals may leave the cloth much more porous and therefore not as efficient.

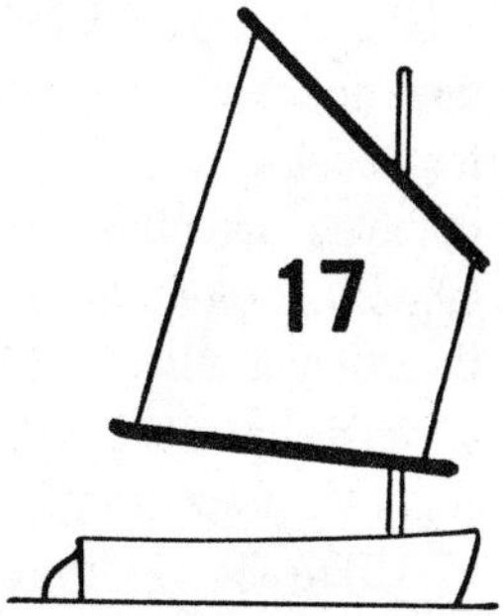

Sailing Equipment

There is other canvaswork besides sails that is the concern of the sailmaker. More sailcloth items are either essential or desirable equipment for a properly found yacht. It is almost impossible to make sails without producing some waste cloth. The overall shape and the fact that cloths have to go right across without joins and are then cut at odd angles means that there are inevitable pieces left which are unlikely to all be used in sails, even for patches. Other items can be made from these offcuts, although some equipment is better made from stouter fabric.

The most obvious ancillary items are sail bags. There should be a bag for every sail. The main and head sails of a dinghy may be packed together and there will be little difficulty in knowing which is which, but larger sails might be confused if packed more than one to a bag.

The usual sail bags may be made from the same cloth as the sails, although a stouter fabric will provide more protection and be more suitable for hard use, particularly if the sails have to be stored alongside other harder and rougher items.

A bag should be considerably bigger than the sail when tightly rolled. It is better for the sail to be loosely packed and there are many circumstances when the sail will have to be pushed into its bag with little opportunity to fold or roll it. Plenty of space will be welcomed. Some neatness may be desirable, but if a seasick crew on a heaving deck wants to stow a sail quickly, neatness is not the first consideration.

MAKING BAGS

The simplest bag is made from folded cloth (Fig. 17-1A), but it does not have much capacity. Small bags of this type have their uses for keeping small things together. Reserve sail hanks, shackles, thimbles, and other hardware may go in a bag made from a scrap of fabric. Another similar bag may have the block of beeswax, reels of thread, and other small items inside the large repair bag.

The basic bag is made inside-out. The first job is tabling the top edge. If a drawstring is to be used, make the tabling fairly wide (Fig. 17-1B) to allow for the bunching up of cloth when the string is pulled. Either heat seal the edges or turn in and sew the ends of the tabling (Fig. 17-1C) to prevent fraying. One line of stitches along the side and bottom will probably be sufficient (Fig. 17-1D). Cut edges ought to be heat sealed to prevent fraying, but if the bag is not intended to have a very long life, this may not matter. Another treatment is to cut the edge with pinking shears (Fig. 17-1E).

Turn the bag back the right way to bring the edges inside (Fig. 17-1F). Pull a draw string through the tabling with a bodkin, blunt needle, or a safety pin. So the ends do not pull back into the tabling, tie them together (Fig. 17-1G).

If the bag is made by hand sewing, the tabling is turned under and sewn, then the other edges joined by round stitching (Fig. 17-1H) and the bag turned the right way. Making these little bags by hand provides practice in the techniques that may have to be used afloat in emergency repairs to sails.

A bag is given much more capacity if a round bottom is fitted (Fig. 17-2A). Besides allowing a greater circumference than the sail is expected to require allow some excess length so the top can be drawn close without being at all tight on the folded sail. If battens are to be packed with the sail, it is probably their length that will govern the length of the bag (Fig. 17-2B). Letting battens project is bad practice. Fortunately, precision is not important. The distance around the bag is a little more than three times the intended diameter, plus a little for making the seam. The bottom is the intended size of circle, with enough around for the seam to the tubular part of the bag.

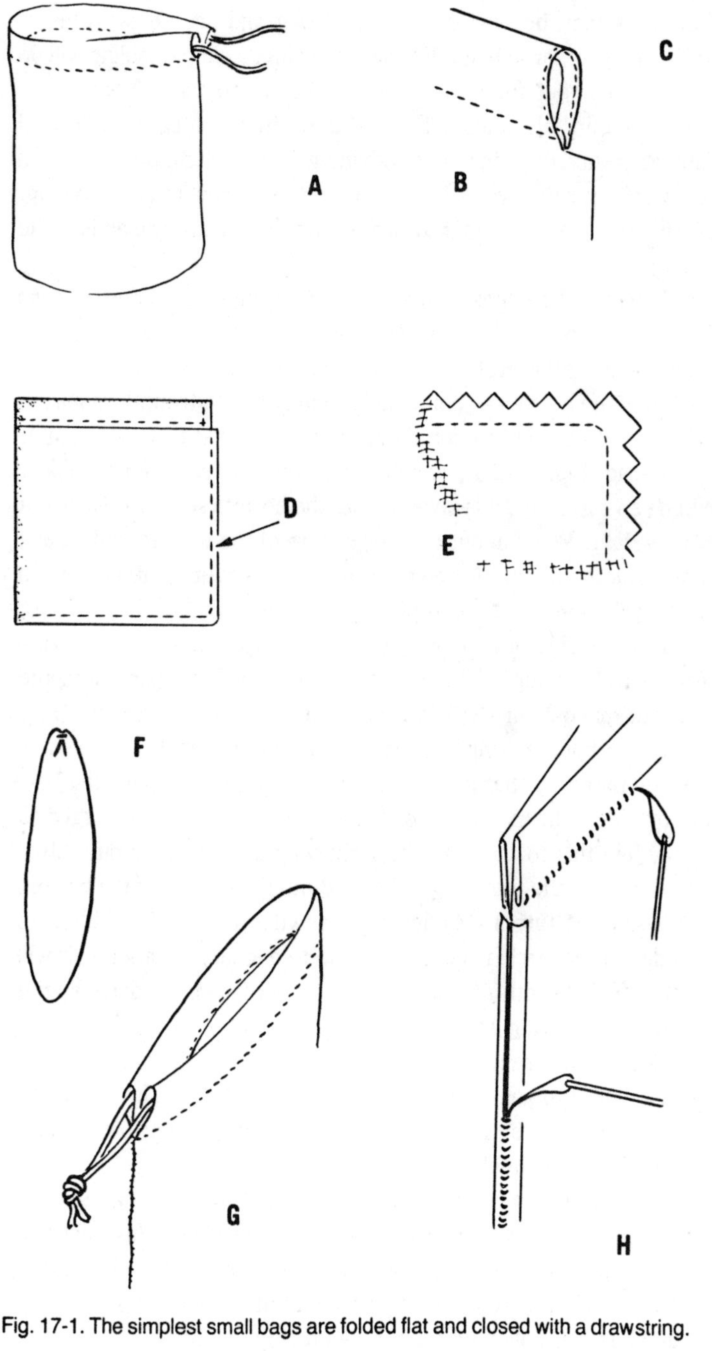

Fig. 17-1. The simplest small bags are folded flat and closed with a drawstring.

The top of the bag may be closed with a drawstring, but eyelet grommets may be preferable in any bag and are certainly more satisfactory for large bags. For a drawstring, a simple tabling will do (Fig. 17-2C), but for grommets it is better to turn in enough to include a third thickness (Fig. 17-2D). In most cases a row of stitches around the edge of the tabling will be enough, but a bag for a heavy sail may be strengthened with an extra row of stitches (Fig. 17-2E). If there is to be a drawstring, turn in and sew the ends of the tabling.

Join the tube edges with a flat seam, using sealed edges or turn them in. Make up the bag inside out, so the tabling will be on the outside during the first assembly (Fig. 17-2F).

How the bottom is joined in depends on the strength required. In the simplest construction there is one row of stitches—straight, not zig-zag (Fig. 17-2G), which result in the edges coming inside. When sewing around it is unlikely that the bottom seam will work out exactly right. When about three-quarters of the way around, check on what cloth remains and adjust more or less overlap of the bottom to bring the length of the remainder of the seam right.

A single row of stitches around the bottom may not be considered strong enough. There could be a second line parallel to the first, but this only provides a reserve if the other stitches fail (Fig. 17-2H), without sharing any strain until that happens.

Another way that increases initial strength is to have the bottom outside. Cut the circle for the bottom an inch or so bigger all round. Join this to the tube the right way out, but turn out only a narrow part of the tube (Fig. 17-2J). Bend the excess of the bottom up the side and turn in its edge to be sewn around (Fig. 17-2K). As the edge of the circle is being pulled in to a smaller diameter, it will pucker. If the width of this seam is kept reasonably narrow, the amount of puckering will be kept less than if a wide seam is used. As the edge is sewn, regulate the creasing so it is evenly spaced around the bag. This type of seam could be made with the bag inside-out so the puckering will be hidden inside, but letting the bottom turn up outside the tube should give better protection.

Another way of making a round bag avoids the use of a separate bottom piece. This was used in the seaman's ditty bag—his small bag for rope and canvas working tools. Instead of cutting the bottom of the tube straight across, it is cut into a number of triangles, after enough has been allowed for the seam (Fig. 17-2L).

Six is a reasonable number. If the sides of the triangle are the same length the bottom will be almost flat, but if deeper triangles are used it will run down to a point, while rounding the edges of each triangle can produce a curved bottom (Fig. 17-2M).

When the tube has been sewn up, have the bag inside-out and pull the triangles together with a row of straight machine stiches or by hand sewing round seams (Fig. 17-2N). Turn the bag the right way and fix grommets.

If grommets are used instead of a draw cord through the tabling, the neck will pull closer and tighter if there are plenty of grommets. The minimum is six for even a small bag, but there could be many more for a large bag. It is important that there is an even number (Fig. 17-2P), otherwise a cord passed through will have one end inside and one outside. Knot or join the ends to prevent loss of the cord, but allow plenty of slackness so the neck of the bag is not restricted when putting in or removing the sail or other things.

A bag for tools or other heavier items is better made from stouter cloth than is used for sails. It does not have to be polyester or other synthetic material and the bag might be better for its purpose and easier to sew if a cotton canvas of about 8 oz. grade was used. However, the limit may be the capacity of the available sewing machine, unless the bag is to be sewn by hand.

A tool bag may be round. If it is to be taken aloft, this is probably the best shape as there is little risk of it tipping if it is carried and suspended by its drawstring. However, for work on deck, a flatter open-topped or side-opening bag is more convenient because the contents are more easily seen and sorted.

It is an advantage if the bag has some rigidity so it is better made of canvas stouter than sailcloth, while extra thicknesses will also help to hold its shape. There is often an advantage in having the bag waterproof. Although proofed fabric may be used, there could be leaks through the sewn seams. One way of reducing this risk is to fold the canvas to shape so there are few cut edges to be sewn. You may not wish to carry water in the bag, but a watertight bag can be put down on a wet surface or splashed with waves without risk of the contents becoming wet.

An open bag with handles can be folded from a single piece without cuts (Fig. 17-3A). To get its shape, draw the base size with extending lines (Fig. 17-3B). Allow enough length one way to suit

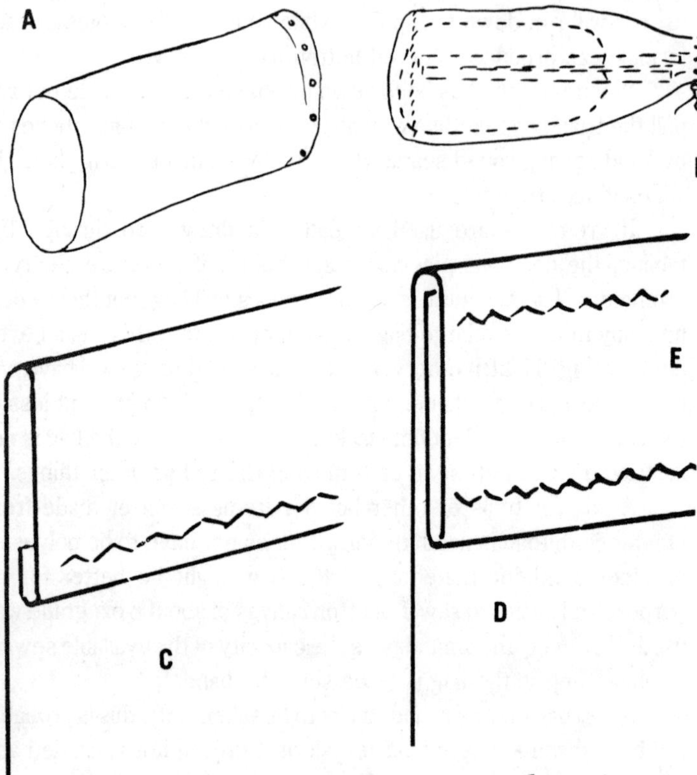

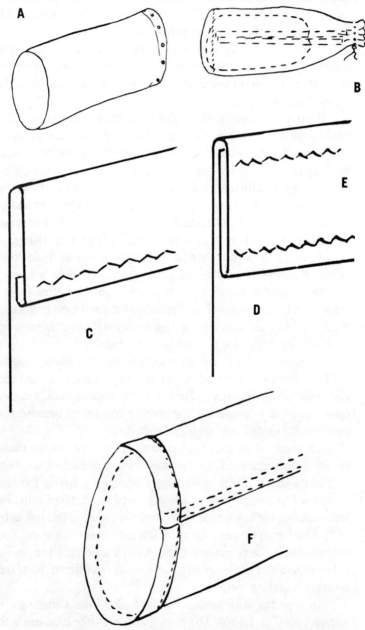

Fig. 17-2. A round-bottomed bag may have an inserted bottom or segments of the side material. There should be an even number of grommets at top. (Continued on next page.)

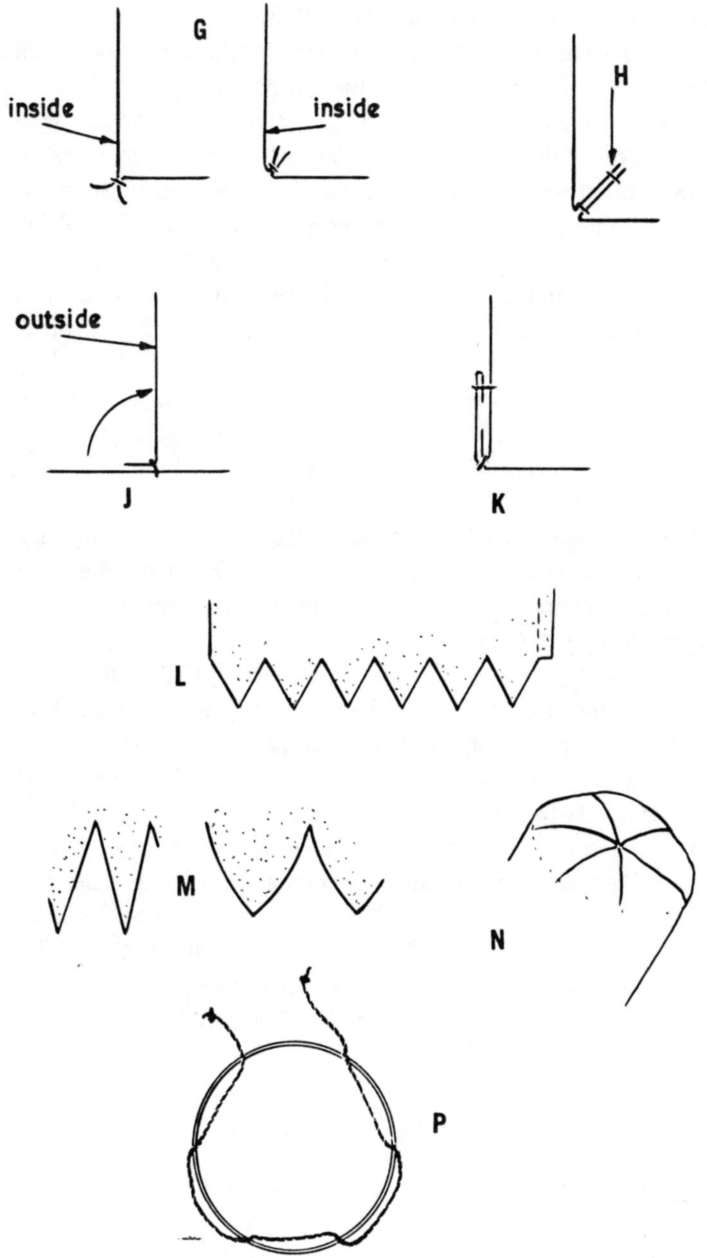
G
inside
inside
H
outside
J
K
L
M
N
P

the height with enough for tabling (Fig. 17-3C), and enough the other way to make up the width with something for the overlap of a seam (Fig. 17-3D). Mark triangles for the bottom fold up.

Use a seam rubber on the fold lines and bend up the canvas to shape. Try the fit of the parts. If tabling is to be done first, open the canvas after testing the size and shape, otherwise pin or use a few large sticking stitches to hold the seams in place. Leaving tabling until after making up the bag allows for correcting any discrepancies, but it is easier to hold for sewing while flat. Flat seams are used to join the edges, then the triangles turned up and sewn (Fig. 17-3E).

If hand sewing is used, the neatest seams are obtained by stretching each as it is sewn, with the sail hook. Meantime, you have the work over your knees, which are protected by a stout apron or a piece of scrap canvas, while one hand stretches and the other sews.

The turned-up triangles should come on the outside, but the tabled top edge should be inside. It can be sewn with the bag inside-out. Rub down the folds at the corners. There may be some advantage in reinforcing them with strips of tape sewn on to stiffen and protect them from chafe.

Although independent handles attached only to the sides might be satisfactory for light loads, the greatest strength comes from carrying them underneath. Cut a strip of canvas long enough to wrap around with enough above to make the handle loops. The ends will meet under the bag. The handles are given shape with pieces of rope and it is the diameter of this that governs the width of strip. A reasonable thickness is needed for comfort in carrying. The rope should be not less than 1/2 inch diameter and could be 3/4 inch. Make the canvas wide enough to go around this almost twice (Fig. 17-3F), so it can be turned in until the edges meet.

Pieces of rope about 6 inches long should make a comfortable handle. Seal the ends or whip them. It would be best to scrape away some of the fibers at each end of the rope to give it a slight taper (Fig. 17-3G), but this is not usually done.

Fold the length of fabric and rub down the seams hard. Position a piece of rope and sew the edges together over it. This can be done with a simple baseball stitch (Fig. 17-3H) or it is easier to get a tight close fit if herringbone stitches are used (Fig. 17-3J). In both cases start with a knot under one side and use doubled thread. Let the stitches continue for a short distance past each end of the rope.

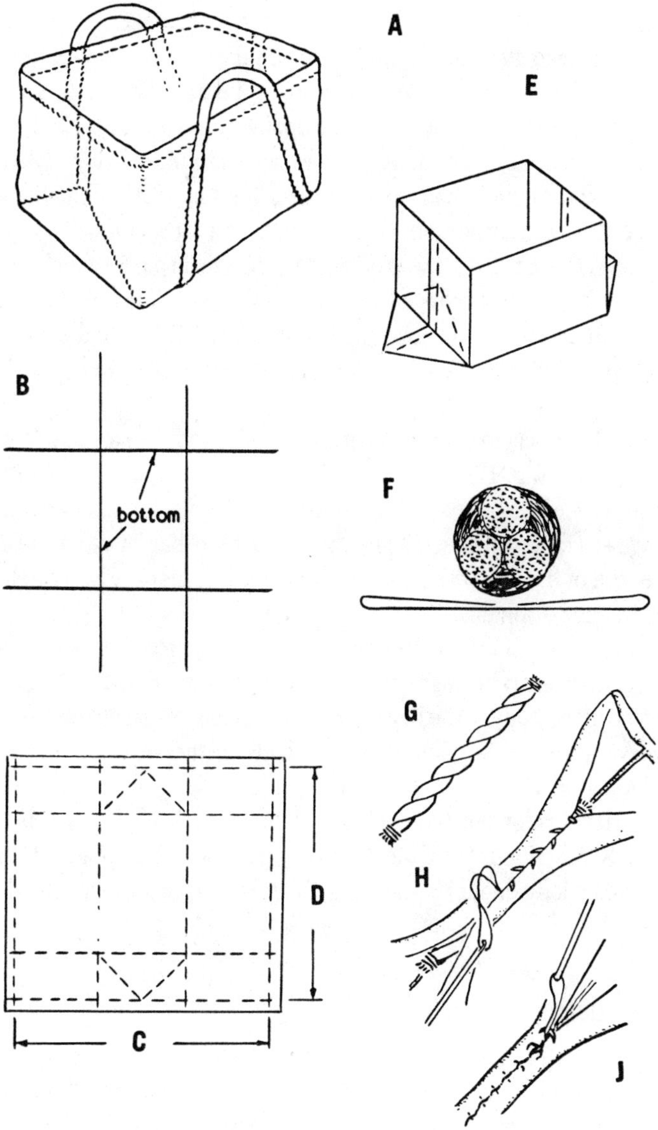

Fig. 17-3. A strong bag can be made without cuts. Roped handles are comfortable and strong.

Position the handle strip on the bag. It is a help to pencil its location and use a few strike-up marks or hold the strip in place with a few large sticking stitches. Sew along the edges by machine or hand.

Watch that the folded strip remains parallel and the creases do not vary.

A similar type of bag may be given flaps to overlap on the top (Fig 17-4A). The folded construction can be used, when the flaps in both directions are made by extra cloth in the length (Fig. 17-4B). An alternative is to make the ends from separate pieces (Fig. 17-4C).

In the simplest bag the ends are joined in with round stitching while the bag is inside-out (Fig. 17-4D). In a stronger arrangement the bag is kept the right way outwards, then main parts of the bag are sewn with some surplus edge (Fig. 17-4E), which is then turned in for another line of stitches (Fig. 17-4F). With light cloth the corners may be folded and sewn, but for stouter fabric a miter will have to be cut.

A large bag may not keep its shape unaided. It may help to sew in divisions (Fig. 17-4G). A piece of plywood could be made to form a base. It need not be fixed, but it should be a close fit in the bottom. If there is a long stiff article to be carried in a tool bag, it can be held to the side of the bag with tapes and studs or fasteners (Fig. 17-4H) so it provides stiffness.

Compartments can be made inside the bag to take tools, which can conveniently be pushed into loops or pockets (Fig. 17-4J). These can be in the body of the bag or under a flap, but be careful there is no risk of a tool sliding out. Pocketed ends to the stowage may help (Fig. 17-4K).

Handles for this type of bag may be of fabric enclosing rope, as already described, but if the bag is to be carried single-handed, they should be long enough to meet, even when the bag is over-full (Fig. 17-4L).

SAIL COVERS

If a main sail is left on its boom, it should be protected by a cover, which may be made of sail cloth or stouter fabric. The lowered triangular sail settles with considerably more thickness near the mast than at the clew, so the cover has to allow for this. It is not a straight taper and there will be a hollow curve up towards the mast end. It is usual to make the cover to fasten around sail and boom, with a flap around the mast (Fig. 17-5A).

Because of the shaping it is best to make the cover in halves with a seam along the top. The bottom should not come close, but there should be space for ventilation. This is also important if part of the sail is wet. An overlapping cover would seal in moisture, with a risk of mildew starting.

Measure around the boom and sail at intervals. It will probably be best to make a paper template of half the cover from these measurements (Fig. 17-5B) and try it in position. At the mast there should be a fairly tight sleeve to prevent the water running down the mast from finding its way into the sail (Fig. 17-5C). The length should be enough to cover the clew of the sail, but the limit will usually be set by metal fittings near the end for sheet or topping lift.

Some sail covers have the edges meeting under the boom joined with a zip fastener. While this is neat and effective, so long as the zipper continues to function correctly, it seals the cover too much for ventilation. If the zipper fails or jams, there is no convenient alternative way of joining the edges. It is more seamanlike to use ties, which could be cord sewn on (Fig. 17-5D), but strips of fabric are preferable (Fig. 17-5E). Another way is to have grommets along the edge of the cover and lace along with one piece of cord (Fig. 17-5F).

Use the template to mark out one side. Make an allowance for the top seam and for tabling the bottom edge. If necessary, use flat seams to join cloths to make up the length. A sail cover can often be made from offcuts left from making a sail, with seams as necessary. Mark the opposite sides together. Allow for turning in a tabling across the clew end and for tabling at the mast end or a flap to wrap around the mast (Fig. 17-5G).

Do the tabling on the two halves then join them along the top seam. Make up the sleeve to go around the mast. It is best for any shaping to conform to the bundled sail to be in the basic cover, so the sleeve is a parallel piece which can go around in one piece (Fig. 17-5H). If there has to be some shaping in the sleeve, it will have to be made in two parts (Fig. 17-5J). On some sail covers the sleeve goes quite far up the mast. This has the advantage of allowing three or more ties to give a firm fastening, but a distance up the mast equal to the distance around it is a reasonable shape (Fig. 17-5K)

The flap to go around the mast is stitched to one side and there may be ties attached to it or arranged to go over it (Fig. 17-5L). Ties can be made from strips of canvas. Use one line of stitching near the edges (Fig 17-5M). Fasten a safety pin to one end and use this to pull

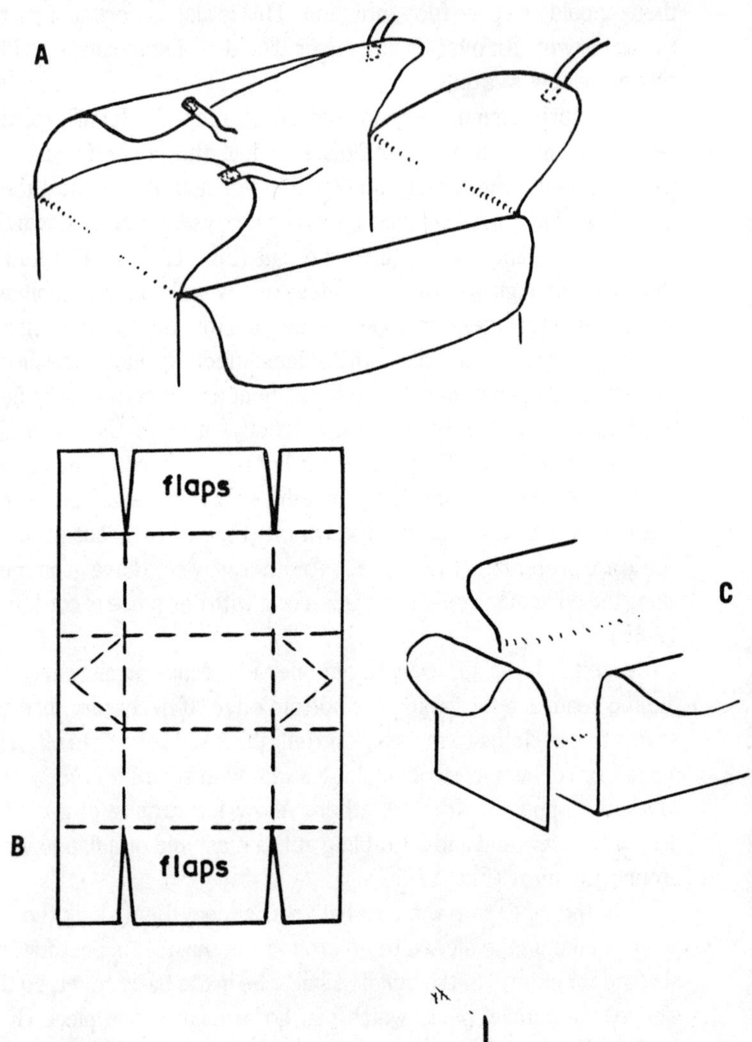

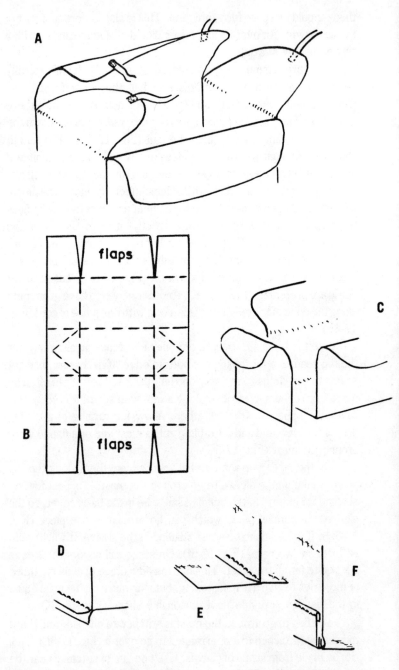

Fig. 17-4. A bag may have flaps to close it and be fitted with stowage for tools and other gear. (Continued on next page.)

G

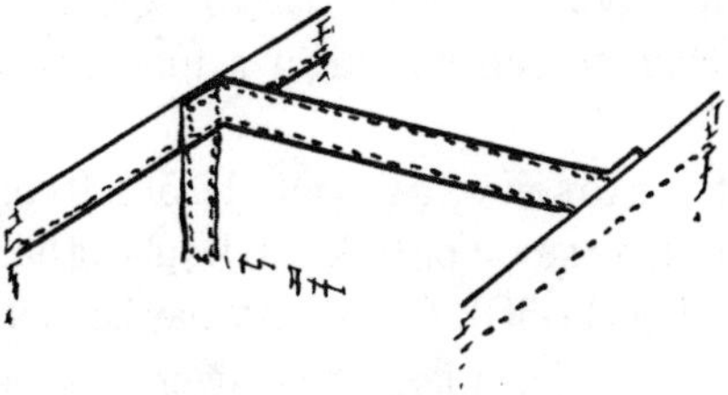

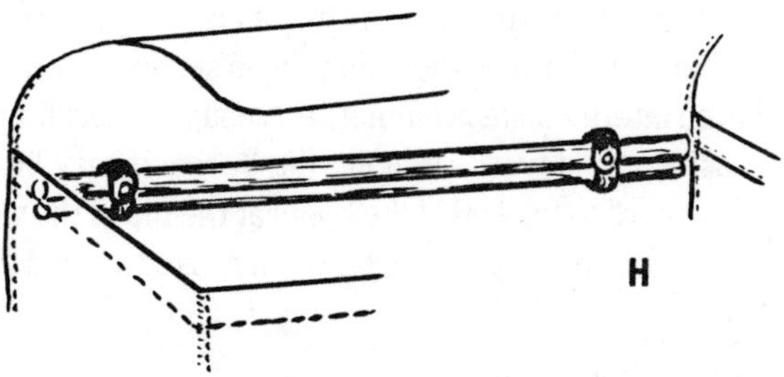

H

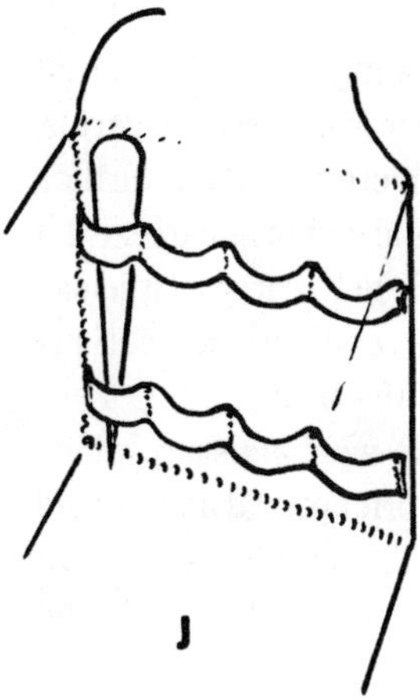

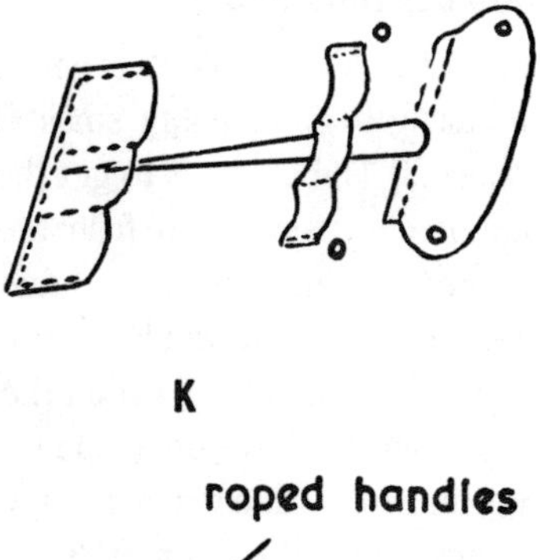

K

J

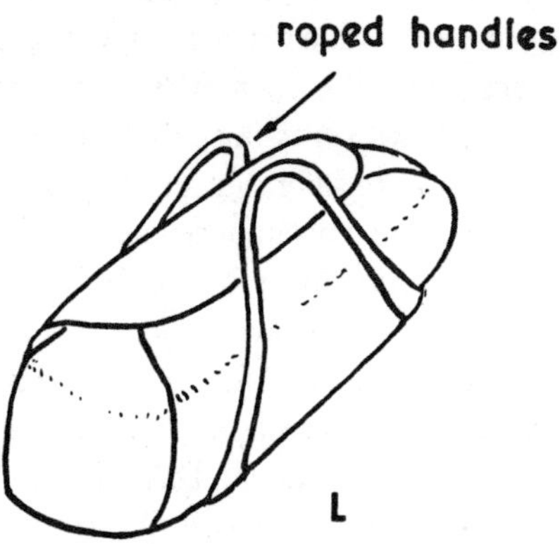

L

the tube inside-out (Fig. 17-5N). How easy this is to do depends on the grade and stiffness of the cloth. You may have to experiment with a scrap piece of the cloth to see how tight a tube can be reversed.

Use several rows of stitches to sew on a tie (Fig. 17-5P). If cord is used, seal and whip its ends, then sew it on by hand. Doubling back the end gives extra security (Fig. 17-5Q). Grommets may be metal eyelet types through the tabling. For a large sail cover they are better sewn. If continuous lacing is used, the end of the cord should be spliced to one end grommet to prevent loss. For a very long cover it may be better to arrange the lacing line in sections, with a new part spliced to an intermediate grommet. It is usual to start fitting a cover at the mast end and work aft along the boom. It may be helpful to have a tie or cord to the end of the boom at the top of the clew end so the cover can be stretched along before it is fixed around the sail and boom.

TRAPEZE HARNESS

The use of a trapeze is becoming increasingly common as an aid to sailing a great many small craft. Many racing classes permit trapezes. The object is to get the weight of a crew member further outboard by using a wire from the mast, thus allowing him to exert a greater righting moment and therefore continue to carry a large sail area in winds that would have compelled a reduction of sail if his weight had been kept within the bounds of the boat.

Trapezes have developed from a simple webbing sling, which was uncomfortable to use for anything but a brief period and it could be unsafe for the user. More elaborate webbing harnesses have been made with crossing parts that held the user more securely and were therefore safer, but anything built up of comparatively narrow parts becomes uncomfortable in a short time, so the better harnesses still have webbing to take the load. The seat part is made more comfortable with canvas, though.

There are metal fittings which are essential and the design of these affect construction. The main load is taken by a central plate with some sort of hook. This engages with a ring in use and is the only attachment to the wire. When this is disengaged, all the harness stays on the wearer. There will also have to be buckles or other adjustment for the webbing which goes over the shoulders. The

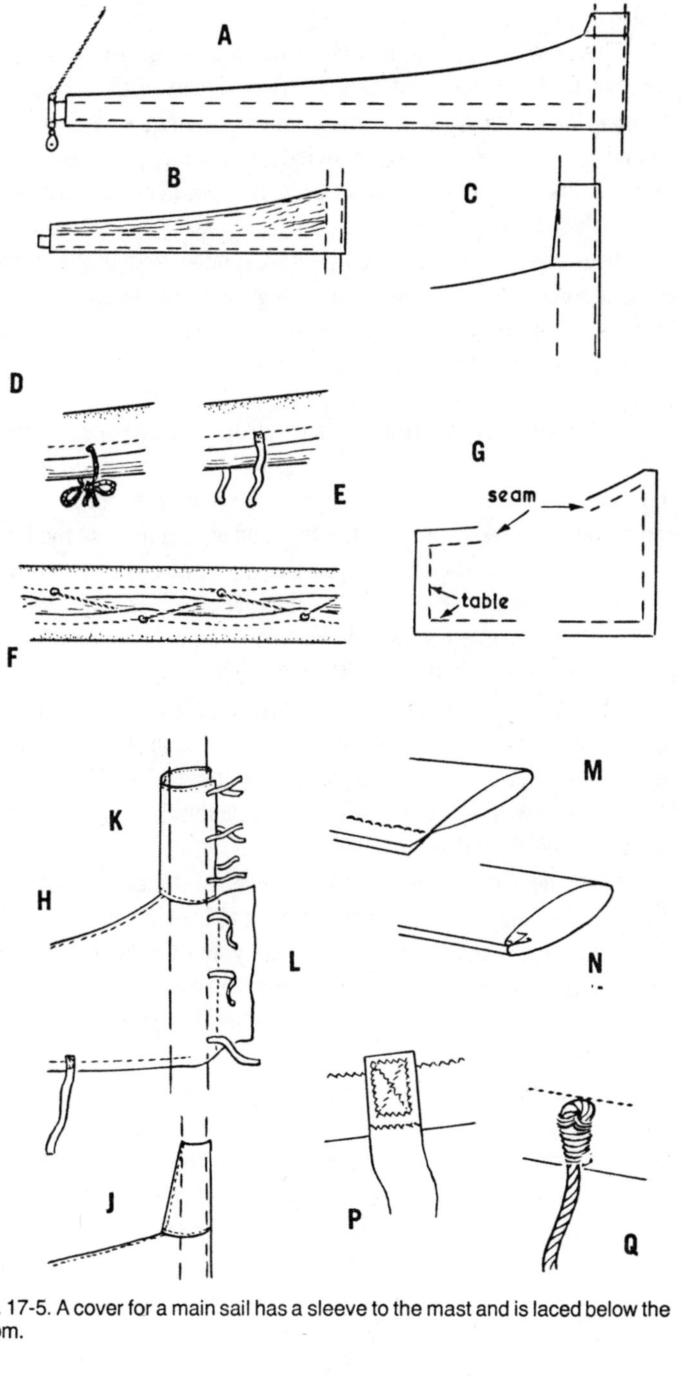

Fig. 17-5. A cover for a main sail has a sleeve to the mast and is laced below the boom.

webbing used will be about 2 inches wide, but this must be matched to the metal fittings obtained.

There are variations in harness design, but basically the hook plate has to come just above the center of gravity of the wearer and the main load when he is near horizontal is taken by a webbing band around his seat, with canvas provided as a concession to comfort (Fig. 17-6A). Shoulder straps keep the harness in place and provide some safety by doing this.

Sizes are best obtained by using a model—either the regular crew or someone estimated to be as big as anyone likely to use the harness. There may be an adjustment provided around the seat and between the legs, but these vital strength parts are better without breaks.

The important construction is the seat. Make a paper template and experiment with shape. The user will be near straight most of the time, not sitting, although he must be able to bend. Shape the canvas outline to come around the hips and almost meet at the front. Let it be as high as the waist behind, and far enough down to reach the top of the thighs (Fig. 17-6B). The piece between the legs may be webbing, but the canvas can be cut so some shaping provides comfort by spreading the load (Fig. 17-6C).

The canvas should be reasonably stout. It may be synthetic or natural fiber around 10 oz. grade. Two or more thicknesses can be used and sewn together by diagonal lines of stitching (Fig. 17-6D). There can be a thin layer of plastic foam sandwiched between (Fig. 17-6E). Tape the edges.

It may be satisfactory to sew on pieces of webbing at each side (Fig. 17-6F), with many rows of stitching to provide strength. This allows the canvas seat to mold comfortably, but webbing all round is stronger (Fig. 17-6G). The webbing may cross and be sewn under the seat. If the plate has rollers in the slots this allows the wearer some sideways movement.

The shoulder part of the harness is made up something like trouser suspenders. At the back the webbing is sewn to the seat canvas and there is usually a crosspiece to prevent the straps from slipping off the shoulders (Fig. 17-6H). At the front a central piece of webbing goes up to meet the shoulder straps just above waist level. Some metal fittings for this part have a buckle arrangement at this point and the two straps adjust there, or one strap may pass through

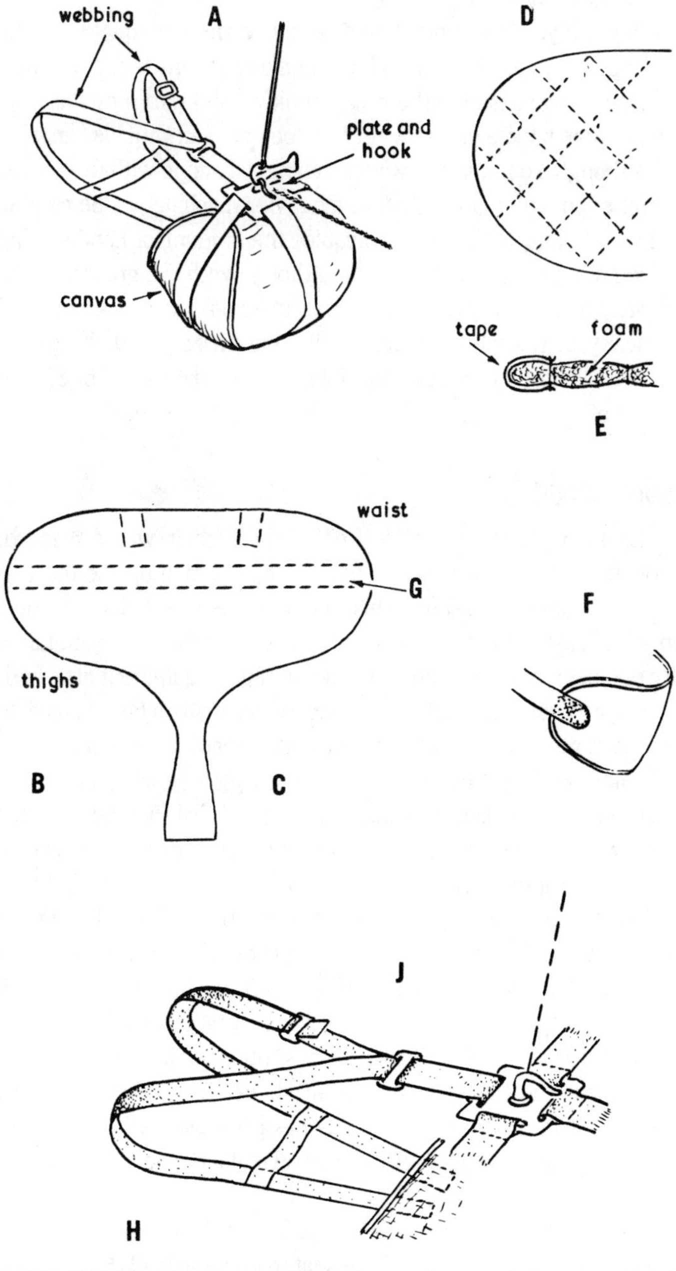

Fig. 17-6. Webbing takes the main load in trapeze harness, but canvas spreads support.

a slot in the fitting and go to meet the other part at a buckle where adjustment is made (Fig. 17-6J).

Obviously, all sewing should be more then adequate, as the wearer depends on the fact that all the many strains that come with trapezing being passed to the single hook will not part it on the way. He has a grab handle on the wire, but does not sail with his hands on this. Although a domestic sewing machine may cope with the canvas sewing, even with foam included, a heavier machine will be needed for the webbing. If this is unavailable, the amount of hand sewing involved need not prove laborious, although with the greater thickness of materials a larger needle than is used on sails will be required and facility in the use of a palm will soon be acquired. Keep the tension on stitches as even as possible. Knot the line at the beginning and end of each line of stitches so they cannot pull out.

BOSUN'S CHAIR

Traditionally the bosun's (Boatswain's) chair was a piece of wood roped at the corners and used to haul a man up the mast to make a repair (Fig. 17-7A). This may have been satisfactory for a ship with masts made from trees, but on a yacht with a metal or softwood mast and much comparatively fragile equipment attached, such a thing being bumped up the mast with a man on board could do some damage, even with the yacht fairly steady at a dockside.

The alternative was a rather uncomfortable bowline tied in the end of a rope, or a plain webbing loop (Fig. 17-7B) that did not offer much more comfort. A better bosun's chair has something in common with a trapeze harness.

The seat is a broad canvas band with a pair of large D rings or other metal fittings to take the hoisting rope. The passenger has a belt and a strap between the legs (Fig. 17-7C). The canvas band is 9 inches or more across its widest part, then tapers at the sides to about half that at the top. The size is best obtained by using a man as a model, but the top should come at about chest level. Anything higher might be inconveniently in front of the face, while anything lower would interfere with arm action and make the gear slightly less stable.

Use stout canvas if possible—12 oz. or 15 oz. is suitable. If there is a webbing band around the seat to take the load (Fig. 17-7D) stoutness of the canvas is not as important, but if the canvas is to

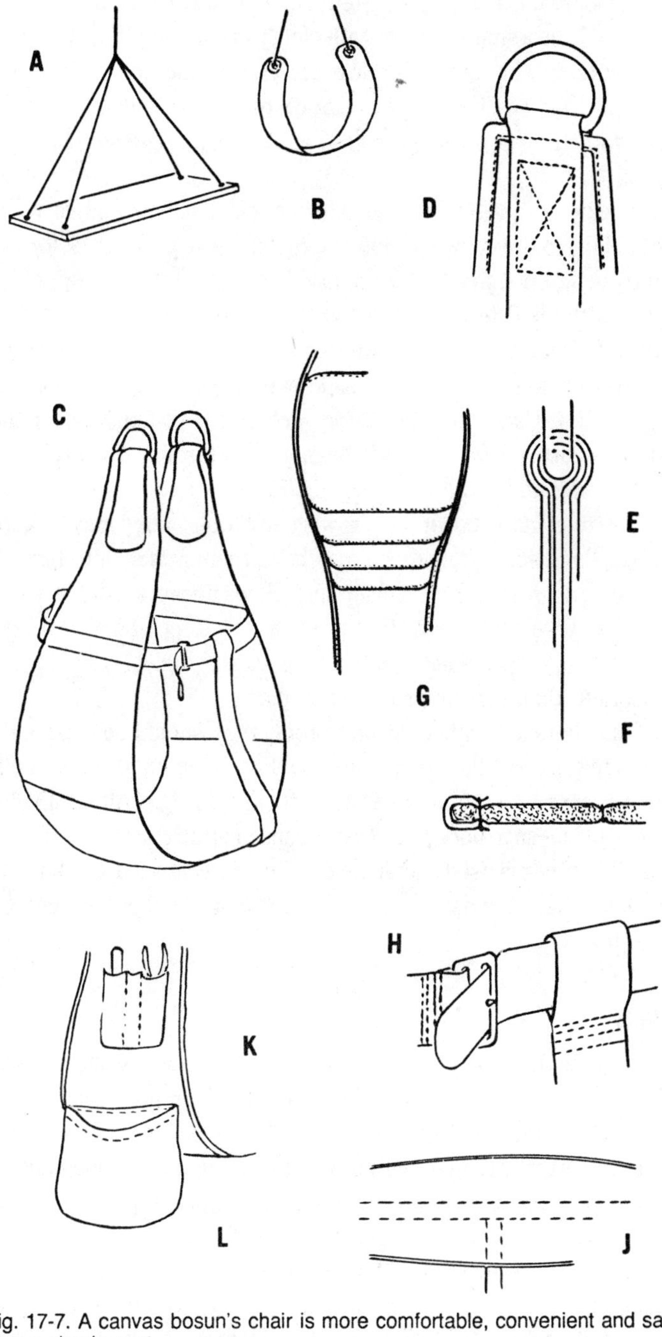

Fig. 17-7. A canvas bosun's chair is more comfortable, convenient and safer than a simple seat.

tace the load, it is better fairly stout and the patches for the hanging rings should be a similar grade, with plenty of stitching (Fig. 17-7E).

There can be an extra thickness around the seat, with foam between (Fig. 17-7F), or there can be more than one extra thickness, with the edges staggered (Fig. 17-7G). Tape or table the edges.

The belt is a webbing strap with a buckle, securely sewn at the right height to the canvas. Allow enough fullness at the back for the user to sit far enough back for the load to come across the tops of his thighs. If the belt forces him forward he may be uncomfortable or unsafe. Arrange the buckle to one side of the front and let the other piece of webbing have a loop to slide over the other side of the belt (Fig. 17-7H). Carry the end of this webbing far enough under the seat for secure sewing and it will be more comfortable if it reaches at least halfway under the seat (Fig. 17-7J).

The man in the bosun's chair will need tools. They may be kept in a bag slung separately or he may have them attached to himself with lanyards, but a broad canvas sling allows pockets to be sewn on in order to take some tools. Of course, a tool dropped from a height can be lethal, so providing closed end pockets (Fig. 17-7K) is more appropriate than merely providing loops.

If pockets are to take straight tools they should be located on the straight side of the seat. Bags could be sewn on at one or both sides to carry other things needed aloft (Fig. 17-7L). Alternatively, there could be snap hooks or other means of attaching bags or larger tools. Whatever is used should be capable of being secured. With an open hook there is a risk of something being dropped or knocked out of the hook.

APRON

Anyone doing much work on sails or other fabric work needs an apron. It may be the ordinary bib type apron, either reaching the knees or cut off at the top of the thighs (Fig. 17-8A). Many workers favor the latter arrangement as it does not restrict movement. If hand work is being done while sitting, a piece of scrap canvas is put over the knees to protect them from needle jabs.

The apron is best made of quite stout canvas and given a narrow tabling around the edges. Tape is used in a loop around the neck and tied around the waist. The bottom of the front is turned up to make a pocket about 6 inches deep, usually divided with a row of stitches down the center (Fig. 17-8B). This takes all the odds and ends needed while working, except there may be a pencil pocket (Fig. 17-8C) and a piece of thick soft cloth is put on the bib to take needles (Fig. 18-8D). A sharp needle is not a thing to carry loose in the lower pocket and a pad high on the bib is in a position where the hand is unlikely to get scratched.

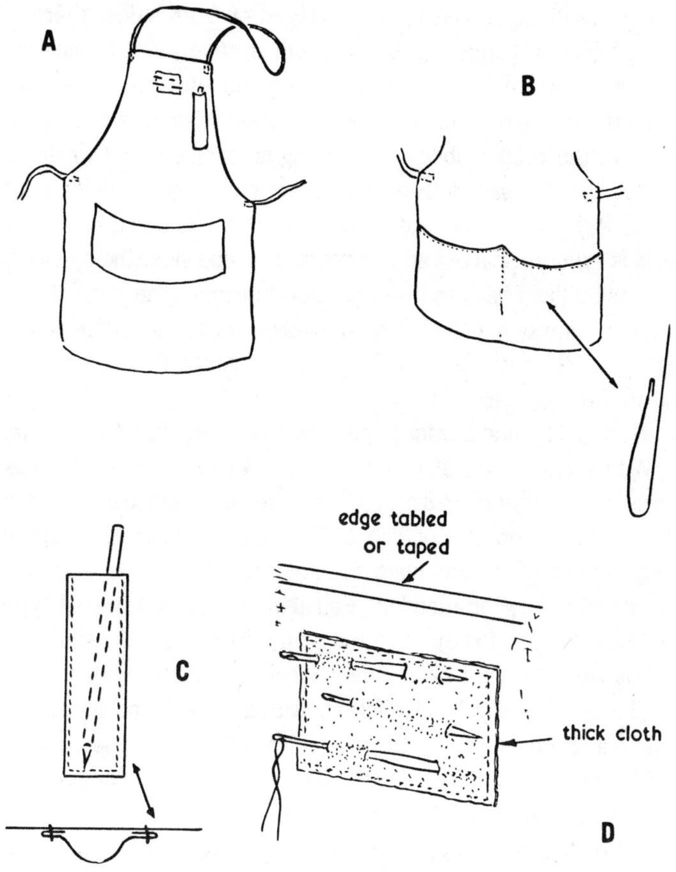

Fig. 17-8. A sailmaker needs a strong apron, with stowage for his tools.

If a longer apron is preferred, it can be made any length and the pocket sewn on. Protection is usually only needed in the front and it is helpful to be without restrictions when bending and kneeling, so do not make the apron too wide. Two feet should be enough.

INSIGNIA AND NUMBERS

Having a badge or emblem on a sail was once a rarity, then it became usual on racing classes, but now there are many general-purpose and cruising craft that proudly display the insignia of their class or even the personal marks of their owner. If yachts are registered within their class there will be a number as well. With some of the popular classes the number may be quite high. As it is necessary to have the insignia and number large enough to be seen at a reasonable distance and to be displayed on both sides, there is often a problem of arranging this on a comparatively small main sail.

With most established classes there are drawings available showing the size and arrangement to be followed, so the sailmaker is relieved of the responsibility of planning an arrangement to suit a particular sail. No sail cloth is opaque so what is on one side may show through to the other side in some light if not at all times. If an insignia is symmetrical or can be reversed on one side, the opposite sides may be fixed back to back, but at other times the insignia and numbers on one side have to be arranged clear of those on the other side (Fig. 17-9A and 17-10). It is usual to have the higher arrangement on the starboard side.

In the past some markings have been painted directly onto the sail. With some types of natural fiber cloth this was sometimes successful. Synthetic fibers are non-absorbent and paint on the surface would soon run or rub off. It may be possible to spray through a stencil, but any color applied direct to synthetic cloth is suspect and not recommended. Felt pens of the waterproof type have been used, but they have the same drawbacks as paint.

It is much better to apply the insignia or number with colored cloth. There are self-adhesive fabrics with a peel-off backing, some originally intended for domestic use, which will serve. Choose material with a smooth surface and of the appropriate color. Mark out the pattern in reverse on the backing sheet, then cut it out. Do not peel off the backing until immediately before fixing. Mark where the insignia is to come on the sail. Position the insignia or number and press down with the side of the hand, working from one edge while lowering the rest of the material with the other hand (Fig. 17-9B). The sail should be stretched flat on a firm surface. Get it right the first time, if possible. If there is an air bubble or something is wrong, the material can be peeled and repositioned, but adhesion is better if it is not disturbed. Air from an air bubble may escape through the cloth. If the material cannot be lifted and the air worked out to an edge, prick the bubble with a needle and press down around and towards this small hole, which will not show afterwards.

Another type of self-adhesive fabric needs heat to set it. This is treated in the same way, but a warm iron is used to seal the joint. Do not use any more heat than necessary, as excessive heat may damage the polyester sailcloth.

The self-adhesive material may bond sufficiently tightly so no more treatment is needed. Edges can be sewn as well. If colored cloth that is not self-adhesive is used, it may be advisable to position it with a few spots of adhesive before sewing. Edges may be sewn entirely through the insignia (Fig. 17-9C) or over the edge with zig-zag stitches (Fig. 17-9D).

These added pieces may have to go over seams and will probably be secure, but if they can be arranged to come in smooth panels it will be better.

It is difficult to remove all evidence of insignia and numbers if the sail is no longer used for its class and its markings have to go, particularly if any adhesive has been used. Even when the numbers have only been sewn, there may be a change of color due to the

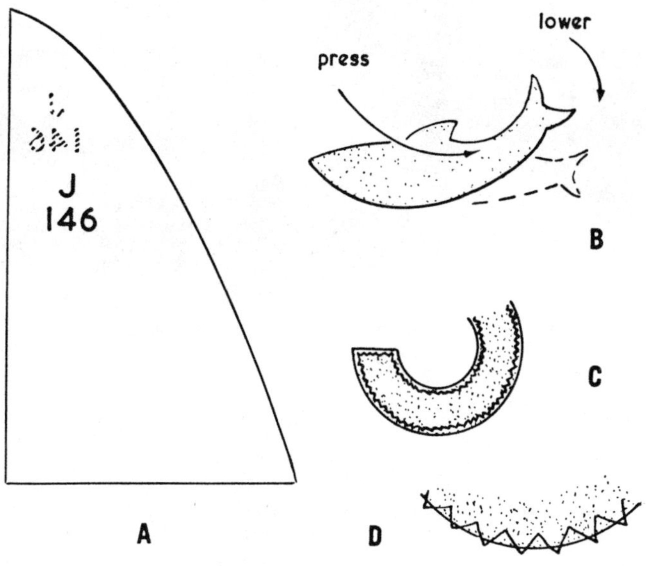

Fig. 17-9. Insignia and numbers go both sides and may be stuck as well as sewn.

Fig. 17-10. The Heron insignia on the left-hand boat is arranged back to back, but the other insignias and numbers are staggered on opposite sides. The markings are higher on the starboard (right) sides. The widths at the top of the main sails due to head boards can be seen on two of the sails.

effect of sunlight. It is possible to put the markings on separate cloths and sew them on, but these necessarily fairly large pieces of cloth, usually with their weave not matching the sail, may affect performance.

Other Canvaswork

There are other cloth, fabric, or canvas items about a boat or yacht that are not necessarily associated with sails, but their making is akin to sailmaking. Any sailmaker, whether amateur or professional, can expect to find that much of the work he has to do is concerned with these things. Many of the items will be for a boat that has no sails. Any well-found motor cruiser has many canvas items, either as part of its normal equipment or connected with ancillary items.

Some of the items can be made with offcuts from sails, but others have to be heavier. The material may still be polyester or nylon, but for many purposes there is some advantage in the bulkiness of traditional cotton or other natural fiber canvas, which should have been proofed during manufacture. In the usual grades this is stiffer and appears to have more substance than synthetic fibers, so it may be preferred for such things as dodgers and screens.

There are other fabrics which have been given a coating of plastic. There are some sheet plastics that have no fabric backing. They may have some uses, but without the back-up of woven fabric, they might distort and stretch or tear uncontrollably, so durability is doubtful and something made from this material may have to be replaced after a short time.

Fabric-backed plastic may have a fairly thick layer of plastic on the side intended to take wear, while the other side may have a thin wash of the same plastic or the woven fibers of the backing cloth may be exposed. The coating is usually made of polyvinyl chloride (P.V.C.), although other plastics are used. The backing may be a cotton fabric, but nylon or other synthetic fiber woven fabrics are used. If cotton fabric is coated both sides, there should be no fear of rot, but if it is exposed one side, this should be treated with proofing solution for use afloat.

The coating of plastic restricts any stretch in the woven fabric, but there is some. For most purposes the small amount of stretch is of little account, but if a screen or dodger is to be tensioned, it may be possible to choose fabric with its greater stretch in the right direction. Some cloths have a greater tendency to stretch in the length than the width. Many have stretch in the width and very little in the length.

P.V.C. is affected by heat. When it is cold, it is very stiff. At normal temperatures it is reasonably flexible, but if it is to be stretched or molded to shape it can be heated almost to the point where it becomes uncomfortable to touch. At this stage it is possible to stretch it over a compound curve. As it cools to normal temperatures, its tendency to shrink should ease out any puckers. Obviously there are limits and these are controlled by the type of fabric backing, but the technique works on the compound curvature of a canoe hull.

Contact cement, such as that used for fixing plastic laminate material to wood, will adhere P.V.C. fabrics. There are also special P.V.C. adhesives, which may allow more flexibility in the joined fabrics. Most adhesives intended for other materials are unsuccessful on P.V.C. If the plastic coating is another type, follow the advice on adhesives given by the makers. There are some plastics for which there is no trustworthy adhesive.

Although some of these coated fabrics can be stuck, most of them will also have to be sewn, but it is useful to be able to assemble joints with adhesive that will keep them in the right relation to each other while being sewn.

For things like covers, which have to conform to an awkward shaped object, there is an advantage in elasticity. Elastic cord (shock cord, bungee) can be used instead of ordinary rope for lacing. The ends can be fitted with hooks or other fasteners, which may need a special tool for fixing. Make sure they are a type suitable for damp conditions. Alternatively, the end can be looped through a grommet and seized with a tight whipping. A free end should also be whipped tightly for a sufficient distance to make a stiff narrow point, that is more easily thrust through a line of grommets.

Elastic webbing is sold for chair upholstery. This has possibilities in some boat canvaswork. It can be used in place of ordinary webbing where some stretch is desirable to get a good fit. This is strong material and not able to stretch very much. Its intended use is in a woven pattern below a seat cushion. When used afloat, the limits of stretch should be allowed for.

COVERS

Protective covers may be needed for such things as ventilators in heavy weather, outboard motor propellers on trailed boats, a steering console when out of use, a spotlight when not needed, and an anchor windlass that might damage anything knocked against it.

In many cases the cover can be an inverted bag and its construction is the same as the bags described earlier. Sometimes there has to be some shaping. It is unusual to make a closely fitted cover. There should be some slackness, but a simple bag that makes no concessions to the shape it enclosed may have an undue amount of looseness.

If a cover is made of two flat pieces sewn together, there will be some slackness after fitting (Fig. 18-1A). This is unavoidable. It is better to follow the round bag technique, with a sewn-in end (Fig. 18-1B). If there is any shaping to the object being covered, this may not be enough to avoid excessive bagginess. The next step is to have two or three seams so some of the panels can be shaped (Fig. 18-1C).

A further problem comes when part of the object is large, yet where the bag is to be closed it is much narrower. The bag has to be large enough to go over the thickest part, yet there could be an excess of cloth in the neck of the bag if it was made like a sail bag.

It may be satisfactory to have a parallel bag, but it would be difficult to gather up all the slack in the neck with a normal drawstring or a line through grommets, so as to make a close and secure fastening around the narrow part of the object. This can be eased if the tabling is divided into sections (Fig. 18-1D). How wide the gaps are depends how much gathering in there is to be, but making the remaining tabling and the gaps about the same width should be satisfactory. The method can be used with a drawstring through the tabling, or with lacing through grommets. Two grommets in each piece should be satisfactory (Fig. 18-1E).

This sort of neck can be used if there are projections that can be used to hold the cover in place (Fig. 18-1F), even when the reduction in size is not such an important considerations. Instead of using a drawstring, it may be neater and more convenient to use tape or webbing through the tabling, with some sort of press or hook fastener (Fig. 18-1G). However, make sure it is not the sort of fastener dependent only on a spring, that may give way under strain and the cover could come off.

Another way of getting a close fit on a shaped part is to include a zip fastener, preferably of the heavy plastic type. If a cover has to go over a large part and be fastened at a reduced part, the zip fastener may go some way from the neck of the bag, so it can be put in position. Then with the bag fitted, the zip closed leaves only a narrow neck to be fastened (Fig. 18-1H). A zip fastener is not waterproof, so if the cover is intended to keep out water, let the zip come on the underside.

A cover like that needed to prevent the exposed propeller of a motor on a trailed boat causing damage, may be zipped in a convenient position, then the neck closed by a strap (Fig. 18-1J). If the cover is long and narrow, even when it does not require shaping, as with the case for a fishing rod, it is easier to use if a zip fastener goes part way along the side (Fig. 18-1K). It is then possible to open the bag sufficiently to select the part of the contents needed without having to tip everything out through a narrow opening.

Some covers are more conveniently arranged to open along one side, similar to a cover for a main sail on its boom. Lacing gives the best fit and allows adjustment so the cover is still a good fit whether the contents are neatly packed and dry or pushed in untidily while wet in an emergency. The obvious method of lacing is a zig-zag arrangement of grommets (Fig. 18-2A), but this is not always best. For a finer control of adjustment, it is better to have grommets opposite each other. Lacing then pulls across to get the edges closer together (Fig. 18-2B). Usually, it is possible to hold each crossing line while the next crossing is being tensioned, but greater control comes from using the lacing in the same way as one method of attaching a sail to a spar, with half hitches at each position (Fig. 18-2C).

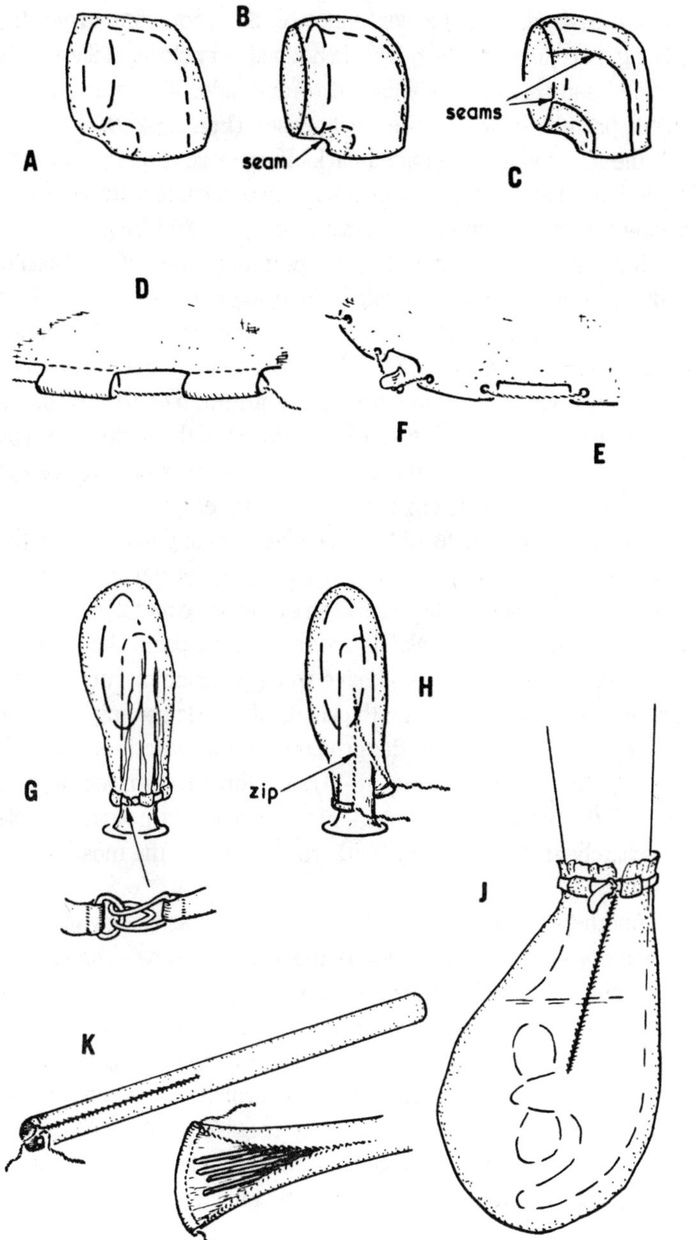

Fig. 18-1. Covers may be made in several ways and cut to allow fitting and securing.

Two edges may be merely drawn together and this may be all that is required, but the contents are not protected under the opening, particularly if the edges do not pull very close. A flap can be provided and this is best attached to one side. The other side is tabled, preferably with three thicknesses (Fig. 18-2D). The part with the flap has a piece folded back. If equivalent strength to the other side is required, it may be advisable to include a strip of fabric or tape for the grommets to pass through (Fig. 18-2E).

If a laced cover is merely a wrap-around, the action of lacing tends to pull in the ends if nothing is done about it. If part of the thing being covered extends past the covering, the lacing can be carried further along and attached, but if it is a closed end, it may be possible to sew on a flap large enough to carry a grommet to provide an anchorage (Fig. 18-2F). If the construction is of the folded bag type described in Chapter 17, the end of the triangular flap can be left unsewn to make a neat position for a grommet (Fig. 18-2G).

Grommets can be fixed to woven fabric of any thickness in the same way as when fixing grommets to sails, but letting flaps of fabric turn up to be gripped by the parts of an eyelet-type metal grommet is not practicable with most plastic-coating fabrics, particularly for the smaller grommets. A hole will have to be punched or cut. If it is a very firm material, due to the thickness of plastic coating, the hole may be a fit on the neck of the grommet. Otherwise it is better to punch the hole undersize (Fig. 18-2H) and force it open with a spike (Fig. 18-2J), then spring the neck of the grommet through the hole immediately after the spike is withdrawn to make the most secure fixing.

Another method of fastening that has possibilities in some methods of closure or securing is the use of Velcro—the type of fabric with a hooked surface so two of these faces meeting will interlock. There can be a piece of Velcro on one part and a piece on the other (Fig. 18-2K). One part can be longer if adjustment is needed (Fig. 18-2L), but the material is probably most convenient for a positioned fastening or one only requiring moderate adjustment. A long piece of Velcro hanging loose may attach itself to other cloth. It would not damage the other cloth, but it could be a nuisance.

SCREENS

There are places on motor and sail yachts where permanent protection is not required, yet it is sometimes necessary to keep out

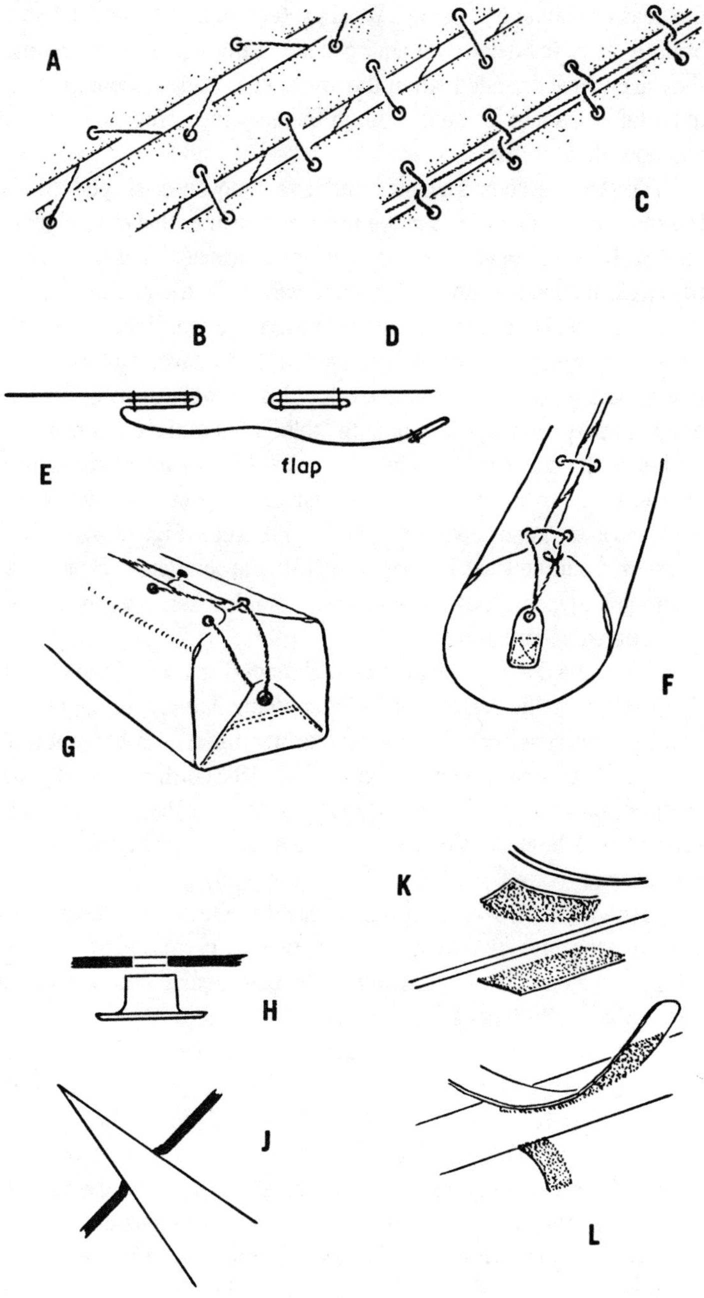

Fig. 18-2. Bags can be secured by lacing, with end flaps for end tension. Grommet holes may be expanded. Velcro can be used for some fastenings.

the seas or maybe only spray. Wind protection may be needed on a bridge. This can be done with quite simple canvas panels. However, they are usually needed when the weather is bad, so construction must take this into account, both in the way the screens are made and how they are fixed.

The basic screen is a panel, either rectangular or shaped to suit the space it is to fit, with its make-up very similar to that of a sail (Fig. 18-3A). It has to stand up to very similar conditions. If it is necessary to join cloths, make seams in the same way as for a sail. Table edges that are parallel to the weave by turning in the edge. If there is much shaping to an edge so the cut comes across the weave, use an applied tabling with material cut from the edge. Fixing will usually be strong enough with grommets through the tabling, but at the corners it will be better to use small patches (Fig. 18-3B). In many cases the strains likely to be imposed may warrant roping, with the rope enclosed in tape and carried all round in one piece (Fig. 18-3C). Such a screen mounted fairly low, as when fitted around the cockpit of an ocean-going yacht, may have to resist solid water, and should be constructed accordingly.

It may be that the dodger can be threaded on a wire hand rail. In that case the edge can be treated something like the luff of a head sail. The cloth itself can have a broad tabling, but it is probably better to use a broad strip of cloth sewn on (Fig. 18-3D). If this is liable to chafe, it could be stouter than the material used for the dodger. It will probably still be necessary to strain the edge by using grommets at the corners.

Although this sort of screening can be made in a long length, it is often more convenient to have it in sections. This may allow a better fit around a complex area, or part of the screening can be erected when the whole length is not required.

Edges may meet and be laced through closely-spaced grommets (Fig. 18-3E). They can be overlapped so the lacing goes through pairs of grommets (Fig. 18-3F). A variation of this is to use "Dutch" lacing. One part has grommets, while the other part has loops of cord opposite the grommets. The loops may be merely sewn on or they can be taken through sewn grommets in the same way as reef points (Fig. 18-3G). A single line is used in place of the bottom loop. Each loop goes through its mating grommet, then each one is taken through the loop coming from above (Fig. 18-3H) and

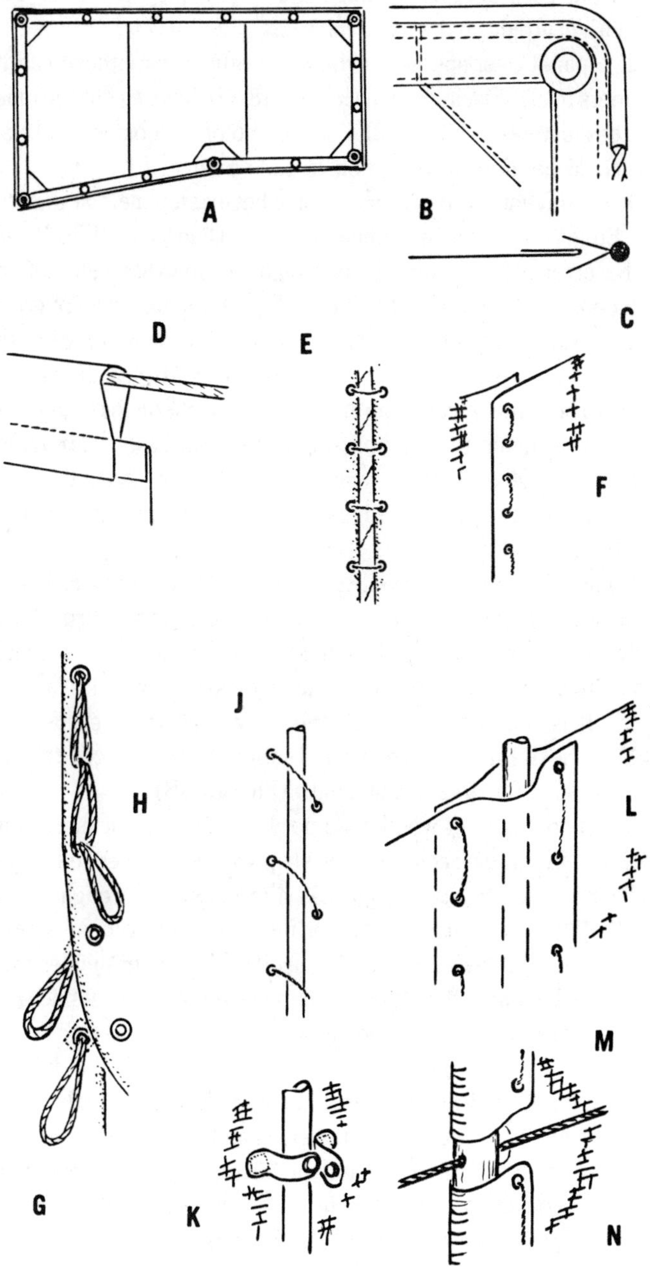

Fig. 18-3. Screens and dodgers are made like sails and may be secured to each other and to stancheons by lacing.

the bottom cord is taken through the lowest loop and tied. This makes a very tight and secure joint.

If a panel overlaps a stancheon or other post, there can be grommets to allow lacing around it (Fig. 18-3J). There could be tapes and press fasteners (Fig. 18-3K). If the end of the post is accessible there could be a pocket sewn on to slide over it.

It is convenient to arrange a joint between panels at a stancheon. Edges may come up to the stancheon, then lacing (Fig. 18-3E) may be arranged so alternate parts go on opposite sides of the stancheon. Another way is to give each part a double row of grommets, then lacing goes through the overlapping grommets to join the panels and secure them to the stancheon (Fig. 18-3L). If only one panel is to be fitted, it can wrap around the stancheon for lacing (Fig. 18-3M). This means that the spacing between the rows of grommets should be enough to allow for wrapping a single part, and if there are any intermediate wires the edges should be cut to allow for them (Fig. 18-3N).

Sometimes a canvas dodger has to be fixed to wood. It may have its lower edge permanently attached along the forward edge of a bridge and the canvas kept folded down in good weather, then it is laced up to a rail in bad weather. Merely tacking to wood is unsatisfactory. It is better to sandwich the canvas between strips (Fig. 18-4A). Adhesive may be used as well as screws and the edge should be turned back for greatest strength (Fig. 18-4B).

The two pieces of wood need not be the same thickness (Fig. 18-4C) and in some places a narrow strip will be screwed to existing woodwork. The strongest edge has a metal strip through tabling (Fig. 18-4D). There may be another metal strip over it and screws through that or the screws may be used with washers under their heads. The best attachment uses a cup washer over a flat one (Fig. 18-4E) so pressure comes over a good area.

A yacht's name on her transom may be traditional, but it is not much use for identification, even at a short distance in harbor. It is better to have the name large at the sides and a convenient seamanlike way of arranging this is to have the letters on the dodgers at the sides of the cockpit of a sailing yacht. They are sewn to the canvas in the same way as the numbers and insignia on a sail.

MAST COAT

When a mast goes through a deck and is stepped on the bottom, the hole through the deck has to be larger than the mast diameter,

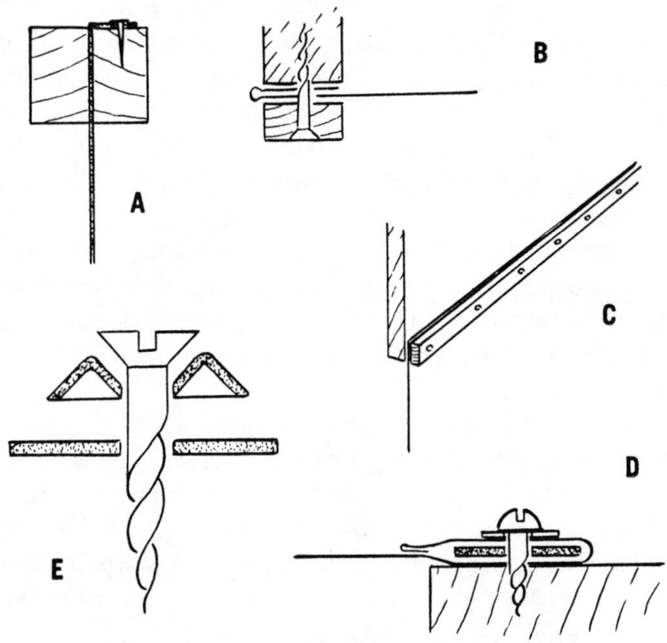

Fig. 18-4. Canvas is fixed to wood by holding under strips or using screws through washers.

particularly if mast angle is to be adjustable by its stays. This means that there is a gap which has to be made watertight. In a modern yacht there are other ways of doing this, but in a traditional yacht there was a canvas mast coat, which may have to be replaced (Fig. 18-5A). This is a conical sleeve fixed around the mast and to the deck. It is simple to make, but the difficulty is in getting the shape. It is probably best to start with a paper template, which may go half or all round the mast.

Draw a side view of the coat. Extend the sidelines to meet (Fig. 18-5B). This is the center for drawing the shape. Draw curves on this center through top and bottom. Project from the center to mark one edge of the joint (Fig. 18-5C). Measure about 3 1/2 times the width of the side view around the outside curve to give the approximate position of the other side of the joint (Fig. 18-5D). Cut a paper template to this shape and try it in position. Make any adjustment necessary, then add enough on one edge to make a seam, enough at the bottom to go under the ring and plenty at the top for turning inside (Fig. 18-5E).

Sew the seam the full length. It should not be necessary to sew the other edges. If a plastic-coated fabric or other material with one good side is used, remember that the coat will go on the mast upside-down and inside-out. The coat is normally fitted to the mast before it is stepped, but if a new coat has to be made with the mast in position, the seam will have to be sewn by hand with the canvas around the mast.

The coat is fixed to the mast with a secure lashing (Fig. 18-5F). The surplus canvas at the top is turned downwards. The lashing need not be very wide, but it should be very tight, preferably using a serving mallet to put on the strain. If one of these old tools is unavailable a piece of wood can be used (Fig. 18-5G).

Turn the cone down to the deck. There may be a continuous wood or metal (often lead) ring. If so, this should be put over the hole before the mast is stepped. There may be a wooden ring in two parts with overlapping joints (Fig. 18-5H). Fixing is done with screws. Traditionally, the canvas was coated on both sides with paint and the ring screwed down while this was wet, but it would be better today to use a flexible jointing compound.

There is no need to treat a polyester mast coat, and a P.V.C. fabric will need no attention, but ordinary canvas should be given a coat of proofing solution. A wooden ring should be adequately protected with paint or varnish, even if the coat needs no treatment.

BOAT COVERS

When a boat is out of use it is best left covered. Even a larger decked craft may have covers over its cockpit and any other open parts. It may even be advisable to have fitted covers over cabins to protect them from hot sun or the attention of birds.

A common fault is to find covers sagging inwards so they collect rain water, or accumulate debris if it is a dry situation. This means it is advisable to arrange a cover so all parts slope away to the edges. Sometimes the cover itself can be planned to do this, but more often it is necessary to provide some sort of ridge pole, which is either one of the boat's spars or a special strip of wood or a metal tube. Of course, a cover has to be arranged so any water on it runs overboard, either directly or via the deck. A cover that finishes inside a cockpit coaming or has only a slight overlap on the edge of cabin may let in some of the water it is intended to keep out.

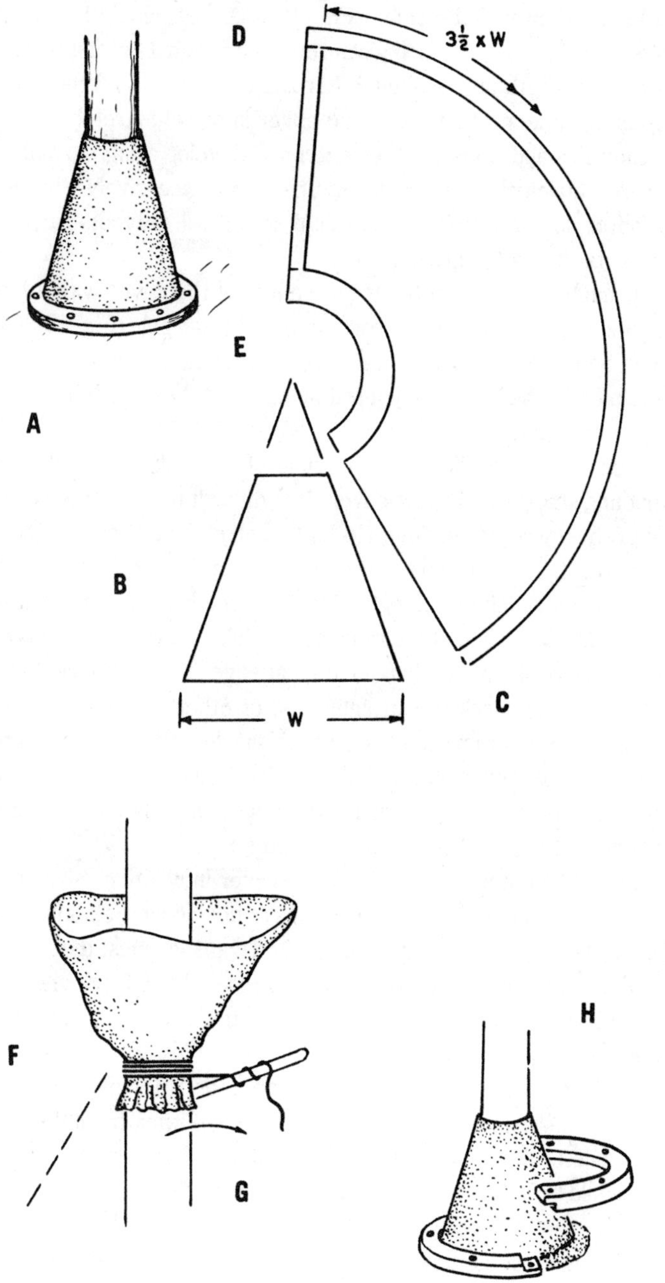

Fig. 18-5. A mast coat is a cone that seals the gap between mast and deck.

A dinghy or other small open boat needs a cover to go all over and be laced around the sides (Fig. 18-6A). Lacing can be to half cleats (Fig. 18-6B). The lacing can remain through its grommets for most of its length and hooked under the cleats as it is fitted, then tensioning done at the ends. If the cover is merely stretched over the gunwales and transom, the center will develop a sag, no matter how great an initial tension is given. Stretching excessively is bad for any fabric, so it is better to make a cover that will serve its purpose without the need for great tension.

It might be possible to lift the center of the cover with a few uprights, but it is better to have a lengthwise ridge pole (Fig. 18-6C). It may be possible to lash oars, join a boathook and an oar, use a single metal tube, or have jointed aluminum tubes, such as those used for tent frames.

Because of the difference in angle of slope there is a slightly compound shape to this boat cover. It is difficult to get a true shape by merely sewing up enough cloths and stretching them over the ridge pole. It is better to have a seam along the center. Make seams crosswise to build up the length. Make up one half and stretch it in position. Mark the line of the ridge pole. Make a few marks to show the gunwale position, but do not trim that edge yet. Put the cloth flat on the floor and check the straightness, or otherwise of the line of the ridge pole. How far out of straight this is depends on the amount of sheer of the gunwales (sweep up towards the ends). With little sheer, the line may be assumed to be straight, but otherwise a slight curve along the seam should be allowed for.

Sew the center seam and put the cover in position. Stretch it moderately all round. Use spikes or pins to position it. Self-adhesive tape may be useful. Draw the gunwale and transom lines, then allow enough outside for the overlap and tabling the edges. Do the necessary tabling, but allow for strengthening at the corners. Patches inside may take the pressure (Fig. 18-6D).

At the corners of the transom, box around with an overlap (Fig. 18-6E). The stem may be dealt with in the same way, but if there is much angle to the stem, this may result in a rather narrow overlap and it would be better to use another strip of cloth or tape there (Fig. 18-6F).

Closing in all corners means the cover will have to be sprung into place. This is satisfactory for many craft, but a tighter fit can be obtained with lacing or a strap and buckle at the transom corners

(Fig. 18-6G). On a very broad transom, arrange half cleats or allow for the center of the cover to be held down to a rudder fitting.

If the open boat has a mast that will remain stepped, the cover can be arranged to shed water without the need for a ridge pole. The

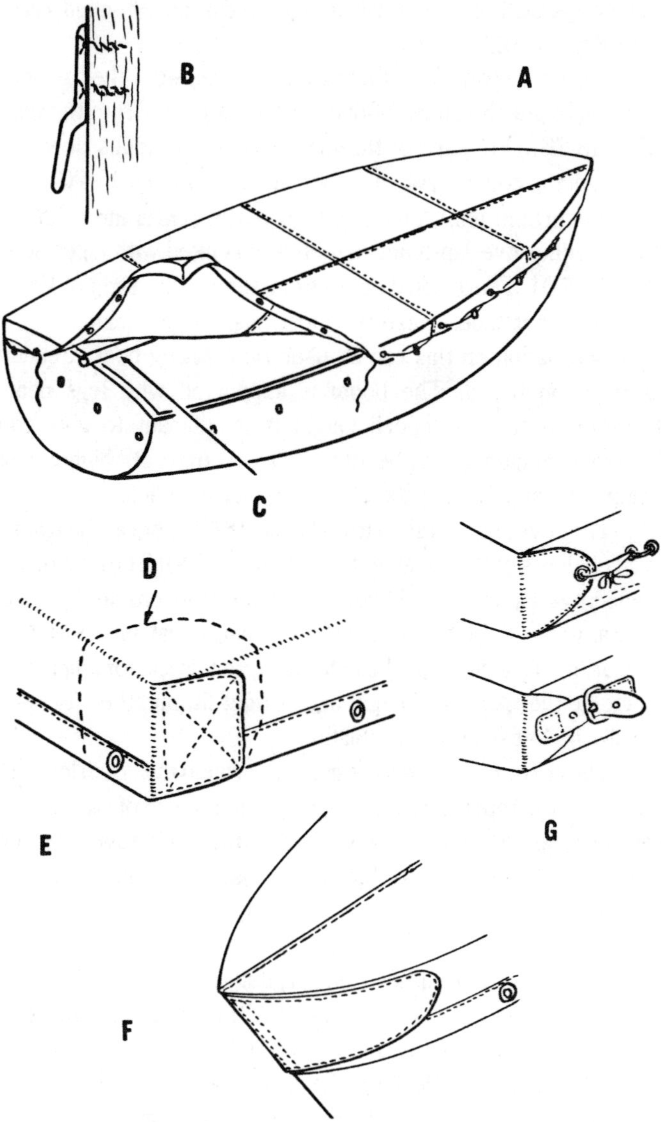

Fig. 18-6. A boat cover should fit closely and be held with lacing. A pole prevents sagging.

cover fits around the gunwales in the same way as just described. At the mast it has a sleeve that can be lashed around. Even if the boom does not remain attached to the mast the gooseneck fitting may stop the cover slipping down, but it may be available to provide a loop so the main halliard can be used to keep the cover up (Fig. 18-7A). In some ways the boat cover can be regarded as an extended sail cover (See Fig. 17-5).

Stretch a string from the mast to the center of the transom and use this to get the shape of one half of the cover from the mast aft (Fig. 18-7B). Forward of the mast the cover slopes down to the stem. All the cover forward of the mast opens (Fig. 18-7C). For the most watertight joint, one side follows the centerline to the stem, but the other overlaps considerably and is fixed with tapes sewn on (Fig. 18-7D). There could be press fasteners or a strip of Velcro on each part, but tapes make the most positive fastening.

A variation on this can be used on a sailing boat intended for camping on board. The boom is supported with legs near the transom. If the gooseneck height is insufficient to give enough headroom at night it may be attached to the mast at a higher position when camping. Having the aft end higher also helps.

The cover fits in a similar way (Fig. 18-7E), but at the transom it is given doors of the usual tent type (Fig. 18-7F). These should have a good overlap and should come over the transom deep enough to shed any rain. If the boat is used for camping afloat and it swings to an anchor, it will normally lie head to wind, so it is the forward part that has to be the more watertight and airtight fit, and the aft doors can usually be left open for ventilation.

The cover may have to be cut to fit around the boom legs, if they extend. If the topping lift is still in position, the end of the ridge of the tent may be attached to it. Otherwise it may be advisable to have tapes or other ties inside the top to fasten around the boom like reefing ties, to prevent movement of the canvas and the boom in relation to each other.

For use in hot weather a similar, but simpler, cover can be used over the boom to give shelter in part of a boat on moorings or over the cockpit of a larger yacht (Fig 18-7G).

If there is partial decking, the cover may still be carried over the gunwales, but if there is a coaming, the cover can be put over this and any water that runs off will go on to the deck and then overside.

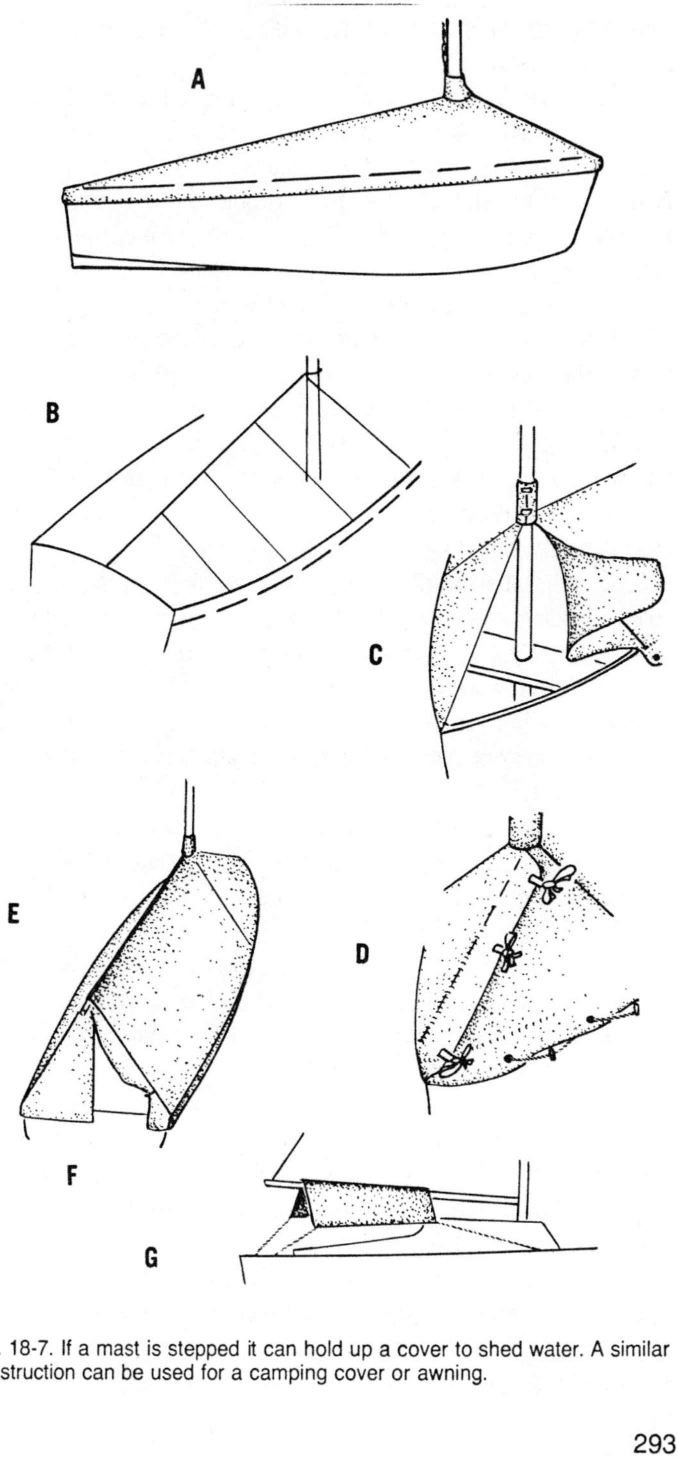

Fig. 18-7. If a mast is stepped it can hold up a cover to shed water. A similar construction can be used for a camping cover or awning.

This arrangement is often possible with a cockpit cover for a sailing or power cruiser.

The cover is fixed to a higher cabin top, which usually slopes forward, and any water on it will run that way. The cover is brought down to the coaming and fixed with lacing, spring fasteners, or other fastenings (Fig. 18-8A). The main problem is the possibility of sagging, particularly towards the aft end. Because of the slope the initial fitting may result in a good enough run-off, but later stretch may result in sag and the collection of water.

A ridge pole can hook on to the center of the rear coaming and rest on the center of the cabin edge (Fig. 18-8B). If there is much width or a cabin hatch prevents use of a central pole, use two.

Much use is made of folding covers, often fitted to tubular folding frameworks, that swing down and take the canvas with them. Construction is done by the usual canvas working methods, but the main difficulty is getting satisfactory shapes for the parts. This can only be done satisfactorily with the framework erect, possibly with strings holding it in position, while paper patterns are made (Fig. 18-8C). Usually a top is made with joints across each support. The top extends a few inches down the sides and side curtains fit under this edge and down to come outside the coaming (Fig. 18-8D). There may be transparent panels in the side curtains and in the back of the top (Fig. 18-8E).

There may be a lifting panel at the rear to give access to an outboard motor, if it is that type of craft. The flap should have a good overlap with provision for tapes to be secured from inside (Fig. 18-8F).

This type of cover is usually made of plastic-coated fabric and all joints should be stuck as well as sewed. Some of this fabric has an initial tendency to shrink slightly, after which it is stable, so make the cover an easy fit at first. Fasteners should be at an easy spacing that does not cause creases. Attachment to the framework may be done by pockets sewn inside, where it is possible to slide the parts through (Fig. 18-8G). In other places there may be straps held by fasteners (Fig. 18-8H). If the folded cover has to be pulled up by the front edge, it may be advisable to use webbing attached to the rear coaming and the tubular framework inside the cover (Fig. 18-8J), so this takes the strain instead of the covering material.

Some light awnings rely on internal stiffening to give them shape. A light sun awning across a boom, may be held out by battens

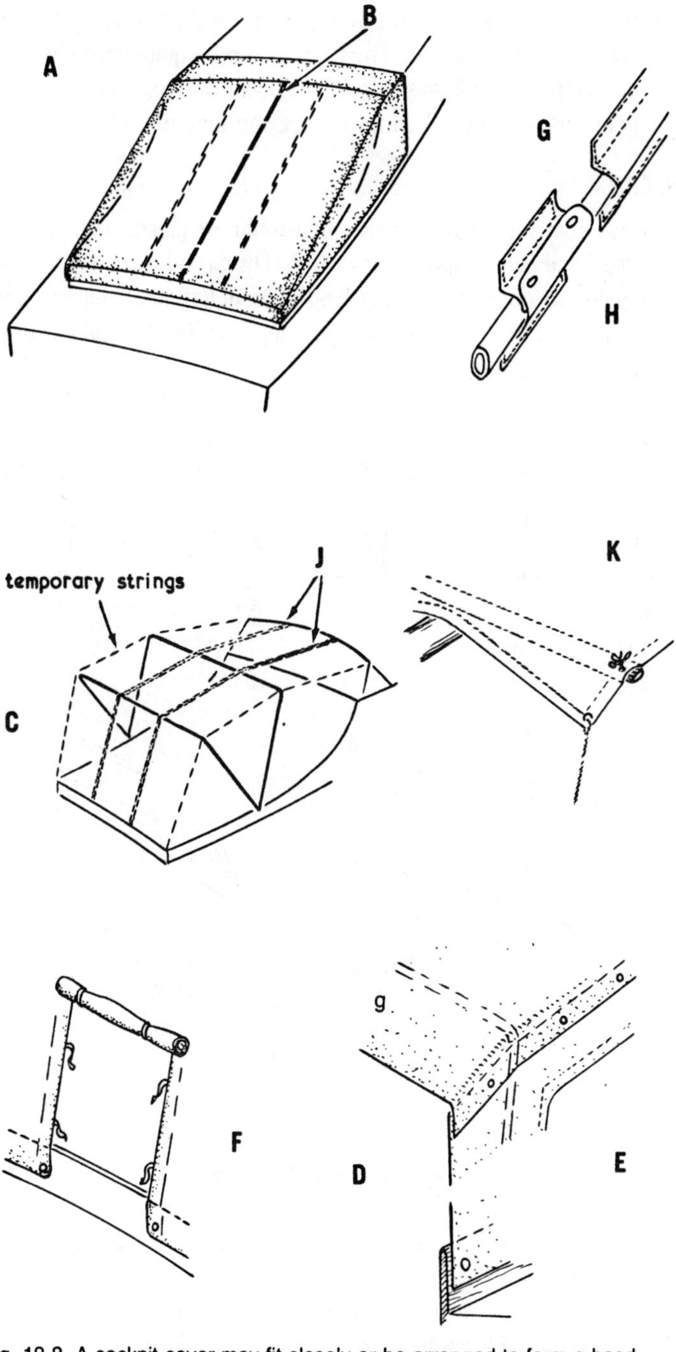

Fig. 18-8. A cockpit cover may fit closely or be arranged to form a hood.

in pockets (Fig. 18-8K), with guy ropes taken diagonally from the corners to tension the fabric. The battens can be quite light section and be planed to an elliptical section. The pockets are similar to those for sail battens and there can be ties at one or both ends.

FENDERS

Most boat fenders are made of rubber or plastic today, but there are rope and canvas ones, too. Discarded auto tires will probably do the job as well as anything, although their appearance is against them for use anywhere except perhaps the dockside at the home moorings.

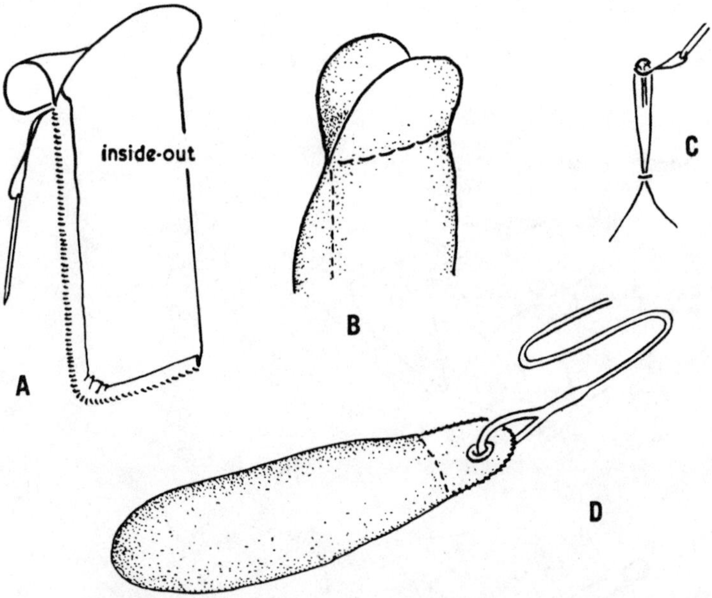

Fig. 18-9. A stuffed canvas fender is simple to make.

A canvas fender is a stout bag. It may be sewn up as a round seam across bottom and sides (Fig. 18-9A) inside out and pushed into shape with a hammer handle or something similar. Leave some surplus at the top for finishing. Traditionally, these fenders were made of very stout offcuts of canvas and stuffed with teased out pieces of worn-out rope. Probably, small pieces of plastic foam or oddments of rubber would be better today. Pack the bag fairly tightly, ramming the contents well down to the bottom.

A few sticking stitches can be put across above the stuffing to keep it out of the way while the top is finished (Fig. 18-9B). Turn in the top to make a rounded shape and oversew by hand (Fig. 18-9C) or run a line of machine stitching parallel with the edge. However, it may not be possible to work machine stitching as close to the sides as needed, so there may have to be some hand stitching.

Fit a grommet and splice on a lanyard (Fig. 18-9D). A metal grommet will usually do, but a sewn type can be made, or the lanyard may be sewn direct to the canvas. However, a trailing fender trapped between a moving boat and a dockside can cause considerable strain on the attachment of the lanyard and this should be really secure.

Rope fenders have a traditional feel and appearance. They are effective and appropriate to oldtime craft or reproductions of them. The main snag is their tendency to harbor dirt and grit, which may mark the topsides of the yacht. The making of rope fenders is outside the scope of this book, but covering them to reduce the tendency to collect grit is within our province.

Smooth plastic coated fabric makes the cleanest covering. The edges can be left as cut. If canvas is used, there must be an allowance for turning in all edges. The covering goes all round the fender for the full length of the parallel part (Fig. 18-10A). There is no need to turn in edges and sew them like tabling. Sewing to the fender will secure the folds.

Turn under the top and bottom edges and rub them down to make firm creases. Put the canvas around the fender and turn under

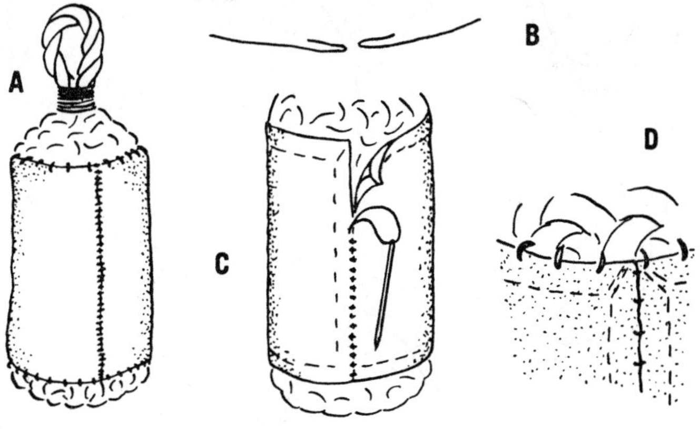

Fig. 18-10. A canvas cover around a rope fender keeps the boat and fender clean.

the meeting edges (Fig. 18-10B) so they do not quite meet when pulled tight. Pull these edges together with herringbone stitching (Fig. 18-10C). If necessary the tension of the canvas can be adjusted by varying the amount that is turned under.

With the band of canvas tightened around the fender, put more stitches around the turned under top and bottom into the rope to prevent the cover slipping. The stitches can be quite large and should be regulated to suit the spacing of parts of rope that come near the canvas (Fig. 18-10D).

An auto tire with a rope lanyard passed through a hole and tied to a piece of wood inside (Fig. 18-11A) makes a functional fender. If it is covered in canvas its appearance is improved. In particular, smaller tires can be made into quite attractive fenders. Cut two circles of canvas large enough to go over the tire and meet with a couple of inches to spare, to allow for turning in (Fig. 18-11B). Sew slightly more than half the circle (Fig. 18-11C). Any more would prevent the tire from being forced in. The amount of sewing depends on how much the tire will flex—the further the first stitching can be taken, the less final hand sewing has to be done.

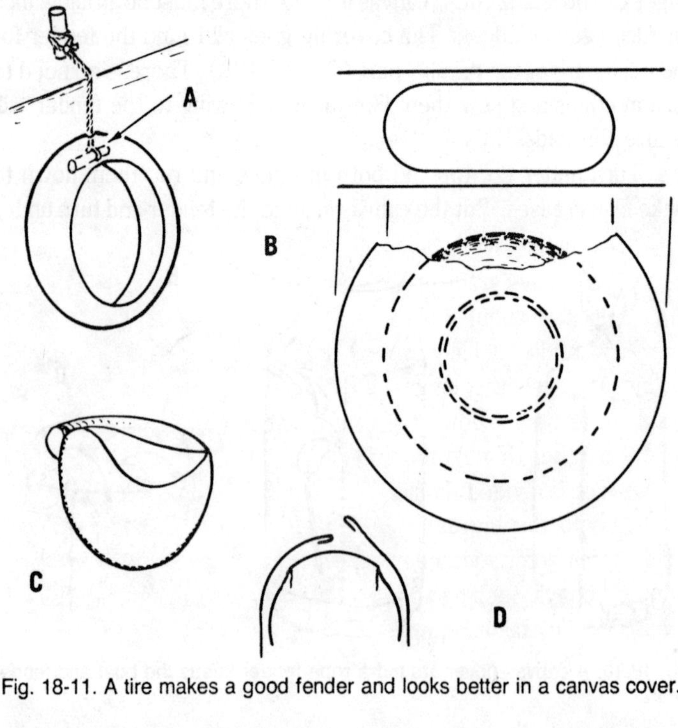

Fig. 18-11. A tire makes a good fender and looks better in a canvas cover.

Have the tire prepared with its lanyard in place. Make sure it is firmly fixed to the wood inside, as this will be out of reach in the finished fender. With the tire in place, bring the edges together and turn them under as you oversew by hand from each side twoards the lanyard at the top (Fig. 18-11D). Adjust the amount of turning in to get a good tension on the canvas so it is tight over the tire. Stitch and knot the thread several times close to the lanyard.

SEA ANCHOR

In heavy weather when a stage is reached that a yacht has to heave-to, a sea anchor may be used to keep the boat head to wind. The usual form is an open-ended conical bag, streamed over the bow on a long line. As the wind tries to blow the yacht astern, the resistance of the sea anchor pulling on the line holds the bow to windward so the yacht lies in what should be the safest and most comfortable position. There may be another light line from the small end of the cone, which is left slack, but is used to turn the bag around and haul it in small end first when the anchor has to be recovered.

The best sea anchor is probably one with a rigid circular end, but this is bulky to stow and there are folding versions, including one with a square section and two crossbars, that can be taken out or folded on each other. Sizes of sea anchor vary, but the largest that can be conveniently carried is advisable. A length of 5 feet and an open end nearly 2 feet across is the sort of thing to consider. For small boats there can be smaller versions and some quite small ones are provided with life rafts. Apart from their lighter construction the method of construction is the same.

A sea anchor should be made as strong as possible. This means using a fairly heavy grade of cloth, which may be polyester or natural fiber. Polyester about 5 oz. and cotton about 10 oz. are suitable. There is a bridle, usually in four parts which are seized around a thimble to which the long wrap is secured (Fig. 18-12A). This continues as roping down the sides of the bag (Fig. 18-12B) and there is another thimble to take the tripping line (Fig. 18-12C).

Opinion is divided about the size of the opening at the small end in relation to the big end. Circumstances change and yachts of different characteristics need differing amount of drag, but there must be enough opening to allow some water to pass through.

If a rigid metal or laminated wood ring is to be used at the large end that will settle the size there. It should be possible to turn in the cloth itself (Fig. 18-12D), with a small amount of puckering. The alternative is to use a stout tape (Fig. 18-12E). Draw the shape of the cone (Fig. 18-12F). The lines can be extended to find the center for drawing the developed shape (Fig. 18-12G).

If the taper is slight, extending the lines may take the center too far away for drawing a curve to be practicable, although quite a long compass can be made with a strip of wood (Fig. 18-12H). The alternative is make a template of the side view and use this in a total of four positions to get a shape (Fig. 18-12J) with a curve sprung through the points. This will give slightly too much width, but surplus can be removed when the cone is brought to shape to match the ring.

If cloths have to be joined, make the seams lengthwise along radial lines (Fig. 18-12A). For further reinforcement there may be false seams along the lines of the roping, so a joining seam will take one line and the other ropes come over false seams. Alternatively there may be strips of cloth sewn on, then the roping sewn outside that. The small end is tabled.

At the big end the ropes may go through sewn grommets if there is room in the taping beside the enclosed ring. A laminated wood ring may have holes to take the roping. The rope is then sewn down the outside of the sea anchor in the same way as roping is sewn to a sail (Fig. 18-13B). Alternatively it may be taken through pockets, like batten pockets, and sewn securely to the canvas at each end or for the full length (Fig. 18-13C).

A square sea anchor can be made of four tapered panels joined with broad flat seams along each edge and with the roping sewn outside (Fig. 18-13D). As there is no ring around the large end this should be strengthened with tabling and roping (Fig. 18-13E). Some weighting may be called for. This can be lead shot or other small pieces of lead in a pocket across one side (Fig. 18-13F).

Some strengthening of the corners is advisable and this can be one or more patches in each place, like those used on a sail (Fig. 18-13G). The pocket for weights can be made as an extension of a pair of patches.

The wooden crossbars should be stout hardwood and may be fixed at the corners permanently with screws through washers. At the center shallow notches locate the parts at right angles when the bolt is tightened, but allow slackening and turning in line for packing

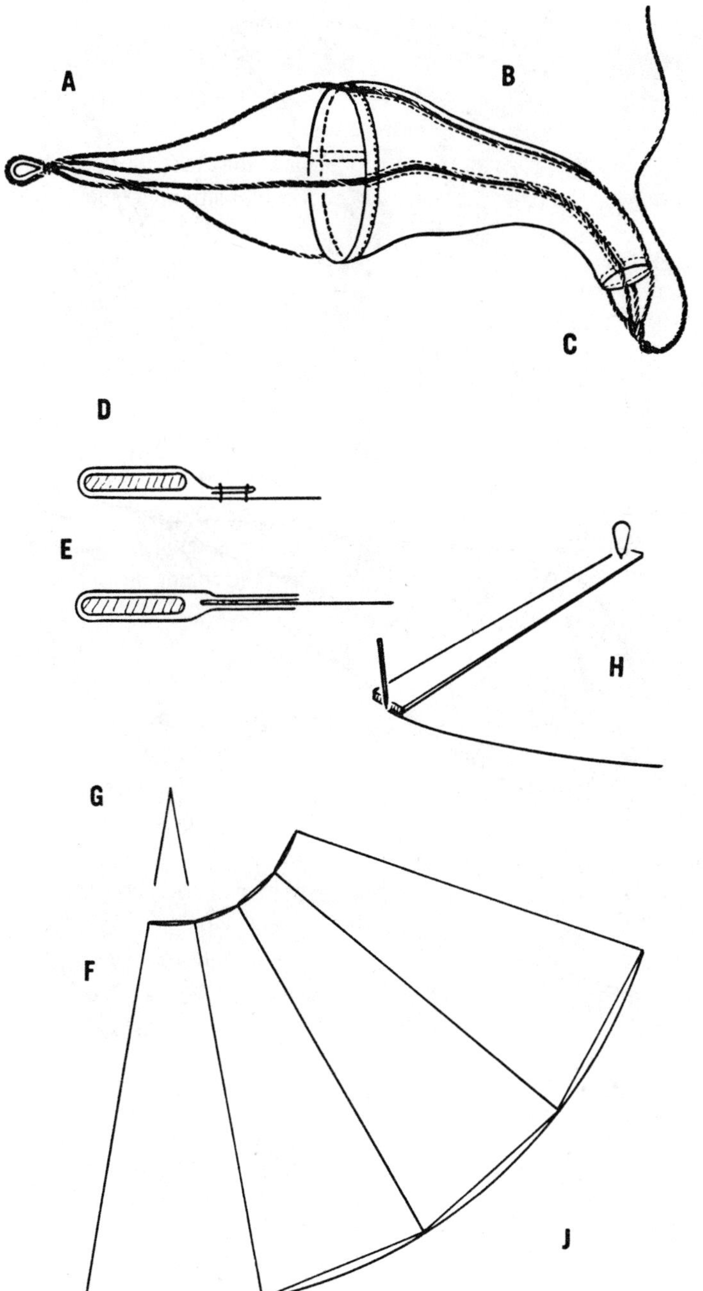

Fig. 18-12. A sea anchor is a stout conical canvas bag with a rope bridle secured to it and a rigid ring used to keep the large end open.

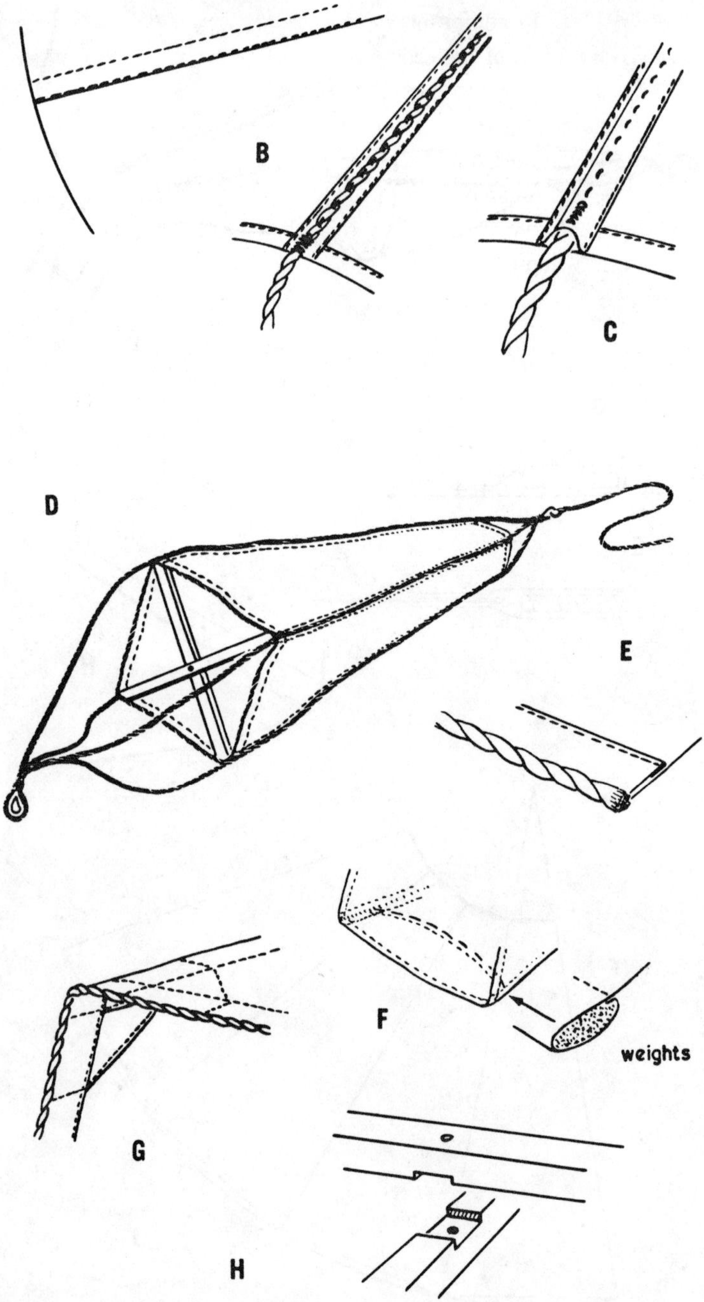

Fig. 18-13. Roping is used to strengthen a sea anchor, which can be made to fold if wooden struts are used to keep a large square end open.

(Fig. 18-13H). In a different construction the bridle parts go through holes in the ends of the crossbars.

Smaller sea anchors need not be so robustly made, but there must be a means of keeping the large end in shape. A bridle is needed to get an even pull, but there may be no need for the roping to go down the bag. It can be spliced to the large end. A small sea anchor may not require a tripping line, as the bag can be recovered by a direct pull when the conditions no longer call for the use of a sea anchor.

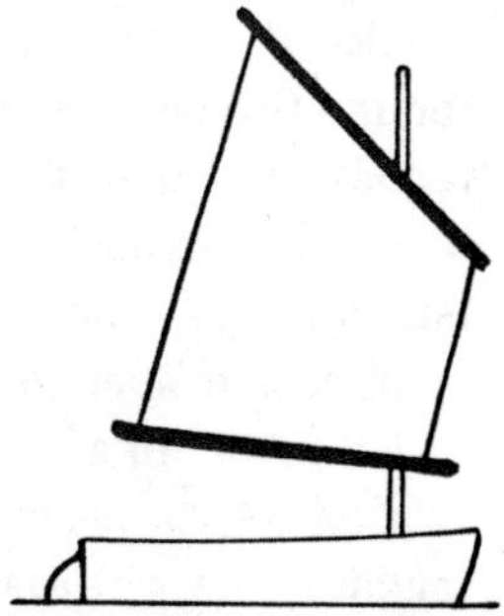

Glossary of Sailing and Sailmaking Terms

Anyone concerned with making or repairing sails and dealing with other canvaswork used on board a boat needs to understand a few technical terms. Much of the language of the sea is a carry-over from the days when sail was the only power other than oars and a large craft carried a multiplicity of sail and rigging, all of which has to be identifiable. Those days have gone, but some of the names live on. The meanings of some have been altered to suit modern rigs and this sometimes leads to confusion.

There is sometimes a tendency for sailing people to use terms which are really obsolete and not always strictly applicable to the circumstances being described. If there is any doubt about a particular term it is usually better to use a plain language description so both parties know what is meant, even if this does not sound very nautical.

This list gives terms applicable to modern sailing craft. Although there are a few square-rigged craft about, it is very unlikely that the reader will be concerned with their sails, and the very large number of terms only applicable to square rig have been omitted as they might be confused with the same or other terms used now for fore and aft rigs. Some alternatives have been quoted, where it is possible that different names or spellings may be met.

The terms quoted are applicable to the sails and their rigging, and equipment associated with sailing, together with some that affect other canvaswork. Parts of a boat and other equipment not associated with sailing, sailmaking or other canvaswork are not included.

Aback—Having the wind on the wrong side of the sail.

About—Change direction from one tack to the other.

Aerodynamics—Study of the effects of solid bodies moving through air, applicable to sails in a similar way to aircraft wings.

Aspect ratio—The relations between the breadth and depth of a plane in relation to the air it is passing through. The relation to luff to foot of a main sail.

Awning—A canvas cover to keep off sun or rain.

Backstay—A wire stay aft of a mast.

Baggywrinkle—Anti-chafe padding, usually on standing rigging where a sail might rub.

Balanced lug—A four-sided fore-and-aft sail with yard and boom both going forward of the mast.

Balloon jib—A very fully-cut head sail. A reacher.

Bare poles—A vessel driven by the wind when no sail is set.

Batten—Strip of wood or similar material used to stiffen the edge of a sail, as in the roach along the leech.

Batten pocket—Sewn-on canvas strip to hold batten.

Beam—The greatest width of a boat.

Beating—Sailing to windward by tacking.

Beeswax—Wax commonly used on sailmaking thread to toughen and waterproof.

Before the wind—Sailing with the wind aft.

Belay—Secure or make fast a rope.

Belly—The central body of a sail. The bunt.

Bend a sail—Fix a sail to its spars.

Bendy mast—Unstayed mast designed to bend so as to affect the set and fullness of its sail.

Bermudan (Bermudian)—Jib-headed main sail.

Board—One leg sailed when tacking.

Bobstay—Stay below a bowsprit.

Bolt rope—Rope around the edge of a sail.

Bonnet—Extra canvas attached to the foot of a sail.

Boom—Spar along the foot of a sail.

Boom vang—Tensioning cable diagonally from boom to bow point on mast to prevent boom rising. Also called a kicking strip.

Bowsprit—A spar projecting forward over the bow.

Brace—Rope used to swing a yard.

Broad seam—Flat seam made wider than usual, sometimes only towards one edge to produce taper.

Bunt—Body of a sail. Its belly.

Burgee—A small flag which may be swallow-tailed or a triangular pendant (pennant).

Carry away—Break a rope or spar.

Cat boat—Single-masted single-sail boat, with unstayed mast close into bow.

Center of effort—The balancing point of a sail or of a combined sail plan.

Center of lateral resistance—The balance point of the underwater area of a hull.

Chains, chain plates—Attachment points on boat sides for shrouds.

Cleat—Wood or metal device, usually two-pronged, used for belaying a rope.

Clew—Lower aft corner of a sail, to which the sheet is attached.

Clew liner—Patch extended along the sides from the clew.

Close-hauled—Sailing at as close an angle towards the wind as possible.

Concave—A hollow curve.

Convex—An outward curve.

Crank—A craft unable to carry much sail with safety. Opposite to stiff.

Cringle—Rope loop worked into the edge of a sail.

Cross, cutting on—Cutting diagonally to weave.

Cross stitch—Zig-zag machine stitch.

Crutch—Support for lowered boom or gaff when lowered.

Cunningham control—Arrangement at tack of main sail for gathering in cloth to adjust sail.

Cutter—A single-masted rig with a main sail and more than one sail forward of the mast.

Dacron—Trade name for a polyester material.

Dart—Gather in a triangular piece at the edge of a sail.

Dipping lug—Four-sided fore-and-aft sail with the tack forward of the mast and the sail having to be moved to the other side of the mast at each change of tack.

Douse sail—Lower sail quickly.

Downhaul—Line to assist in pulling down a sail.

D-ring—Metal D-shaped ring which may be taped to a sail.

Duck—Good quality light cotton canvas.

Earing—Rope attached to a cringle.

Egyptian cotton—Good quality cotton fabric used for traditional sails.

Eyelet—Two-part metal ring for fixing in a sail. A grommet.

Eye splice—Loop in the end of a rope with the strands tucked back into the standing part of the rope.

False seam—Cloth folded back and sewn to give the appearance of a flat seam.

Fender, fend-off—Padding hung over edge of vessel to prevent chafing.

Fid—Wooden spike.

Finishing—All the work that follows the sewing of a sail.

Flat seam—Joint made by overlapping and sewing the edges of cloths together.

Flax—Coarse natural material used for sail cloth.

Flow—Curve induced in a sail by its cut.

Flying jib—Other jib where there are several sails forward of the mast.

Foot—Bottom edge of a sail.

Foot liner—Patch extending along foot of sail.

Foresail—Head sail.

Forestay—Forward stay of a mast.

Fore staysail—Inner head sail of a cutter.

Full—Sail drawing well.

Full and bye—Sailing close-hauled with all sails full.

Fully-battened sail—Sail with battens right across it.

Furl—Stow a sail on its boom.

Gaff—Spar to support head of sail, entirely aft of mast.

Gaff-headed—Four-sided sail with head requiring a gaff.

Gallows—Crutch to support boom when lowered.

Gear—General name for all equipment needed for sailing.

Genoa—Large head sail overlapping main sail.

Gibe, gybe—Sudden change of sail from one side to the other with the wind aft.

Gooseneck—Universal joint between end of boom and mast.

Goose-winged—Sailing downwind with sails set on opposite sides.

Go about—Change tack by turning into wind.

Grommet—Metal or sewn edged hole in sail.

Groove, luff or foot—Groove in spar to take roped edge of sail.

Guy—Controlling rope to restrict movement of a spar, usually led forward.

Halliard, halyard—Rope used for hoisting.

Hank—Spring clip, attachment of sail to stay.

Harden—Flatten in sheets.

Headboard, headstick—Wood or metal plate set in head of jib-headed sail.

Head of sail—Top edge of sail.

Head sail—Sail forward of mast.

Headstay—Foreward supporting stay for mast. Forestay.

Heave to—Turn into wind in heavy weather to make minimum progress ahead or astern.

Heel—Tilt sideways. Bottom of mast.

Helm up or down—Moving tiller towards or away from wind.

Hemp—Natural fiber used for rope and canvas.

Horse—Arrangement, usually metal, across deck to take sheet.

In irons—Turn head into wind with sails flapping.

Insignia—Badge or emblem on sail.

Jib—One of the head sails of a cutter, but commonly applied to a single head sail.

Jib-headed—Main sail with pointed head.

Jib snaps—Clips attaching luff of jib to forestay.

Jib topsail—Highest of three head sails on cutter.

Jigger—Extra sail aft. Mizzen sail.

Junk rig—Fully battened sails based on those of Chinese junks.

Jury—Temporary or emergency, as Jury rig.

Jute—Natural material used for coarse fabric.

Ketch—Two-masted rig with mizzen mast forward of the rudder head and mizzen sail smaller than the main sail.

Lateen sail—Triangular sail with very long head supported by a spar.

Lee—Side away from wind. sheltered.

Leech, leach—Aft edge of sail.

Leech line—Line through leech, which can be used to adjust tension.

Lee helm—Necessity to sail with tiller towards lee side of boat to maintain a straight course.

"Lee-ho"—Statement that tiller is to be put over so boat goes about on to other tack.

Leeward (pronounced "loo-ard")—Direction away from wind.

Leeway—Movement sideways as well as forward.

Leg-o-mutton sail—Obsolescent term sometimes applied to balanced lug or jib-headed sail.

Linen—Good quality cotton cloth.

Liner—Strengthening patch along edge.

Long splice—End-to-end joint between ropes that does not increase their thickness.

Loose-footed—Sail without boom or only attached at clew and tack to boom.

Luff—Forward edge of a sail.

Luff, to—To turn a boat towards the wind.

Lug sail—Four-sided fore-and-aft sail.

Main sail—Largest sail. Normally the one aft of a single mast.

Make sail—Set the sails.

Marconi sail—Jib-headed main sail.

Marline—Light lashing line.

Marline spike—Metal spike.

Mast hoops—Wood hoops attached to luff of main sail and sliding on mast.

Mildew—Form of rot, leaving dark spots on sail.

Miss stays—Fail to go about between tacks and go into irons.

Miter cut—Head sail with a seam bisecting the clew angle.

Mizzen mast and sail—Aft sail in two-masted rig.

Needle—Tool for sewing, usually triangular for sailmaking.

Nylon—Elastic synthetic fiber.

Off the wind—Reaching.

On the wind—Sailing close-hauled.

Outhaul—Line for pulling sail along spar.

Palm—Leather fitting for hand, with metal pad for pushing needle through cloth.

Parachute spinnaker—Very fully-cut spinnaker.

Parrels—Balls, usually wood, on loops of light line attached to the luff of a main sail and running on the mast. Alternative to mast hoops.

Patch—One or more strengthening pieces sewn into the corner of a sail.

Pay off—Let vessel go away from wind.

Peak—Highest point of a gaff-headed sail.

Pendant, pennant—Small triangular flag.

Piston hank—Hank for attaching luff of head sail to forestay, using a spring-operated piston to secure and release.

Plain sail—All normally-used sails set.

Polyester—Synthetic fiber used for sail cloth, Dacron, Terylene.

Port—Left side of shop when facing forward.

Preventer—Rope to limit movement of a spar.

Punch and die—Tools for setting eyelet-type grommets.

Raffee—Triangular sail set above square sail.

Rake—Slope of mast.

Reacher—Large jib or head sail. Genoa.

Reaching—Sailing with wind on beam.

Reef—Reduce the area of sail.

Reef band—Strip across sail to take reef pendants.

Reef pendant—Light line attached to sail for gathering up surplus at foot when sail is reefed.

Reefing, roller—Method of reefing by rolling sail around boom.

Rig—General arrangement of spars and sails on a sailing vessel. The action of setting up all of the sailing gear.

Rigging—All the lines needed to support masts, hoist and control sails.

Roach—Edge of sail given a curve, usually a convex one held to shape by battens, as on a main sail leech.

Roping—Strengthening the edge of a sail with rope, either sewn to the side or enclosed in tape.

Round seam—Joint between cloths done with a single line of stitches while the work is inside out.

Rubber—Tool made of wood, bone or plastic for rubbing down creases in cloth for seams.

Running—Sailing with the wind astern.

Running backstays—Pair of backstays taken to the gunwales aft. Only the stay on the weatherside is set up and this has to be released and the other set up when the main sail changes sides.

Running rigging—Ropes used to hoist and control sails.

Sail hook—Steel hook with lanyard, used to stretch a seam during hand sewing.

Schooner—Vessel with two or more masts. Unlike a ketch or yawl the largest sail is not necessarily on the forward mast.

Scotch cut—A miter cut head sail with cloths parallel with leech and foot.

Seam—Sewn joint between cloths.
Selvedge—Manufactured edge of cloth.
Serve—Bind light line over a rope as protection.
Set up—Tighten rigging etc.
Sewn eyelet, grommet—Hole edged by stitched ring, as distinct from metal eyelet fixed with punch and die.
Sheet—Rope used to control a sail, normally attached to the clew.
Shift, to—Change sails etc.
Shoot—Turn directly into the wind deliberately, as when coming up to a buoy.
Shorten sail—Reduce the amount of sail in use, either by reefing, changing to smaller sails or lowering one or more sails.
Shrouds—Mast stays brought down to the gunwales opposite the mast.
Slack in stays—Sluggish when going about.
Sleeved sail—Main sail with a long pocket to fit over the mast.
Slide, slug—Metal or plastic piece attached to a sail to run along a track.
Sloop—Single-mast rig with a main sail and one head sail.
Snug down—Stow sails.
Sny—Toggle.
Spike—Pointed tool for splicing or opening holes.
Spinnaker—Large light balloon-shaped head sail for use in light airs.
Splice—Ropework involving tucking strands instead of knotting the complete rope.
Spring stay—Top stay between masts.
Sprit sail—Four-sided sail supported by a spar (sprit) diagonally across it.
Square sail—Four-sided sail hung from a yard and set across the vessel.
Stancheon, stanchion—Upright support for hand rail.
Standing lug—Four-sided sail with the head and its yard going forward of the mast and the boom and foot coming to a gooseneck at the mast.
Standing rigging—Supports for mast.
Starboard—Right side of vessel when facing forward.
Stay—Support for mast.
Staysail—Lower head sail.

Stays, in—Going about.
Step—The seat for the foot of the mast.
Sternboard, sternway—Going astern.
Sticking—Large up and down hand stitches through cloths to hold them in position for final stitching.
Stiff—Able to carry plenty of sail safely.
Straight stitch—Normal machine stitch, as distant from zig-zag or cross stitch.
Strainer—Long patch to spread load.
Strike-up marks—Marks made on adjoining edges when marking out and cutting cloths as a check that they register when being sewn.
Tabernacle—Support for foot of mast, so the mast can be lowered by swinging down on a pivot.
Tabling—Strengthened edge of sail by turning cloth over or adding a strip of cloth.
Tack—Lower forward corner of a sail.
Tack angle—Angle between foot and luff, usually about 87 degrees.
Tack back—An angle cut back at the tack of a main sail to give clearance for the gooseneck and a neater set to the sail.
Tacking—Sailing to windward by sailing close-hauled alternately in each direction.
Tack line—Line attached to the tack of a sail, as when the tack of a balanced lug sail has to be hauled back to the mast.
Tail—End of a rope.
Taped sail—Sail strengthened around edge with tape instead of by roping.
Tapered rope—Rope unlaid and some fibers removed, then laid up again to make a reduced end.
Tapered seam—Increasing the width of a seam towards an edge to produce a reduced edge and flow in the sail.
Terylene—Trade name for a polyester material.
Thimble—Metal or plastic piece to fit in a rope eye.
Throat—The angle between luff and head of a gaff-headed sail.
Tiers, ties—Rope or canvas straps for securing a furled sail to a boom.
Toggle—Wood or plastic peg fixed across an eye in the end of a rope, usually to make a connection to an eye in another rope.

Topping lift—Line from end of boom over sheave at mast head and used to take the weight of the boom while sail is hoisted or lowered.

Top sail—Sail set above a gaff main sail.

Traveler—Metal ring to travel on mast. May have a hook to engage with a yard and a ring for the halliard.

Triatic stay—Stay between two masts.

Trice—Hoist.

Truck—Top of mast or a cap on the top of the mast.

Try sail—Heavy weather sail used in place of main sail.

Tuck—A dart.

Turnover—Sewn grommet fitted with a metal ferrule or liner.

Una rig—Single rail rig.

Unhand—Cast off.

Under way—Moving through the water.

Under weigh—With the anchor about to be disengaged from the bottom.

Unrig—Dismantle the whole rig.

Up helm—Move the tiller towards the windward side.

Vang, vane, whang—Steadying rope from gaff or other spar.

Vertical cut—Cloths arranged parallel with leech.

Warp—Yarns running lengthwise in a piece of cloth.

Way—Movement, particularly of a boat through the water.

Wear—Change direction of sailing so the boat turns a complete circle. Used when sailing off the wind to bring the boom to the other side as an alternative to a gibe.

Weather helm—When the tiller has to be held to windward to maintain a straight course.

Weather side—The side of a vessel towards the wind.

Weft—Yarns running crosswise in a piece of cloth.

Whipping—Binding the end of a rope to prevent it unlaying.

Window—Transparent plastic let into a sail.

Windward—Direction towards the wind.

Wing and wing—Goosewinged, sailing downwind with sails on opposite sides.

Wire luff—Flexible steel cable let into the luff of a head sail.

Yankee—Large light head sail.

Yard—Spar to support the head of a sail, that crosses the mast, as distinct from a gaff which is entirely aft of it.

Yaw—Go from side to side instead of keep on course.

Yawl—Two-masted rig with the mizzen mast aft of the rudder head.

Zig-zag stitch—Machine cross stitch.

Index

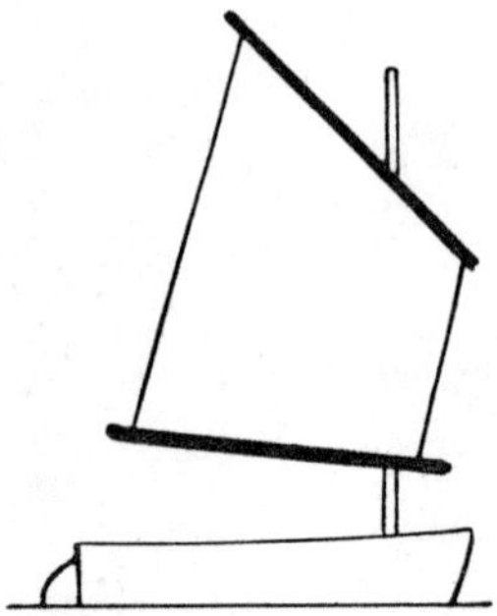

Index